# THE GLOBAL DIFFUSION OF HUMAN RESOURCE PRACTICES: INSTITUTIONAL AND CULTURAL LIMITS

# ADVANCES IN INTERNATIONAL MANAGEMENT

Series Editors: Joseph L. C. Cheng and Michael A. Hitt

ADVANCES IN INTERNATIONAL MANAGEMENT
VOLUME 21

# THE GLOBAL DIFFUSION OF HUMAN RESOURCE PRACTICES: INSTITUTIONAL AND CULTURAL LIMITS

EDITED BY

## JOHN J. LAWLER
*Institute of Labor and Industrial Relations*
*University of Illinois at Urbana-Champaign, USA*

## GREG HUNDLEY
*Krannert School of Business*
*Purdue University, USA*

Emerald
JAI

United Kingdom – North America – Japan
India – Malaysia – China

JAI Press is an imprint of Emerald Group Publishing Limited
Howard House, Wagon Lane, Bingley BD16 1WA, UK

First edition 2008

Copyright © 2008 Emerald Group Publishing Limited

**Reprints and permission service**
Contact: booksandseries@emeraldinsight.com

**British Library Cataloguing in Publication Data**
A catalogue record for this book is available from the British Library

ISBN: 978-0-7623-1401-0
ISSN: 1571-5027 (Series)

Awarded in recognition of
Emerald's production
department's adherence to
quality systems and processes
when preparing scholarly
journals for print

INVESTOR IN PEOPLE

# CONTENTS

# LIST OF CONTRIBUTORS

| | |
|---|---|
| *Gayle Allard* | IE Business School, Maria de Molina, Madrid, Spain |
| *Alexandre Ardichvili* | Department of Work and Human Resource Education, University of Minnesota, St. Paul, MN, USA |
| *Shyh-jer Chen* | Institute of Human Resource Management, National Sun Yat-sen University, Kaohsiung, Taiwan |
| *Khalil M. Dirani* | Department of Lifelong Education, Administration, and Policy, The University of Georgia, Athens, GA, USA |
| *Tony Edwards* | Department of Management, King's College London, London, UK |
| *Frank M. Horwitz* | Graduate School of Business, University of Cape Town, Cape Town, South Africa |
| *I-Chieh Hsu* | Department of Business Administration, National Changhua University of Education, Changhua, Taiwan |
| *Greg Hundley* | Krannert School of Management, Purdue University, West Lafayette, IN, USA |
| *Harish C. Jain* | School of Business, McMaster University, West Hamilton, Ontario, Canada |
| *John J. Lawler* | Institute of Labor and Industrial Relations, University of Illinois, Champaign, IL, USA |

*Francisco Llorente-Galera*        Department of Econometrics, Statistics
                                   and Spanish Economy, Facultad de
                                   Ciencias Económicas y Empresariales
                                   Universitat de Barcelona, Barcelona,
                                   Spain

*Mary Mathew*                      Department of Management Studies,
                                   Indian Institute of Science, Bangalore,
                                   India

*Luis Ortiz*                       Department of Political Science and
                                   Sociology, Universitat Pompeu Fabra,
                                   Barcelona, Spain

*Ming Piao*                        Department of Management, David Eccles
                                   School of Business, University of Utah,
                                   Salt Lake City, Utah

*Carlos Sánchez Runde*             IESE Business School, Barcelona, Spain

*Kan Shi*                          Management School of Graduate
                                   University, Chinese Academy of Sciences,
                                   Beijing, China

*Cristina Simón*                   IE Business School, Maria de Molina,
                                   Madrid, Spain

*Fred Walumbwa*                    Department of Management, Arizona State
                                   University, Phoenix, AZ, USA

*Peng Wang*                        Miami University at Oxford, Oxford,
                                   OH, USA

*Miao Zhang*                       Kingston Business School, Kingston
                                   University, Surrey, UK

# INTRODUCTION

Greg Hundley and John J. Lawler

Discussions about transferring human resource practices across national borders inevitably raise the question as to whether practices in different countries will converge on a common model or whether they will be characterized by continued divergence. The convergence hypothesis is a product of the landmark study by Kerr, Dunlop, Harbison, and Myers (1960), who sought to understand the forces shaping national industrial relations systems by analyzing the experiences of national economies at various stages of industrialization. They predicted a convergence of practices as industrial societies adopted plural market economies in which major actors shared beliefs about the nature of industrialism, the efficacy of the market economy, and the need for mechanisms to reconcile the interests of employers, the public, and workers.

Nonetheless, recent decades have seen plenty of support for continued divergence. For example, a comprehensive study of trends in established and emerging economies by Locke, Kochan, and Piore (1995) showed continuing cross-national differences in employment practices, traceable to the different ways in which decision makers in different institutional environments respond to the pressures of global competition. They observed considerable heterogeneity in human resource practices within nations and noted the growth of specific employment practices, including team-based production, decentralized decision making, employee participation, pay for performance, and new patterns of skill acquisition and training.

Two influential bodies of literature support the case for cross-national divergence. First, there is the research in the tradition of Hofstede's (1980)

**The Global Diffusion of Human Resource Practices: Institutional and Cultural Limits**
**Advances in International Management, Volume 21, 1–7**
Copyright © 2008 by Emerald Group Publishing Limited
All rights of reproduction in any form reserved
ISSN: 1571-5027/doi:10.1016/S1571-5027(08)00012-0

work on the features of national cultures. These studies emphasize the ways that nations are distinguished by supposedly permanent differences along important dimensions of national culture, such as individualism/collectivism and belief in hierarchy. Second, there is the literature on national business systems (Whitley, 1999) that describes major differences in organizational governance, owner–manager relationships, patterns of interfirm cooperation and competition, and approaches to human capital formation and skill development.

For several reasons, divergence should not be accepted a priori. The cultural difference approaches are under attack by scholars such as McSweeney (2002), who point to shortcomings in the theoretical and methodological underpinnings of Hofstede's work, and by research showing that major cultural attributes vary more within than between nations (Au, 1999; Gerhart & Fang, 2005). The studies that link the extent of the use of specific practices to national culture are susceptible to the ecological fallacy so that the statistical effects of national level measures may easily be a reflection of national attributes other than the cultural characteristic purportedly measured. Whereas distinctive features of national business systems are easily discerned, there is little guidance as to if or how these attributes affect human resource practices. Moreover, there are questions as to how durable these institutional features are. Although business system characteristics are fixed by unique aspects of national history and tight linkages with other national institutions, recent history demonstrates that the broader sociopolitical environments of some of the most populous countries, such as the post-Communist transition nations (including China) and India, have been subject to momentous change.

The nature of the global arena and the ways in which firms compete in it have changed in ways that shape how firms approach the transfer of management practices. The global corporation is now conceptualized as a network of units engaged in developing and transferring knowledge for the advantage of the overall corporation premium (Bartlett & Ghoshal, 1998). Accordingly, the decision to localize practices can no longer be left to a simple consideration of local efficiencies and acceptability. Instead, competitive advantage depends on the development of a strong global corporate culture that promotes coordination and the generation and sharing of knowledge throughout the system. Thus, there are strong pressures for human resource systems to converge within the global corporation, at least to the extent that they promote sharing of corporate values and the movement of knowledge and talent throughout the firm. The management of diversity, unmentioned in earlier debates, assumes great importance as organizations compete for increasingly scarce talent and for ways for individuals from diverse backgrounds to work together most effectively. Further, there is an increase in the number and diversity of firms occupying the competitive landscape. Where earlier discussions were mainly about global firms headquartered in traditional centers of economic power, notably North America and Europe, subsidiaries of these multinationals can now be observed to compete and cooperate with indigenous companies in the developing world markets. The substantially different national origins of these firms (along with their relative newness) may well generate new ways of competing in global markets.

The changing global arena raises new and important challenges for researchers. There is a need for a better understanding of the processes for transferring practices, including how local and global managers go about crafting the transfer of practices to different nations and regions. Investigation of specific issues and practices is needed, including the management of global diversity and the retention of top talent. Whereas institutional accounts of global transfer of work practices (Tempel & Walgenbach, 2007) ignore the notion of competitiveness and work-related outcomes, such as employee well-being and attitudes, strategies and practices must be evaluated for their effects on these outcomes.

The papers in this volume address these research challenges. An eight-country comparison by Hundley and Sanchez (Cross-national Differences in the Determination of Pay Fairness Judgments: Do Cultural Differences Play a Role?) demonstrates that aggregate measures of national culture have little role to play in explaining managers' judgments regarding the acceptability for determining pay differences. Instead, cross-national differences in reactions to management practices may have more to do with beliefs about how the systems will work that are conditioned by the recent experiences or expectations of participants and less to do with presumed deep-seated cultural values that endure across the generations. Dirani (Individualism and Collectivism in Lebanon: Correlations with Socio-economic Factors and Effects on Management and Human Resources Practices) explores factors that affect within-country variations in culture in a nation that, on the basis of meager evidence, has been classified as collectivistic in nature. They show that the degree of individualism varies across groups, with students being more individualistic than employees, and increases with age, providing an indication that Lebanese society has become more individualistic in the past quarter century.

The processes and methods associated with localization of management practices in specific national economies are examined in three papers.

Edwards and Zhang (Multinationals and National Systems of Employment Relations: Innovators or Adapters?) provides an insight into the role of cross-national corporations in transferring management practices across borders. Their work (a study of a large U.S. manufacturer in China and a careful analysis of other studies) supports an institutional perspective that assigns an important role to strong home-country pressures for standardization even when local conditions (such as lower costs, production for local markets) seem appropriate for regional segmentation. They show how local conditions strongly influence how the definitive corporate practices (diversity policies, teamwork methods, performance management policies) are implemented as managers strive to ensure acceptability to key local players while preserving meaning for top stakeholders in the United States. Horowitz and Jain (Managing Human Resources in South Africa: A Multinational Firm Focus) explores the issues posed for multinational companies that flow from a historic period of intense discrimination against the majority workforce, a dual labor market with a well-established formal sector supplemented by an even larger, faster growing informal sector, and intensification of global competitive pressures that place a premium on skill development and organizational learning. An array of subsidiary challenges, including the need to address employee relations problems due to continuing perceptions of racism among Black employees and reverse discrimination among Whites in the context of compliance with employment equity legislation, which focuses demands for compliance on numerical goals. Horowitz and Jain highlight policy prescriptions, including the creation of organizational cultures in which diversity is valued as a competitive advantage, and programs for skill enhancement encompassing the development of more basic skills as well as advanced competencies. They advocate processes to support learning from other situations in which best operating practices have been transferred to local companies and techniques that build trust and social capital in organizations while contributing to societal needs. Ortiz and Lorente (Two Failed Attempts and One Success: The Introduction of Teamwork at SEAT–Volkswagen) address the factors affecting the transfer of HR practices from a parent to local institutions. The successful introduction of teamwork into a Spanish plant following two earlier resounding failures at installing a similar model is associated with structural factors – particularly changing demographics, moving from older workers and managers steeped in the traditional way of doing things to younger actors; political processes of local union and local labor–management relations; supportive management policies; engaging union leaders in a more respectful way; and much closer attention to implementation, including supportive HR policies in the area of training. The convergence of subsidiary practices to the host country is very much conditioned by structural and political factors at the host-country level and the astuteness of management at the local and host levels at installing the teamwork practices.

Human resource practices and policies of both local companies and multinationals in the same market are examined by Mathew and Jain (International Human Resource Management in the Indian Information Technology Sector: A Comparison of Indian MNCs and Affiliates of Foreign MNCs in India) and by Chen (The Adoption of HR Strategies in a Confucian Context). Mathew and Jain's investigation of the IT sector in India enables a comparison of the way Indian and foreign multinational corporations affect an organization's business culture and the implementation of specific HR practices. They find no evidence of differences between U.S., European, and Indian companies in India in types of HR practices in the major areas of training and development, staffing practices, compensation practices, and employee empowerment. Indian IT companies who go global maintain active strategies of learning from IT sectors in other countries, particularly the United States. Chen tackles the dynamics by which companies in an emerging economy adopt specific management policies. He finds that companies are characterized by a range of combinations of practices ranging from traditional Confucian practices (informal staffing based on relationships, seniority-based pay and hierarchy, no employee involvement) toward a full commitment to rigorous selection, extensive training, performance-based pay, job autonomy, and high involvement in decision making. Chen reports that all firms are part way along the continuum from traditional to high-involvement practices and his results provide strong guidance in the convergence versus divergence debate, with the movement toward high-involvement practices coinciding with more individualist attitudes (especially among the younger Taiwanese) and the influence of Western universities and business scholars. In general, those firms with high-involvement practices demonstrate superior financial performance compared to those managed along Confucian lines. A third study, by Ardichvili and Dirani (Human Capital Theory and Practice in Russian Enterprises) extends that theme of intranational variation by analyzing the forces affecting the development of HR practices and strategies in an important transition economy. Consistent with the short-term orientation often associated with firms in an uncertain economic and legal environments, Russian firms take a demand-driven approach characterized by acquisition of current job-based skills, rather than the development of capacities to learn and grow – a practice especially pronounced in areas of rapid economic growth, where firms struggled to meet current demands and job market conditions. A longer-term strategic orientation characterizes larger firms, especially in the case of management development, and there is evidence of firms trying to coordinate human resource practices and placing a greater emphasis on employee work–life balance.

Competitive pressures unleashed by globalization direct attention to the roles played by specific aspects of human resources in affecting business competitiveness and employee outcomes. Hsu and Lawler (Toward a Model of Gender Diversity in the Workplace in East Asia: Preliminary Evidence from Manufacturing Industries in Taiwan) shows that firms with a higher percentage of females in managerial and professional occupations perform better, whereas gender diversity in manual and nonsupervisory occupations does not affect performance. Simon and Allard (Competitiveness and the Employment Relationship in Europe: Is There a Global Missing Link in HRM?) show that a national-level index of global competitiveness is strongly associated with personal well-being (including job satisfaction) and feelings of greater autonomy and freedom, including more say in workplaces and greater freedom to influence decisions on jobs. Wang, Lawler, Shi, Walumba, and Piao (Family-Friendly Employment Practices: Importance and Effects in India, Kenya, and China) examine the incidence of a range of family-friendly policies characteristic of North American-based multinationals in three collectivistic, developing countries. The study of local banking operations within each country explores the incidence of family-friendly policies and relates their use and employee reactions to them to particular national characteristics showing, for example, that family leave for child care is less important in China with smaller families and a tradition of parents helping with offspring. The study relates the outcomes of family-friendly policies to a range of factors, including family composition (including hypothesized negative effects on those without dependents).

# REFERENCES

Au, K. Y. (1999). Intra-cultural variation: Evidence and implications for international business. *Journal of International Business Studies, 30*(4), 799–812.

Bartlett, C. A., & Ghoshal, S. (1998). *Managing across borders: The transnational solution.* Boston, MA: Harvard Business School Press.

Gerhart, B., & Fang, M. (2005). National culture and human resource management: Assumptions and evidence. *International Journal of Human Resource Management, 16*(6), 971–986.

Hofstede, G. (1980). *Culture's consequences: International differences in work-related values*. Beverly Hills, CA: Sage.

Kerr, C., Dunlop, J. T., Harbison, F. H., & Myers, C. A. (1960). *Industrialism and industrial man*. Cambridge, Mass: Harvard University Press.

Locke, R., Kochan, T., & Piore, M. J. (Eds). (1995). *Employment relations in a changing world economy*. Cambridge, MA: MIT Press.

McSweeney, B. (2002). Hofstede's model of national cultural differences and their consequences: A triumph of faith – a failure of analysis. *Human Relations*, *55*(1), 89–118.

Tempel, A., & Walgenbach, P. (2007). Global standardization of organizational forms and management practices? What new institutionalism and the business systems approach can learn from each other. *Journal of Management Studies*, *44*(1), 1–24.

Whitley, A. (1999). *Divergent capitalism: The social structuring and change of business systems*. Oxford: Oxford University Press.

# COMPETITIVENESS AND THE EMPLOYMENT RELATIONSHIP IN EUROPE: IS THERE A GLOBAL MISSING LINK IN HRM?

Cristina Simón and Gayle Allard

## ABSTRACT

*Competitiveness is an often ill-defined concept that is key to economic success. This chapter focuses on the links between competitiveness and the employment relationship (ER). It ranks European countries by their specialization in high-technology, skilled labor sectors to yield a competitiveness ranking and examines workers' values and attitudes to identify common ER features of the "competitive" countries. Results show that workers in competitive countries enjoy greater flexibility and autonomy. Some conclusions are raised regarding what companies can do from the HRM perspective to optimize employee capabilities, leading to more productive and competitive working environments.*

The Global Diffusion of Human Resource Practices: Institutional and Cultural Limits
Advances in International Management, Volume 21, 9–32
ISSN: 1571-5027/doi:10.1016/S1571-5027(08)00001-6

# HUMAN RESOURCE MANAGEMENT (HRM) AND GLOBAL COMPETITIVENESS: IS THERE A COMMON DENOMINATOR?

The debate about the existence of a global HRM model has continued for years, and several models have proposed where the "limits of uniqueness" of the HRM model should lie. Several approaches have been adopted in this exercise of differentiation, with a series of relevant contributions to the literature coming from cross-cultural management (Hofstede, 1998, 2003; Franke, Hofstede, & Bond, 2001; Hofstede & Hofstede, 2004) and institutional theory (Whitley, 2006). Particularly focusing on HRM practices and systems, the following debates could be outlined:

- The identification of *sociocultural differences on a national level* that may act as stumbling blocks to the exportation of HRM practices. In this respect, several authors have strongly argued the need to vindicate a particular European HRM style (Guest, 1997; Budhwar & Sparrow, 2002; Brewster, 2004; Morley, 2004). These works emphasize the differences in social conceptions of the community and the individual and the role played by unions as insuperable factors that make it difficult to implement specific U.S.-born HR practices such as performance evaluation and leadership styles in Europe. Another interesting line of research explores what could be called an "Asian style of HRM" (Warner & Zhu, 2002; Warner, 2004), placing the emphasis on the interaction between socio-ideological principles and the evolution of technology and economic development as a differentiating factor among HRM models.
- The search for *organizational fit* of the HRM system, including the social and demographical context in which the specific company operates, whether a local company or a branch of a foreign multinational (Baron & Kreps, 1999).
- The consideration of *distinctive business features* hindering the implementation of HRM policies in a homogenous way. The pioneering work of Youndt, Snell, Dean, and Lepak (1996) in the manufacturing sector fostered successive research on strategic business peculiarities that might lead to a proper choice of practices.

All these research efforts have produced interesting outcomes that help to set the frontiers of a global HRM model, close to the universalistic, best-practices approach born in the United States in the 1980s (Pfeffer, 1994;

Delery & Doty, 1996). From a different standpoint there is the contingency model (Hendry & Pettigrew, 1992; Baron & Kreps, 1999), which states that any arrangement of HRM practices could be effectively implemented as long as the strategic conditions of alignment and consistency are fulfilled, thus requiring a careful adaptation to the organizational context and structure.

The present work casts new light on this convergence debate by integrating these approaches and proposing a different point of view centered on the concept of *competitiveness,* because it:

- Provides a common set of criteria for comparing countries with its proposed Competitiveness Index as an alternative to Michael Porter's Business Competitive Index or the IMD Global Competitiveness Yearbook, which are widely used by academics and practitioners all over the world.
- Keeps the discussion close to business essentials, which remain an imperative in HRM regardless of the nature and characteristics of the human capital the companies may require for their operations.
- Introduces the logic of the economic discipline, which enriches the analysis of HRM efficiency by bringing interdisciplinary views to bear on the relationships between economic indicators and citizens' (employees') attitudes and behaviors.

If competitiveness is studied as a potential "common denominator" for a global HRM model, we must start by recognizing that the concept is often ill-defined and overused (Porter, 1998). Yet its importance is undeniable. Whether on a company or a country level, the drive to become and remain competitive underlies much business activity and is one of the key ingredients of economic success. Hence one of the pressing questions for business and economics is: What makes a company or a country competitive?

There is some evidence from research by Hofstede, Pedersen, and Hofstede (2002) that national culture does contribute to economic growth, although there seems to be a moderating effect of technological break-throughs. They also reported that cultures with a long-term orientation are more likely to grow faster than countries under other value models. A step further would lead us to the HRM debate: Is there any link between competitiveness and workers' perceptions and behaviors? And between competitiveness and the way those workers are managed?

Along these lines, this chapter joins the quest for answers by focusing on the links between competitiveness and the employment relationship. It first develops a definition of competitiveness by selecting some variables that evidence a country's transition to the high-technology, skilled-labor-intensive sectors that economic theory predicts will be the future market niches for developed nations. It combines these variables in an index to yield a ranking for European countries. The study then proceeds to examine the values and attitudes displayed by workers in those countries, to see what features are common to the "competitive" countries.

The results contradict some frequent suppositions in the public debate over worker values, preferences, and perceived welfare and offer directions for reform at the macro- and microlevels. Individuals in competitive countries are more satisfied with their environment, their public services, and their work. Above all, the competitive countries display in these surveys elements of an employment relationship that involves more give and take, more flexibility, and greater autonomy for the worker.

The results also point to a new employment model that may be emerging in Europe, characterized by greater flexibility and associated with greater competitiveness. Such a model demands an HRM architecture that respects heterogeneity of local socio-legal differences while keeping a set of design principles based on providing greater levels of autonomy and flexibility to employees.

## WHAT IS COMPETITIVENESS? DEVELOPING AN INDICATOR FOR THE 21ST CENTURY

What is competitiveness? The word is employed frequently and it undergoes subtle redefinition with each use, so that its meaning has become elusive. This chapter opts for a simple working definition:

> To be competitive is to be prepared to maintain and even expand one's global market niche in the rapidly changing world of the 21st century.

To move to a more specific definition, then, requires some speculation over what that world will be like. In this respect, economic models have ventured some guidelines that are broadly confirmed by experience. One classical model sketches the outlines of a world in which countries' areas of specialization and competitiveness, and consequently the patterns of international trade, are determined by the human, capital, and natural

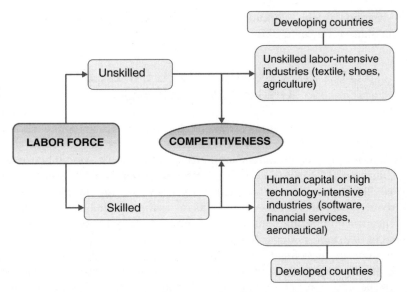

*Fig. 1.* The Patterns of Trade and Comparative Advantage, Heckscher–Ohlin Model.

resources they possess. Specifically, countries in which unskilled labor is in abundant supply will occupy market niches for labor-intensive goods, such as farming and foods, textiles, footwear, and other basic manufactures. On the other hand, countries with abundant skilled labor will develop products, services, and technologies that use that type of labor intensively. Thus they will specialize in what are referred to as high-technology or high value-added products, for which the skills of those workers are the key and essential input. The basic pattern of global production projected by the model is shown in Fig. 1.

Emerging patterns of global production and trade broadly confirm this general interpretation of the model. Increasingly, countries in which unskilled labor is cheap and abundant are expanding their global market shares of lower-technology products, and this process is expected to continue. The challenge for developed countries, and hence the key to their global competitiveness, is to shift their production away from these low-skilled industries and specialize in sectors that employ more advanced technologies and skills. Porter (1998) has long worked on the development of national competitiveness indexes from this standpoint, calling for a definition of competitiveness that starts from the sources of prosperity and goes beyond purely economic conceptions based on national product market shares (Porter, 2005).

## TOWARD A COMPETITIVE INDEX BASED ON HUMAN CAPITAL

The first task of this study[1] was to determine which countries were progressing toward the competitiveness demanded by this global division of production. Porter's Global Competitive Index and its "micro" correlate, the Business Competitive Index (Porter, Sachs, & Warner, 2000; Porter, 2005), provide an extensive overview of the multidimensional nature of competitiveness, as well as a well-grounded and established reference for comparing countries. The present study focused on a smaller range of variables that could be considered to be forces driving competitiveness as defined above. An index was designed for this purpose, which incorporated a series of macroeconomic indicators emphasizing human capital variables that affect competitiveness dynamics within national businesses (Simón & Allard, 2005). The indicators chosen for the index were the following:

(1) Productivity per hour worked[2] is a key indicator of economic success and the source not only of market competitiveness, but also of living standards over time. Labor productivity is also relatively straightfor- ward to measure for a wide sample of countries. Hence it became one of the key points of reference in this study and its conclusions.

(2) The proportion of exports in the high-technology sector[3] shows whether an economy is moving to occupy the market niche that corresponds to developed countries, as defined above. This is another key indicator of competitiveness in this study.

(3) The Human Development Index (HDI)[4] reflects various aspects of welfare in different countries, including GDP per person, educational attainment, and health indicators. This index is relevant for competi- tiveness because countries with a high HDI not only are showing evidence of economic success in material terms (GDP per capita), but also provide a fertile market for local companies to launch new products. Individuals in these countries are also presumably better equipped for skilled work, due to their better education and health.

(4) Annual private-sector spending on research and development, adjusted for the size of the country's population,[5] gives an idea of how actively a

country's businesses are preparing themselves to occupy their global market niche by developing new products and improving existing ones. Public spending on R&D is excluded because it reflects public effort rather than the private initiative that is essential to competitiveness.

(5)  The number of patents registered in the U.S., Japanese, and EU patent offices, adjusted for the size of the economy,[6] is another indication that the private sector is seeking the new technologies, processes, and product differentiation that will open up and conserve its global market niche in the future.

(6)  The percentage of university degree holders among the 25- to 34-year-old population[7] reflects the preparation of younger workers to move into higher skilled tasks and sectors.

(7)  The percentage of all university degrees that are in sciences and engineering[8] is further evidence of the preparation of workers for jobs with a high technical or technological content.

(8)  The percentage of immigrants with higher education[9] reflects not only the fact that a country is drawing new skilled workers into its pool of human capital, but also that the sectors that require highly skilled workers are in expansion. Thus the country is probably progressing toward the type of specialization required in the global environment.

Finally, in line with the work of Porter et al. (2000)[10] on the role of variables that may condition a country's capacity to compete in the medium and long term, three institutional indicators were included in the index to represent whether the local business environment permitted the flexibility and adjustment that rapidly changing, dynamic industries would require. Those indicators were the following:

(9)  Time required to start a company.

(10) Time required to shut down a company.

(11) Employment Rigidity Index, which combines various features of the legal requirements for hiring, firing, and reassigning workers.[11]

Clearly, some of the variables selected (e.g., education of the labor force or the indicators of the institutional environment) represent inputs into the production and competitiveness process. Others, such as R&D spending and patent activity, represent an intermediate phase, whereas high-tech exports, productivity, and the HDI are evidence that the drive to competitiveness is bearing fruit. Without a doubt, there is endogeneity among these variables, and it is impossible to determine which have generated competitiveness and which are the products of a more competitive economy.[12] Taken together,

however, they give a good picture of how well an economy is poised to meet
the challenges common to developed countries in the 21st century.

The variables listed above were first combined into an index by
transforming the corresponding values into $Z$ scores for every variable and
entering each of them as adding (indicators 1–8) or subtracting (indicators
9–11) according to the estimated direction of the force for fostering
competitiveness. The index was calculated for 24 countries, which included
the United States, Japan, China, and other non-European countries. The
ranking (see Appendix) yielded few surprises, with the possible exception
of the position of China, which joined the eastern and southern European
countries at the bottom of the ranking, indicating that its market niche
is still clearly in the lower value-added sectors predicted by the model.
Another interesting feature of the ranking was that the most competitive
countries included economies with both high and low levels of social
spending, as Fig. 2 shows. The suggestion that social spending is not
an important contributor to economic success will be discussed in more
detail later.

If competitiveness in the global environment of the 21st century is to be
evaluated, countries should be compared with a wide range of trading
partners from various regions, as in the ranking above. Indeed, comparing

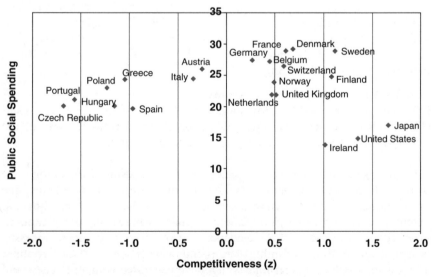

*Fig. 2.*   Public Social Spending and Competitiveness.

***Table 1.*** Competitiveness Ranking, 20 EU Countries.

| Country | Position | Standard Score |
|---|---|---|
| Sweden | 1 | 1.29 |
| Finland | 2 | 1.24 |
| Ireland | 3 | 1.14 |
| Denmark | 4 | 0.85 |
| France | 5 | 0.83 |
| Switzerland | 6 | 0.75 |
| Belgium | 7 | 0.61 |
| United Kingdom | 8 | 0.61 |
| Norway | 9 | 0.61 |
| Netherlands | 10 | 0.57 |
| Germany | 11 | 0.45 |
| Austria | 12 | −0.15 |
| Italy | 13 | −0.28 |
| Spain | 14 | −0.83 |
| Greece | 15 | −0.99 |
| Slovenia | 16 | −1.13 |
| Hungary | 17 | −1.18 |
| Poland | 18 | −1.24 |
| Portugal | 19 | −1.5 |
| Czech Republic | 20 | −1.64 |

European countries only with one another omits the leading countries from the sample (Japan, the United States) and thus deprives the study of valuable information on how different models and attitudes may have influenced economic success. However, because the detailed survey data used in the second half of the study was available only for EU member states plus Switzerland and Norway, non-European countries were dropped from the index. A ranking was elaborated for 20 European countries for which data could be obtained for all of the competitiveness indicators. The results are shown in Table 1.

The European ranking was generally as expected. The Scandinavian countries and Ireland moved into the top slots, whereas the southern and eastern European countries remained in the lowest positions; and Germany trailed France. The countries exhibited certain features that confirmed suspicions about the types of activity and environment that enhance competitiveness. For instance, education was a key predictor of high productivity and strength in high-technology sectors, as was R&D spending. Complex administrative structures, on the other hand, were associated with lower productivity and smaller high-tech export shares.[13] All of the countries at the bottom of the index were characterized by a relatively complex bureaucracy for business. In other words, the correlations among variables confirmed the selection of indicators for the index and the features that would be typical of countries that are successfully competing on a global scale. This also suggests that key items on the agenda for national policymakers should include boosting education and seeking more flexible institutional environments for business.

What underlying factors in the economy determine the positions of various countries in this ranking? Obviously there are myriad factors, some of which are not observable and cannot be quantified, such as cultural attitudes toward work, risk, and excellence (Hofstede et al., 2002). This study focused on only one broad factor that was considered to be most important in determining competitiveness, which is the human factor. With the ranking completed, this study proceeded to its second task, which was to determine whether certain attitudes, values, and especially working patterns were associated with success, as defined in the first part of the report.

## MOVING TO A MICRO FOCUS: WHAT ATTITUDES AND VALUES ARE ASSOCIATED WITH COMPETITIVENESS?

The European Social Survey (ESS), the source of the data for the second half of this research, is a wide-ranging annual social survey that began in 2002 and that explores the interactions between institutions and the attitudes, opinions, and values of citizens across the European Union. This study selected the questions that were related to citizens' perceptions of their own subjective satisfaction or happiness, their views on the quality of public institutions, their perceptions of their working environment, and the expression of the values that were most important to them. To facilitate the contrasts between attitudes and competitiveness, the questions were grouped into four indices, which were the following (Table 2):[14]

1. Index of Personal Well-being (IPW), which incorporates the individual's expression of satisfaction, happiness, and health.
2. Index of Perceptions of Public Institutions (IPPI), which reflects satisfaction with the national legal, educational, and health systems and the state of the economy in general.

***Table 2.*** Opinions Included in the Indices.

| Item | Index |
|------|-------|
| Legal system | Index of perceptions of public |
| Environment economic | institutions (IPPI) |
| Health system | |
| Educational system | |
| Estimation of the level of personal satisfaction | Index of personal well-being (IPW) |
| Estimation of the level of personal happiness | |
| General perception of subjective health | |
| Perceived flexibility in relation to the work schedule | Index of perception of the working |
| Perceived autonomy in relation to the personal organization of work | environment (IPWE) |
| Perceived capacity of influence in the workplace | |
| Perceived capacity of decision making | |
| Perceived capacity to make changes in the workplace | |
| Perception of employability | Index of perception of employability (IPE) |

3. Index of Perception of the Working Environment (IPWE), which includes questions related to perceived flexibility and autonomy and the ability to influence decisions in the workplace.
4. Index of Perception of Employability (IPE), which reflects the individual's perception of his/her market value and employment possibilities.

The results for each of these indices were compared with the competitive position of each country, to determine whether any clear relationships emerged.

Additionally, following the structure laid out in the Schwartz Value Survey,[15] 15 questions were selected from the ESS that provided information on respondents' motivational structure, and they were classified into 8 of the 10 values defined by Schwartz (1999).[16] The values are power, achievement, hedonism, stimulation, self-direction, universalism, benevolence, and conformism. Schwartz classifies these values into two orthogonal dimensions, which are "toward oneself" or "toward others" (power and achievement vs. universalism and benevolence) and "openness to change" vs. "conservatism" (self-direction and stimulation vs. conformism). Again, the results of the values classification were contrasted with the competitiveness ranking to see whether patterns emerged.

Globally, our results were startling. For each of the indices described above, the most important predictor of satisfaction was the country's degree of competitiveness on the EU ranking. The countries at the top of the competitiveness ranking showed higher degrees of satisfaction on the IPW, as Fig. 3 indicates. Achieving competitiveness appears to raise the subjective welfare of citizens in economically successful countries.

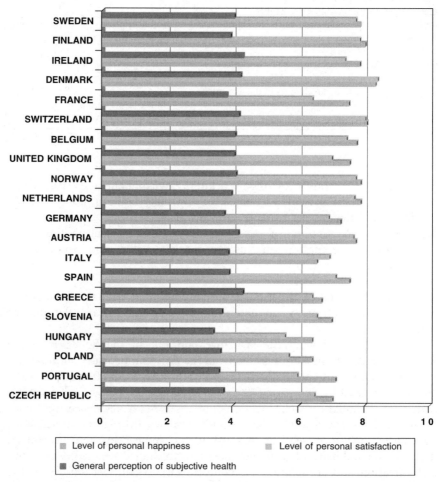

*Fig. 3.* Personal Well-being and Competitiveness (Countries Ranked by Competitiveness).

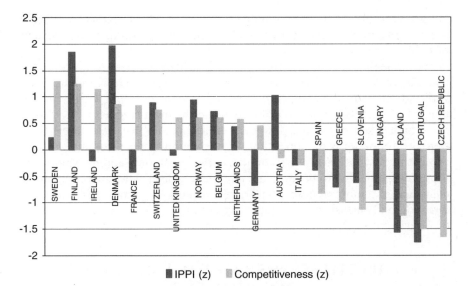

*Fig. 4.* Satisfaction with Public Institutions and Competitiveness (Countries Ranked by Competitiveness).

In a similar way, citizens in the most competitive countries express greater satisfaction with the quality of public institutions in their countries. Although there is a group of more "critical" countries (France, Germany, Ireland, Sweden, and the United Kingdom), where satisfaction with public institutions is lower than would be predicted by their competitiveness levels, in general there is a clear positive relationship between competitiveness and perceptions of the quality of public institutions and services, as can be observed in Fig. 4.

In this regard, it is interesting to note once again that, whereas the perception of the quality of public services correlates highly ($r = 0.614$, $p = 0.004$) with competitiveness as defined in this study, its correlation with the level of public spending or social spending is much lower ($r = 0.416$, $p = 0.076$). Ireland, for instance, is a country high on the competitiveness ranking and one of the ones in which satisfaction with public institutions is highest; yet public social spending is the lowest for the countries in the sample.[17] The finding presents an interesting paradox. Could it be that more competitive countries have better public services because they apply the same high standards and quest for quality and innovation to their public institutions as they do to their products? Or is competitiveness simply so important to the satisfaction of individuals that its effect on their well-being overwhelms other considerations, such as the size of spending or the extent of public services?

The values study extracted from the ESS yielded less clear results than the two indices described above. Some of the values expected to correlate highly with indicators in the competitiveness index – for example, creativity and number of patents – failed to do so. Nor did the most competitive countries show higher scores for the power or achievement values. However, there were certain patterns of values that were common to the most and the least competitive countries. In all countries, the most outstanding values are those corresponding to benevolence and universalism. The most competitive countries are more focused on values related to stimulation and self-direction, in contrast to less competitive countries, which are more centered on values linked to power and achievement.

## COMPETITIVENESS AND THE EMPLOYMENT RELATIONSHIP

The key objective of this study was to discover whether certain characteristics of the labor relationship were associated with competitiveness. The answer appears to be yes, and the findings in this area are the most remarkable. The IPW, defined above, showed that workers in the most competitive countries felt that they had more say in their workplaces and enjoyed a greater freedom to influence decisions on the job. The relationship can be observed in Fig. 5. Table 3 shows the ranking by countries.

The variables of this ranking show a high positive correlation with the key indicators of economic success, such as productivity ($r = 0.81$, $p = 0.000$), research and development spending ($r = 0.75$, $p = 0.000$), and the share of exports coming from high-tech sectors ($r = 0.54$, $p = 0.013$). Unsurprisingly, they correlate negatively with the administrative rigidities of the index, especially with employment rigidity.

This finding is in line with what might be expected to be the requirements of an employment relationship in a world in which the key input for success is highly skilled labor. Contemporary managers in higher-tech sectors would be more likely to seek feedback from workers and would allow them greater autonomy so that they could fully employ their skills. In this sense, the study shows that the less competitive countries show evidence of a more hierarchical, rigid working relationship that may be becoming a relic of the past in the more competitive sectors. Leading countries, on the other

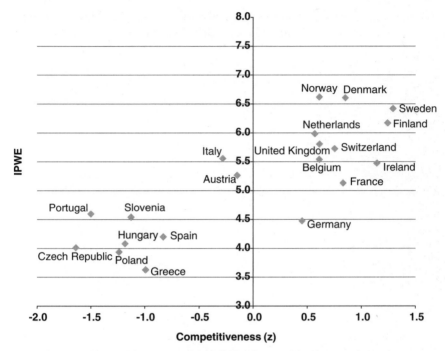

*Fig. 5.* Competitiveness and Flexibility in the Working Environment.

hand, either have made the transformation to a new model or have always enjoyed the advantage of a more open working environment that bears a resemblance to the "new labor contract" described in some U.S. literature (Capelli, 1999; Osterman, 2001). Once again, the results point to important changes that could be implemented in the workplace and the employment relationship that might help companies and countries to achieve greater economic success. These types of changes resemble the research lines on employees' participation practices, empowerment, and structures and policies aiming at what is being called organizational democracy (Gratton, 2005; Malone, 2004).

An important sidelight to the variables discussed above is their relationship with hours worked, for which data were available for all of the countries in the study.[18] Hours worked was not included in the competitiveness index because the variable serves as the denominator to productivity per hour worked, and the two effects are inseparable. Whereas there are countries, such as the United States and Ireland since the 1990s,

**Table 3.**    Ranking of Countries by Perception of Working Environment,
from Most to Least Positive.

| | |
|---|---:|
| Norway | + |
| Denmark | |
| Sweden | |
| Finland | |
| Netherlands | |
| United Kingdom | |
| Switzerland | |
| Italy | |
| Belgium | |
| Ireland | |
| Austria | |
| France | |
| Portugal | |
| Slovenia | |
| Germany | |
| Spain | |
| Hungary | |
| Czech Republic | |
| Poland | − |
| Greece | |

that show rising employment and gains in productivity at the same time, it is also true that higher unemployment is normally associated with rising productivity, because the denominator in the productivity equation is falling. Hence any link between trends in hours worked and productivity must be interpreted with caution.

However, the study did find that individuals in countries with longer working hours expressed less satisfaction with their job environment. Hours worked also showed a (small) negative correlation with variables such as the percentage of high-tech exports, R&D spending, and patents.

More important than the number of hours worked is the perception of workers that they enjoy some control and flexibility over how much and when they work. This perception, which formed part of the IPWE discussed above, was linked to higher productivity levels ($r = 0.831, p = 0.000$). At the same time, workers who have more schedule flexibility perceive themselves as more employable. They are also more likely to suggest changes in the work situation to their superiors, and those suggestions are more frequently listened to and put into practice. Other attitudes associated with innovation were also linked to the perception of time flexibility, such as entrepreneurship and interest in continued training and education. All of these relationships suggest that providing a margin of working-time flexibility is clearly in the long-term interests of the firm.

# CONCLUSIONS: TOWARD A GLOBAL HRM MODEL UNDER THE COMPETITIVENESS IMPERATIVE

The associations uncovered in this study between variables characterizing competitiveness and certain attitudes and features of the employment relationship throw some light on the debate over the existence of a global HRM model and to what extent this can be implemented in different contexts with comparable outcome levels.

First, competitiveness has proved a fruitful concept in coming up with a set of common aspects that should characterize HRM policies regardless of geographical or cultural differences. In an increasingly global business model, the search for the imperative of competitiveness poses a set of guidelines for HR, allowing implementation details to be further adapted to regional or cultural differences. Under this assumption, competitiveness demands greater autonomy and flexibility for the employee to maximize the human capital contribution to corporate performance. This type of scenario, based on the organizational democracy metaphor, is being debated more and more in the HRM literature that questions the limits and cost–benefit balance of such strategies (Kerr, 2004; Harrison & Freeman, 2004). Even authors such as Gratton (2005), who represent a highly employee-oriented approach to the "democratic enterprise," point up some troublesome factors on the horizon, such as:

– The need for managers to develop different leadership styles fostering employee empowerment and autonomy,
– The call for mature employees to accept accountability and obligations and to establish a psychological contract based on an adult-to-adult relationship, and
– The need for companies to evolve toward more open, less control-based structures and to optimize the use of technologies to create a more autonomous environment.

Probably because of these reasons, the steps forward have not yet been taken in most organizations, despite the "evolution toward democracy" that authors in different disciplines claim is occurring as a condition of modernization in Western countries (Inglehart, 2003). Some of the study's conclusions on worker perceptions and expectations have still to be proven effective and real.

The study also offers relevant conclusions regarding national policies and regulations that have an impact on employees and HRM policies from a long-term standpoint. If, as this study shows, the satisfaction of individuals and their perception of the quality of national institutions depend more on the productivity of their country than on public spending, then policies that enhance competitiveness are the best way to raise national welfare. If, in addition, the laws that protect workers from dismissal are actually leaving them "trapped" in an outdated, hierarchical employment relationship, and these laws are associated, in addition, with lower levels of productivity, there are few good arguments against their deregulation and reform. If excessive bureaucracy is a drag on competitiveness, this too needs to be made more agile. If working long hours is associated with poorer performance on competitiveness indicators and additionally reduces the perceived welfare of workers and their sense of influence and employability, longer working days should not be used as a device to make a firm or a country more competitive.

The reform agenda that this series of findings sets out is clear. National governments should pay more attention to longer-term elements that are keystones in the business environment, such as institutional quality and education, rather than using stopgap measures such as selective subsidies, government R&D spending, or even social spending to try to achieve competitiveness.

This study suffers from limitations posed by the data. In particular, leaving non-European countries out of the survey omits access to a rich variety of experience in countries like Japan and the United States, which rank at the top of the competitive index and have shown much faster productivity growth than the EU average in recent years. A logical direction for future research is to bring some of these countries into the sample, to see whether the attitudinal links identified in this study are unique to Europe or can be generalized to countries with different social and cultural models. In addition, in an exploratory study of this nature the problem of causality was not addressed. It is possible that many of the factors identified actually caused higher levels of productivity, whereas others are the results of better productivity performance. This study attempts to demonstrate only that a relationship does exist between indicators, without venturing into the question of in which direction causality runs.

Even with these limitations, the study makes an important contribution to the literature on how the human factor can play a role in competitiveness. It points to important directions for future research and identifies possible reforms at the business and national level that can help countries achieve that elusive objective of competitiveness.

## NOTES

1. This study was partially funded by Adecco Spain and the Instituto de Empresa Business School Foundation.
2. Data for 2002. IMD World Competitiveness Yearbook (2003).
3. Data for 2001. IMD World Competitiveness Yearbook (2003).
4. Data for 2000. IMD World Competitiveness Yearbook (2003).
5. Data for 2001. IMD World Competitiveness Yearbook (2003).
6. Data for 2004. OECD.
7. Data for 2001. IMD World Competitiveness Yearbook (2003).
8. Data for 1999. IMD World Competitiveness Yearbook (2003).
9. OECD.
10. Porter et al. (2000). *Executive Summary: Current Competitiveness and growth competitiveness* in the Global Competitiveness Report 2000, New York: Oxford University Press for the World Economic Forum.
11. World Bank Database, "Doing Business."
12. See the Appendix for correlation matrix.
13. The employment rigidity index and the time involved in starting or closing a business correlated negatively with educational attainment, R&D spending, patents, high-tech exports, and productivity. See the Appendix for details.
14. See the Appendix for details on each of these indices and correlation matrices among the questions included.
15. Schwartz (1992). Universals in the content and structure of values: Theoretical advances and empirical tests in 20 countries.
16. See the Appendix for details on the questions included in each of these value types.
17. Data on public social spending are not available for all countries in the study.
18. OECD.

## BIBLIOGRAPHY

Baron, J., & Kreps, D. M. (1999). *Strategic human resources: Frameworks for general managers.* New York: John Wiley & Sons.

Brewster, C. (2004). European perspectives on human resource management. *Human Resource Management Review, 14*, 365–382.

Budhwar, P. S., & Sparrow, P. R. (2002). An integrative framework for understanding cross-national human resource management practices. *Human Resource Management Review, 12*, 377–403.

Capelli, P. (1999). *The new deal at work.* Cambridge: Harvard Business School Press.

Delery, J. E., & Doty, D. H. (1996). Modes of theorizing in strategic human resource management: Tests of universalistic, contingency, and configurational performance predictions. *Academy of Management Journal, 39*(4), 802–835.

Franke, H. R., Hofstede, G., & Bond, M. H. (2001). National culture and economic growth. In: *Handbook of cross-cultural management* (pp. 5–15). Blackwell Publishers Limited.

Gratton, L. (2005). Managing integration through cooperation. *Human Resource Management, 44*(2), 151–158.

Guest, D. (1997). Towards jobs and justice in Europe: A research agenda. *Industrial Relations Journal, 28*(4), 344–353.

Harrison, J. S., & Freeman, R. E. (2004). Is organizational democracy worth the effort? *Academy of Management Executive, 18*(3), 49–53.

Hendry, C., & Pettigrew, A. (1992). Patterns of strategic change in the development of human resource management. *British Journal of Management, 3*, 137–156.

Hofstede, G. (1998). Attitudes, values and organizational culture: Disentangling the concepts. *Organization Studies, 19*(3), 477–492.

Hofstede, G. (2003). *Culture's consequences, comparing values, behaviors, institutions, and organizations across nations* (2nd ed.). Newbury Park, CA: Sage Publications.

Hofstede, G., & Hofstede, G. J. (2004). *Cultures and organizations: Software of the mind: Intercultural cooperation and its importance for survival.* New York: McGraw-Hill.

Hofstede, G. J., Pedersen, P., & Hofstede, G. (2002). *Exploring culture: Exercises, stories and synthetic cultures.* Yarmouth, Maine: Intercultural Press (http://www.interculturalpress.com/).

IMD World Competitiveness Yearbook. (2003). *IMD World Competitiveness Yearbook.* Lausanne, Switzerland: IMD.

Inglehart, R. (2003). How solid is mass support for democracy and how can we measure it? *Political Science and Politics, 36*, 51–57.

Kerr, J. L. (2004). The limits of organizational democracy. *Academy of Management Executive, 18*(3), 81–95.

Malone, T. (2004). *The future of work: How the new order of business will change your organization, your management style and your life.* Boston: Harvard University Press.

Morley, M. J. (2004). Contemporary debates in European human resource management: Context and content. *Human Resource Management Review, 14*, 353–364.

OECD – Organisation for Economic Cooperation and Development. Available at http://www.oecd.org

Osterman, P. (2001). Employers in the low wage/low skill labor market. In: K. Richard & M. Mare (Eds), *Low wage workers in the new economy.* Washington: Urban Institute.

Pfeffer, J. (1994). *Competitive advantage through people: Unleashing the power of the work force.* Boston, MA: Harvard Business School Press.

Porter, M. E. (1998). *The competitive advantage of nations.* New York: The Free Press.

Porter, M. E. (2005). *Building the microeconomic foundations of prosperity.* Ch. 2. The Global Competitiveness Report 2003–2004. Oxford University Press for the World Economic Forum, New York.

Porter, M. E., Sachs, J. D., & Warner, A. M. (2000). *Executive summary: Current competitiveness and growth competitiveness.* The Global Competitiveness Report. Oxford University Press for the World Economic Forum, New York.

Schwartz, S. H. (1992). Universals in the content and structure of values: Theoretical advances and empirical tests in 20 countries. In: M. Zanna (Ed.), *Advances in experimental social psychology* (Vol. 25, pp. 1–65). New York: Academic Press.

Schwartz, S. H. (1999). A theory of cultural values and some implications for work. *Applied Psychology: An International Review, 48*, 23–47.

Simón, C., & Allard, G. (2005). La competitividad en el Siglo XXI: Una comparativa Europea. IE Business School sponsored by Adecco Spain. Available at http://www.hrcenter.org/WF_Investigacion.aspx?id = 6

Warner, M. (2004). Human resource management in China revisited: Introduction. *International Journal of HRM, 15*(4), 617–634.

Warner, M., & Zhu, Y. (2002). Human resource management 'with Chinese characteristics': A comparative study of the People's Republic of China and Taiwan. *Asia Pacific Business Review, 9*(2), 21–42.

Whitley, R. (2006). Understanding differences: Searching for the social processes that construct and reproduce variety in science and economic organization. *Organizational Studies, 27*(8), 1153–1177.

WORLD BANK (2006). Database doing business. Available at http://rru.worldbank.org

Youndt, M. A., Snell, S. A., Dean, J. W., & Lepak, D. P. (1996). Human resource management, manufacturing strategy, and firm performance. *Academy of Management Journal, 39*(4), 836–866.

# FURTHER READING

Djankov, S., La Porta, R., Lopez-de-Silanes, F., & Shleifer, A. (2002). The regulation of entry. *Quarterly Journal of Economics, 117*, 1–37.

ESS – European Social Survey (2006). Available at http://www.europeansocialsurvey.org

EUROSTAT Yearbook (2004). Available at http://epp.eurostat.ec.europa.eu/portal/page?_pageid = 1073,46587259%26_dad = portal%26_schema = PORTAL%26p_product_co de = KS-CD-04-001

Freeman, R. (2005). *Labor market institutions without blinders: The debate over flexibility and labour market performance.* NBER Working Paper no. 11286.

Gratton, L. (2004). *The democratic enterprise: Liberating your business with freedom, flexibility and commitment.* London: Prentice Hall.

Lindert, P. (2004). *Growing public: Social spending and economic growth since the eighteenth century.* Two volumes. Cambridge University Press.

Lundvall, B. (2007). National innovation systems – analytical concept and development tool. *Industry and Innovation, 14*(1), 95–119.

Rousseau, D. (1995). *Psychological contracts in organizations: Understanding written and unwritten agreements.* Thousand Oaks, CA: Sage.

Rousseau, D., & Schalk, R. (2000). *Psychological contracts in employment: Cross-national perspectives.* Newbury Park, CA: Sage.

Schneider, B. (1987). The people make the place. *Personnel Psychology, 40*, 437–453.

Schneider, B., Goldstein, H. W., & Smith, D. B. (1995). The ASA framework: An update. *Personnel Psychology, 48*, 747–773.

Sparrow, P., & Cooper, C. L. (2003). *The employment relationship: Key challenges for HR.* Butterworth-Heinemann.

# APPENDIX

***Table A1.*** Competitiveness Groups.

| High Competitiveness Group | Middle Competitiveness Group | Low Competitiveness Group |
|---|---|---|
| Sweden | Norway | Spain |
| Finland | United Kingdom | Greece |
| Ireland | Belgium | Slovenia |
| Denmark | Netherlands | Hungary |
| France | Germany | Poland |
| Switzerland | Austria | Portugal |
| | Italy | Czech Republic |

***Table A2.*** Ranking Including Non-EU Countries.

| $Z^a$ | Position | Country |
|---|---|---|
| 1.71 | 1 | Japan |
| 1.37 | 2 | United States |
| 1.11 | 3 | Sweden |
| 1.07 | 4 | Finland |
| 1.01 | 5 | Ireland |
| 0.68 | 6 | Denmark |
| 0.61 | 7 | France |
| 0.59 | 8 | Switzerland |
| 0.51 | 9 | United Kingdom |
| 0.49 | 10 | Norway |
| 0.47 | 11 | Netherlands |
| 0.45 | 12 | Belgium |
| 0.27 | 13 | Germany |
| 0.00 | 14 | Israel |
| −0.24 | 15 | Austria |
| −0.34 | 16 | Italy |
| −0.96 | 17 | Spain |
| −0.97 | 18 | China |
| −1.04 | 19 | Greece |
| −1.15 | 20 | Hungary |
| −1.18 | 21 | Slovenia |
| −1.22 | 22 | Poland |
| −1.56 | 23 | Portugal |
| −1.68 | 24 | Czech Republic |

[a]Standard score.

**Table A3.** Correlation Matrix: Macroeconomic Variables.

| | | Labor Productivity | Working Hours | High-Tech Exports | Business Expenditure on R&D | Science Degrees | Human Development Index | Higher Education Achievement | Highly Educated Foreign Born | Starting a Business Time | Rigidity of Employment Index | Closing a Business Time |
|---|---|---|---|---|---|---|---|---|---|---|---|---|
| Working hours | * | -0.69 | | | | | | | | | | |
| | ** | 0 | | | | | | | | | | |
| High-tech exports | * | 0.47 | -0.15 | | | | | | | | | |
| | ** | 0.04 | 0.52 | | | | | | | | | |
| Business expenditure on R&D | * | 0.65 | -0.3 | 0.54 | | | | | | | | |
| | ** | 0 | 0.21 | 0.01 | | | | | | | | |
| Science degrees | * | 0.18 | -0.4 | 0.11 | 0.2 | | | | | | | |
| | ** | 0.44 | 0.08 | 0.63 | 0.39 | | | | | | | |
| Human development index | * | 0.92 | -0.65 | 0.51 | 0.72 | 0.19 | | | | | | |
| | ** | 0 | 0 | 0.02 | 0 | 0.42 | | | | | | |
| Higher education achievement | * | 0.66 | -0.39 | 0.62 | 0.52 | 0.11 | 0.67 | | | | | |
| | ** | 0 | 0.09 | 0 | 0.02 | 0.64 | 0 | | | | | |
| Highly educated foreign born | * | 0.77 | -0.39 | 0.62 | 0.64 | 0.07 | 0.77 | 0.93 | | | | |
| | ** | 0 | 0.11 | 0.01 | 0 | 0.78 | 0 | 0 | | | | |
| Starting a business time | * | -0.54 | 0.25 | -0.52 | -0.54 | -0.26 | -0.42 | -0.21 | -0.35 | | | |
| | ** | 0.01 | 0.28 | 0.02 | 0.01 | 0.26 | 0.06 | 0.38 | 0.16 | | | |
| Rigidity of employment index | * | -0.26 | -0.2 | -0.29 | -0.35 | 0.32 | -0.14 | -0.12 | -0.16 | 0.49 | | |
| | ** | 0.28 | 0.39 | 0.21 | 0.13 | 0.16 | 0.55 | 0.63 | 0.53 | 0.03 | | |
| Closing a business time | * | -0.44 | 0.61 | -0.23 | -0.11 | 0.02 | -0.42 | -0.44 | -0.43 | 0.05 | -0.22 | |
| | ** | 0.05 | 0 | 0.34 | 0.66 | 0.94 | 0.07 | 0.05 | 0.08 | 0.83 | 0.36 | |
| Triadic patent | * | 0.5 | -0.29 | 0.49 | 0.93 | 0.27 | 0.62 | 0.36 | 0.53 | -0.49 | -0.23 | -0.08 |
| | ** | 0.02 | 0.22 | 0.03 | 0 | 0.25 | 0 | 0.12 | 0.02 | 0.03 | 0.33 | 0.74 |

*Pearson correlation.**Significance (bilateral).

*Table A4.*   Correlation Matrix: Social Index.

|        |     | IPW    | IPWE   | IPPI   |
|--------|-----|--------|--------|--------|
| IPWE   | r   | 0.246  |        |        |
|        | p   | 0.000  |        |        |
|        | n   | 16,258 |        |        |
| IPPI   | r   | 0.415  | 0.191  |        |
|        | p   | 0.000  | 0.000  |        |
|        | n   | 27,653 | 15,505 |        |
| IPE    | r   | 0.193  | 0.258  | 0.182  |
|        | p   | 0.000  | 0.000  | 0.000  |
|        | n   | 16,180 | 16,067 | 15,446 |

*Table A5.*   Values: Factorial Analysis.

|             | Item                                  | Type of Value  |
|-------------|---------------------------------------|----------------|
| Factor I    | Treating people equally               | Universalism   |
|             | To understand different people        | Benevolence    |
|             | Concern for the environment           | Self-direction |
|             | To worry about others' well-being     |                |
|             | To be creative                        |                |
|             | To make one's own decisions           |                |
| Factor II   | To show ability and be admired        | Power          |
|             | To have authority over others         | Achievement    |
|             | To be successful                      |                |
|             | To be rich                            |                |
| Factor III  | To have a good time                   | Hedonism       |
|             | To look for amusement and pleasure    | Stimulation    |
|             | To prove new things                   |                |
| Factor IV   | To behave correctly                   | Conformism     |
|             | To obey and to follow the rules       |                |

# MULTINATIONALS AND NATIONAL SYSTEMS OF EMPLOYMENT RELATIONS: INNOVATORS OR ADAPTERS?

Tony Edwards and Miao Zhang

## ABSTRACT

*Do multinational companies (MNCs) transfer employment practices across their operations in different countries? In other words, are they innovators in national systems of employment relations or do they adapt to them? This question lies at the heart of much research in the field of international HRM, yet the debate is characterized by two quite different approaches to this question – the "global – local" perspective and the "segmentation" thesis – that have not engaged satisfactorily with one another. Drawing on data from a case study of an American multinational in China, we argue that analysis must be sensitive to the sector-specific conditions that create variation between MNCs in this respect. Specifically, the way that multinationals build international processes of production and service provision is a crucial factor in shaping whether they look to transfer practices and, therefore, whether they are innovators or adapters.*

The Global Diffusion of Human Resource Practices: Institutional and Cultural Limits
Advances in International Management, Volume 21, 33–58
Copyright © 2008 by Emerald Group Publishing Limited
ISSN: 1571-5027/doi:10.1016/S1571-5027(08)00002-8

# INTRODUCTION

Multinational companies (MNCs) are becoming ever more influential in the global economy. The stock of foreign direct investment increased fivefold between 1990 and 2004 (UN, 2005), meaning that MNCs have direct control over a growing amount of production and service provision. In addition, many MNCs are key players in the creation of coordinated global "webs" or "chains," in which cross-border trade links operating units in various countries both within MNCs and between MNCs and other firms. These growing interlinkages have thrown the issue of the impact of MNCs on national systems of employment relations into sharp relief. One key question concerns the extent to which MNCs transfer human resource (HR) practices across their subsidiaries in different countries. Do they system-atically engage in such transfer, thereby acting as innovators in national systems of employment relations? Alternatively, do they see little benefit in transferring practices across borders, meaning that their role is that of adapting to national systems?

An assumption underpinning one strand of research in this area has been that MNCs can reap benefits from the consistency that global, or at least international, HR policies provide but that these must be balanced against the advantages of sensitivity to the local context that is achieved through adapting to the system of employment relations concerned. This "global – local" issue is very prominent in the international human resource management (HRM) literature (Edwards & Kuruvilla, 2005). However, some writers have questioned whether this is an appropriate starting point, casting doubt on the assumption that MNCs will see benefits in global HR policies. In an increasingly integrated global economy, so an alternative strand of the literature argues, MNCs segment their production so that distinct parts of the process are located in different countries. In these circumstances, there is little incentive to develop standardized policies for groups of workers who differ in terms of their skill levels, the nature of the technologies they operate, the level of discretion they are subject to, and so on. Thus this perspective sees variation in employment practices between national operating units of MNCs arising not from local constraints but rather from the segmentation of the production or service provision process.

These contrasting perspectives are particularly evident in relation to developing nations. MNCs are seen by some as a force for development in such countries, acting as carriers of efficiency-enhancing practices; others see them as contributing little to the growth or enhancement of the economy but rather as taking advantage of cheap and unprotected labor forces. In the

Chinese context this is neatly summarized by Cooke (2005, p. 4). She argues that "the increasing presence of MNCs in China may on the one hand act as a driving force for disseminating 'best practice' of HRM." On the other hand, MNCs may use "China as a low-cost mass production base that can be replaced when its comparative advantage declines ... (which serves) as a disincentive for a high commitment model of HR policy."

In this chapter we seek to shed light on the role of MNCs as innovators or adapters. Using data from a case study of an American engine manufacturer in China, we explore the way that the firm's international production process shapes the extent to which managers try to balance global and local influences. We argue that analysis of this issue needs to be sensitive to the sector-specific conditions that create variation between MNCs in the incentive that managers have to develop global HR policies. Specifically, we contend that a crucial distinction is whether MNCs are characterized by standardized or segmented production processes internationally. The chapter is structured as follows: the next section summarizes the two key strands in the literature referred to earlier, the method is outlined in the third section, the findings are presented in the fourth, the discussion in the fifth section examines the sectoral variation between firms that can help to reconcile contrasting findings in the literature, and conclusions are drawn in the sixth section.

# THE GLOBAL – LOCAL QUESTION AND ITS CRITICS

As mentioned above, one well-established approach to the issue of whether MNCs are innovators in employment practices has been to focus on the contrasting pressures for global integration on the one hand and local adaptation on the other. This approach revolves around whether MNCs build globally standardized HR policies or look to respond to the pressures from the local environment.

Models of HRM in MNCs provide a variety of sources of a global dimension to management style. One argument is that MNCs should search for a degree of uniformity to make sure that the nature of employment practices across countries is consistent with a global business strategy. Another incentive for a strong global aspect to HRM is to ensure that the firm is taking advantage of best practice across its operations by transferring practices that are perceived as enhancing efficiency to other parts of their operations. In this vein, the influential model developed by Taylor, Beechler, and Napier (1996, p. 960) suggests that MNCs should construct global HR policies that are based on "specific organizational competencies that are critical for securing competitive advantage in a global environment." An additional source of a global dimension to HR policies is less deliberate than the two identified above and arises from the range of ways in which MNCs retain strong roots in their original national base. The domination of senior managerial positions by individuals from the home country and the retention of key strategic units there mean that most MNCs exhibit a country-of-origin effect at the international level (Ferner, 1997).

The global pressures must be balanced against local constraints, however. It is commonly argued that decisions on many HR issues are best handled by experts in the local context who are more favorably placed than their counterparts in the corporate headquarters (HQ) to make sure that employment practices are adapted to respond to national peculiarities. The most widely cited aspect of these national peculiarities that researchers have argued leads firms to decentralize decisions to nationals in the host countries is culture; the myriad ways in which a set of taken-for-granted assumptions and values informs the way that organizations function in a particular nation cannot be easily understood by an outsider who is remote from the country in question. Employment regulations and institutional require-ments, so this approach argues, are also best dealt with by local managers who are equipped with the requisite knowledge. In short, to be able to go with the grain of a host business system, MNCs need to allow for a significant local dimension to their management style.

A large body of empirical work is predicated on the assumption of a global – local trade-off. For example, much of the literature on U.S. MNCs has shown how a strong American element to international HRM exists, something that is evident in the transfer of domestically conceived practices in the areas of variable pay and direct communication with staff. However, these central influences have had to be adapted to the requirements of host systems, which shows through in the evidence concerning the anti-union sentiments of U.S. MNCs (see Edwards & Ferner, 2002, for a review).

Many of the empirical studies of MNCs in China also demonstrate this tension between global and local influences. Ngo, Turban, Lau, and Lui's (1998) postal survey of U.S., British, and Japanese firms in Hong Kong produced evidence of a global aspect in the form of national cultural influences from the parent countries leading to significant differences between the national groups. Similarly, Bjorkman and Lu (2001) also found a strong global element in their analysis of Chinese–Western joint ventures in China. In contrast, Gamble's (2003) analysis of a British retail firm in China suggested that institutional and cultural features of the host environment – local factors, in other words–explain the nature of employment practices in the firm better than does a focus on the country of origin influence. Other studies have emphasized the combination of global and local effects. For instance, Ding, Fields, and Akhtar (1997) considered the extent of HQ control over HR policies in foreign-owned firms in the Shenzen region and argued that MNCs have moved away from some practices that have a long history in China, such as lifetime employment and egalitarian pay, but in other areas they are still strongly influenced by "Chinese socialist ideology," such as limited pay differentials between occupational groups. In a similar vein, Farley, Hoenig, and Yang (2004) on the basis of a survey of American, German, and Japanese MNCs in China argued that HR practices of the Chinese units of MNCs reflect both "push" factors to do with ownership, control, and nationality and "pull" factors to do with adapting to the Chinese system. And continuing along this line, Sanyal and Guvenli (2000) show that the pressures on American firms in China to adapt to the Chinese system were greater in some areas, such as the setting of pay and benefits, than in others.

Although these empirical studies come to differing assessments of the balance between global and local pressures, they all share the assumption that MNCs face the dilemma of balancing the advantages of global policies with the need to adapt to local constraints. This literature has been criticized on a number of grounds, such as the unconvincing use of culture as a catchall for national effects (see Edwards & Kuruvilla, 2005 for a review). A more fundamental problem, however, is the key assumption underlying the global – local question. Specifically, it assumes that MNCs will see inherent advantages in a global aspect to management style; this approach treats the absence of a global dimension as evidence that local constraints are more influential. This has been strongly questioned by a quite different approach that focuses on the way that MNCs segment their production or service provision processes so that different activities are carried out in different countries.

The notion that countries fulfill distinct roles within international trade is far from new, of course, dating back to the early theories of comparative advantage developed by Ricardo and others. It was also a central part of the "new international division of labor" that foresaw a trend toward parts of the production process of manufactured goods becoming delinked from one another, with the labor-intensive functions being located in countries offering a pool of cheap and compliant workers (Froebel, Heinricks, & Kreye, 1980). More recently, an analytical tool that has been used to explain the internal division of labor in MNCs is that of global "commodity chains"

(Gereffi & Korzeniewicz, 1994) or global "value chains" (Kaplinsky, 2001). Over the past decade or so a large body of research in the field of development studies has examined the way in which the production of many agricultural and manufactured goods that was hitherto carried out either within one country or through arm's-length international trade has become internationally integrated. This has occurred through the creation of global chains that are generally governed by a "lead" firm, normally a multi-national, which externalizes some activities through subcontracting and franchising and keeps other activities in-house. As Gereffi and Sturgeon (2004) put it, the "cumulative effect is that cross-border linkages between economies and firms have grown more elaborate" (p. 2). Among those activities retained within the firm, the production process is broken up and its constituent parts are concentrated in those countries that offer the most favorable circumstances for the particular activity in question.

Where there is an international segmentation within MNCs – with the labor-intensive operations in developing nations in which wages are lowest and the capital-intensive operations in developed countries in which highly skilled labor is most readily available – then MNCs are likely to deploy quite different practices across their operations, with the nature of these differences being shaped by the technology and skills involved in the work process. Accordingly, Marginson (1994) argues that the process of European integration has made it easier for MNCs to stratify their operations across countries and that a consequence of this is that those countries, such as the United Kingdom, that seek to attract FDI on the basis of a cheap and deregulated labor force will tend to attract the labor-intensive, low-skill activities of MNCs. This approach – which we refer to as the "segmentation thesis" – has led some writers to argue that cross-national variation in employment practices should be seen more as the multinational company taking advantage of what each country offers than as a reluctant adaptation to local constraints.

One prime example of this is Dedoussis (1995), who argues that understanding the way Japanese firms do or do not transfer practices across borders "may be approached as an issue of devising appropriate managerial strategies for different segments of the global workforce" (1995, p. 732). Drawing on data from the Australian subsidiaries of nine Japanese manufacturing firms, he argues that their internationalization strategies represented the extension of the core-periphery distinction in Japan between large firms and others that were dependent on them. The practices that were deployed in the Australian operations reflected this periphery status; as the author puts it, "little evidence of anything especially 'Japanese' could be found in the case of smaller firms" (1995, p. 742). Even in larger Japanese MNCs in Australia, transfer was restricted to practices that were low cost to establish, such as job rotation, whereas the "key but rather high cost practices" characteristic of Japanese firms, such as "tenured employment, seniority based remuneration and the provision of extensive welfare benefits," were not transferred or were applied only to Japanese expatriates. Overall, the author argues that "the transfer of Japanese management practices is primarily affected by economic considerations rather than socio-cultural constraints as has frequently been argued in the literature" (1995, p. 731).

This line of analysis also features strongly in Kenney and Florida's (1994) study of Japanese controlled "maquiladoras" in Mexico, principally in the consumer electronics industry. They argued that there was little evidence of the transfer of the Japanese-style employment practices that attracted so much attention in the West in the 1980s and early 1990s. For example, there was very little in the way of continuous improvement activities; rather, work processes were highly standardized and there was very little training for workers. Transfer from Japan was limited to "the more superficial aspects of the Japanese production-management system, such as the use of company uniforms" and "aspects of the Japanese open office system." Their explanation for this is that "the labor process in Tijuana was typical of that performed by part-time and temporary workers in Japan" (1994, p. 33). The nature of the labor-intensive assembly operations that produce goods for export into the United States in product markets characterized by intense price competition severely curtailed the incentive that management had to transfer other aspects of the Japanese system (see also Kenney, Goe, Contreras, Romero, & Bustos, 1998, for a similar argument concerning Japanese consumer electronics firms in Mexico).

A further study focusing on the international segmentation of production is Wilkinson, Gamble, Humphrey, Morris, and Anthony's (2001) analysis of Japanese electronics firms in Japan and Malaysia. The authors found marked variations between the two sets of plants: those in Japan were characterized by job security, some autonomy for workers, and opportunities for employees to undertake training and development; in contrast, jobs in the Malaysian plants were much less secure, monitoring of work was more notable, and training was much more restricted. The findings were explained not with reference to national constraints but rather to the internal division of labor within the Japanese firms controlling the production processes. The domestic operations of the Japanese MNCs, which carried out the design and development roles that account for a significant proportion of the "value added," deployed relatively complex technology that requires specialist knowledge and skills from employees. The HR practices in the Japanese plants reflected management's attempt to operate with a stable and motivated workforce for this type of plant. The Malaysian units, on the other hand, carried out the more labor-intensive production work and used less complex technology that can be operated by largely unskilled workers. The HR practices that meshed with this type of operation focused on cost minimization, including numerical flexibility, tight supervision, and little in the way of training. In an extension of this work, Wilkinson and Morris (2001, p. 2) make a similar argument based on data from the clothing as well as the consumer electronics sector in Malaysia and China. As they put it: "When firms locate facilities beyond their own national borders, attempts to simply replicate home country activities are quite unlikely to occur, and not just because foreign tastes and consumption patterns may be different. Rather, different activities are likely to be undertaken in different countries as part of a more or less complex international division of labour."

This strand of the literature appears to offer an influential critique of the logic of the global – local question, but there are problems with it, too. One problem relates to the rejection of institutional influences in favor of an "economic" explanation, as favored explicitly by Dedoussis (1995) and Wilkinson and Morris (2001). Recognizing that firms may concentrate their activities within a segmented international process does not mean that firm strategy will not be shaped by institutional influences. Whitley (1996), for example, has argued that the way that value chains are coordinated and managed reflects the influence of the business system in which the "lead" agent is embedded. Thus decisions over how to construct an international chain of operating units are informed by institutions and, therefore, it is not sensible to think about separating institutional explanations from economic ones; the two are inextricably linked. An arguably more fundamental problem, however, concerns the extent to which MNCs are characterized by segmented processes of production and service provision. Many MNCs evidently are characterized by the segmentation that Dedoussis (1995), Kenney and Florida (1994), and Wilkinson et al. (2001) describe, largely on evidence from the electronics industry. However, it is less clear that this will be the case in other sectors; in some industries, such as hotels and catering, MNCs seem to have constructed their international operations on a standardized basis in that firms have expanded into other countries by setting up mini-replicas of existing operations. In such circumstances MNCs may well see a logic in developing a global element to their HR policies.

These considerations suggest that the extent and nature of international integration within MNCs are crucial aspects of the context in which decisions on international HR issues are made. We look to shed light on this through a case study of an American engineering firm in China. The details of the process of data collection are summarized in the next section.

# METHOD

Given the aims of this chapter, it is crucial that the method is equipped to shed light on both the extent and the logic of a global element to HR policies and the way that local institutions inform the nature of practices at site level. In addition, it is also crucial that the method allows an investigation of the international production process and the way that this informs a firm's approach to managing its international workforce. An in-depth, multilevel case study is particularly appropriate for such a situation.

The case study, Engineering, Inc., is a medium-sized U.S.-based multinational that produces engines for vehicles. The research on which this chapter is based is an extension of a wider study that examined the ways in which the embeddedness of U.S. MNCs in the American business system shapes the way they operate internationally (see Almond & Ferner, 2006 for more details). The firm is typical of a large number of American MNCs in the manufacturing sector in that it grew domestically in the early part of the 20th century and internationally in the second half. As we have demonstrated elsewhere, Engineering, Inc., is a firm that has been characterized by a strong central influence over HR in its international operations and has moved in recent years toward greater formalization of international HR policy that appears to extend across its global operations (Edwards, Colling, & Ferner, 2004).

The primary focus of this chapter is on the firm's Chinese operations. Engineering, Inc., has 350 directly employed workers in its operations in Beijing who are involved in the firm's HQ for the East Asia region, performing tasks such as financial control, sales and marketing, and HR. The production operations consist of six joint ventures with state-owned firms that are scattered across the country and in total employ 2000 people. Of the six joint ventures, three are 50–50, two are 55–45 with Engineering, Inc., as majority owner, and one is 75–25 with Engineering, Inc., as majority owner. The fieldwork took place at both the East Asian HQ and one of the production sites. In total, 16 interviews were conducted with a range of respondents, three of whom were posted at the firm's corporate HQ at the time of the research. Some interviews were conducted in English and some in Mandarin, but all were recorded and transcribed in English. Some material from the wider case study of the firm, which consisted of a further 28 interviews in the United States and the United Kingdom, is used to throw light on the nature of the firm's global HR policies and the extent to which the production process is internationally integrated. The interviews all covered three areas of employment practice that the initial fieldwork suggested were those for which the HQ had a clear and distinct vision and appeared to exert a strong influence across the firm's operations. These were workforce diversity, teamworking, and performance management.

Two key aspects of the research design need to be justified, the choice of country and the choice of sector. In relation to the first of these, China has witnessed a sharp increase in FDI over the 2 decades or so since the initiation of the Open Door policy. In 1980 the stock of FDI into China was valued at just over $1 billion; by 2004 it had risen to over $245 billion. In terms of flows, China accounted for 9% of FDI in 2004, the third highest national figure (UN, 2005). Consequently, there are parts of the Chinese economy in which foreign firms are increasingly dominant, particularly the Special Economic Zones and the big cities where large numbers of workers, especially young ones, are used to working for MNCs. This has been a part of a wider transformation of the economy, which has had many dimensions, including marked changes to employment practices. These have included fixed-duration individual and collective contracts rather than jobs for life; remuneration becoming influenced by performance, post, and skill levels and not just seniority; and new welfare schemes in which employees and employers are required to pay into funds for pensions, industrial accidents, maternity, unemployment, and medical insurance that have reduced the reliance on the state welfare system (Cooke, 2005, p. 20). These changes appear to have created a context in which MNCs have more scope to transfer practices from their Western operations. The significance of this is that if the case study data were to yield little evidence of transfer, then such a finding would be unlikely to be due solely to local constraints. In relation to the choice of sector, the engineering industry provides an interesting contrast with the electronics industry, from which much of the evidence relating to the segmentation thesis is drawn. In electronics, MNCs appear to have constructed global value chains in which distinct parts of the production process are stratified across countries. As we have seen, this means that the technologies that workers operate are quite different, as are the basic tasks and skills required to carry out these tasks. In the vehicle manufacturing sector, in contrast, the dominant model among MNCs is to use production sites to service the national markets in the countries in which they are located (Ivarsson & Alvstam, 2005). In these MNCs, the technological context and the nature of skill requirements are similar to those of their counterparts in other countries, creating commonalities in the context of work organization and employment relations that make them much more likely to perceive an advantage in transferring HR practices. Thus the choice of country and sector means that this case study can be seen as a key test of whether MNCs do indeed seek to develop a global element to HRM: the changes in the host system afford some scope for such global HR policies, and the sector exhibits conditions that may be conducive to this approach.

The data exhibit some limitations. Most obviously, the research design of a single case study does not permit contrasts to be drawn between firms. However, the need for a contrast with firms in differing contexts is fulfilled through examining other comparable studies of MNCs, particularly those discussed earlier in the literature review. As we will see, this proves to be highly revealing. A further limitation is that it was difficult to secure access to carry out interviews with employees in the Chinese production site in the way that we had done in the U.K. site, meaning that we rely principally on accounts from managers. Although this constrains our ability to provide a "view from below" on the nature of employment practice in the site in question, we do nevertheless have data from key informants at a number of levels that were crucial in constructing a picture of the issues at the heart of this chapter. Moreover, the data possess many strengths. In-depth interviews of this sort are still relatively rare in MNCs in China, or in MNCs in developing nations more generally, and provide a depth that some other techniques cannot provide. The variety of levels at which the research took place – from global corporate HQ to employees in production sites – provides a scope that is unusual in studies of this phenomenon. Most importantly, the data are highly suitable for an analysis of the utility of both the global – local tension and the segmentation thesis in interpreting the way the firm manages its international workforce.

# FINDINGS

Our starting point is to establish the key elements in the international production process at Engineering, Inc. To what extent is there a clear division of labor across countries involving national operating units specializing in distinct tasks? There was some evidence of such a specialization. This was most evident in relation to R&D, for which the main center is located in the firm's heartland in the Midwest of the United States. Some development work takes place in other countries, but this is generally restricted to adapting products to the national market. For example, in China the products need to be adapted for 6-speed heavy vehicles as opposed to the 12-speed model that is common in the United States and the United Kingdom, something that is the responsibility of a small applied engineering department. In the main, though, R&D is heavily concentrated in the United States. A further indication of locating specialist functions in particular countries is the firm's move to increase the extent to which it concentrates routine administrative work in a small number of locations. One example is the plans by the HR department to create one call center for the global operations that would be located in India and operate the firm's HR information system.

This specialization of distinct activities was very limited, however. The dominant pattern in the firm's international operations is for production to be carried out by local sites that sell a high proportion of their output in the national or regional market. Thus the U.K. site that formed part of the case study had the role of producing a particular type of engine for the European market. It was evident that senior management was keen for its performance to be benchmarked against a similar American plant, but the mandates of the two sites were primarily regional in scope. The Chinese operations were heavily geared toward selling in the national market. In fact, exporting was negligible; the site we looked at exported only 1% of its products. The firm does import significantly into the Chinese market, mainly for sales to foreign MNCs located in China, which prefer to buy Engineering, Inc.'s products that have been produced elsewhere, apparently because they perceive there to be quality problems with the goods produced in the Chinese joint ventures. However, this cross-border trade is not increasing; in fact, the firm is seeking to reduce the extent to which they have to import products into China by raising the capability of the Chinese plants.

A consequence of this is that in the main the firm's international production process is not segmented. That is, it is not characterized by low-technology assembly operations involving routinized work being concentrated in some countries and high-technology manufacturing operations involving skilled workers using considerable initiative and discretion being concentrated in others. Rather, national operating units carry out a range of activities similar to those of their counterparts in other countries. Thus the process exhibits a high degree of standardization across countries in that there is a series of comparable plants carrying out production activities that have strong similarities. This is a very important part of the context because it indicates that the national operating units have similar ranges of occupational groups with workers undertaking comparable tasks.

It is in light of this that the strong corporate influence over employment practice in the firm's international operations should be seen. In some cases this took the form of mandatory policies for all global operations. This was the case for the handling of cases of sexual harassment, whereas other issues, such as a code of conduct on business ethics and a corporate statement of values, were also set centrally. There was another range of HR decisions that could be made locally but which were heavily constrained by higher levels of management. Those relating to promotion and recruitment at the director level and the size of the annual pay budget fell into this category. The role of the central HR department appeared to be growing and becoming more formalized. In the past there were a number of HR policies that were nominally global but which operating units were free to ignore in practice; the HQ would simply announce that they were to cover the firm's operations across the world but would not monitor their implementation or operation. In the years immediately prior to our research, however, management at HQ had sought to formalize policies and to take steps to ensure that they were enacted, making it more difficult for subsidiaries to deviate from company policy. Evidently, there is a strong global dimension to HR policies.

Data relating to the three substantive areas of employment practice on which we focus in this chapter confirm this picture of central attempts to build global HR policies. The first of these is workforce diversity. The corporate emphasis on this issue in part reflects the ideological commitment of the founding father, who had gone to some lengths to promote the benefits of "valuing difference" within the organization. It also reflects the nature of antidiscrimination legislation in the United States that has created institutional pressures on firms to take a proactive stance in dealing with equality issues. Such pressures do not exist in anything like the same form in China, yet the evidence confirms the existence of a strong central influence in this area.

One manifestation of this was the requirement that each set of national operating units was required to present a Business Case for Diversity. This involved a range of practices that would operate at the national level and some targets for increasing diversity. In China one such target was to reach a ratio of six men to four women in management positions, though the ratio at the time of our research was a long way from this. Another aspect of the Business Case was to seek to increase "regional diversity." This represented an attempt by Chinese managers, who were faced with a highly homogenous population ethnically, to provide a functional equivalent of ethnic diversity, which was something they knew the corporate HQ was keen to promote. The expectation that all of the firm's sites globally should have, or be planning to establish, a Diversity Council – a body that meets regularly to discuss local diversity issues – was also in evidence in China, with the joint venture production site studied having such a council in place. In addition, all "direct" employees in China had to go through diversity training, though those in joint ventures did not face this requirement.

These data provide evidence not only of a global element to the handling of diversity issues but also of a local element. This is clear in the way in which local managers were encouraged to think about what diversity might mean in the Chinese context, hence the focus on regional diversity. The HR Director for China argued that he was encouraged to "tailor the corporate definition of diversity into the local situation." The local dimension also comes through in the active resistance by local actors to global diversity policies. One illustration of this is the attempt by senior management at corporate HQ to apply at the international level the Domestic Partners Benefits policy first developed in the United States. This consisted of extending the rights that had previously accrued only to the wives and husbands of the firm's employees – primarily medical insurance but also entitlement to use company facilities – to unmarried heterosexual and homosexual partners. Many managers saw this as an important element of the firm's global approach as it represented a symbol of tolerance and the respect the firm exhibited for various ways of life. In China the policy met with stiff resistance, however. Local managers argued that such a policy would be highly controversial and might even be illegal. Following repeated arguments, the HQ agreed to drop their demand that the policy be formally implemented in China on the condition that local management operate "the spirit of the policy."

The second issue that we look at is teamworking. Analysis of data on this issue shows that, in keeping with the topic of workforce diversity, central attempts had been made to transfer a corporate model but that this operated in a way that reflected local constraints. A key part of the context of the firm's global policies in this respect was the Engineering, Inc., Production System, which consisted of tightly defined specifications of how production should take place. One element of this was a substantial manual setting out in some detail guidelines for engineers to implement locally concerning the layout of the production process. Another element consisted of the firm's emphasis on teamwork through a "star system." The idea behind this was that each employee would occupy a position at one of the points of the star and would take on responsibility for a particular aspect of the team's work. This was a mandatory part of the production system. Accordingly, this form of teamwork had been implemented throughout the production sites in China even though this required management of Engineering, Inc., to convince the management of its joint venture partners of the virtues of this approach.

The data also demonstrate, however, the way in which local peculiarities present difficulties in transferring practices in this area. One such difficulty was the lack of a tradition of workers taking on responsibility in the way that the firm's approach required. Respondents at the site level described how the Chinese tradition of teamwork involved very little real participation and that this had meant that, despite concerted attempts by management to instill a spirit of teamworking, teams operated with a dominant leader. As one put it, "they are more a group not a team; it has a leader, the leader decides and the group does it." Our respondents also emphasized the difficulties in introducing teamworking given the Chinese tradition of guanxi, in which individuals prefer to deal with those with whom they have a preexisting family or social link. The expectation on the part of the parent company that employees should share responsibility in teams with other employees with whom they may have no such link presented a further difficulty to management.

The third issue is that of performance management, which also demonstrates the importance of both global and local factors. The firm had for many years operated a performance management system that was based on a forced distribution of employees into three categories: the top 10%, the middle 80%, and the bottom 10%. During our research the system was revamped in a number of ways, including being converted to operate electronically and to incorporate a focus on competencies in assessing individuals. Perhaps more significantly, in a less favorable financial climate the system was reinterpreted with the bottom 10% no longer being treated as in need of counseling and development but rather being put "at risk." The shift toward seeing the performance management system as a way of identifying staff for the sack was highly controversial in all of the parts of the company that we examined. For example, several Chinese managers echoed the unease of their counterparts elsewhere in arguing that the policy could not go on indefinitely without eating into very solid performers. However, it was seen by senior management as a crucial element in convincing those within the firm and especially external shareholders that performance was being taken very seriously.

The Chinese part of the firm had implemented this new corporate-wide performance management system in the year or so before our research. This comprised the harsher approach to those in the bottom 10% of the forced distribution. In China a formal requirement was that half of those in this category be put on a six-month correction plan and if there was no improvement then they had "to walk out," as one of our respondents put it.

There was, though, evidence that the system did not operate in quite the same way as in the United States and the United Kingdom. In particular, at the production sites the performance management system is patchy in its coverage and operates subtly differently. The International HR Director described the suspicion on the part of the Chinese joint venture partners of the performance management system, particularly when it involved the bottom 10% being put at risk. Gaining acceptance from managers in the partner companies had been very challenging and was achieved only very gradually. As she put it, "for those 10% right now we're trying to let them go and with joint ventures it's very difficult." Concessions had been made by managers in Engineering, Inc., to get the system implemented partially, resulting in it not covering all employees, whereas the correction plan for those in the bottom 10% did not entail the same danger of job loss as envisaged by American managers.

There was also evidence indicating that managers at the East Asian HQ in Beijing had some scope to ameliorate what they perceive as the negative consequences of the performance management system. For those concerned about the pressure to sack those who found themselves in the bottom 10%, the buoyant labor market for professional workers presented an opportunity to manipulate the system. Specifically, a degree of labor turnover that is found in buoyant labor markets reduced the pressure to cull workers, but even where the pressure remained managers could categorize those who left as poor performers even if they were not. This space from higher levels of management is likely to be greater for the Chinese operations than for, say, those in Britain because of the linguistic and cultural distance between China and the United States.

In sum, this evidence does not indicate that the multinational is using its operations in developing nations as low-cost production sites at which there will be little incentive to transfer practices used in the country of origin. Rather, the production processes in operating units in different countries share many similarities, creating scope for practices to be transferred across borders, in particular, and a global dimension to HR policies more generally. Accordingly, the data point to the existence of a country-of-origin effect in relation to diversity, teamwork, and performance management. This was felt most strongly for the professional workers in the firm's administrative center, but also at the production sites even though they were only jointly owned. In part, it stemmed from a deliberate attempt by senior management to ensure that the firm was able to present a united face to some global customers and also to ensure that the firm was actively spreading across their operations those practices that managers perceived to be efficiency enhancing. The global influence also stemmed from a deep-rooted country-of-origin influence arising from the embeddedness of the firm in the United States in terms of its shareholder base, the concentration of R&D, the nationality of senior management, and so on. This central influence had endured over a long period, creating a legacy that was slow to change. The focus on the global influence did not extend to all areas of HRM. Most obviously, pay levels were adapted to the national context and the low labor costs in China were of course one of the attractions of producing in that country. Nevertheless, a global dimension, shaped in part by home country institutions, was an important part of the story. As we have seen, these attempts to transfer practices came up against institutional barriers from the local context. This was particularly evident in relation to the issue of workforce diversity, for which local laws and institutions were major constraints, but is also evident for performance management and teamwork. A key theme of the data was of Chinese actors opposing those global policies that they saw as clashing with the local environment, and their ability to do so was enhanced by the ownership structure of the production sites. The need for a set of employment practices to be approved by the Government Labor Bureau in China enabled the joint venture partners to use their allies in the bureau to help slow down the introduction of new practices or modify the way they operate. As one respondent put it, "The joint venture partners are resistant, many times they are very suspicious of what you're trying to do ... I remember in one joint venture we ... said we were going to reduce this many people, this is the way we're going to reduce. The partner actually went to the (Labor Bureau) and talked to them and said what kind of instability we would create to the city." Local institutions were clearly also a key part of the story.

## DISCUSSION: THE ROLE OF SECTOR-SPECIFIC CONDITIONS

Overall, the findings did not support the arguments of those writers who have advocated the rejection of an "institutional" approach to transfer in favor of an "economic" one. Specifically, the idea that the international division of labor within MNCs gives management little incentive to transfer practices across quite different operations had little analytical purchase in this case. How, then, can we reconcile the findings of those authors who have argued that MNCs have little incentive to transfer practices across sites with those from the case study and a large body of other evidence that confirms that many MNCs do just this? The answer partly lies in understanding sector-specific conditions that lead some MNCs to *standardize* and others to *segment* their operations across borders.

The issue of variation between sectors is a factor that is commonly overlooked in both of the main strands of the literature. For example, many of the survey-based studies in the global – local perspective, such as Farley et al. (2004), are of firms from a range of sectors, yet the significance of this is not addressed. Similarly, some of the evidence provided by the segmentation school pays little attention to the role of sector. Dedoussis's (1995) study of nine Japanese MNCs, for example, comprised two in consumer electronics, two in motor vehicles, two in "wool sourcing and top making," one in optical lenses, one in telecommunications equipment, and one in air conditioning systems. Taylor's (2001) analysis of Japanese MNCs in China, which straddles the two main schools, raises the issue of variation between groups of MNCs. Specifically, his conclusion was that the extent of transfer in the 20 plants in the study was "complex and uneven"; whereas many Japanese firms encountered barriers to the transfer of practices from the host country, for others the location decision was geared toward saving labor costs and there was little apparent desire to apply Japanese management techniques in these cases. The role of sector-specific conditions is one possible cause of this variation, but is not addressed by the author.

However, the role of the sector is not ignored entirely in the literature. One example of this is Elger and Smith's (2005) study of Japanese electronics MNCs in the United Kingdom, in which the features of the sector, and variations within it, are central to their analysis. Another example is Kenney and Florida's (1995) account of differences in the extent of transfer by Japanese MNCs in the United States between the electronics and the automotive sectors. These authors argue that the automotive transplants had successfully engaged in transfer of the central features of the Japanese system of production and work organization with only modest adaptation, whereas most of the electronics transplants had not sought to transfer employment practices from Japan. They point to differing skill requirements as a source of these differences between sectors, but can this line of explanation be pushed further?

As we have argued, MNCs in some sectors tend to deploy standardized production processes that involve the international firm being organized around a series of comparable sites that perform most aspects of the process themselves and outsource others to suppliers in the country concerned. Such a process involves foreign operations taking the form of mini-replicas of existing sites; each of these exhibits a similar occupational profile, with workers performing tasks that resemble those performed by their counterparts in other countries. We point to two key factors that create conditions that are conducive to a standardized approach. The first of these is where firms need a physical presence in a market to serve it, something that is the case in many service sector industries in which there is an immediacy between producer and consumer, such as hotels and restaurants. It is also true in those areas of manufacturing for which establishing a local presence is important in generating greater visibility in the eyes of customers. This factor is important where governments prefer to buy politically sensitive goods from firms that have a local presence, as may be the case in defense or health-related products. The second key factor that creates conditions conducive to a standardized approach is where it is difficult technologically to separate parts of the production process into different geographical areas. In some sectors the manufacturing process cannot be segmented across borders because of the perishable nature of the products, as is the case in some parts of the food manufacturing sector, or because regulations concerning hygiene and safety prevent this, as is the case to some extent in pharmaceuticals. In other sectors, just-in-time (JIT) production processes require spatial proximity between different parts of the process, something that constrains, but does not eradicate, the international segmentation of MNCs in the automotive industry.

As we have also seen, in other sectors segmented production processes are more common. These are based on the role of sites being differentiated according to the costs and skill levels of the local workforce, so that the firm is characterized by a chain of specialized operating units, each with distinct functions and contrasting occupational profiles. Significant cross-border intrafirm trade occurs within these MNCs. Following the logic above, if the need for a firm to have a physical presence in the market in order to serve it gives rise to standardized processes, then the corollary is that segmented processes will be more common where this need is reduced or nonexistent. In these circumstances, MNCs have some scope to concentrate production or service provision in certain countries and serve some national markets with operations in others. This appears to be increasingly true of textiles. For example, Bair and Gereffi's (2001) study of the blue jeans industry in North

America showed how U.S. retailers and brand-name designers control value chains in which much of the production is carried out in Mexico. The second key factor in leading to standardized MNCs – a high degree of difficulty in separating distinct parts of the production process over different geographical areas – also has a corollary here. In sectors such as the manufacturing of electronic goods and textiles the constraints to segmenting the process in this way are much less significant; products are not perishable, health and safety constraints are not significant, and production is generally not organized around JIT. Accordingly, there is greater scope for segmentation across countries.

This distinction between standardization and segmentation is not absolute, of course. In other words, MNCs are not either wholly standardized or wholly segmented. Rather, those firms that have a high degree of standardization often have an element of segmentation too, as was the case with Engineering, Inc., in relation to design and development, for example. Moreover, in MNCs that appear to be largely standardized there may well be subtle but important variations between plants; features such as the capital–labor intensity of the sites are likely to differ, leading to significant variations in the context in which employment practices operate. Similarly, those MNCs that are highly segmented have some aspects of their international workforces who perform tasks similar to those of their counterparts in other countries, something that was illustrated by the expatriates in Dedoussis's (1995) study.

Although the balance between these tendencies is important in shaping the approach of MNCs, it should not be seen as a straight continuum because there are other pressures at work, too. For example, it might be argued that a third pressure is for a "differentiated" approach in which variations between countries in consumer tastes and product regulations create significant differences in the nature of products and services. Thus in these sectors we might expect there to be stand-alone national operations, with each of these carrying out the full range of functions in the process as is the case with standardized MNCs, but with the HQ adopting a highly decentralized approach to operational issues, including HR and industrial relations (IR).

Turning to the wider literature on MNCs, the importance of sectoral conditions is a central feature of Colling and Clark's (2002) analysis of the British operations of an American engineering services firm. They point to a number of features of the sector that were key influences on HR practices. The importance of teamworking, for example, was not the product of an influence from home-country managers but rather was integral to the design process in the sector that required "interaction across the full range of disciplines throughout the design process" (2002, p. 315). They conclude that, first, there is a need to incorporate a focus on sectoral specificities into analysis of home- and host-country effects and, second, that the characteristics of the sector, and particularly how it meshes with the host business system, endow subsidiary actors with expertise that can give rise to local "charters" within MNCs. How can this line of analysis be applied to the issues at the heart of this chapter?

Three points can be made. First, although we have argued that sectoral specificities are central to understanding how firms develop international production and service provision processes, the home business system is also a key factor in shaping this dimension. The embeddedness of the parent firm in its country of origin means that the strategies and practices of MNCs are inevitably influenced to a greater or lesser degree by their links with institutions in the home country. Accordingly, we noted earlier that the way in which global value chains are constructed reflects the home country influence from the lead agent. One illustration of this is Sturgeon's (2002) analysis of U.S.-based firms in the electronics sector that have created production networks that differed from those employed by firms in other countries. Specifically, the "modular" networks that are found in American firms are distinguished by their open character, in which mutual dependence is more limited than is the case in Japanese firms. Thus sectoral and home-country factors interact in shaping the way that international production and service provision occur.

Second, sectoral specificities also interact with features of the host country. One aspect of this is how the nature of national business systems in general and the role of the state in particular result in the operating units of MNCs being well placed to fulfill some functions but not others. In some developing countries, such as many of those in Latin America, the state has been willing to accept foreign capital at almost any price; in contrast, in others the state has been active in setting the terms on which MNCs can engage with the national economy in question (Amsden, 2001). In relation to the latter group, in many Asian countries, of which China is an excellent example, MNCs have been denied entry to a country until local firms have developed to a certain stage and are only then allowed to participate in the economy through joint ventures and alliances with these local firms. Arguably, the former context is likely to entice MNCs to locate the low-value-added activities relying on cheap and unskilled labor; the latter, in contrast, is better placed to attract a wider range of activities given the greater capabilities of firms and workers. Thus the nature of the host-country business system affects the issue of transfer, not only by presenting constraints on MNCs wishing to implement practices in that country, but also by shaping the place of the subsidiaries of MNCs located in their nation within the overall production or service provision process.

Third, the nature of the interaction between national and sectoral influences shapes the context in which actors look to carve out niches for themselves within the wider international firm. Writers such as Birkinshaw (2000) use the term "charters" to refer to units that have unique expertise or capabilities on which the rest of the firm depends, giving them scope either to be free from corporate requirements that apply to other units or to exert influence on the rest of the firm. In a similar vein, analysts of global value chains attach much importance to where within the international process there are economic "rents," defined as the profit earned by producers over and above the normal rate of profit in an activity. These rents tend to arise in those parts of the production process that enjoy the protection of barriers to entry (Kaplinsky, 2001). Crucially, the interaction between sectoral conditions and the characteristics of the host business system is a key factor in shaping whether actors in a particular operating unit are unique, or at least unusual, within the multinational. Highly distinctive institutions that support an important function and for which alternative locations are very limited are an important source of such rents. For example, the pool of highly skilled labor and the existence of a network of productive and competent suppliers were key factors in the Danish plant of APV being able to position itself to play a key role in generating innovations that were taken up within the rest of the firm (Kristensen & Zeitlin, 2005). The significance of this lies not only in shaping where innovations come from but also in shaping terms and conditions of employment. We might expect that those operating units within the chain that earn the highest rents would be characterized by relatively favorable terms and conditions and a developmental, "high road" management style; in contrast, those operating units not enjoying rents are much more likely to exhibit a cost-minimization, "low road" style.

## CONCLUSION

At the beginning of the chapter we posed the question of whether MNCs are likely to be innovators or adapters to national systems of employment relations. As we have seen, the principal stream of the international HRM literature assumes that innovation – which is considered to be the process by which MNCs bring to a country new practices that represent a departure from prevailing norms – will occur to some extent. More specifically, this approach assumes that there are inherent advantages to a multinational in transferring practices from other parts of the firm, but that these should be balanced against the need to be responsive to the local context. The findings from the case study in this chapter are broadly consistent with this line of analysis; Engineering, Inc., had gone to some lengths to ensure that a range of HR practices were implemented in China that were consistent with global policies.

An alternative perspective, which we have referred to as the segmentation thesis, argues that MNCs organize their international operations around the opportunities presented by differences between national systems. This counter-literature has argued that MNCs make a virtue of going with the grain of each system in which they operate by locating the part of the production or service provision process that meshes most neatly with the country in question. The evidence presented by authors from this school has suggested that China, in keeping with most other developing nations, has received low-value-added, labor-intensive operations that rely on low-cost, disposable workforces. Thus adaptation – defined as the process in which a firm becomes naturalized to a new environment – is seen as the dominant tendency. One qualification to this adaptation argument is that when MNCs carry out only low-value-added activities in a country, they may not closely resemble local firms that undertake a wider range of activities (design, development, and testing, say, as well as low-cost assembly). In other words, local firms may be characterized by a broader mix of practices for a wider range of occupational groups. Another qualification is that those MNCs that seek to locate their low-value-added operations in countries offering cheap labor may look to pay below the local going rate and to ignore those employment regulations they perceive to impose costs on them. MNCs that look to stretch local norms in this way are clearly not adapting fully.

The argument developed in this chapter is that whether they innovate or adapt is contingent upon the nature of the firm's international production or service process and that there is significant variation by sector in this respect. In particular, we have presented evidence from a sector in which there are strong pressures on MNCs to develop standardized production across borders and contrasted this with evidence from previous studies in sectors in which the context leads MNCs toward segmenting their international operations. We have also flagged a third possibility, namely sectors in which the conditions lead MNCs to a differentiated approach. This emphasis on sector-specific conditions is in keeping with the conclusion of

Wilkinson et al., who note that work "organization and related human resource management and development practices must increasingly be understood in relation to the international production networks associated with specific industries" (2001, p. 692). We would go one step further in arguing that the interrelationship between sector-specific conditions and the peculiarities of national business systems should be the focus of analysis. In doing so, researchers should avoid a choice between adopting either an institutional or an economic approach in favor of an integrated explanation that recognizes they are inseparable.

Our main focus has been on the operations directly owned by MNCs. The concepts of global value chains and economic rents within these chains raise the issue of linkages between MNCs and their suppliers and how these shape the tenor of employment relations in the latter. Whereas data on the scale of the linkages between MNCs and suppliers are less reliable than data on FDI, all the indications are that global value chains are growing in scale and in geographical reach. For example, the UN (2004) World Investment Report highlights the growing trend toward the "offshoring" of services, such as call centers and data processing units, terming this the "next global shift," the most important contemporary development in the increasingly integrated nature of production and service provision. This is a trend that has significant implications for employment, yet is one that the field of international HRM has scarcely touched on. The concepts developed in this chapter may prove useful in research that addresses this area.

## ACKNOWLEDGMENTS

The case study work in Britain was part of an ESRC-funded project on American MNCs in the United Kingdom. We are particularly grateful to Trevor Colling and Anthony Ferner, who were involved in the fieldwork in the firm's British operations, for permission to use these data. We thank Virginia Doellgast for helpful comments on an earlier draft of the chapter.

## REFERENCES

Almond, P., & Ferner, A. (Eds). (2006). *American multinationals in Europe: Managing employment relations across national borders*. Oxford: Oxford University Press.

Amsden, A. (2001). *The rise of "The rest": Challenges to the West from late-industrializing economies*. Oxford: Oxford University Press.

Bair, J., & Gereffi, G. (2001). Local clusters in global chains: The causes and consequences of export dynamism in Torreon's blue jeans industry. *World Development, 29*(11), 1885–1903.

Birkinshaw, J. (2000). *Entrepreneurship in the global firm: Enterprise and renewal.* London: Sage.

Bjorkman, I., & Lu, Y. (2001). Institutionalization and bargaining power explanations of HRM practices in international joint ventures – The case of Chinese–Western joint ventures. *Organization Studies, 22*(3), 491–512.

Colling, T., & Clark, I. (2002). Looking for "Americanness": Home-Country, sector and firm effects on employment systems in an engineering services company. *European Journal of Industrial Relations, 8*(3), 301–324.

Cooke, F. (2005). *HRM, work and employment in China.* London: Routledge.

Dedoussis, V. (1995). Simply a question of cultural barriers? The search for new perspectives in the transfer of Japanese management practices. *Journal of Management Studies, 32*(6), 731–746.

Ding, D., Fields, D., & Akhtar, S. (1997). An empirical study of HRM policies and practices in foreign-invested enterprises in China: The case of Shenzen special economic zone. *International Journal of Human Resource Management, 8*(5), 595–613.

Edwards, T., Colling, T., & Ferner, A. (2004). Comparative institutional analysis and the transfer of employment practices in multinational companies. Paper presented at conference entitled 'Multinationals and the International Diffusion of Organisational Forms and Practices', July 15–17th, Barcelona.

Edwards, T., & Ferner, A. (2002). The renewed "American challenge": A review of employment practice in US multinationals. *Industrial Relations Journal, 33*(2), 94–111.

Edwards, T., & Kuruvilla, S. (2005). International HRM: National business systems, organizational politics and the international division of labour in MNCs. *International Journal of Human Resource Management, 15*(1), 1–21.

Elger, T., & Smith, C. (2005). *Assembling work: Remaking factory regimes in Japanese multinationals in Britain.* Oxford: Oxford University Press.

Farley, J., Hoenig, S., & Yang, J. (2004). Key factors influencing HRM practices of overseas subsidiaries in China's transition economy. *International Journal of Human Resource Management, 15*(4/5), 688–704.

Ferner, A. (1997). Country of origin effects and HRM in multinational companies. *Human Resource Management Journal, 7*(1), 19–37.

Froebel, F., Heinricks, J., & Kreye, O. (1980). *The new international division of labour.* Cambridge: Cambridge University Press.

Gamble, J. (2003). Transferring human resource practices from the United Kingdom to China: The limits and potential for convergence. *International Journal of Human Resource Management, 14*(3), 369–387.

Gereffi, G., & Korzeniewicz, M. (Eds). (1994). *Commodity chains and global capitalism.* Westport, CT: Praeger.

Gereffi, G., & Sturgeon, T. (2004). Globalization, employment and economic development: A briefing paper. Sloan Workshop Series in Industry Studies, Massachusetts, June 14–16.

Ivarsson, I., & Alvstam, C. (2005). Technology transfer from TNCs to local suppliers in developing countries: A study of AB Volvo's truck and bus plants in Brazil, China, India and Mexico. *World Development, 33*(8), 1325–1344.

Kaplinsky, R. (2001). *The value of value chains: Spreading the gains from globalisation.* IDS working Paper 110. Institute of Development Studies, University of Sussex, Brighton.

Kenney, M., & Florida, R. (1994). Japanese maquiladoras: Production organization and global commodity chains. *World Development*, *22*(1), 27–44.

Kenney, M., & Florida, R. (1995). The transfer of Japanese management styles in two US transplant industries: Autos and electronics. *Journal of Management Studies*, *32*(6), 789–802.

Kenney, W., Goe, R., Contreras, O., Romero, J., & Bustos, M. (1998). Learning factories or reproduction factories? *Work and Occupations*, *25*(3), 269–305.

Kristensen, P., & Zeitlin, J. (2005). *Local players in global games: The strategic constitution of a multinational corporation*. Oxford: Oxford University Press.

Marginson, P. (1994). Multinational Britain: Employment and work in an internationalised economy. *Human Resource Management Journal*, *4*(4), 63–80.

Ngo, H., Turban, D., Lau, C., & Lui, S. (1998). Human resource practices and firm performance of multinational corporations: Influence of country of origin. *International Journal of Human Resource Management*, *9*(4), 632–652.

Sanyal, R., & Guvenli, T. (2000). Human resource issues in American firms in China. *Journal of Asia-Pacific Business*, *2*(4), 59–82.

Sturgeon, T. (2002). Modular production networks: A new American model of industrial organization. *Industrial and Corporate Change*, *11*(3), 451–496.

Taylor, B. (2001). The management of labour in Japanese manufacturing plants in China. *International Journal of Human Resource Management*, *12*(4), 601–620.

Taylor, S., Beechler, S., & Napier, N. (1996). Toward an integrative model of strategic international human resource management. *Academy of Management Review*, *21*(4), 959–985.

United Nations (UN). (2004). *World investment report: The shift towards services*. New York: United Nations.

United Nations (UN). (2005). *World investment report: Transnational corporations and the internationalization of R&D*. New York: United Nations.

Whitley, R. (1996). Business systems and global commodity chains: Competing or complementary forms of economic organisation. *Competition and Change*, *1*, 411–425.

Wilkinson, B., Gamble, J., Humphrey, J., Morris, J., & Anthony, D. (2001). The new international division of labour in Asian electronics: Work organization and human resources in Japan and Malaysia. *Journal of Management Studies*, *38*(5), 675–695.

Wilkinson, B., & Morris, J. (2001). Economic logic and institutional explanation: MNCs, production organization and human resource management in China and Malaysia. Paper presented at ESRC Conference on Multinational Companies, September 11–13th, Warwick University, Coventry.

# TWO FAILED ATTEMPTS AND ONE SUCCESS: THE INTRODUCTION OF TEAMWORK AT SEAT–VOLKSWAGEN

Luis Ortiz and Francisco Llorente-Galera

## INTRODUCTION

The debate concerning the convergence or divergence of human resource management (HRM) and industrial relations has grown in parallel with the importance of multinational companies (MNCs) in OECD countries. The "country-of-origin effect" and "host-country effect" are two obvious poles of this debate (Ferner & Quintanilla, 1998). The country-of-origin effect claims the ability of MNCs to shape industrial relations and HRM practices in their subsidiaries abroad, frequently in accordance with industrial relations practices and institutions in their country of origin. Conversely, the host-country effect stresses the resilience of industrial relations institutions at both the national (Whitley, 1999; Hall & Soskice, 2001; Katz & Darbishire, 2000) and the regional or local levels (Belanger, Berggren, Björkman, & Köhler, 1999; Ortiz, 2002). Yet, the possibility that each one of these effects could prevail under different circumstances has hardly been considered. Moreover, the roles of politics and structure within

The Global Diffusion of Human Resource Practices: Institutional and Cultural Limits
Advances in International Management, Volume 21, 59–87
Copyright © 2008 by Emerald Group Publishing Limited
All rights of reproduction in any form reserved
ISSN: 1571-5027/doi:10.1016/S1571-5027(08)00003-X

the organization (Edwards, Almond, Clark, Colling, & Ferner, 2005), as well as the role of *local* culture, have often been ignored.

This chapter shows evidence of the importance of some of these factors by comparing three attempts to introduce teamwork in SEAT, the Spanish subsidiary of the Volkswagen Group. After two failed attempts to introduce teamwork between 1991 and 1993, SEAT surprisingly succeeded in its third attempt, carried out in 2004–2005. The latter attempt reveals the effectiveness of the country-of-origin effect, which existed only in this final attempt. The reform of the Spanish labor market in 1997 certainly helped companies to introduce functional, as well as numerical, flexibility and the companies constituting the environment of SEAT, both within and outside the Volkswagen Group, were increasingly introducing teamwork by the end of 1990s and the beginning of the next decade (Llorente, 2004). But the most decisive factor in smoothing the introduction of this change was a more respectful approach to the role of the unions at the workplace level by a completely new HRM direction, a different climate of labor relations at the plant level, the renovation of cadres and leaders in the two main trade unions' branches, and the political maneuvering of SEAT management in this context. In sum, politics and structure had a positive effect on the company's ability to introduce teamwork.

The next section will discuss the various theories explaining the transfer of corporate HRM norms and practices across borders. The interest of this case study in light of this literature will be highlighted. An introduction to the company will follow. The evolution of employment relations at SEAT will then be described, as well as the structure of employee representation in the company. After the three attempts to introduce teamwork are described, possible reasons accounting for the different outcomes will be discussed. Finally, this discussion will be related to the theoretical discussion initially developed in the chapter.

# THEORETICAL FRAMEWORK

The increasing importance of multinationals in postindustrial societies and economies has favored a rich debate on the multinationals' ability to transfer management practices across borders. At one pole of this debate, some scholars have held that such transfer will be successful enough to lead eventually to a convergence around the same management techniques. Advocates of convergence base their arguments on the liberalization of international trade, the increasing integration of production at an international level by MNCs, and the increasing competition within the sectors that are dominated by these companies. These forces would eventually overwhelm any institutional resistance to convergence. At the opposite pole of the debate, other scholars stress the resilience of the culture or the institutions constituting the host environment of the multinationals investing abroad: subsidiaries would *adapt,* rather than *import,* management techniques encouraged by the corporation.

Among the various positions advocating this persistent divergence, the *culturalist* approach came first. Given cross-national differences in values and norms, HRM practices could not be readily exported to a country in which these values and norms are different; on the contrary, sensible multinationals would try to *adapt* these practices and norms to those of the host country (Hofstede, 1980, 1988; Newman & Nollen, 1996).

The *institutionalist* approach criticizes the culturalist approach on the grounds that culture is not just difficult to conceptualize, but also to operationalize. Moreover, different cultures may coexist in a given subsidiary and even in a given plant (Ferner & Quintanilla, 1998). According to the institutionalist approach, it is not culture that really matters for explaining the behavior of individuals within organizations, but institutions, because institutions ultimately shape culture and, in turn, managers' and employees' behavior. Moreover, institutions can be more clearly differentiated, measured, and compared than culture.

Susaeta (2004) distinguishes between an early institutionalism and a theoretically more sophisticated one (neo-institutionalism) (Susaeta, 2004). Early institutionalists looked at institutions and clusters of institutions for stressing the host-country or the country-of-origin effect. These clusters of institutions have been more or less inclusive, from *systems of industrial relations* or *employment relations system* (Lane, 1989; Streeck, 1985) to *business systems,* which includes vocational training and education, government, interfirm relations, and direct relations with employees (Whitley, 1999), or, more recently, *varieties of capitalism,* which encompasses industrial relations, education and vocational training, corporate governance, and the financial system (Hall & Soskice, 2001).

The "new institutionalist" school of organizational analysis emphasizes the adaptation of the organization to its environment, an outcome labeled "isomorphism" (DiMaggio & Powell, 1983; Zucker, 1977). The process can be related to different environments surrounding the company (Ferner & Quintanilla, 1998; Rosenzweig & Nohria, 1994). Local isomorphism would be roughly equivalent to the host-country effect; the company is embedded in an immediate, local institutional environment and conforms to it.

Cross-national isomorphism would support the idea of a country-of-origin effect; the institutional environment in which isomorphism occurs is the one surrounding the headquarters of the company (Edwards & Ferner, 2002; Ferner, 2000). MNCs would thus export the institutional environment that characterizes their home country. Corporate isomorphism implicitly regards the MNC as a self-contained institutional environment capable of molding other subsidiaries taken over by the firm. Finally, global intercorporate isomorphism would capture the idea of global convergence: "major MNCs are subjected to isomorphic pressures from their key competitors and international markets" (Ferner & Quintanilla, 1998, p. 713).

Both early and neo-institutionalism have been criticized on different grounds: for their functionalism, the static nature of their reasoning, and the difficulty of establishing the origin of the different clusters of institutions they are proposing (Ferner & Quintanilla, 1998). As happens with institutionalism in general, a theoretical explanation for *institutional change* is lacking. Moreover, some recent research has even pointed out the importance of institutions below the national level (i.e., regional or local institutions) (Ortiz, 2002). Beyond these criticisms, institutionalism does not account for the roles of *structure* and *politics* in conditioning the likelihood of diffusion of HRM policies and practices across borders. First, there are structural features of both subsidiaries and parent companies that may play an important role in the diffusion of some HRM policies and practices from the MNC headquarters: the character of the subsidiary as a greenfield or brownfield site, its age, its size, its dependence on local resources, and the rate of union membership among its workforce (Rosenzweig & Nohria, 1994). Second, all the previous approaches seriously underestimate the roles of political actors in the diffusion of MNC practices and policies across borders. The *political approach* has already been explored by Edwards, Rees, and Coller (1999). A more thorough account of the various strategies used by organizational actors "in direct response to the institutional processes that affect them" is provided by Oliver (1991), who establishes the following "strategic responses": acquiescence, compromise, avoidance, defiance, or manipulation.

Beyond the exclusion of structure and politics from the discussion, both the advocates of convergence and those of divergence support their respective claims on the basis of empirical evidence that usually has not considered time as a possible explanatory variable. In fact, different case studies have often been compared at the same point in time, to support either the convergence or the divergence thesis. A question thus remains relatively unanswered: are the host-country or country-of-origin effects permanent? If not, which factors determine whether one or the other prevails at different points in time during the history of organizations? As we will argue in answering this latter question, structure and politics gain particular relevance.

By comparing three different attempts to introduce the same change in the same subsidiary of a multinational automobile manufacturer, our research will contribute to this debate. First, it will add a rarely assumed temporal dimension to the research on cross-national transfers of HRM practices; second, it will explore the reasons the company failed in introducing teamwork in the first two instances and succeeded in the last. In doing so, the research will shed light on the importance of *structure* and *politics* in making either the host-country or the country-of-origin effect prevalent.

## Note on Research Methods

Ideally, the research question would be answered by resorting to panel data that included information about organizational change, structure, and organizational politics for organizations belonging to different sectors. Such survey data, recorded for a sample of organizational units at a series of discrete points in time, would enable an event-history analysis of organizational change, as well as of the roles of politics and structure in this change. It would be similar to the research by Hannan, Carroll, Dobrev, Han, and Torres (1998a, 1998b) on organizational mortality. Unfortunately, a similar endeavor addressing organizational change (and, more specifically, cross-border transfer of HRM practices) has not been carried out yet because such data do not exist. Were the data to exist, though, such a research design may still not be efficient as a case study for *disentangling* the precise political dynamics that may promote or depress the host-country or the country-of-origin effect in different times.

Thus, the research question will be preliminarily answered here by resorting to a case study in which the same change was attempted at three points in an organization's recent history, resulting in different outcomes. The Spanish car manufacturer SEAT first attempted to introduce teamwork as a pilot scheme in 1991. Similarly, teamwork was also attempted unilaterally in 1993 by SEAT in its Martorell factory. Both were unsuccessful experiences (see below). Quite recently, in 2004–2005, SEAT made another attempt and surprisingly succeeded in smoothly negotiating with trade unions a change that had formerly been quite difficult to negotiate and implement.

This research further explores findings from Ortiz (1999a, 1999b) and Llorente (1997, 2004) as regards unions' reaction to teamwork. The empirical evidence gathered for building this case study is constituted, on the one hand, by a series of interviews held with managers and union leaders at the two main factories of the company between 1993 and 1996,[1] and on the other hand, by a series of follow-up interviews that were recently held with the managers chiefly responsible for the latest attempt to introduce teamwork, as well as with the union leaders of the two main unions represented in the SEAT works council.[2] In both the 1993 and the 2006 interviews, the information provided by the interviewees was complemented by internal documents that were provided by the company and the two main unions.

## From a State-Owned Company to a Subsidiary of a German Multinational

In 1951, the Spanish National Industry Institute (Instituto Nacional de Industria, INI), a state agency founded in 1951 by the Francoist regime to create a diverse, self-sufficient manufacturing sector and promote import substitution, established the Spanish Society for Automobile Manufacturing (Sociedad Española de Automóviles de Turismo or SEAT) (Martín Aceña & Comín, 1991). For a long period, SEAT enjoyed a de facto monopoly of this strongly protected market (Castaño, 1985; Solé, 1994). Such a monopoly, in turn, fostered a strong vertical integration. Ninety percent of the components used by SEAT were also produced in Spain, and the range of products was sufficiently large and diversified to meet the needs of the Spanish market.

This favorable situation, and the organization and production strategy derived from it, soon became disadvantageous when the Spanish market progressively opened to foreign car manufacturers throughout the 1960s and 1970s. SEAT lacked the economy of scale newcomers in the sector, like Citroen, Renault, or Peugeot, enjoyed. The situation worsened when the automobile sector in Spain gave signs of exhaustion for the first time. Quite unfortunately, this situation coincided both with the arrival of the two main American multinationals, Ford and General Motors, and with the oil crisis of the 1970s.

SEAT soon went into a deep crisis that revealed the urgent need to integrate the company into the commercial and production strategy of a multinational, if jobs and production were to be saved. Given the huge losses accumulated by SEAT, the sell was difficult. Unsuccessfully attempted with FIAT,[3] SEAT was finally taken over by the Volkswagen

Group in 1986 (Martín Aceña & Comín, 1991, p. 552). But losses soon appeared again (see the appendix for graphical information on the financial evolution of the company from 1990 onward). The 1993 exercise was closed with huge losses (see Graphs A4 and A5). As a result, the old, legendary plant of SEAT in Zona Franca (Barcelona) was almost closed, keeping only minor operations, mostly as a subsidiary of the new Martorell plant.[4] A minor car manufacturing plant in Landaben (Navarra) was sold to Volkswagen. A plant opened in Martorell assumed most of SEAT's production.[5]

The Volkswagen Group is the result of an amalgamation of formerly independent car manufacturers progressively taken over by the old Volkswagen company. The firm is currently divided into two groups: Audi and Volkswagen itself. The latter is constituted by the old Volkswagen company, plus Skoda and Bugatti; the former, by Audi, Lamborghini, and SEAT. This division is driven by production and commercial reasons, but HRM corporate policies are shared by the whole group (HRM Manager, Martorell plant, February 9, 2006). The Audi subgroup aims at manufacturing cars with a "more sportive" look and profile.

After Volkswagen's takeover, SEAT progressively specialized in the production of a range of low-cost cars. But this production soon began to compete naturally with Skoda's production (Llorente, 1997). This might have been one of the reasons SEAT was slowly transformed into a producer of cars with a sporty look and a slightly higher quality than before. It might also be the reason SEAT was moved into the Audi subgroup in 2002 (Llorente, 2004). This move was accompanied by the arrival of a new management team from Audi, in whose plants teamwork was more widespread.

Immediately after being integrated into Audi, 10% of SEAT production was transferred to the plant of Volkswagen in Bratislava (CCOO, March 29, 2006). This transfer was an attempt by the new management team to transform 5 days that had been previously "hired" to the works committee[6] into working days. These days formed the so-called *jornada industrial*. Formally, they were holidays, but the works committee had agreed in the past to "lend" them to the company under the condition that they would be used in a given period of time. Otherwise, the company would lose the right to make them working days, unless approved again by the works committee. By 2002, the company had exceeded this time limit. With the union elections soon to be held, the two main unions represented in the works committee (CCOO and UGT) rejected the possibility of working these days. The company retaliated by taking much of the production of the Ibiza model, the core of SEAT's production at the Martorell plant (Table 1), to Bratislava.

***Table 1.*** SEAT–Martorell Production by Models (Number of Units).
Period: 2000–2005.

|  | 2000 | 2001 | 2002 | 2003 | 2004 | 2005 |
|---|---|---|---|---|---|---|
| Arosa | 28,403 | 22,980 | 19,627 | 13,814 | 9,368 | 0 |
| Ibiza | 199,279 | 188,427 | 197,311 | 200,328 | 163,255 | 163,426 |
| Córdoba/Vario | 94,740 | 75,847 | 57,871 | 59,348 | 46,821 | 37,568 |
| León | 79,722 | 91,939 | 93,606 | 96,400 | 90,850 | 98,130[a] |
| Toledo | 0 | 8,660 | 39,503 | 36,026 | 38,962 | 20,600 |
| Inca | 20,741 | 20,079 | 15,681 | 10,132 | 0 | 0 |
| Altea | – | – | – | 136 | 67,125 | 65,174 |
| Polo Classic/Variant | 56,670 | 32,598 | 0 | 0 | 0 | 0 |
| Caddy | 36,591 | 39,515 | 32,078 | 20,749 | 0 | 0 |
| Total production Martorell factory | 516,146 | 480,045 | 455,677 | 436,933 | 416,381 | 384,898 |
| Vehicles SEAT produced by other factories of VW Group | 96,802 | 65,509 | 26,308 | 43,856 | 42,083 | 20,121 |

[a]In 2005, León I: 44,889 and León II: 53,241.
*Source:* SEAT.

This event acted as a warning to the main trade union confederations represented in SEAT and to the company. According to some sources, part of the management was subsequently laid off and substituted by those who are in key positions of management at SEAT nowadays. One of the new managers is the HRM director of the Martorell plant. The new management team was key in the process of negotiation and implementation of teamwork at SEAT–Martorell.

The other milestone in the recent history of SEAT is the New SEAT project to renovate the company. One of its ingredients was the implementation of teamwork. Quite meaningfully, two of the new members of the current management team of SEAT–Martorell arrived at SEAT from the gearbox manufacturing plant of Volkswagen at Kassel, a plant well-known inside the group for its thorough introduction of teamwork (CCOO, February 8, 2006). These two members were essential in the negotiation and implementation of teamwork at SEAT–Martorell.

## Employment Relations at SEAT

### Employment Relations at SEAT Until the 1993 Crisis
Ironically, SEAT was once labeled the "model company" of the Francoist regime. Soon, it became one of the foci where the Spanish trade union

movement originated and developed during the 1950s and 1960s, a point of reference for workers' mobilizations in other companies of the sector (Miguélez, 1977). The struggle for basic union and workers' rights in the 1960s and 1970s coincided in SEAT with a more basic struggle for the improvement of working conditions at the company level. This mobilization, and its successes, generated a strong pride among SEAT workers. According to a trade union leader interviewed in the mid-1990s, "SEAT was the cutting edge of trade union movement in Spain" (CCOO November 9, 15, 1996).

The lack of competitiveness during the 1970s and 1980s (see above), the decrease in sales, and the necessity of making the company appealing for any eventual buyer forced management to consider job cuts throughout both decades. A chronic state of labor unrest settled among an already heavily mobilized workforce. Although trade unions finally accepted the process of restructuring of the workforce, the agreement always arrived too late, when further job cuts were required. The SEAT workforce always seemed to be oversized.

The political evolution of the works council in SEAT–Zona Franca suffered from this long process of restructuring. There was a progressive radicalization of the workforce at this plant, expressed in the composition of its works council (Ortiz, 1999a, pp. 346–349). The composition of the SEAT–Martorell works council was quite different from the very beginning. Most workers here were indirect (maintenance) workers, foremen, and technicians, traditionally more inclined to vote UGT[7] than CCOO,[8] although the core of what would become the new factory kept the most radical section of CCOO. Some of them were eventually expelled from the union branch and joined CGT[9] (Ortiz, 1999a, pp. 349–350).

The result of the development of an early union movement, along with the struggle within the company around many different issues, was a thick, very detailed collective agreement. Customarily, collective agreements at the company level in Spain usually *add* new issues and articles to what has been agreed upon in previous negotiating rounds. In this way, collective agreements literally get thicker and thicker. This was the case with SEAT and the reason, compared with other manufacturing companies that settled in Spain afterward (i.e., Ford or General Motors), that its collective agreement accumulated a vast number of guarantees that curtailed the maneuvering of human resources managers. The detailed "professional" classification, preventing workers from doing tasks outside the realm of their professional categories, and the restrictions to functional mobility in general are particularly relevant for the introduction of teamwork (Ortiz, 1999a, pp. 350–351).

### Employment Relations in SEAT from 1993 Onward

Employment relations at SEAT changed radically from 1993 onward. After SEAT–Zona Franca was almost closed, most of its workers, who constituted the rank and file of CCOO and UGT and struggled against the company during the 1980s, were moved to the new plant in Martorell. As revealed by some of the sources recently interviewed, these workers "made the collective agreement binding" in Martorell. It was necessary because the younger workers initially hired for SEAT–Martorell were not as knowledgeable of their "rights" and the way to make them effective as the older workers.

But the company did not give up in its attempts to gain tighter control of labor relations. As a result of an initiative by UGT in November 2001, SEAT struck a deal with the joint works council for the progressive introduction of contratos relevo. Such a measure enabled workers above 60 years of age to work just 15% of the year while still earning the total amount of their salaries; the other 85% of the salary would be paid by the Spanish Social Security System. At the arrival of their formal retirement age, it would be considered that they had worked *full-time until their retirement age;* that is, there would not be any reduction in the pension they would be entitled to receive. For every old worker asking for such a scheme, SEAT would hire a young one who would get an indefinite contract after working 6 months in the company. Both the company and the SEAT employees benefited from this scheme; the cost was basically assumed by the state.[10] The implementation of the scheme began in April 2002 and was very successful in reducing the mean age of the workforce[11] (Llorente, 2004, pp. 453–457). According to one of our sources, from 2002 to 2005 not fewer than 5000 workers joined the contratos relevo.[12] As Fig. 1 shows, by 2005 the age distribution of the SEAT workforce had become clearly bimodal, young workers becoming clearly predominant.

The contratos relevo scheme gave SEAT the opportunity to obtain workers with higher initial training, higher productivity, and lower labor costs, because they would receive less money from the company as compensation if they were laid off in the future. The scheme was also very advantageous for many old affiliates and supporters of UGT and CCOO, but it had an adverse effect both in the organization of union branches and in the strong union culture so far prevalent in SEAT (see below) (HRM Manager, SEAT–Martorell).

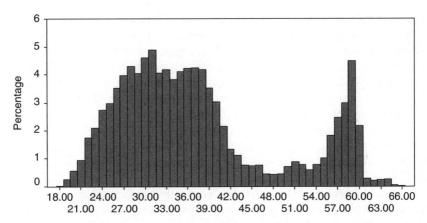

*Fig. 1.* The Age Distribution of the SEAT Workforce in 2005. *Source:* CGT (2005).

## EMPLOYEE REPRESENTATION AT SEAT

Workers' representation at the workplace level in Spain is formally dual. On the one hand, works councils, elected every 4 years, represent workers at the company and/or workplace level *regardless* of their union membership. On the other hand, union branches, recognized by the Organic Law on Trade Union Freedom (Ley Orgánica de Libertad Sindical, LOLS), represent all workers belonging to a given union in a company or a workplace. Successive union elections revealed the ability of the main trade unions to get most of the seats at works councils (Martínez Lucio, 1992, 1998). Formally dual, this system of representation is de facto dominated by trade unions.

The long history of negotiations with the company and the richness of the collective agreement in SEAT resulted in the establishment of *functional commissions* beyond this formal structure of representation. Functional commissions were formed by works council members *and* representatives of the company and relieved works councils from some of their work by specializing in and negotiating specific issues (holidays, productivity, etc.).

The Workers' Statute and the LOLS grant both the normal members of the works councils and the "union delegates" 40 h a month off their duties at the company.[13] It became customary that these hours were concentrated among the first members of any union list in union elections, so that they could become *full-time* representatives for the workers and their affiliates. Even so, the number was clearly insufficient for a workforce as large as the one in SEAT and with so many issues to negotiate and administer. For this reason, in companies with a long tradition of union organization and workers' mobilization, like SEAT, an informal union structure was usually created, linking the works committee with the workforce. This was the union "shop council," constituted by the direct representatives of the workers. A member of any UGT or CCOO shop council was normally a representative of 30 or 35 members of the union in a given shop. Not recognized by any piece of labor legislation in Spain, the shop council was just the result of a long organizational effort carried out by trade unions at the workplace. UGT and CCOO shop council members were usually workers with charisma and leadership among their peers and usually veterans in negotiating with the company and getting involved in mobilizations called by trade unions. They worked closely with the members of the works council and trade union branches.

The introduction of the contratos relevo negatively affected the shop councils. First, their members were reluctant to be as aggressively demanding in relation to the company as they used to be: they were soon to leave the company and they thought that young workers ought to be the ones playing the leading role in claiming some improvements in working conditions, not them. Second, once they left the company as the result of the contratos relevo, it was difficult to find other union cadres as experienced as them. All this had the effect of dismantling the workshop councils, or lessening their activity.[14]

But generally, the main effect of reducing the age of the workforce, by means of generous early retirement schemes and hiring new, young, more qualified workers, was a crisis of representation in the two trade union branches. The executive committees of both UGT and CCOO branches at SEAT–Martorell went through episodes of turmoil between 1995 and 2002 that ended up with new teams leading them both. The main positions in the executive committees of both trade union branches are now occupied by young workers who entered SEAT after 1990 and who did not experience the adversarial climate of labor relations that was common in the company during the 1980s.

*Two Failed Attempts and One Success: The History of Teamwork at SEAT*

*Pilot Schemes (1991–1993)*
Before the current introduction of teamwork at SEAT, the company made two failed attempts to introduce this change. The first took place at the

bargaining of the 1991 collective agreement, signed by CCOO and UGT. The agreement included a compromise to introduce this form of organization progressively among the whole workforce. Pilot schemes for this purpose were designed at the plants of Landaben (Navarra) and Zona Franca (Barcelona). These pilot experiences would take place in 1991 and 1992 (Ortiz, 1999a, p. 357).

According to some union leaders interviewed in 1993, the negotiation of teamwork was "not a major issue."[15] The procedure and topics to be discussed were settled there, but no formal agreement was made for a definitive change in the organizational structure. The agreement consisted of only opening future negotiations on teamwork.

A steering committee, constituted by representatives of management and the two signatory trade unions, would discuss the salient issues related to teamwork as the pilot schemes unfolded. By the end of these schemes, it was thus expected that the main issues at stake would be clear, as well as the positions of both the company and the trade unions. A negotiation for a thorough, deep implementation of teamwork would then be ready. The list of topics initially proposed by trade unions was the following:

• Collective workload in the group (team) and job rotation within it;
• Demand for higher professional qualification and job promotion;
• Demand for further training for those workers involved in teamwork;
• Suppress monotony;
• Supervision of pilot schemes;
• Control of selection of personnel for the pilot experiences.

This list, agreed to by the two main trade union confederations, tells what the demands of the trade unions were when teamwork was more clearly proposed by the company.

If the bargaining for the start of these pilot schemes was unproblematic, problems appeared soon after the pilot schemes were under way. The first pilot scheme took place in Landaben, in October 1991. It was preceded by a specific agreement in which, for the first time, the roles of the "coordinator" (team leader) and the "supervisor," above the coordinator, appeared as a matter of concern for trade unions. The coordinator's role was deliberately left undefined and vague, by having no specified functions; but it was made clear that in no case would coordinators become spokespersons for "personal or labor problems of the workers in the team." At least in these pilot schemes, nothing indicated that coordinators were not to be elected by the company.

Unlike the coordinator's role, the supervisor's was detailed in an appendix to the agreement. Both the coordinator's and the supervisor's roles seemed to have been the major issues at stake. Later on, while the pilot schemes were taking place, trade unions made new complaints. The company was first denounced for not meeting the agreements previously made with trade unions. Supervisors and coordinators, it was said, were obeying the company's orders without trade unions having anything to say. Moreover, trade unions expected promotions and pay increases for those workers who, as a result of job rotation, performed tasks corresponding to higher job categories than the ones they formally held.

It had been planned that pilot schemes would continue at Zona Franca, but these plans were vetoed by trade unions, on the grounds that prior commitments made by the company had not been fulfilled in Landaben. According to trade union leaders, the company had acted unilaterally. The agreements for the pilot schemes were denounced.

On April 25, 1992, a new agreement for the development of a pilot scheme at Zona Franca was struck. CGT denounced it as the result of "private" meetings that CCOO and UGT held with the company. There were some meaningful differences in relation to the previous agreement. First, the selection of both the supervisor and the coordinator was more carefully outlined. As regards the supervisor, she/he would be selected by the company, but the company would need to comply with detailed rules in this selection. As regards the coordinator, his/her "category, wages, profile, and selection" would ultimately be determined by the *Agreement on Teamwork,* which would be based on lessons from these pilot schemes. As for these schemes, there would be two procedures to select the coordinator: either the supervisor selects one among a short list of team members proposed by the group as candidates or the group selects one among a short list of three proposed by the supervisor. In either case, candidates would need to pass an exam. Second, the collective workload, unproblematic in the first agreement, became another issue at stake. As in the initial agreement, the collective workload would be the sum of individual workloads in the team, but it would not be established just by the supervisor, but by him/her *and the Technical Services of the company,* strongly monitored by the works council. Moreover, the steering committee would have detailed information on the computation of the collective workload for every team. Finally, as regards economic incentives, some of the interviewees declared that they would only be given bonuses received by all members of the pilot teams on top of their wages, whereas others declared there would be promotions.

Four places at SEAT–Zona Franca were designated to carry out the pilot schemes: the press shop, body shop, assembly line, and engine shop. Except for the first shop,[16] the schemes in the other three were completed, but not renewed. Even worse, the schemes did not have the projection of a pervasive, complete change of organizational structure at SEAT–Volkswagen. The steering committee apparently kept on working and meeting, beyond the completion of the schemes, but the crisis of 1993 was so deep that it almost automatically discouraged any attempt to proceed with the change.

The two pilot experiences in SEAT between 1991 and 1993 revealed the major concerns of both CCOO and UGT in regard to teamwork: a possible reduction in the number of jobs, work intensification, a marginalization of trade unions at the shop floor level, and, last but not least, the possibility of making workers perform jobs above their professional category without being properly rewarded. Subsequently, their main claims were related to the election of the team leader, or coordinator: the promotion of workers when they performed jobs belonging to higher categories, as it was ruled in the collective agreement, and the recognition of team leaders as workers within a specific, proper category (Ortiz, 1999a, pp. 386–399).

*A Unilateral Introduction of Teamwork at Martorell (1993)*
Almost at the same time that the company was negotiating the introduction of teamwork as a pilot experience in the plants of Landaben and Zona Franca, it was opening a brand new plant in Martorell. SEAT hired Clive Griffith, former manager of a Nissan plant in Sunderland (UK) and quite knowledgeable of Japanese management techniques and lean manufacturing, to introduce dramatic changes in work organization at this factory.

The Nissan plant at Sunderland (UK) had become famous for introducing teamwork that was deliberately aimed at reducing the power of trade unions (Garrahan & Stewart, 1992). And so Griffith attempted to introduce teamwork at Martorell unilaterally, avoiding any negotiation with trade unions: "where there was a clash, we would work it out [individually, not with the assistance of trade unions]" (HRM Manager, Martorell plant, July 15, 1994).

Many elements of teamwork initially introduced at Martorell by Griffith formally broke the collective agreement at SEAT. For example, coordinators and supervisors were introduced without their roles having been agreed upon and recognized in the collective agreement. Teams also had a collective workload, although such a thing had not been agreed upon beyond pilot experiences nor existed in the collective agreement.

Despite these irregularities, Griffith initially succeeded in his attempt. He hired 1400 new employees who received extensive training on teamwork. These new employees were meant to be the backbone of the new organizational structure the company was unilaterally implementing: they would fill the positions of supervisors and coordinators required by teamwork. Because the factory was brand new, trade unions did not seem to have much opportunity to oppose the unilateral introduction of teamwork at SEAT–Martorell.

But the 1993 crisis completely changed the scenario. The old, legendary plant at Zona Franca was almost dismantled and many of its workers were transferred to Martorell. Young workers with temporary contracts, specifically trained to work in teams, had to be dismissed, to allow for old workers from Zona Franca to keep their jobs. These workers were moved to SEAT–Martorell. They had a strong union culture and a good knowledge of their rights, acquired through long struggles in the past decades. Almost immediately, they enforced the collective agreement and made teamwork untenable.

*A Thorough Introduction of Teamwork from 2004 Onward*
The legacy of teamwork persisted in areas where it was technologically more feasible (i.e., the press shop at SEAT–Zona Franca), but teamwork was generally dismissed until trade unions officially took the initiative and asked for this change themselves during the negotiation of the 2004 collective agreement. An internal document of the union branch of CGT at SEAT reveals that teamwork had already been discussed in early March of 2003 (CGT, 2003). In fact, other sources recently interviewed for this research talked about trips made by the main leaders of the new executive committees of the CCOO and UGT union branches in SEAT–Martorell to plants of Audi and Volkswagen where the implementation of teamwork was more advanced. These visits would have taken place before teamwork was formally proposed by the SEAT works councils, controlled by UGT and CCOO. IG Metall union officials also visited SEAT–Martorell before SEAT–Martorell formally requested teamwork. These might be signs that the request by the works councils (and, implicitly, by the main trade unions represented in them) may have been orchestrated by both the company and the trade unions after negotiating and exploring the opportunity of introducing teamwork in 2004.

Teamwork is now defined as the "collaboration of several workers in carrying out a collective responsibility clearly delimited in its content and its geographical area of application" (SEAT, 2005a, *Teamwork Handbook,*

p. 5, authors' translation). The new version of teamwork had roughly the same elements as prior ones: functional flexibility is to be developed among team members, so that they are able to carry out as many direct and indirect tasks as possible within the group; training would be provided so that this aim is accomplished; a skill matrix would show how skillful each team member is in performing the different tasks the group (or team) is to carry out; the team leader is supposed to be the member who has already mastered the whole range of tasks to be carried out by the group, so that he/she is able to train other teammates in carrying them out and substitute for them in case of absenteeism; team leaders are also responsible for calling team meetings to discuss process and product improvements and enhance the efficiency of the team in this way. The team is collectively responsible for a given workload and has a number of targets to accomplish in various dimensions that are carefully measured. Roughly, these were the main elements of teamwork in any of the attempts previously described. In other words, we can be sure we are dealing with the same change.

There were other similarities to previous attempts to introduce teamwork. After the formal request made by the works committee at the 2004 collective bargaining, a steering committee was set up to supervise the introduction of the change in the whole factory of SEAT at Martorell. The steering committee was formed by the President of the company, the Production Manager (Vicepresidente de Producción), and the HRM Manager (Vicepresidente de Recursos Humanos), that is, the two top managers most affected by the change to be introduced. Below this steering committee, there was a team for the consolidation of teamwork. This latter team consisted of the top manager of the shop in which teamwork would be initially introduced, another top manager of the HRM department, and an expert on teamwork transferred from the plant in Wolfsburg (Germany) to help the process in Martorell.[17] This group of three managers handled the daily process of planning, introduction, etc., and negotiation with the representatives of the works councils. For the latter purpose, a supervisory team, constituted by members of the two main trade union branches, was also established. The team for the consolidation of teamwork worked closely with this supervisory committee of union representatives.

Although the basics of the change are the same as in previous endeavors, the process has been completely different. The best way to distinguish this last attempt to introduce teamwork from previous ones is by its *thoroughness*. As a first example, a detailed calendar was established. A period of "preparation" and the initial implementation in Shop 9 was to last the whole year of 2004. During this period, the whole workforce in the shop was split into teams. It was also the period of training, and this is the second sign of the thoroughness that differentiates this attempt from previous ones. The year 2005 saw the full implementation in all areas of the factory.

The second feature exemplifying the thoroughness of this third attempt to introduce teamwork was investment in training, not just among the ultimate performers of teamwork, but also among would-be supervisors, team coordinators, and members of support teams, constituted by workers who would help coordinators to handle meetings and acquire basic management skills. Throughout the year 2004, team coordinators received 48 h of training (basics of teamwork, handling of indicators, and setting up objectives and negotiating social relations inside the team); supervisors received 27 h a year in the same themes, and support teams received 48 h a year (SEAT, 2005a).

As a third sign of thoroughness, handbooks of teamwork were carefully drafted and agreed upon by representatives of the workforce. A general handbook was written, along with one more specific for the indirect workforce (SEAT, 2005a, 2005b). The company was trying to introduce teamwork not just among its direct workers, but among the workforce as a whole, including administrative workers.

Fourth, the company invested in spaces for team meetings, so that teams could meet periodically. Team areas were built throughout the factory, with boards and computer terminals, so that every team could be connected to an intranet ex professo created to measure teams' performance and to give a clear view of how each team was performing on every one of the established indicators (see below).

Fifth, time was reserved for team meetings. In previous attempts, the company had been reluctant to make these breaks and facilitate these meetings for the teams. This changed in the last attempt. Teams met more frequently during the phase of preparation. Even during the full speed of functioning teamwork, it is expected that teams meet at least 15 min a month. These meetings are part of the continuous improvement process teamwork had always included.

Finally, indicators were carefully established so that the company and teams could know the extent to which the teamwork was being implemented. Moreover, there was to be a process of auditing: teams would be measured. This included the establishment of indicators (of quality, personnel, order and cleanliness, and costs) to measure how well the group was working as a team. Finally, clear, specific measures were established to know the cost incurred by every team during a month (SEAT, 2005a, *Teamwork Handbook*, p. 24).

The interviews held with both managers and union officials did not reveal major differences between the two parts in the process of planning and implementing teamwork. The chapter on teamwork in the 2004 collective agreement again reveals a concern for the method by which team leaders were selected. In this sense, unions' concerns were the same as in previous attempts. There was also some concern to show that teamwork would have economic advantages for team members and coordinators, but these economic rewards were more symbolic than anything else. But teamwork was introduced without some of the guarantees formerly sought by union officials, like the preservation of very constraining norms on job classification present in SEAT's collective agreement. Trade unions were certainly involved in the process, and the role of the team leader was carefully discussed (both trade unions and workers had a say in the election of the team leader), but the demands made by the trade unions did not hinder teamwork as they had in the previous attempts. For instance, job classification did not appear in the result of the negotiations as something "sacred," as before (Ortiz, 1999b).

# DISCUSSION

In the period between 1991 and 1994, union officials at SEAT saw the same advantages and disadvantages of teamwork as union officials at Opel Spain (Ortiz, 1998) or Renault (Ortiz, 2002). The only difference consisted of a strong union culture that made union officials in SEAT especially confident of their capability to stop the change or, at least, mold it as they pleased. SEAT was thus just another case confirming that the unions' reaction to teamwork was shaped by Spanish labor relations institutions at the workplace level. It also constituted a further confirmation that trade union officials were quite able to maintain these institutions (Ortiz, 1999a). Quite surprisingly, in 2004 the same trade unions, far from resisting teamwork, formally proposed it, even renouncing some of the claims they had formally formulated in relation to it. In any case, they showed a much more positive stance toward the changes brought about by teamwork, even though the change in work organization was basically the same in all three of these attempts.

The thoroughness of the third attempt to introduce teamwork could have certainly contributed to its success. Moreover, guarantees of trade union activity at the shop floor level were again provided. In this sense, there are still reasons to believe the host-country effect was still there. The factors highlighted by the advocates of convergence could have also been felt by union leaders more strongly in 2004. As we have seen, there were signs that SEAT was in a difficult position, even within the Volkswagen Group. The competition from Skoda was steep, and the transfer of production between subsidiaries had gotten increasingly easier. However, the trade unions' hindrance of the introduction of teamwork in 1993 happened when the situation of the company was perceived as particularly vulnerable: the SEAT–Zona Franca plant had been almost closed and the SEAT–Landaben plant had been sold to the Volkswagen Group. Diverse indicators of the financial situation of the company (see the appendix) reveal that the situation between 1991 and 1993 was far worse than in 2004, when teamwork was negotiated for the third time. In sum, even if trade union officials had been perfectly aware of coercive competition between plants *within* the corporation, and even between different competitors in the international car market, this would not have been enough to explain the difference between the 1991 and 1993 attempts and the 2004 attempt. The SEAT case reveals the importance of structural, cultural, and political factors that are usually dismissed by neo-institutionalism.

In the first place, the contratos relevo, and the subsequent rejuvenation of the workforce, were decisive. Young workers seemed to be more receptive to working in teams; they also had a different culture as regards their relationship with the company and their approach to work. Old workers, once the majority at Zona Franca (and the majority in SEAT–Martorell when the factory in Zona Franca was almost dismantled), had fought hard in the past to get improvements in working conditions from management teams usually very reluctant to attend to their claims. These claims were related to Fordist methods of production; workers had been concerned with work pace, wages, mobility, job classification, promotions, etc. Old workers had been historically successful, not just in these claims, but also in leading a labor movement that brought many other advantages to metal workers both in Catalonia and outside Catalonia and, ultimately, basic rights for workers and union representation at the workplace.

The progressive absence of these workers due to early retirement schemes such as the contratos relevo also had an effect on trade union branches. First, the shop councils were possibly depleted of the more battle-hardened members. Second, and more important, a distance grew between the rank and file of younger and younger workers and the executive committees formed by old, veteran union leaders, quite adversarial in their stance and approach toward the company. Between 1995 and 2005, this led to a renewal of the executive committees. Again, old union leaders, well accustomed to adversarial labor relations and to dealing mainly with specific issues, were replaced by young leaders possibly more ready to bargain over other issues because they considered some (i.e., job classification) to be less salient.

Parallel to this renewal, there was an increasingly closer position of both trade unions on many political issues at the workplace and company level. Possibly, CCOO had to make more of an effort in getting closer to the positions of UGT than vice versa. This proximity was part of a recent evolution of Spanish labor relations that implied, first, a distancing between trade unions and political parties and, second, a rapprochement between UGT and CCOO. In the case of CCOO, it has meant a moderation of the political stance shown during the 1980s and "a more pragmatic involvement by CCOO in bargaining over work organisation issues at the company level" (Martinez Lucio, 1998, p. 437).

Fourth, there were minor crises of production in the period between 1993 and 2004. Technological improvements within the Volkswagen Group made it easier to move production between different subsidiaries of the group. In this context, 10% of the production of the main model manufactured in SEAT–Martorell was moved in 2003 to the Audi plant in Bratislava. This transfer of production was seen as a possible sign of the loss of competitiveness of SEAT *within* the Volkswagen Group. Its former role as a low-cost producer was being progressively assumed by Skoda, another manufacturer of low-cost vehicles (CGT, 2005).

Fifth, a new management team, recently arrived at SEAT as a result of its integration in Audi, could have used the "Bratislava Crisis" as an opportunity to induce changes in top management that facilitated the introduction of teamwork. Some members of the new management team had much experience with teamwork at the plants they came from. There are also reasons to suspect that the Bratislava Crisis was handled in such a way that changes in the executive committees of the two main trade union branches at SEAT occurred. Knowing the importance of SEAT for their respective organizations, neither the Federation of Metal Workers Union of CCOO nor the corresponding federation within UGT wanted to risk losing jobs. A good way of preventing this loss was to foster changes in the leadership of their trade union branches in SEAT–Martorell. With more (CCOO) or fewer (UGT) difficulties, these changes took place from 1995 to 2002.

Finally, the new management team established a new climate of labor relations at the company level, trying to replicate as much as possible the good relationships IG Metall has traditionally had with the company in Germany and the involvement of this trade union in basic management policies (i.e., teamwork). Aware that this kind of relationship had been decisive in introducing teamwork in many German factories, the new management team at SEAT made an effort to import this style of management. Interviewees in both unions agreed that SEAT management had become closer and more receptive to trade union necessities than ever. The word "codetermination" was explicitly mentioned in the interviews[18] and in company documents (SEAT Yearly Report, 2004,[19] 2005). Although no similar institution was actually implemented at the workplace level, there were signs that the new CCOO and UGT members of the works councils received special treatment[20] and entered into a much closer and less adversarial relationship with management than their predecessors had. All the interviewees agreed that, along with changes in top management and the executive committees of CCOO and UGT, nothing would have changed if this new climate of *trust* had not been forcefully implemented in SEAT.

## CONCLUSIONS

Empirical evidence gathered at three different points in time, shortly after the three different attempts made by SEAT to introduce teamwork, has allowed us to shed light on the persistence of the host-country or country-of-origin effect as an explanation of the ability of MNCs to transfer HRM policies across borders. As we have seen, whereas the host-country effect prevailed in the first two attempts to introduce teamwork, between 1991 and 1994, the country-of-origin effect was more prevalent in the last attempt. In other words, we have found at least preliminary evidence that the host-country effect is not necessarily persistent.

Moreover, the detailed analysis of the SEAT case study has enabled us to shed light on the factors that made the country of origin *more* effective in the last instance. The case could simply show that the country-of-origin effect *surpasses* the host-country effect when the level of internationalization and the threat of investment diversions reach a certain limit. The transfer of HRM practices would be initially led by the host-country effect, but ultimately guided by the country-of-origin effect. In terms of the neo-institutionalist approach, local isomorphism was superseded by corporate isomorphism,[21] cross-national isomorphism, or even global intercorporate isomorphism. Yet, the trade union officials' perceptions of the coercive comparisons between plants *within* the corporation, and between different competitors in the international car market, might not be enough to explain the difference. At the end of the day, the 1993 crisis already imposed a strong perception of the plants' vulnerability on the trade union leaders of SEAT.

The history of the introduction of teamwork in SEAT might reveal the importance of structural and political factors in making the forces in favor of the country-of-origin effect prevail. A structural element, like the mean age of the workforce, eased crucial changes in the trade union branches and, more importantly, entailed a cultural change that facilitated the acceptance of teamwork by trade unions.

An unexpected finding of theoretical relevance is this intermingling of structural and cultural elements. How did *culture* become so salient if, as argued in the theoretical framework, culture may be regarded as the *result* of a number of institutions? The findings give a possible explanation: institutions also survive because values and norms keep them alive. Many institutions that had traditionally configured SEAT's collective bargaining, and general labor relations inside SEAT, were alive insofar as workers who had fought for some issues, such as tight job classification, claimed the strict application of tradition. Young workers who joined the company during the 1990s and the first years of the next decade were not as knowledgeable and aware of the importance of these "rights" as their older workmates. In sum, the case illustrates the importance of culture in instilling life into institutions.

Political factors are even more decisive in turning a given scenario, such as that formed from competitive pressure by other Volkswagen subsidiaries and a younger workforce, into a suitable scenario for the introduction of teamwork. The Bratislava Crisis could be seen as just a sign of the forces in favor of convergence, but it had to be smartly handled by the new management team at SEAT to induce further changes in management and among the executive committees of the main trade union branches. These changes left aside old bargainers, not fully committed to teamwork and more used to adversarial industrial relations. It was also a political decision to accompany such a "stick" element in the micro-politics of SEAT with the "carrot" of a more conciliatory style of management, deliberately imported from plants of the group in Germany. German industrial relations, and the relatively good relationship between trade unions and management, had been key to the successful introduction of teamwork in these other plants, and the new management team that came from Audi knew this.

A case study has obvious shortcomings in regard to the ability to generalize its findings. Yet, it is suitable for exploring possible factors that determine a phenomenon. Moreover, political factors and dynamics are not always sufficiently disentangled through statistical research methods. Even so, such research methods would allow in the future a more general and solid confirmation of the preliminary argument stated here, about the importance of structure and politics in favoring a host-country or country-of-origin effect. A large-scale longitudinal survey with a sample of multinational corporations with different countries of origin *and* their subsidiaries in host countries would be an ideal basis for such research. In addition to time, country of origin, and host country, special attention would need to be paid to building good indicators of the factors once highlighted by the convergence advocates, such as the liberalization of international trade affecting the sector where the production unit is located, the relative importance of production yielded by MNCs within this sector, or the competition to which the unit is subjected. Structural factors such as sector, age, size, dependence on local resources, rate of union membership, etc., would be much easier to collect than information on politics at the organizational level: changes in the management team, origin of the managers more directly involved in changes in HRM practices, conflicts related to such practices and policies, etc., as well as increases or reductions in production models, volume of production, and number of personnel employed at the production unit. Finally, information would need to be gathered on policies and practices susceptible to being transferred across borders. These policies and practices would eventually constitute the dependent variable, and the likelihood of successfully importing such practices would need to be referred to in terms of both time and many of the factors that have just been mentioned.

# NOTES

1. Four managers of SEAT–Zona Franca and 2 managers of SEAT–Martorell were interviewed in 1994. Between 1994 and 1996, 8 members of the executive committees of UGT at both factories were interviewed; 11 members of the CCOO executive committee and 11 from the CGT were also interviewed.

2. Three managers of SEAT–Martorell were interviewed in the first months of 2006, along with one representative from UGT and two representatives from CCOO. One manager from SEAT–Zona Franca was also interviewed.

3. It was the most "natural" MNC to sell SEAT to, because SEAT had been producing automobiles under FIAT's design from the very beginning. At the end of the 1970s, the agreement between FIAT and the Spanish INI had been reached. Also caught by the 1979 oil crisis, FIAT renounced the agreement at the last minute.

4. The plant of SEAT at Zona Franca (Barcelona), once the core of the company, became a "supplier of the car manufacturing plant of Martorell" (CCOO, March 29, 2006). According to some sources, the SEAT management had decided to close down its plant in Zona Franca well before 1993, at the same time that it planned to expand

its production by opening a new plant in Martorell (Costa, Callejon, & Giraldez, 1991; Llorente, 1997, 2004).

5. The building of this plant partly explains the increase of indebtedness around 1993 (Graph A2), as well as the huge losses of the company, given that the debt of SEAT to the group had to be paid in DM (Graphs A4 and A5).

6. UGT (February 1, 2006).

7. The most moderate union, formerly associated with the Spanish Socialist Workers Party (Partido Socialista Obrero Español).

8. Formerly close to the Spanish Communist Party (Partido Comunista de España).

9. To the left of CCOO, CGT is a minor trade union, vaguely heir to the anarchist-inspired National Confederation of Work (Confederación Nacional del Trabajo).

10. SEAT was not the only company that implemented such a scheme. In 2000, UGT successfully proposed this early retirement scheme (contratos relevo) as a general benefit for companies and workers of the automobile sector in Spain (Llorente, 2004, p. 454). But SEAT was the company that more thoroughly negotiated and applied it.

11. Llorente reflects on the similarities between the contratos relevo and the 5000 × 5000 Project, implemented by Volkswagen in its main factory in Wolfsburg in August 2001. Quite interestingly, this project was negotiated between Volkswagen and the main German metal workers union (IG Metall), under the threat of transferring part of the Wolfsburg production to either Portugal or the Czech Republic (Lung, 2002).

12. UGT (February 1, 2006). It should be borne in mind that the workforce of SEAT at the Martorell plant is around 9000 workers.

13. Union delegates are members of the works council with a voice but without the right to vote. Trade unions that get at least 10% of the votes in union elections at the workplace may get as many as four union delegates in the works councils. The number depends on the number of employees (Ley Orgánica de Libertad Sindical, November 1985).

14. CCOO (February 8, 2006).

15. UGT–Martorell (June 24, 1994) thought teamwork had been of "hardly any" importance, among the other issues that were dealt with for the collective agreement to be signed in 1991. According to them, this was due to the fact that the point was just to "create the basis" for a major change that would eventually take place in the near future. CCOO–Zona Franca (June 4, 1994) confirmed this point: "the company raised the issue at the last moment, when the agreement was about to be struck. Trade unions did not make many objections."

16. The pilot scheme here was interrupted shortly after it had begun. The reason was that the shop manager himself was already implementing changes in this line.

17. The three of them were interviewed by the authors of this chapter.

18. UGT (February 1, 2006), CCOO (February 8, 2006). Another CCOO official (March 28, 2006) agreed that this was the obvious intention of the company, although he also pointed out that the codetermination institutions in Germany had not been introduced in SEAT.

19. "Therefore, co-determination is a well-established reality that favours both the company and its employees, since it offers them a greater autonomy to perform the tasks in their jobs" (SEAT Yearly Report, 2004, p. 20).

20. All kinds of facilities were provided to CCOO and UGT leaders, so that this climate of trust was built, at least provisionally, among them.

21. Teamwork was relatively common in the different companies and plants of the Volkswagen Group (Labit, 1999).

# REFERENCES

Belanger, T., Berggren, C., Björkman, T., & Köhler, C. (1999). *Being local worldwide: ABB and the challenge of global management*. Ithaca & London: Cornell University Press.

Castaño, C. (1985). *Cambio Tecnológico y mercado de trabajo en la industria del automóvil*. Madrid: Instituto de Estudios Laborales y de la Seguridad Social.

CGT – Confederación General del Trabajo. (2003). *Desarrollo del Trabajo en Equipo*. Internal Document of the SEAT union branch, mimeographed, March.

CGT. (2005). *Informe Expediente SEAT-VW*. Barcelona: CGT (Gabinete de Estudios Confederal), internal document, December 7.

Costa, M.T., Callejon, M., & Giraldez, E. (1991). *Estudio de la Organización Productiva y del Impacto generado por la Ubicación de la empresa SEAT en Martorell*. Barcelona: CEP.

DiMaggio, P. J., & Powell, W. W. (1983). The Iron Cage revisited: Institutional isomorphism and collective rationality in organizational fields. *American Sociological Review, 48*, 147–160.

Edwards, T., Almond, P., Clark, I., Colling, T., & Ferner, A. (2005). Reverse diffusion in US multinationals: Barriers from the American business system. *Journal of Management Studies, 42*(6), 1261–1286.

Edwards, T., & Ferner, A. (2002). The renewed 'American Challenge': A review of employment practice in US multinationals. *Industrial Relations Journal, 33*(2), 94–112.

Edwards, T., Rees, C., & Coller, X. (1999). Structure, politics and the diffusion of employment practices in multinationals. *European Journal of Industrial Relations, 5*(3), 286–306.

Ferner, A. (2000). The underpinnings of bureaucratic control systems: HRM in European multinationals. *Journal of Management Studies, 37*(4), 521–540.

Ferner, A., & Quintanilla, J. (1998). Multinationals, national business systems and HRM: The enduring influence of national identity or a process of Anglo-Saxonization. *International Journal of Human Resource Management, 9*(4), 710–731.

Garrahan, P., & Stewart, P. (1992). *The Nissan enigma. Flexibility at work in a local economy*. London: Mansell.

Hall, P., & Soskice, D. (Eds). (2001). *Varieties of capitalism: The institutional foundations of comparative advantage*. Oxford: Oxford University Press.

Hannan, M. T., Carroll, G. R., Dobrev, S. D., Han, J., & Torres, J. C. (1998a). Organizational mortality in European and American automobile industries, Part II: Coupled clocks. *European Sociological Review, 14*(3), 279–302.

Hannan, M. T., Carroll, G. R., Dobrev, S. D., Han, J., & Torres, J. C. (1998b). Organizational mortality in European and American automobile industries, Part I: Revisiting the effects of age and size. *European Sociological Review, 14*(3), 279–302.

Hofstede, G. (1980). *Culture's consequences: International differences in work related values*. Beverly Hills: Sage.

Hofstede, G. (1988). How institutions think. *Organization Studies, 9*(1), 122–125.

Katz, H., & Darbishire, O. (2000). *Converging divergences: Worldwide changes in employment systems*. Ithaca & London: Cornell University Press.

Labit, A. (1999). Group working at Volkswagen: An issue for negotiation between trade unions and management. In: J.-P. Durand, P. Stewart & J. J. Castillo (Eds), *Teamwork in the automobile industry: Radical change or passing fashion?* (pp. 395–410). London: Macmillan.

Lane, C. (1989). *Management and labour in Europe. The industrial enterprise in Germany, Britain and France*. Aldershot: Edward Elgar.

Llorente, F. (1997). Las estrategias de los fabricantes de automóviles: El caso de SEAT, 1980–1995. In: D. Roca (Ed.), *La formació del cinturó industrial de Barcelona* (pp. 275–289). Proa: Institut Municipal d'Historia de Barcelona.

Llorente, F. (2004). *La innovación como estrategia de competitividad empresarial en el sector automovilístico: Los casos de SEAT y los proveedores directos en Cataluña de los fabricantes de automóviles*. Ph.D. dissertation, University of Barcelona, Barcelona.

Lung, Y. (2002). The changing geography of the European Automobile System. 10th GERPISA International Colloquium, June 6–8, Palaçe du Luxembourg, Paris.

Martín Aceña, P., & Comín, F. (1991). *INI, 50 años de industrialización en España*. Madrid: Espasa Calpe.

Martínez Lucio, M. (1992). Spain: Constructing institutions and actors in a context of change. In: A. Ferner & R. Hyman (Eds), *Industrial relations in the New Europe* (pp. 482–523). Oxford: Basil Blackwell.

Martínez Lucio, M. (1998). Spain: Regulating employment and social fragmentation. In: A. Ferner & R. Hyman (Eds), *Changing industrial relations in Europe* (pp. 426–458). Oxford: Basil Blackwell.

Miguélez, F. (1977). *SEAT, la empresa modelo del régimen*. Barcelona: Dopesa.

Newman, K., & Nollen, S. (1996). Culture and congruence: The fit between management practices and national culture. *Journal of International Business Studies, 27*(4), 753–779.

Oliver, C. (1991). Strategic responses to institutional processes. *Academy of Management, 16*, 145–179.

Ortiz, L. (1998). Union response to teamwork: The case of Opel Spain. *Industrial Relations Journal, 29*(1), 42–57.

Ortiz, L. (1999a). *Convergencia o permanencia de los sistemas de relaciones laborales: reacción sindical a la introducción del trabajo en equipo en la industria del automóvil*. Ph.D. dissertation, Universidad Complutense de Madrid & Centre for the Advanced Social Sciences, Juan March Institute, Madrid.

Ortiz, L. (1999b). Unions' responses to teamwork: Differences at national and workplace level. *European Journal of Industrial Relations, 5*(1), 49–69.

Ortiz, L. (2002). The resilience of a company-level system of industrial relations: Union responses to teamwork in Renault's Spanish subsidiaries. *European Journal of Industrial Relations, 8*(3), 277–299.

Rosenzweig, P., & Nohria, N. (1994). Influences on human resource management practices in multinational corporations. *Journal of International Business Studies, 25*(2), 229–251.

SEAT Yearly Report (2004). *SEAT, S.A. (Departamento de Balances y Cierres)*. Barcelona: SEAT, S.A.

SEAT, S.A. (2005a). *Manual de trabajo en equipo [Teamwork Handbook]*, internal document. Barcelona: SEAT, S.A.

SEAT, S.A. (2005b). *Manual de trabajo en equipo (Mano de Obra Indirecta) [Teamwork Handbook, Indirect Workforce]*, internal document. Barcelona: S.A.

Solé, E. (1994). *SEAT, 1950–1953*. Barcelona: Ediciones de la Tempestad/Actualidad.

Streeck, W. (1985). *Industrial relations and industrial change in the motor industry: An international view*. Working Paper. Industrial Relations Research Unit, University of Warwick, Coventry, UK.

Susaeta, L. (2004). *El proceso de transferencia de políticas y prácticas de RRHH en la empresa multinacional: un modelo ecléctico*. Working Paper XXXIX. Asamblea Anual de CLADEA, EAE (Escuela de Administración de Empresas), Barcelona.

Whitley, R. (1999). *Divergent capitalisms: The social structuring and change of business systems*. Oxford: Oxford University Press.

Zucker, L. (1977). The role of institutionalization in cultural persistence. *American Sociological Review, 42,* 726–743.

# APPENDIX

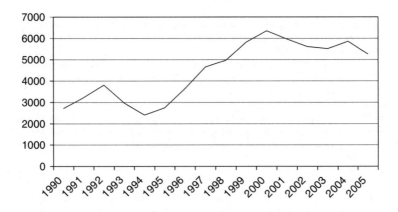

*Graphs A1.*　Sales (1000s of Euros).

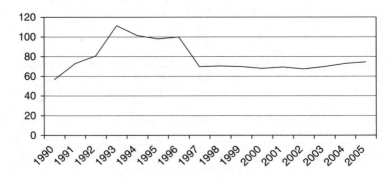

*Graphs A2.*　Indebtedness (%).

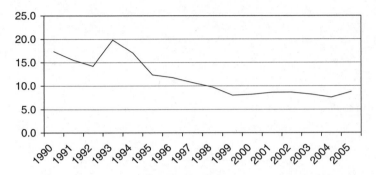

*Graphs A3.* Cost of Employees/Operating Revenues (%).

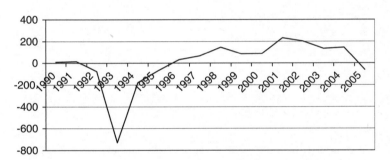

*Graphs A4.* Income (Loss) for the Year (1000s of Euros).

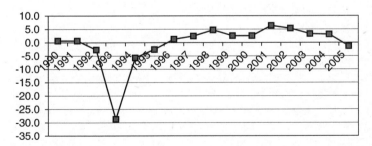

*Graphs A5.* Economic Profitability (%) (Income (loss) for the Year/Total Assets).

# MANAGING HUMAN RESOURCES IN SOUTH AFRICA: A MULTINATIONAL FIRM FOCUS

Frank M. Horwitz and Harish C. Jain

## INTRODUCTION

Two key developments exert an important influence on the nature of human resource management (HRM) in South Africa (SA). The first is two seemingly conflicting imperatives, sometimes and arguably wrongly juxtaposed: that of developing a high-growth, globally competitive economy with fuller employment and the sociopolitical imperative of redressing past structural inequalities of access to skilled, professional, and managerial positions, as well as ownership opportunities. The first development is the related influences of globalization and multinational corporations (MNCs), information technology, and increased competition, which have become very prominent in postapartheid SA. South Africa has a dual labor market, with a well-developed formal sector employing some 8.5 million workers in standard or typical work and a growing informal labor market. In the case of the formal, knowledge-based economy, the World Wide Web, and increasing communication that the Internet has made possible, has influenced changes at the organizational level. A second development is that these changes and changing patterns of employment are having a dramatic impact on HR policies within organizations. In a knowledge-based

The Global Diffusion of Human Resource Practices: Institutional and Cultural Limits
Advances in International Management, Volume 21, 89–123
Copyright © 2008 by Emerald Group Publishing Limited
All rights of reproduction in any form reserved
ISSN: 1571-5027/doi:10.1016/S1571-5027(08)00004-1

economy, organizations rely on knowledge that is embedded deeply in the individual and in the collective subconscious. It is the property of an individual and cannot be taken away from that person (Harrison & Kessels, 2004). He or she would agree to put it in the service of the collective whole, which is known as organizational citizenship behavior (OCB). In technology-driven advanced firms in SA, there are several themes among the various models of citizenship behavior: helping behavior, sportsmanship, organizational loyalty, organizational compliance, initiative, civic virtue, and self-development (Podsakoff, MacKenzie, Paine, & Bachrach, 2000). Many of these themes overlap with the common competencies demanded by advanced MNCs. Thus OCBs rest upon a recognition of mutuality of interest and of responsibility between the organization and the individuals. Increasing globalization and worldwide competition and the knowledge-based economy have their greatest impact on business strategies, process, and practice involving, among others, management of human resources. In this chapter we examine factors influencing the management of human resources in SA and their impact on human resource practices in organizations.

We begin with the contextual factors, including a description and analysis of the gross domestic product (GDP), the ethnically diverse population, and employment/unemployment, followed by the major stockholders (employers, unions, and government), in the new (since 1994) SA. In the second part of this chapter, we outline and discuss the theoretical perspectives regarding HRM and multinational companies in SA. This is followed, in the third part, by emerging trends in the labor market and the discriminatory legacy of apartheid, HIV/AIDS, etc. This includes employment relations and legislative developments (especially postapartheid) such as the Labour Relations Act, the Skills Development Act, and the Employment Equity Act (EEA), as well as the Broad-Based Black Economic Empowerment Act, and their impacts on human resource policies, managing diversity, and changing managerial styles. The final section contains our conclusions and implications.

## CONTEXTUAL BACKGROUND

South Africa attracts over 60% of the foreign direct investment (FDI) to the African continent. It has a population of almost 47 million (SA Statistics, 2005) and in 2003 a GDP of 160.1 billion U.S. dollars (South Africa, 2004). GDP growth for 2003 was 1.9% and in the prior 3 years had been around 3%, slightly above the global average (South Africa, 2004). In 2005, the

GDP rose from 4.5 to 5% and was expected to rise for the next 3 years to 6% (Joffe, 2005; Shezi, 2005a, 2005b). As a matter of fact, according to the Reserve Bank, the GDP reached 5% in the second quarter of 2005 and the economy is on course to achieve 6% economic growth by 2010 (Mde & Ensor, 2005). Inflation was below 10% over the period 2002–2008. In 2003, average consumer price inflation was 7.9% (South Africa, 2004) and for July 2005, it was 3.4% (SA Statistics). The South African Reserve Bank (June 2005) indicated that the inflation rate (CPIX) would amount to an annualized rate of 4% in the first quarter of 2005. Mboweni, Governor of the Reserve Bank in South Africa, forecasts that inflation will peak at 5.25%. *The Sunday Times* (Twine, 2005) carried a banner headline, "SA's wealth explosion – number of dollar millionaires skyrockets to 37 000 from 25 000 in 2002." Twine (2005) suggests that the rise in the value of the Rand since 2002 had largely created the "explosion." Virtually every week the papers also carry reports of mouth-watering empowerment deals. Similarly, the *Financial Mail* (2005) indicated that the African share of high income exceeding R 30,000 per month had risen from 25% in 2001 to 31% in 2004, with a growth rate of nearly 13% per annum. Similarly, the African share of middle incomes between R 10,000 and R 30,000 per month was presented at 42%, compared with 44% for Whites. The source of the information, according to this article, was the Labour Force Survey and an Old Mutual Insurance team analysis. At the same time, the media also carried stories of abject poverty and deprivation deepening, largely as a consequence of unemployment and HIV/AIDS and also due to globalization resulting in retrenchments in industries such as clothing and textiles. However, Schlemmer (2005) suggests that "class breakdowns and associated trends are far more complex than the media hype allows for. Africans are making progress but it is slower than most people think ... The good news is that deep poverty is not increasing as many people fear ... The extension of social grants has indeed stopped the socio-economic rot at the lower levels of livelihood."

Formally employed people in 2003 numbered 8,373,761 in the labor force (in the formal sector); MNCs employed between 10 and 15%. The labor force in the formal sector consisted of almost 60% Africans, 15% Colored, 5% Indian, and 22% White (SA Statistics and 2003 Annual Employment Equity report). There has been an increase in the nature and characteristics of the informal economy in developing countries. This has been driven by an increase in size, in absolute terms, of the informal economy and by the increasingly important role that informal activity can play in the generation of income-earning opportunities in developing countries. In SA, the

participants in the informal economy have increased from 1.9 million in
1992 to 3.5 million in 2002, an increase of roughly 84%. The increase in
informal activity should be seen against the background of a declining
labor force absorption rate of the formal economy – from 82.1% in 1981 to
38.2% in 2002 – and the exceptionally high level of unemployment.
According to the labor force survey (SA Statistics, 2004), it is estimated
that unemployment ranges between the strict definition estimate of 27.8%
and an expanded definition estimate of 41.2%. From 1994 to 2002, the size
of the informal economy ranged between 7.2 and 8.4%. A unidirectional
causality ran from the informal economy GDP1 to the GDP, implying that
causality ran one way from GDP1 to GDP and not the other way. This
could indicate that an increase in the size of the informal economy
contributed to the increase in the GDP in SA from 1994 to 2002 (Saunders
& Loots, 2005).

There is a rapidly growing informal and casual worker sector, this
especially following large-scale retrenchments in industries such as mining,
clothing, and textiles. Low-cost Chinese imports in the latter sectors have
led to a serious economic crisis, with more than 70,000 jobs lost over the
period 2005–2008. Historically, the economy was dependent on the mining
industry, including gold, coal, and other minerals. Over the first decade of
the 21st century the GDP contribution of these sectors declined to under
35% as industrial and export strategies in the auto assembly, manufacturing, and agriculture sectors were aggressively pursued. Although SA has
made a relatively successful transition from a resource-based economy to a
manufacturing- and export-oriented model, it has not created significant
formal employment (Fraser, 2002), although the postapartheid open
economy saw significant growth in the tourism and hospitality industries.
While the economic fundamentals of macroeconomic policy appear sound,
high unemployment persists.

As noted earlier, SA remains a highly unequal society, with nearly two-
thirds of its labor force earning less than 250 U.S. dollars per month, due to
the country's legacy of discriminatory access to education, skilled jobs in the
labor market, and ownership of stock and assets. According to the UN
Development Program's *Human Development Report,* two-thirds of the total
income is concentrated in the hands of the richest 20% of the population,
leaving the poor with a mere 2% (South Africa, 2004, p. 23). Crime and an
HIV/AIDS epidemic are pressing social problems for organizational and
HRM policy choices. The estimated shrinkage from the year 2002 to 2015 of
real GDP owing to AIDS ranges from 2.8 to 9.6% (ABSA Bank and ING
Barings, 2002).

South Africa is an ethnically diverse society. English, Xhosa, Zulu, Sotho, and Afrikaans are the most widely spoken languages. Black people (Africans, Colored people, and Indians) comprise over 75% of the population. Since its establishment as a trading post by the Dutch East India Company in 1652, SA has had colonial governments from Britain and the Dutch (Afrikaaner) settlers. Racial discrimination and wars for control over territories and land were a feature of SA's history for over 2 centuries. Apartheid was formally instituted as a political system by the Nationalist Party in 1948 and abandoned in 1994, with the country's first democratic election, after decades of a continuing political struggle by the African majority and its representative parties such as the African National Congress. The latter and other opposition groups had been banned from the 1960s until the release from prison of Nelson Mandela and other political prisoners in 1990.

The industrialization of SA began with the discovery of gold and diamonds at the end of the 19th century. Preference for skilled and managerial work was given to White workers, who were given trade union and collective bargaining rights by the Industrial Conciliation Act (1924). African workers were excluded from these rights until 1980. Access to training and skilled work was denied to Africans. The legacy of institutionalized workplace discrimination has meant that organizations in the "new South Africa" now have to develop a skilled and productive workforce, which has been underutilized, poorly trained, and alienated from performance improvement and competitiveness goals. This is a vital challenge for HRM today.

Major stakeholders in HRM and labor relations are represented in the tripartite National Economic Development and Labour Council (Nedlac). Employers may belong to employer organizations represented nationally by bodies such as the SA Chamber of Business. Trade unions belong to union federations such as the Congress of South African Trade Unions (COSATU), with some 3 million members in its affiliates. Nedlac is an important statutory body aiming to foster a social partnership among organized business, labor, and the state through joint consensus-seeking on national labor market policy issues and proposed labor legislation such as skills development, employment equity, and labor relations laws. Nedlac also has a chamber in which small businesses can be represented as an interest group. Many human resource practitioners are members of a professional association, the Institute for People Management (IPM), which together with the SA Board for Personnel Practice (SABPP), seeks to enhance the professional standing of the HR profession by providing professional accreditation and standards of ethical and professional conduct. The IPM provides an educational function running seminars, providing diploma and advanced programs, and disseminating relevant information through newsletters to members. The SABPP is accredited with the national skills and qualification authority and has played a key role in the formation of this body. The IPM has its own HR magazine, *People Dynamics,* aimed at practitioners. It hosts a large annual conference with local and international experts as speakers. Many industrial relations specialists belong to the Industrial Relations Association of SA, an affiliate of the International Industrial Relations Association based at the ILO in Geneva.

## THEORETICAL PERSPECTIVES: HUMAN RESOURCES AND MULTINATIONAL COMPANIES IN SOUTH AFRICA

The global – local debate concerns how MNCs can or should balance the pressures to develop globally standardized policies with the pressures to be responsive to the peculiarities of the local context (Edwards & Kuruvilla, 2005). Edwards and Kuruvilla identify three conceptual weaknesses restricting research in this field: (1) inadequate conceptualization of the national effects, which results in culture being used as an unsatisfactory "catchall" for national differences; (2) lack of attention to the influence of internal organizational politics; and (3) the internal division of labor within MNCs, which lacks focus. The global – local policy question arises first from pressure from global uniform or standardized practices arising from a legacy of the MNC's embeddedness in the original national base; thus the influence of the home national base of the firm, particularly the cultural influence, creates a "country-of-origin" effect; second, and conversely, MNCs also face pressures that lead them to decentralize decision-making on HRM issues to managers in their national context, allowing the firm to respond to national peculiarities – the "local" pressures. The latter pressure toward decentralizing decision-making on HR issues arises from the need to abide by national-level regulations and institutions in the labor market (Boxall, 2003). This additionally concerns the link between production strategies and industrial relations institutions, for example, where there is considerable internal diversity within many national economies, particularly marked in large countries. For instance, in the United States, a key source of variation is the existence of some "right to work" states in the South, where it may be more difficult for unions to organize; similarly, wages and working conditions vary considerably between Chinese provinces and in India. Various institutional differences in the business environment between northern and southern Italy, for example, are well known. Nevertheless, despite some variations by region, the national level is useful as a conceptual tool; national governments play a lead role in developing the framework of legal regulation of collective bargaining, employment policy, and training provisions with common regulatory requirements across an economy.

The continuing relevance of three factors, institutional, industry sector, and cultural context, shows the limitations of the convergence/divergence debate. This emphasizes the importance of studying internal firm-level work process dynamics and the notion of "crossvergence" in the development and implementation of hybrid practices (Horwitz, Kamoche, & Chew Keng-Howe, 2002). The notion of convergence is therefore tempered by opposite theoretical constructs of divergence/particularism relating to country and local context, including cultural variables, regulatory environment, labor market attributes, skills supply and level, and industry structure. Globalization creates compelling pressures for homogenization of MNC policy and work practices. This process is arguably mitigated by contextual factors with a concomitant need to focus on contingency approaches and mediating variables affecting firm-level execution. The importance of stakeholder interests such as trade unions, power dynamics within and between organizations, and the organizational reality of other competing groups needs to be taken into account. This is particularly important in South Africa. Noting the complexity of research on comparative and international HRM, Budhwar and Sparrow (2002) found both common and country-specific attributes of HRM. In South Africa, the nature of the domestic labor market is important, including the degree of voluntarism or regulation of employment practices such as fair/unfair labor practices, recruitment and selection, pay determination, union influence, human resource development policy, and dismissal law. This reinforces an understanding of the complexity of environmental context.

South Africa has experienced a dramatic transformation in the postapartheid era. Socio-legal and political context is particularly important in labor relations, given different regulatory systems, collective bargaining institutions, and relative power of stakeholder interests. Although these factors are not static or immutable in time, they may impede or enable change in a particular cultural and industry context. Trade unions in South Africa retain a relatively important influence over the choice and implementation process of HRM practices. Labor legislation in South Africa is protective of worker interests with respect to organizational rights, collective bargaining, and the principle of unfair labor practices such as arbitrary dismissal and unfair employment discrimination. Statutory institutions, such as bargaining councils, the labor court, and the Commission for Conciliation, Meditation and Arbitration (CCMA), play a prominent role in the conduct of industrial relations. The regulatory context is an important mediating variable and co-contributing factor in limiting the arbitrary introduction of HRM practices by MNCs and enabling hybrid outcomes. Some of the South African MNCs have introduced productivity measures successfully learnt in the African context, most of which are adapted from lean manufacturing, Total Quality Management (TQM), and other Japanese practices, thus supporting the crossvergence construct. Thus, whereas a convergent/divergent analytical framework is important, it can be built on by adding the construct of crossvergence. This appears to be a more robust way of analyzing the actual nature of the change process in cross-cultural adoption of High Performance Work Practices (HPWPs), particularly in the type and degree of hybridization that appears to occur in the Southern African context and clearly has far-reaching implications for the broader African context.

Some propositions may be helpful in summarizing the above discussion.

1. Firms in a host country with a strong regulatory and institutional framework are more likely to adopt hybrid than other forms of HRM practices.
2. The greater the internal cultural diversity of the host country, the more likely that hybrid rather than other forms of HRM will be adopted.

Considerable research has been done on the issue of cultural factors in the diffusion of HRM practices in MNCs (Debrah & Smith, 1999; Jackson, 2000; Kamoche, 1997a, 1997b, 2000) and Horwitz and Smith (1998) have done such work in SA. A facet of this research is a focus on integration/ divergence of work values cross-culturally. The question of cultural influence on work values and HRM practices is important in assessing the extent and type of hybridization that occurs in adopting human resource practices developed elsewhere and how culture and labor market institutions influence such adoption. Cross-cultural variation in the labor market and skills supply for addressing market needs is an important consideration by MNCs in the decision regarding FDI. South Africa and its regional economy have an oversupply of manual, relatively unskilled workers and, as in many emergent economies, a shortage of technological, financial, and managerial skills. The Skills Development Act and EEA have sought to put policy emphasis on human resource development, with levy and grant incentives.

A theme in the literature on MNCs in developing countries is the appropriateness of Western management principles and practices. Many authors have challenged the tendency by MNCs as well as local managers to adopt practices with little consideration of the suitability and relevance of such practices. Some have identified the limitations of concepts formulated in the West (Kamoche, 1993, 1997a; Nzelibe, 1986), whereas others have offered empirical evidence on the nature of extant practices, pointing to their appropriateness or lack thereof (Kamoche, 2000). The importance of family and community are seen in the network of interrelationships, extended family, and mutual obligations. This results in a sense of communalism (Nzelibe, 1986). Some advocate African "ubuntu" as a basis for fostering an Afrocentric managerial culture with regiocentric HRM practices (Mbigi, 2000). The word "ubuntu," literally translated, means "I am who I am through others"; this is in contrast to the Western tenet of "cogito, ergo sum" – "I think, therefore I am." It is this contrasting of a form of communal humanism with individualism and instrumentalism that has a normative appeal for advocates of an African economic and cultural renaissance, and is posited as having the potential to build competitive advantage (Jackson, 2000; Mangaliso, 2001). But a desired future vision may be confused with current empirical reality. The socioeconomic context of management in SA reflects high unemployment, poverty, and illiteracy. At the same time there is a high need to develop people and provide a globally competitive economy (Kamoche, 1997b).

Macro-cultural comparative analyses (Hofstede, 1991; Trompenaars, 1993), however, may have adequate face validity, but often neglect deeper consideration of diversity within certain contexts and the power of organizational culture in MNCs. The latter may act as rival causal factors in the propensity to adopt HR practices successfully cross-culturally. This is particularly relevant in SA, with its diverse cultural and ethnic fabric and where research on cross-cultural diversity in organizational contexts is embryonic. Hofstede's original study in 1980 included SA. With its sample of only one firm, viz. IBM, in SA, which was at the time predominantly White in its staffing composition, the study failed to discern the multi-dimensional nature of even its own model. Additionally, the longitudinal changes in the employment and staffing structure of SA organizations have become more diverse and multicultural at all levels, especially since 1994. It is likely therefore that constructs such as individualism/collectivism, risk taking, and risk avoidance may show quite varied patterns today.

Booysen (2007) investigated perceptions of national culture among retail banking managers from three of the largest banks in South Africa. She found significant differences between African and White racial groups on seven of the eight dimensions of national culture examined. The cultural constellation of the White management group reflected a Eurocentric or Western orientation that emphasized individual self-sufficiency, competition and work orientation, and structure and planning. In contrast, the cultural constellation of African managers reflects high levels of collective solidarity, group significance, valuing harmonious interpersonal and group relations, consensual decision making, building trust and reciprocity, nurturing, and coaching (Mangaliso, 2001) and below average levels of assertiveness (Booysen, 2007). These latter attributes reflect cultural values congruent with Afrocentric management systems. As the profile of executives changes, this will impact too on the evolution of MNC organizational cultures in their local (SA) operations. In contrast, Thomas and Bendixen (2000) found little significant difference among the 586 managers they sampled using Hofstede's dimensions of a national culture model. Their sample included 20 different race/ethnic groups representing the dominant categories of the SA population (e.g., White Afrikaans-speaking males and females, Zulu-speaking males and females, and Asian males and females). The groups were similar on power distance, individualism, and long-term orientation. Thomas and Bendixen (2000) concluded that at the managerial level, there appears to be a common national culture among South Africans. The results of their study indicate a cultural gap between management and lower-level employees. Neither study specifically addressed the impact of national culture on HRM practices. Nor have there been studies within MNC and SA organizations to examine whether a strong organizational culture can mitigate the effects of national culture. Combined, this limited research suggests that a continuing challenge for the development of high-performance HRM practices in SA is how to embrace the reality of the duality of both Western MNC and African cultural identities among the workforce. One sobering conclusion is that there may not be universally applicable HRM practices for all employee groups.

Human resource practices in a country are products not only of national culture and environment, but also organizational culture, diffusion strategies of MNCs and local firms, and organization structure, which in turn influence design, content, and implementation of performance-oriented HRM practices such as staffing, compensation, HR planning, and training/ development. The debate regarding convergence/divergence perspectives in the cross-cultural diffusion of HRM practices is a somewhat simplistic one.

Convergent similarity of HRM practices exists largely at the nominal level, hence the need to explain hybrid HRM practices, for which the notion of hybridization or crossvergence seems apt, especially in a culturally diverse society such as SA. Contextual factors including national and corporate culture, may have a determining effect on design and implementation of HR practices (Jackson, 2000; Mbigi, 2000). In SA, the nature of the domestic labor market is important, including the degree of voluntarism or regulation of employment practices such as fair/unfair labor practices, recruitment and selection, pay determination, union influence, human resource development policy, and dismissal law.

A key strategic imperative is formulating HR strategies at both national and organizational levels to enhance competitiveness and performance improvement. South Africa's reentry into competitive global markets in the 1990s created new managerial challenges. One of these challenges is management of human resources in an MNC subsidiary in SA. SA is highly dependent on FDI. It is estimated that there are 1600 foreign companies in SA (Business Monitor International, 2003). An MBA thesis from the Graduate School of Business of the University of Cape Town investigated HRM practices in multinational companies in South Africa. This research surveyed HR practices in 29 MNCs from Europe, the United Kingdom, the United States, Japan, and South Africa. Of the nine U.S. MNCs, two were joint ventures, three were acquired, and the rest were started by the parent company. Four of the companies did both sales/service and manufacturing, whereas another two were purely sales/service, and two were manufacturing. Five of the companies were doing business mainly on the local market, whereas three did business both locally and internationally. Only one stated that it did business mainly on the international market. The companies had been doing business in SA for a period of 8–80 years (average 35 years). Company size ranged from 35 to 1600 employees. Two of the companies had approximately 8% expatriates among the employees, in both cases either the HR director or an HR manager was an expatriate as well. All companies that were involved in manufacturing had labor unions. The average unionization of the workforce in the U.S. companies was around 3.59%. U.S. and European companies both spent about 50 hours of training on 47 and 41%, respectively, of their management staff. Worker compensation systems seem to have similarities in the United States and Europe. Managers in U.S., European, and SA companies agreed on performance-related salary. As well, in the U.S./U.K./Japanese companies, an employee's seniority was an important factor in determining pay for most jobs. U.S., European, and SA companies shared their financial and/or performance data with their employees. The authors note, with caution, that the results were based on a small sample size, but could also indicate that increasing globalization has resulted in converging HR practices across countries (Grzeschke & Moehring, 2004).

In both MNCs and local firms human resource practitioners in SA see the most important workplace challenges as performance improvement, employment equity, training and development, and managing trade union expectations (Templer & Hofmeyr, 1997). It is estimated that SA organizations spend between 0.5 and 1.5% of the payroll on training compared to 5% of European, 5.5% of American, and 8% of Japanese MNCs. The apartheid legacy in SA created a racial segmentation of the labor market with respect to access to higher level technological skills (Barker, 1999; Isaacs, 1997; Standing, Sender, & Weeks, 1996). Training and development are seen by both managers and frontline employees in the services industry in SA as vital in addressing the skills gap and developing the capacity to meet competitive demands (Browning, 2000). As noted earlier, a feature of macroeconomic policy is to attract FDI and multinational firms, often in joint ventures with local empowerment companies. An important question arises as to whether the influence/power of MNCs is so extensive and penetrative as to override local implementation factors such as the regulatory environment, including legislated employment standards and collective bargaining and cultural factors. Effective diffusion and integration of HR practices will therefore depend on the relative importance of these factors. The stakeholder perspective is relatively well accepted in South Africa's new democracy. The historical exclusion of key stakeholders under apartheid has been replaced by a new emphasis on consultation and involvement of key groups and individuals, for example, in Nedlac. It includes organized business, labor, and government departments in formulating industry and labor market policies. Arguably, the stronger the stakeholder and pluralist perspectives are institutionalized in a society, the more likely that crossvergent or hybrid models of MNC and local HRM practices will develop.

## Emergent Trends in the Labor Market

An HRM imperative is to address the discriminatory legacy of apartheid in removing unfair discrimination in the workplace and enhancing organizational representation of Africans, Colored people, Indians, and women. Apartheid education and skills legislation created a relatively unique basis for skills and earnings inequalities. African access to trades and skilled work was legislatively prohibited by job reservation in favor of White employees in the Industrial Conciliation Act (1956) and the Mines and Works Act. These Acts were repealed in 1980 – some 20 years ago – yet African progress into skilled and managerial work has been slow. A new culture of learning and integration rather than reliance only on "access and legitimacy and discrimination and fairness" perspectives has become necessary to ensure cohesive and productive work group relations in diverse settings (Ely & Thomas, 2001).

A structural inequality in the skill profile exists: a shortage of occupationally and managerially skilled employees is contrasted with an oversupply of unskilled labor, ill equipped for a modernizing economy with increasing knowledge and service sector priorities. South Africa has a rapidly growing and large youth population, which is predominantly African, poor, and lacking in education and skills (Horwitz, Nkomo, & Rajah, 2004). This presents a huge challenge to the state, public institutions, and private sector. The labor market absorption rate for young entrants, given modest growth over the period 2002–2008, has been low. Given the lack of relevant skills in market demand fields, coupled with shrinking formal core employment, youth unemployment is high. Socioeconomic and labor market issues remain pressing managerial and business challenges in the postapartheid transitional economy. The government has relaxed legislative provisions on basic conditions of employment to allow greater flexibility for small firms and is encouraging better education and occupationally relevant skills through the Skills Development Act (1998). It aims at encouraging the provision of opportunities for new labor market entrants to develop skills and gain experience for better employment prospects.

Human resource development priorities and policy challenges in achieving organizational change and capacity building in the labor market are critical to enhancing SA's international competitiveness. In SA, a developing economy, skilled jobs are growing and unskilled jobs are declining. Job losses have occurred due to import liberalization arising from rationalization of production and downsizing of employment often reflecting inefficiencies and comparatively low productivity and high costs in relation to low-wage economies like China (Hayter, 1999; Godfrey, Clarke, Theron, & Greenburg, 2005). In 1996, South Africa lowered tariffs on imported goods significantly and rapidly. As a result, after years of protection, the local clothing industry is increasingly competing directly with those of other countries. These are countries with much lower labor costs producing clothing intended for the lower end of the market. Products from these countries have also been entering SA illegally through its porous borders. Over time, the quantity of clothing beginning at the lower end has spread to the middle and upper market segments. While overall employment in the clothing industry may not have declined as significantly as media reports suggest, closer investigation shows that formal employment has shrunk considerably and informal employment has increased. Employment has shifted from firms registered with bargaining councils (that is, formal employment) to unregistered firms or firms located outside the bargaining council areas, resulting in deterioration in employment conditions, social protection, and pay.

Data on the number of clothing manufacturers in operation indicate that the industry is larger than its formal component. Restructuring has also involved a decrease in the average size of clothing firms (measured in terms of numbers employed). The data on the number of firms and employees make it clear that a process of informalization has accompanied downsizing and retrenchment in the formal clothing industry. Production has been fragmented and relocated away from established manufacturers to smaller operations, some of which are registered cut, make, and trim (CMTs), but many of which are unregistered firms or home-based operations. China now has an 86% market share of clothing imports into SA (Paton & Bisseker, 2005). There is a heated national debate regarding the question of enhancing labor market flexibility, help for small businesses, and lowering the regulatory cost of doing business. The labor absorption capacity of the market for youth employment is limited, resulting in high youth unemployment or employment in nonstandard precarious work. These trends pose serious challenges with regard to compliance with bargaining council agreements and other labor standards. Enforcement of these regulations has become much harder. For example, there has been an increase in the number of noncompliant clothing manufacturers and CMTs. This is sometimes referred to as the "domestic sweatshop phenomenon." Also, in areas that were outside of bargaining council agreements, foreign-owned export-oriented firms have proliferated. These firms have not only prevented the South African Clothing and Textile Workers Union (SACTWU) from organizing workers in some factories, but also illegally refused access to Department of Labour (DOL) and bargaining council inspectors.

The Human Sciences Research Council (HSRC) has identified what it refers to as high, intermediate, and low skills bands in the SA labor market, with the intermediate skills education and training band having the most severe skills shortage and an oversupply of unskilled workers, especially in informal and casual employment. Intermediate skills band shortages include, for example, artisans, technicians, and manufacturing operatives (Kraak, 2004). Supply side provision by educational and training institutions in these skill categories shows a worrying decline. Kraak (2004, p. 65) argues that a skills crisis in the high-level skill band may be exaggerated and misplaced, this given, for example, high unemployment (approximately 1 million) of young graduates attempting to find their first job. Arguably though, some higher level qualifications may see an oversupply at the entry level, for example, human resource practitioners, though others such as actuaries may still be in demand. There is a partial decline in the demand for engineers, which is mirrored in the decline in the training of engineers on the supply side and a decline in university output of engineers since the mid-1990s. Positively, however, 45% of new learnerships registered by the DOL are in the intermediate band (Kraak, 2004, p. 79). Steadily rising economic growth predicted to rise to 5.8–6% from 2006 may accelerate the present muted demand. The HSRC argues that SA needs an economic growth trajectory that includes a significant low-skill, labor-intensive employment strategy (Kraak, 2004, p. 84; Ashton, 2004). This would not preclude the identification of high-performance niche industries requiring high-level skills formation. Hence multifaceted policy solutions are needed. Such policy priorities would need to address the declining output of key "hard" technical areas such as engineers and technical operatives.

Allied to the issues of skills supply and demand, HIV/AIDS has a disproportionately negative impact on the economically active population, on Africans, and on women. The impact is projected to occur unevenly across companies and sectors, and all skill levels will be negatively affected. Capital substitution, poaching, and the importation of foreign skilled labor may occur. HIV/AIDS will adversely affect quantity and quality of education; the achievement of equity targets in skills development, education, and training may be at risk (Human Resources Development Review, 2003). Crime and an HIV/AIDS epidemic are pressing social problems for policy choices. Estimated shrinkage from the year 2002 to 2015 of real GDP owing to AIDS ranges from 2.8 to 9.6% (ABSA Bank and ING Barings, 2002). Although not yet viewed by a majority of South African firms as a strategic issue, the rate of HIV/AIDS in the labor force is viewed by some as having the potential to erode productivity gains made through skill development efforts. According to the Medical Research Council of South Africa about 12–15% of the population is HIV infected. AIDS has become the single biggest cause of death (Dorrington, Bourne, Bradshaw, Laubscher, & Timaeus, 2001). Firms in the mining industry are expected to be hit particularly hard because of the legacy of migrant labor. Some large firms like Anglo Gold have responded by offering employees access to HIV drugs. As the impact of the disease becomes more evident, firms may have no choice but to address it as a strategic HRM challenge.

Templer, Hofmeyr, and Rall (1997, pp. 551–558) found a preference for developing an African model of management, with less reliance on American and Japanese MNC approaches. A comparative study found agreement between human resource practitioners in Canada, South Africa, and Zimbabwe on the need for flexible work practices and cost effectiveness, but significant differences in priorities for South African practices under apartheid focused on personnel administration and industrial relations. This has shifted to emphasizing employment equity, performance management, and organizational restructuring, often resulting in downsizing and retrenchments. The twin challenges of redressing labor market inequalities created by apartheid and simultaneously and rapidly creating competitive capabilities are daunting, often competing, but unavoidable HRM challenges. The magnitude of these challenges are best understood within their historical and stakeholder context. African economic empowerment has become a priority for the new government as a strategy to break through the social closure created by past discriminatory policies. Professional, managerial, and transport occupations account for an increase of around 2 million jobs since 1970. More skilled employees have been absorbed into service industries, due to a structural shift from the primary sector to growth in services, accompanied by rising capital-to-labor ratios. The greatest demand is expected for skills in IT and finance (Bhorat, 1999). The labor absorption capacity into higher skill and managerial jobs is being nudged by supply side measures such as employment equity legislation.

# MNC AND LOCAL FIRM DIMENSIONS OF HUMAN RESOURCE MANAGEMENT

We have earlier evaluated trends dealing with human resource development, skills training, employment equity, and employment relations. Recruitment and selection have become important focal points for seeking both to attract talent and to address equity imperatives. Methods for recruitment and selection have come under scrutiny with respect to fair and nondiscrimi-natory practices. Chapter 2 of the EEA (1998) makes important provisions regarding the use of psychometric and HIV testing that is free of any cultural or ethnic bias. While it is good professional practice anyway, this Act requires an employer to conduct a review of recruitment and selection practices and promotion policies to ensure it does not unfairly discriminate. This has resulted in a more professional approach to recruitment and selection. Recruitment agencies are also required to ensure compliance with the nondiscriminatory provisions of legislation. An applicant for a job is included in the definition of "employee" in employment equity and other labor laws. This means that a job candidate cannot be discriminated against unfairly on grounds such as race or gender.

Remuneration policy and practice have become an important means for an employer to leverage performance improvement (Horwitz et al., 2004). Especially at the executive level, SA firms are increasingly applying and adapting best-pay practices largely from the U.S. MNCs. There is a trend toward performance-based pay, with an increased variable component of pay. Basic pay for executives is declining as a proportion of a total package with more use of share options, profit sharing, and variable and flexible pay measures. At operational levels and often in negotiation with trade unions, skill-based pay has been introduced. Examples include auto assembly, clothing and textiles, and various engineering and manufacturing firms. But in sectors such as building and construction, increased labor subcontracting has resulted in a deterioration of conditions of employment for increasing numbers of workers. Rising earnings differentials are attributable in part to these factors and the legacy of an "apartheid pay gap." It has been difficult to prove that pay differences are exclusively due to racial discrimination and not other factors such as performance, length of service, and relevant experience, even though there is a reverse onus of proof (the employer has to provide a legally valid explanation) in claims of unfair discrimination. Human resource departments are concerned with both pay administration and measures to improve performance management through pay incentives. Increasingly the former is being outsourced and/or replaced with technology as IT and new software packages are designed to do pay administration. For more progressive organizations, this will allow HR functions to concentrate on aligning HR policy and measures with organizational strategy to optimize performance.

The use of job evaluations by HR departments in medium and large organizations is common practice for establishing the relative worth of jobs and ranking jobs as a basis for designing a grading structure. Job evaluation systems were introduced in the mining and beer brewing industries in the early 1970s. Job evaluation systems such as Hay, Peromnes (a widely used locally developed system), and Paterson are variously used in agribusiness, engineering, government, insurance and financial services, manufacturing, mining, and tertiary educational institutions such as universities. As organizations restructure and delayer hierarchies, job evaluation systems have to adapt to deal with processes such as broad banding and multiskilling. Job analysis and work process redesign are increasingly important facets of HR work in SA. Research shows that although Western MNC HRM practices have prevailed for decades in African countries there is an increase in SA firms adopting Japanese and East Asian practices (Horwitz, Kamoche, & Chew Keng-Howe, 2002; Faull, 2000). This is particularly evident in the use of Japanese MNC (such as Toyota and Nissan, which have assembly plants in SA) lean manufacturing, just-in-time methods, and other operations management measures to reduce product defects, stock holdings, inventory, and waste. These measures have also increased in the manufacturing sector, in which firms have introduced kaizen, kanban methods, Nissan-type green areas, Toyota TQM, and production systems and quality improvement teams. However, the adoption of East Asian work practices is seen by many as unworkable. Many firms believe that Japanese MNC work philosophies are rooted in a different cultural context and cannot therefore be copied in African countries (Keenan, 2000, p. 26). There is case-study evidence of forms of functional flexibility in firms such as Pick'n Pay Retailers, SA Nylon Spinners, and Sun International Hotels (Horwitz & Townshend, 1993). However, these practices are less common (under 10%) in relation to use of numerical flexibility such as downsizing and outsourcing and temporal flexibility types such as part-time, temporary, and casual, short-term work (Allen, Brosnan, Horwitz, & Walsh, 2001). Use of flexible work practices, including functional forms of flexibility such as multiskilling and performance-based pay, is more common in MNCs than in local SA firms (Horwitz & Smith, 1998, pp. 590–606). SA organizations tend to emphasize collective and procedural relations, whereas MNC firms in SA have more distinctive, often diffused, HRM practices based on individual relations.

Empirical work in SA on the concept of "effectiveness" in HRM and industrial relations practices has attempted to determine the relationship between these factors and performance measures such as service (Browning, 1998; Horwitz & Neville, 1996; Templer & Cattaneo, 1991; Owens & van der Merwe, 1993). Mediating contextual factors in adoption of HRM have been found in other African countries (Kamoche, 1992). Kamoche (1993) offers a provisional model of HRM in Africa. Considering the notion of "effectiveness" in HRM and industrial relations, a critical challenge is that of moving from discriminatory practices, adversarial industrial relations, and an underskilled workforce toward a fair HRM regime with high performance practices. Consequently, managing diversity, job design, training and development, and performance management seem to be dominant HRM functional areas driving the agendas of both SA and MNC firms in SA.

# EMPLOYMENT RELATIONS AND LEGISLATIVE DEVELOPMENTS

Employment relations in SA have undergone major changes over the past 2 decades (Rajah, 2000). An adversarial race-based dualistic system evolved following labor legislation in 1924, which led to trade unions rights that excluded Africans. Only in 1980 were unions representing African workers legitimized. Inclusive bargaining councils were fostered through the Labour Relations Act in 1995. African unions grew to over 3 million members in 2001 from less than 10% of the formal sector work force in the late 1970s. The largest unions are affiliated with union federations such as the COSATU and the National Council of Unions.

The Labour Relations Act (1995) also established labor and labor appeal courts and the Commission for Conciliation Mediation and Arbitration. The CCMA handles both procedural and distributive or substantive justice in considering the fairness of a matter such as dismissal. The new Act sought to bring employment law in line with the constitution and ratified Conventions of the International Labour Organisation. It aimed to give effect to constitutional rights permitting employees to form unions and to strike for collective bargaining purposes and the right to fair labor practices. Employers have the right to form and join employers' organizations and recourse to the lockout for the purpose of collective bargaining. Strike action is protected only if a specified dispute procedure is followed. Whereas centralized industry-level and decentralized enterprise or plant bargaining may occur, increased devolution and fragmentation of bargaining has occurred in the first decade of the 21st century. The number of bargaining councils has declined to fewer than 80 as employers withdraw from them, favoring plant or enterprise bargaining and increased employment flexibility. This has occurred, for example, in the building and construction industries, as new forms of employment emphasizing flexibility using independent subcontractors, outsourcing, part-time and temporary work, and increased casualization and informalization of work. These practices are associated with a recent decline in private sector union density and some evidence of deterioration in employment standards in certain sectors. The Basic Conditions of Employment Act (1998), however, provides for establishing minimum standards of employment. These conditions cover areas from the designation of working hours to termination regulations and have been extended to farm and domestic workers. Work days lost through strike action have also declined since 1994. Although under apartheid African unions fought for fair labor practices, workers' rights, and better pay and conditions of employment, they also were at the forefront of the struggle for political rights. Once political and labor rights complemented each other in the first democratic elections in 1994, this labor paradox was resolved. This resulted in an intense policy debate within the union movement as to its repositioning in the new SA. The workplace as an arena for political struggle has largely been replaced by an emphasis on measures to try and preserve employment and HR issues such as training and development and employment equity (Horwitz et al., 2004). The Labour Relations Act seeks to promote employee participation in decision making through workplace forums and employee consultation and joint decision making on certain issues. It provides for simple procedures for the resolution of labor disputes through statutory conciliation and arbitration, and through independent alternative dispute resolution services. Amendments to the Act came into effect on August 1, 2002. New forms of dispute resolution were developed to include predismissal arbitration and one-stop dispute resolution known as CON-ARB. Both unions and management have the power to request the CCMA to facilitate retrenchment negotiations to achieve constructive outcomes.

A key challenge in employment relations is the need to shift from a legacy of adversarial relationships to workplace cooperation to compete successfully in the market place. There is evidence in some sectors such as auto assembly that this is understood by both parties. There is increasingly a blurring of the distinction between employment relations and HRM. The new agenda focuses beyond the traditional collective bargaining items and adversarial dismissal disputes to organizational transformation, performance improvement, human resource development, and employee benefits. Trade unions have become more willing to engage employers around these issues. Finding a productive balance between equity and workplace justice imperatives on the one hand, and HR and employment relations strategies enhancing competitiveness on the other, is a vital challenge for mangers and unions.

# EMPLOYMENT EQUITY LEGISLATION
# AND HUMAN RESOURCE PRACTICES

Legislative prohibitions against unfair discrimination are intrinsic to SA's Constitution (1996). Chapter 2 (the Bill of Rights) contains an equality clause, which specifies a number of grounds that constitute unfair discrimination. Additionally, Schedule 7 of the Labour Relations Act (1995) considers unfair discrimination either directly or indirectly as a residual unfair labor practice. Grounds include race, gender, ethnic origin, sexual orientation, religion, disability, conscience, belief, language, and culture. The EEA (1998) focuses on unfair discrimination in employment and HR practices. Employers are required to take steps to end unfair discrimination in employment policies and practices. It prohibits the unfair discrimination against employees, including job seekers, on any arbitrary grounds, including race, gender, pregnancy, marital status, sexual orientation, disability, language, and religion.

The Constitution and prohibitions contained in the EEA and other labor legislation distinguish permissible discrimination from impermissible discrimination. All designated employers (these who employ 50 or more people) have to prepare and submit to the DOL an employment equity plan setting out goals, targets, timetables, and measures to be taken to remove discriminatory employment practices and achieve greater workforce representation, especially at the managerial and skilled category levels. The EEA does not set quotas, but rather enables individual employers to develop their own HR and equity plans. Criteria regarding enhanced representation include national and regional demographic information and special skills supply/availability. The EEA includes provisions against unfair discrimination in selection and recruitment, aptitude testing, HIV/AIDS testing, promotions, and access to training and development opportunities. It is generally accepted that an "apartheid wage gap" saw pay discrimination evolve over some 4 decades or more. More recent equalization of opportunities has not always led to pay parity for work of equal value. Section 27 of the EEA somewhat controversially requires designated employers, as part of a required employment equity plan, to submit to the DOL a statement on the remuneration and benefits received in each occupational category and level of the employer's workforce. Where disproportionate income differentials are reflected in the statement, an employer is required to take measures to reduce such differentials progressively. Measures include collective bargaining, skills formation, compliance with other wage-regulating instruments, and benchmarks set by the Employment Conditions Commission.

As part of a required employment equity plan, designated employers have to review employment and human resources practices to remove provisions or practices that may have an unfair discriminatory effect. This includes recruitment and selection and remuneration. An applicant for a job is included in the definition of "employee," making unfair discrimination in preemployment recruitment and selection practices, such as psychometric assessment and interviews and application form questions that do not pertain directly to the ability of the person to do the job, illegal. South African labor law allows discrimination on the basis of inherent job requirements. But the object of an employer's conduct must be fair, and the means rational. It is in these areas, as well as in the provision of substantive benefits and conditions of employment, that unfair discrimination is most likely. The notions of disproportionate effect and adverse impact are considered in this regard. Once an employee claims discrimination, the evidentiary burden shifts to the employer to show that the discrimination is not unfair. It is nonetheless very difficult for an employee to prove pay discrimination conclusively. In particular, whereas discrimination may occur, an employer may cogently submit that pay and skill differences were not the result of unfair discrimination, but due to factors such as differences in performance, experience, competency, and service. Recent court cases show that even in an environment in which affirmative action to overcome past discrimination is accepted as an appropriate method to achieve equity, there are continuing differing interpretations about its aims and effects on HR practice. Decisions based on race or gender, unless they are related to a genuine skill or occupational requirement, could be found to be arbitrary and unfair labor practices (Van Vuuren vs. Department of Correctional Services, 1998; George vs. Liberty Life Association of Africa Ltd., 1996 cases). Affirmative action, though, is not regarded as unfair discrimination in SA labor law. Both the policy and the organizational context in which the dispute arises are pertinent. This tends to reflect the limitations of the "discrimination and fairness" as well as "access and equal opportunity" perspectives as legalistic and procedural remedies to race and ethnic relations problems in the workplace. Change management and "soft" HR strategies focusing on relationship building and cultural transformation to integrate diversity as a value in itself for effective work group relations have been found to be more effective than reliance on procedural justice approaches alone (Horwitz et al., 2004).

Even when employers explicitly espouse these policies, the consequences of years of systematic discrimination continue to skew both internal and external labor markets. Managers' failure to address both skills and pay practices adequately in the service industry in SA has a direct adverse impact on the service behavior of frontline employees (Browning, 2000). Human resource policies and remuneration practices do not occur in a "neutral" or unbiased context. The institutional environment remains a powerful influence on HRM in SA, mitigated to an extent by the competitive forces of global competition. Table 1 shows that employed Africans, both men and women, tend to be concentrated in lower income levels.

Although changing, with the use of unfair discrimination legal action, a "glass ceiling" still remains for designated groups. According to the 2003 Annual Employment Equity report, workers covered by large (150+ employees) employers under the EEA represented approximately 35% of the total formally employed people in 2003 relative to 8,373,761 in the labor force in the formal sector; as Table 2 indicates, in the formal sector labor force, almost 60% of employees were Africans, 15% Colored, 5% Indian, and 23% White. The percentages for employees in the employment equity returns filed by employers are very similar. African males had the highest relative representation (38%) in the labor force compared to the employment equity (EE) data (Annual EE Report, 2003).

Although there has been upward occupational mobility since the country's first democratic elections in 1994, this has been slower than might have been expected. As Tables 3 and 4 show, in the top employment categories, Whites still hold most executive and managerial posts, occupying 62% of these (males 47%, females 15%). Africans represent 51%

***Table 1.*** Claimed Monthly Household Income by Race 2000.

|  | African | Asian and Colored | White | Total Population |
|---|---|---|---|---|
| R1-R499 | 15.8% | 1.3% | 0.3% | 11.8% |
| R500-R899 | 26.2% | 4.4% | 1.2% | 20.1% |
| R900-R1,399 | 21.2% | 6.4% | 2.9% | 17.1% |
| R1,400-R2,499 | 17.1% | 10.2% | 5.8% | 15.2% |
| R2,500-R3,999 | 8.7% | 12.6% | 9.7% | 9.8% |
| R4,000-R6,999 | 6.8% | 23.7% | 24.2% | 11.5% |
| R7,000-R11,999 | 3.0% | 24.5% | 31.5% | 9.0% |
| R12,000+ | 1.1% | 17.0% | 24.4% | 5.6% |
| (a) All (R) | 100.0% | 100.0% | 100.0% | 100.0% |
| (b) Average (R): 2000 | 1,865 | 7,265 | 9,108 | 3,368 |
| Percentage change: 1999–2000 | 19.3% | 3.4% | 4.2% | 5.7% |

*Source:* South African Advertising Research Foundation, All Media Products Survey, 2000, p. 30.

**Table 2.** Demographics: Population Group and Gender (Labour Force Survey (LFS), 2003 vs. Employment Equity (EE), 2003).

| Population Group | Workforce Profiles | | | | | |
|---|---|---|---|---|---|---|
| | 2003 LFS (formally employed) | | | EE 2003 (permanent employment) | | |
| | Male | Female | Total | Male | Female | Total |
| African | 3,177,503 | 1,726,578 | 4,904,080 | 1,220,153 | 526,753 | 1,746,906 |
| | 61.7% | 53.5% | 58.6% | 64.8% | 49.8% | 59.4% |
| Colored | 669,337 | 533,397 | 1,202,733 | 190,617 | 183,413 | 374,030 |
| | 13.0% | 16.5% | 14.4% | 10.1% | 17.3% | 12.7% |
| Indian | 263,752 | 172,221 | 435,973 | 84,747 | 61,146 | 145,893 |
| | 5.1% | 5.3% | 5.2% | 4.5% | 5.8% | 5.0% |
| White | 1,037,568 | 793,406 | 1,830,974 | 387,276 | 286,893 | 674,169 |
| | 20.2% | 24.6% | 21.9% | 20.6% | 27.1% | 22.9% |
| Total | 5,148,159 | 3,225,601 | 8,373,761 | 1,882,793 | 1,058,205 | 2,940,998 |
| | 100% | 100% | 100% | 100% | 100% | 100% |

**Table 3.** Employment per Occupational Category Comparisons (Labour Force Survey (LFS), 2003 and Employment Equity (EE), 2003).

| Occupational Category | Employees | |
|---|---|---|
| | 2003 LFS (formally employed) (%) | EE 2003 (permanent employment) (%) |
| Executive/Managerial/Legislator | 9 | 4 |
| Professional | 6 | 11 |
| Technical | 13 | 12 |
| Clerk | 14 | 16 |
| Service | 13 | 12 |
| Skilled agricultural | 1 | 1 |
| Craft | 12 | 6 |
| Plant operator | 13 | 16 |
| Elementary | 20 | 22 |
| Total | 100 | 100 |

(males 23%, females 28%) of the people employed as professionals, whereas 86% (male 64%, female 22%) of elementary occupations are also filled by Africans. The African population also accounts for 64% of nonpermanent employment (males 37%, females 27%).

**Table 4.** Employment by Occupational Level.

| Occupational Level | Male | | | | Female | | | | Total |
|---|---|---|---|---|---|---|---|---|---|
| | African | Colored | Indian | White | African | Colored | Indian | White | |
| Top management | 1,741 | 477 | 651 | 10,469 | 568 | 132 | 115 | 1,362 | 15,515 |
| | 0% | 0% | 1% | 3% | 0% | 0% | 0% | 0% | 1% |
| Senior management | 4,829 | 2,062 | 2,538 | 27,397 | 1,899 | 958 | 662 | 7,088 | 47,433 |
| | 0% | 1% | 3% | 7% | 0% | 1% | 1% | 2% | 2% |
| Midmanagement | 55,016 | 10,101 | 10,125 | 88,657 | 45,782 | 5,695 | 4,222 | 38,524 | 258,122 |
| | 5% | 5% | 12% | 23% | 9% | 3% | 7% | 13% | 9% |
| Skilled | 196,875 | 55,454 | 32,853 | 184,536 | 157,342 | 53,256 | 24,166 | 137,055 | 841,537 |
| | 16% | 29% | 39% | 48% | 30% | 29% | 40% | 48% | 29% |
| Semiskilled | 494,638 | 81,554 | 29,319 | 60,996 | 159,701 | 83,715 | 25,232 | 95,826 | 1,030,981 |
| | 41% | 42% | 35% | 16% | 30% | 45% | 41% | 33% | 35% |
| Unskilled | 452,942 | 42,371 | 8,244 | 10,295 | 159,818 | 41,887 | 6,751 | 6,828 | 729,136 |
| | 38% | 22% | 10% | 3% | 30% | 23% | 11% | 2% | 25% |
| Total permanent | 1,206,041 | 192,019 | 83,730 | 382,350 | 525,110 | 185,643 | 61,148 | 286,683 | 2,922,724 |
| | 89% | 88% | 88% | 92% | 85% | 85% | 88% | 91% | 89% |
| Nonpermanent employees | 142,049 | 26,496 | 11,422 | 31,691 | 93,477 | 33,109 | 8,654 | 27,222 | 374,120 |
| | 11% | 12% | 12% | 8% | 15% | 15% | 12% | 9% | 11% |
| Total | 1,348,090 | 218,515 | 95,152 | 414,041 | 618,587 | 218,752 | 69,802 | 313,905 | 3,296,844 |
| | 100% | 100% | 100% | 100% | 100% | 100% | 100% | 100% | 100% |

In addition to the eight occupational categories (Table 4), employers are also required to group employees into seven occupational levels: top management; senior management; professionally qualified and experienced specialists and midmanagement; skilled technical and academically qualified workers; junior management, supervisors, foremen, and superintendents; semiskilled and discretionary decision making; and unskilled and defined decision making.

Three percent of all employees fall into the top and senior management levels, with middle management accounting for 9%. Semi- and unskilled employees account for 60% of the workforce. White employees are more likely to be part of top management than are members of other groups, and both Indian and White employees are more likely to be employed at the top to middle management levels. The majority (68%) of African employees are employed at the semiskilled or unskilled level, and African employees are more likely than other population groups to be employed at the unskilled level (Annual EE Report, 2003).

## BROAD-BASED BLACK ECONOMIC EMPOWERMENT (BEE) AND HUMAN RESOURCE MANAGEMENT

One of the strategies used by the SA government to encourage Black equity in the economy is called broad-based Black economic empowerment. It was introduced in the Broad-Based BEE Act of 2003. It means the economic empowerment of Blacks, including Black women, persons with disabilities, and others, through diverse but integrated socioeconomic strategies including increasing the number of Blacks who manage, own, and control enterprises and productive assets; human resource skills and development; equitable representation in all occupational categories and levels in the workforce; preferential procurement; and investment in enterprises that are owned or managed by Black people.

Broad-based BEE has three components: direct empowerment, human resource development, and indirect empowerment. The human resource development component's beneficiaries are employees and workers through employment equity and skills development. Skills development indicates development of core competencies of Black people to facilitate their interaction in the mainstream of the economy. The broad-based BEE concept has caught on quite significantly. Many industrial sectors have set targets through negotiated charters for BEE and others are implementing EE and skills development to an increasing extent. It is almost daily news (see, for instance, Mathews & Cohen, 2005, p. 1; Rose, 2005; Cokayne, 2005), "Motor industry BEE task team stalls as it awaits revised scorecard," p. 1). According to Navin and Neil (2005) "... the government's black economic empowerment (BEE) program is beginning to pick up pace and fundamental shift in the economic balance of power could be on its way." The government and industrial leaders from several sectors have drawn up industry charters. These charters lay down a series of targets for the proportion of each sector to be controlled by companies owned mainly by Black South Africans. For instance, Navin and Neil (2005) indicate that charters have already been completed for the financial, tourism, and mining sectors, among others. Standard Bank, the country's largest bank, indicated that it would sell a 10% stake to Black empowerment interests; it already has two prominent Blacks on its board of directors. The key targets for the banking industry are to boost the number of Black SA board members to 33% by 2008, up from 25% at present; to increase the number of Black SA executives from 10% in 2003 to 25% by 2008; and to increase procurement from BEE companies from 13% at the end of 2003 to 25% by 2008. The banking and finance sector has also promised to boost Black employment at all levels from 13% at the end of 2003 to 50% by 2008. Additional targets for empowerment are that by 2008 11% of all board members should be Black women and at least 80% of the population must have access to a bank within 20 km of either their home or their workplace by 2008. A study commissioned in 2004 by the Businesswomen's Association and Nedbank found that 14.7% of executive managers and 7.1% of all directors in SA are women; seven, or 1.9%, of CEOs are women and there is not a single female chairperson of listed IT companies in SA (The Top Women in Business and Government, 2005/2006, p. 10). Some of the biggest stumbling blocks in women's progress as directors and chief executives are a lack of serious mentorship, lack of opportunity, and poor self-esteem (The Top Women in Business and Government, 2005/2006, p. 46). However, most women are employed in state-owned enterprises (SOEs) than in the private sector. In SOEs women make up 34.9% of directors and 31.3% of the executive management positions (The Top Women in Business and Government, 2005/2006, p. 73).

The empowerment issue is important for both local firms and MNCs. It is a sensitive issue for the latter, who sometimes question the efficacy of what is perceived as "giving away" an ownership share, especially if the MNC is privately owned, or when this is not the practice in their other international operations. This said, joint ventures are commonplace in countries like China or in other African countries where the state may be a beneficiary. The requirement that BEE should include MNCs is sometimes cited as a barrier to FDI in the country. It would appear that the government is willing to listen to these positions as its policy evolves. MNCs are mostly willing to address the other facets of BEE charters and in some areas, such as training and development, are performing better than many local firms.

## MANAGING DIVERSITY AND CHANGING MANAGERIAL STYLES

Whereas many organizations around the world have implemented managing diversity initiatives in response to the growing heterogeneity of the work-force (Nkomo & Cox, 1996), SA organizations generally lag in the adoption of such practices. In a study of the diversity management in a sample of SA and MNC firms, Strydom and Erwee (1998) found at the time that the majority were best classified as monolithic companies wherein Blacks were expected to adopt the culture of the White dominant group. Hence, most SA organizations and MNCs in the country are still using what Ely and Thomas (2001) describe as the discrimination and fairness paradigm in managing diversity. Organizations that look at diversity through this lens focus on recruitment and selection of Africans, Colored people, and Indians and women employees and on compliance with the provisions of the EEA. Such an approach may be justifiable given the mandate of employment equity legislation, union demands, and the historical exclusion of Africans and women from certain occupations. The fairly slow progress in achieving employment equity is due to management's emphasis on numerical goals and not enough attention to creating organizational cultures and work-places that value diversity as key to competitive advantage. The Report on Employment Equity Registry issued by the DOL in 2000 cited corporate culture as one of the major barriers to employment equity (DOL, 2000). Nevertheless, the specific strategies adopted by firms to value and manage diversity will have to take into consideration the specificity of the local and historical context. An example of such an approach is the one taken by First National Bank. Their unique approach was designed to address the dual challenges of low employee morale due to perceptions of racism among Black employees and feelings of reverse discrimination among White employees and a business need to increase checking account revenues from the growing Black urban population. In addition to cultural diversity awareness training, the program required all managers to spend 2 days in an African township to understand customer needs better. Additionally, the bank institutionalized ongoing staff gatherings and the use of collective decision making in branches (*Sunday Times*, 2002).

Managerial styles reflect organizational and national cultural patterns. In SA, although achievement is valued, group and organization conformity is also important. Whereas there is a paucity of empirical research on managerial culture in SA firms, a masculine dominance is evident across ethnic groups (Horwitz, 2002, pp. 215–217), emphasized by individualist values and a relatively large power distance between groups based on historical racial and ethnic disparities. However, an emergent African middle class has begun to occupy decision-making roles. Class mobility is likely to have an impact on managerial culture and inform strategic choices about appropriate organizational culture, business, and HRM practices in SA. Organization and national culture reflect considerable diversity and pluralism. Managerial styles in SA reflect Anglo-Saxon, Western values based on individualism, meritocracy, and an authoritarian legacy of apartheid. These are often rooted in high-masculinity cultures (Hofstede, 1991). However, indigenous models struggle to assert themselves in the face of a converging global business orthodoxy (Mbigi, 2000).

## CONCLUSIONS AND IMPLICATIONS

Although incremental progress has been made to enhance racial and gender diversity, this has to be supported by coherent human resource development priorities and changes in organizational culture. This is vital at both public policy and organizational levels. Rising income inequalities are beginning to cut across racial and ethnic lines. This could create a new fault line of inequality. An increased earnings gap has an adverse impact mainly on African people, despite increasing diversity and the multiracial character of a growing middle class. The biggest priority must be human resource development and education in skills and competencies needed in a transitional society. Several sectors need both high- and low-level skills. The former are in the information economy and high value adding occupations, whereas the latter are in service sectors such as hospitality. Hybrid forms of HR based on MNC and local firm practices may occur in nomenclature, design, content, and implementation processes. There is some evidence of reverse diffusion. SAB Miller's (South African Breweries owns the U.S. beer company Miller) jointly owned breweries in Poland have successfully implemented best operating practices and management know-how on systems, process, and technology based on Japanese practice and its experience in emergent economies. A balance will need to be struck between indigenous responses to past discrimination and the clear need for high-performance practices.

This conclusion is consistent with Aguilera and Dencker (2004) and Child (2002), who note differing levels of integration across countries, ranging from no integration, to partial integration, to full integration. For example, firms in the United States and the United Kingdom integrate their subsidiaries to a greater extent than do firms in Japan, Germany, and France. Aguilera and Dencker (2004), in positing a strategic fit framework, argue that although at a broad level practices such as pay-for-performance systems are common across market economy types, at a refined level there are nontrivial differences that HR has to manage; for example, a compensation system in the BP–Amoco merger had to be redesigned because the companies differed significantly, and a new job structure framework was established. Thus, even firms in countries within the same market economic type will experience some degree of localization in HRM practices and policies and therefore need to adjust the role of HRM accordingly.

Given the diverse ethnic demography of SA society, most of the underclass is African. Organizations, including MNCs, will need to shift from compliance to a commitment model that has an organizational culture reflecting the notion of ubuntu and capacity building as vital for both competitiveness and equity in the workplace. South Africa faces a double transitional challenge – to redress the historical inequalities by building a democracy based on human rights and tolerance, and to develop, simultaneously and speedily, its human capital capacity to compete in a harsh global economy. Arguably this is a bigger policy and practical challenge than managerial and executive employment equity, on which the focus seems to lie. Skills formation and entrepreneurial development are vital, especially in a country with huge transitional challenges (Horwitz et al., 2004). These can be summed up in one word – "development." National skills policies have introduced mechanisms such as a 1% of payroll levy to finance human resource development to meet national, sector, and organizational development objectives. Particular sector skills formation through Sector Training Authorities (SETAS) and a national qualifications framework (Sparreboom, 2004, pp. 130–131) are encouraged by law. Economic empowerment and employment equity are not possible without human resource development and education as a fundamental national priority. Large-scale labor absorption into a shrinking formal labor market is unlikely, given the shift of employment to service and informal, noncore work mainly outside the ambit of employment equity legislation. The priority of practical policy initiatives by government, private sector firms, labor market institutions such as SETAS, and bargaining councils must be large-scale initiatives to train and retrain for enhancing employability in the changing labor market.

This is supported by Gomez and Sanchez (2005), who conclude that human resources can play a strategic role in building social capital in the process of balancing local and global forces. They argue that HR can be critical in helping MNCs deal with local differences while also helping the company implement practices that are critical for its global strategy and local development needs. Globalization and localization call for different levels of MNC control and coordination of its subsidiaries. One such mechanism used by MNCs concerned with coordination/integration is the creation of social capital – the intangible resources embedded in the network of existing company relationships that assist in the accomplishment of necessary tasks; it allows MNCs to help bridge the gap between globalization and localization of strategic practices. These authors submit that HR practices can create social capital in locally adaptive ways. Even though practices are bound to differ among countries, strategically speaking, companies will want some practice commonalities across their subsidiaries and, more specifically, those practices that are strategically aligned with the organization's mission. Companies specifically transfer organizational practices that reflect their core competencies and espoused corporate values. HR practices are associated with social capital. Practices such as human resource development, fair labor practices and standards, equal opportunity and employee empowerment, equitable wage structures and incentive schemes, cross-functional team development, and performance management systems incentives differentiate firms with high levels of social capital from those with low levels. According to Gomez and Sanchez (2005) certain of these practices may be more appropriate for certain cultural contexts than for others, and in building social capital, MNCs must take into account the cultural and institutional context in which they operate. The same HR practices that build trust in one country context may fail to do so in another – each HR practice that an MNC considers implementing should be filtered through a "localization mesh" that identifies clashes with local values. This analysis, according to the above authors, should allow for modifications that will render the practice culturally fit.

In South Africa this means that local and MNC firms will need to shift from compliance to a commitment model that has an organizational culture reflecting the notion of ubuntu, social capital, and capacity building as vital for both competitiveness and equity in the workplace. South Africa faces a double transitional challenge – to redress the historical inequalities by building a democracy based on human rights and tolerance, and to develop simultaneously and speedily its human capital capacity to compete in a harsh global economy.

# REFERENCES

ABSA Bank and ING Barings. (2002). Special reports on HIV/AIDS in Southern Africa, pp. 1–12.

Aguilera, R., & Dencker, J. (2004). The role of human resource management in cross-border mergers and acquisitions. *International Journal of Human Resource Management, 15*(8), 1355–1370.

Allen, C., Brosnan, P., Horwitz, F. M., & Walsh, P. (2001). From standard to non-standard employment. *International Journal of Manpower, 22*(8), 748–763.

Ashton, D. (2004). High skills: The concept and its application to South Africa. In: A. Badroodien, S. McGrath, A. Kraak & L. Unwin (Eds), *Shifting understandings of skill in South Africa.* Cape Town: HSRC Press.

Barker, F. (1999). *The South African labour market* (23–25). Pretoria: JL van Schaik.

Bhorat, H. (1999) Quoted in Quarterly Trends – National Business Initiative Publication, December, 3.

Booysen, L. (2007). Barriers to employment equity implementation and retention of blacks in management in South Africa. *South African Journal of Labour Relations, 31*(1), 47–68.

Boxall, P. (2003). HR strategy and competitive advantage in the service sector. *Human Resource Management Journal, 13*(3), 5–20.

Browning, V. (1998). Creating service excellence through human resource practices. *South African Journal of Business Management, 29*(4), 125–141.

Browning, V. (2000). Human resource management practices and service-oriented behaviour in South African organisations. Invited paper presented at the Eric Langeard International Research Seminar in Service Management, Toulon France, 5–8 June, pp. 1–16.

Budhwar, P. S., & Sparrow, P. R. (2002). An integrative framework for understanding cross-national human resource practices. *Human Resource Management Review, 12*, 377–403.

Child, J. (2002). Theorizing about organizations cross-nationally: Towards a synthesis. In: M. Warner & P. Joynt (Eds), *Managing across cultures: Issues and perspectives* (2nd ed., pp. 40–56). London: Thomson Learning.

Cokayne, R. (2005). Motor industry BEE task team stalls as it awaits revised scorecard Business Report, September 30, p. 1.

Debrah, Y. A., & Smith, I. G. (1999). Globalisation, employment and the workplace: Responses for the millennium. Employment Research Unit Annual Conference Cardiff Business School, University of Wales, 8–9 September, pp. 1–8.

Dorrington, R., Bourne, D., Bradshaw, D., Laubscher, R., & Timaeus, I. (2001). *The impact of HIV/AIDS on adult mortality in South Africa.* Tygerberg: South African Medical Research Council.

Edwards, T., & Kuruvilla, S. (2005). International HRM: National business systems, organizational politics and the international division of labor in MNCs'. *International Journal of Human Resource Management, 16*(1), 1–21.

Ely, R. J., & Thomas, D. A. (2001). Cultural diversity at work: The effects of diversity perspectives on work group processes and outcomes. *Administrative Sciences Quarterly, 46,* 229–273.

Faull, N. (2000). Manufacturing round table project, Graduate School of Business University of Cape Town.

Financial Mail (2005). *A weekly business newspaper* (p. 1). Johannesburg.

Fraser, J. (2002). Economic transition in SA fails to create jobs. *Business Day,* October 28, 1.

George vs. Liberty Life Association of Africa Ltd. (1996). *Industrial Labour Journal, 17*(3), 571–601.

Godfrey, S., Clarke, M., & Theron, J. with Greenburg, J (2005). On the outskirts but still in fashion: Home working in South African clothing industry; the challenge to organization and regulation. Monograph 2, Labour and Enterprise Project, University of Cape Town. Restructuring in the clothing industry.

Gomez, C., & Sanchez, J. (2005). HR's strategic role within MNCs: Helping build social capital in Latin America. *International Journal of Human Resources Management, 16*(12), 2189–2200.

Grzeschke, C., & Moehring, D. (2004). Human resource practices in multinational companies in South Africa, MBA thesis, Graduate School of Business, University of Cape Town.

Harrison, R., & Kessels, J. (2004). *Human resource development in a knowledge economy.* Hampshire, UK: Palgrave Macmillan.

Hayter, S. (1999). The social impact of globalization. *SA Labour Bulletin,* Vol. 23, November 2, April.

Hofstede, G. (1991). *Cultures and organizations: Software of the mind.* London: McGraw-Hill.

Horwitz, F., & Neville, M. (1996). Organisation design for service excellence. *Human Resource Management, 35*(4), 471–492.

Horwitz, F. M. (2002). Whither South African management. In: M. Warner & P. Joynt (Eds), *Managing across cultures* (pp. 215–220). London: Thomson Learning.

Horwitz, F. M., Kamoche, K., & Chew Keng-Howe, I. (2002). Looking east: Diffusing high performance work practices in the southern Afro-Asian context. *International Journal of Human Resource Management, 13*(7), 1019–1041.

Horwitz, F. M., Nkomo, S., & Rajah, M. (2004). HRM in South Africa. In: K Kamoche, et al. (Eds), *Managing human resources in Africa* (pp. 1–18). London: Routledge.

Horwitz, F. M., & Smith, D. A. (1998). Flexible work practices and human resource management: A comparison of South African and foreign-owned companies. *International Journal of Human Resource Management, 9*(4), 590–607.

Horwitz, F. M., & Townshend, M. (1993). Elements in participation, teamwork and flexibility. *International Journal of Human Resource Management, 4*(4), 17–30.

Human Resources Development Review. (2003). Human Resources Development: Education, Employment and skills in South Africa. Human Sciences Research Council, Cape Town.

Isaacs, S. (1997). *South Africa in the Global Economy.* Durban: Trade Union Research Project (TURP).

Jackson, T. (2000). *Management in Africa: Developing a cross-cultural research agenda.* International Academy of African Business and Development Conference. Atlantic City, NJ.

Joffe, H. (2005). As sectors patterns shift, focus falls on quality of growth. *Financial Mail,* (August 23), p. 10.

Kamoche, K. (1992). Human resource management: An assessment of the Kenyan case. *The International Journal of Human Resource Management, 3*(3), 497–519.

Kamoche, K. (1993). Toward a model of HRM in Africa. *Personnel and Human Resources Management, 3*(Suppl.), 259–278.

Kamoche, K. (1997a). Managing human resources in Africa: Strategic, organizational and epistemological issues. *International Business Review, 6,* 537–558.

Kamoche, K. (1997b). Competence creation in the African public sector. *International Journal of Public Sector Management, 10*(4), 268–278.

Kamoche, K. (2000). *Sociological Paradigms and Human Resources: An African context.* Aldershot: Ashgate.

Kraak, A. (2004). *An overview of South African human resources development* (65–86). Cape Town: Human Sciences Research Council (HSRC) Press.

Mangaliso, M. P. (2001). Building competitive advantage from ubuntu: Management lessons from South Africa. *Academy of Management Executive, 15*(3), 23–32.

Mathews, C., & Cohen, T. (2005). DE Beers shows new face with black MD. *Business Day,* September 30, p. 1.

Mbigi, L. (2000). Making the African renaissance globally competitive. *People Dynamics, 18*(11), 16–21.

Mde, V., & Ensor, L. (2005). Latest figures show economy grew at robust 5% in second quarter of this year: Cabinet approves blueprint for 6% growth by 2010. *Business Day,* October 13, p. 1.

Navin, T., & Neil, F. (2005). Ending economic 'apartheid' in South Africa. *African Business, April*(308), 34–35.

Nkomo, S., & Cox, T. H. (1996). Diverse identities in organizations. In: S. Clegg, C. Hardy & W. Nord (Eds), *Handbook of organization studies* (pp. 338–356). London: Sage Publications.

Nzelibe, C. O. (1986). The evolution of African management thought. *International Studies of Management and Organization, 16*(2), 6–16.

Owens, J., & van der Merwe, J. (1993). Perspectives of services provided by the human resource function. *South African Journal of Business Management, 24*(2), 56–63.

Paton, C., & Bisseker, C. (2005). A stitch in time. *Financial Mail* (April 8), 17–20.

Podsakoff, P. M., MacKenzie, S. C., Paine, J. B., & Bachrach, D. G. (2000). Organizational citizenship behaviours: A critical review of the theoretical and empirical literature and suggestions for future research. *Journal of Management, 26*(3), 513–563.

Rajah, M. (2000). The socio-political and work environment as sources of workplace discrimination: Implications for employment equity. *Southern African Business Review, 4*(2), 77–82.

Rose, R. (2005). Deloitte under fire for 'conflicts' in Nampak BEE deal. *Business Day,* September 30, p. 1.

Saunders, S., & Loots, E. (2005). Measuring the informal economy in South Africa. SAJEMS NS 8, No. 1.

Schlemmer, L. (2005). *Black advancement: Hype outstrips reality.* Focus, South African Institute of Race Relations, Johannesburg, p. 39.

Shezi, A. (2005a). Rand rides high on back of strong growth forecasts: GDP increase of 4% expected to be job boost. *Business Day*, August 23, p. 1.

Shezi, A. (2005b). Domestic demand powers factories. *Business Day*, October 13, p. 1.

Sparreboom, T. (2004). Skills development information systems in demand driven markets: The case of South Africa. *South African Journal of Labour Relations*, 28(1), 130–131.

Standing, G., Sender, J., & Weeks, J. (1996). *Restructuring the labour market: The South African challenge* (1–11, 185–228). Geneva: International Labour Office (ILO).

Strydom, J., & Erwee, R. (1998). Diversity management in a sample of South African companies. *South African Journal of Business Management*, 29(1), 14–21.

South Africa Reserve Bank. (2005). *Quarterly Bulletin*, June, p. 54.

The Top Women in Business and Government. (2005/2006). Cape Town: Publisher Richard Fletcher, Top Companies Publishing (Pty) Ltd.

Templer, A., & Cattaneo, J. (1991). Assessing human resource effectiveness. *South African Journal of Labour Relations*, 15(4), 23–30.

Templer, A., Hofmeyr, K., & Rall, J. (1997). An international comparison of human resource management objectives. *The International Journal of Human Resource Management*, 8(4), 550–560.

Thomas, A., & Bendixen (2000). The management implications of ethnicity in South Africa. *Journal of International Business Studies*, 31(3), 507–519.

Trompenaars, F. (1993). *Riding the waves of culture: Understanding cultural diversity in business*. London: Nicholas Brealey.

Twine, T. (2005). SA's wealth explosion-number of dollar millionaires skyrockets to 37000 from 25000 in 2002. *Sunday Times*, July 17.

Van Vuuren vs. Department of Correctional Services. (1998). Case No: PA 6/98, Labour Appeal Court.

# HUMAN CAPITAL THEORY AND PRACTICE IN RUSSIAN ENTERPRISES

Khalil M. Dirani and Alexandre Ardichvili

## ABSTRACT

*The goal of this study was to test the human capital (HC) theory within the Russian context and explore current HC organizational practices (including training and development, recruitment and selection, compensation, empowerment, diversity, and work/family balance) of Russian enterprises. The data were collected at 270 large, medium, and small enterprises in Moscow and four representative regional centers. The study results suggest that Russian firms tended to emphasize current HC needs, not long-term HC development strategies. The firm size had an effect on differences in training, selection, and compensation practices, with large firms being more long-term oriented. Correlation between elements of the HC management model provided some preliminary evidence that Russian firms tried to coordinate selection, compensation, and training procedures. In addition, firms that empowered their employees were also putting more emphasis on long-term-oriented training, selection, and compensation practices. Finally, there were signs that diversity was gradually becoming an important issue for Russian enterprises of all sizes. However, compared to diversity, companies' emphasis on helping their employees to deal with the work/family balance issue was much stronger.*

The Global Diffusion of Human Resource Practices: Institutional and Cultural Limits
Advances in International Management, Volume 21, 125–144
ISSN: 1571-5027/doi:10.1016/S1571-5027(08)00005-3

# INTRODUCTION

Recent economic history has provided strong evidence that large structural changes are not accomplished without a significant contribution from the human factor. Moreover, there is a growing realization among academics and practitioners alike that in today's business world the only truly unique resource of business firms is their human capital (Von Krogh, Ichijo, & Nonaka, 2000). This perception is grounded in the resource-based view of the firm, which depicts companies as unique combinations of productive resources (Wernerfelt, 1984) and considers human resources as one of the most important contributors to a company's resource-based competitive advantage (Penrose, 1959). People, with their education, skills, and professional experience, determine opportunities and frontiers for organizational development. Several scholars considered that to achieve a competitive advantage through human resources, companies must pursue well-thought-out strategies of investing in human capital (Becker, 1976; Flamholtz & Lacey, 1981).

The human capital strategy is a system that includes inventory and measurement of the existing human resources of the enterprise, identification of strategic human capital development needs, and design of plans for meeting these strategic needs by closing the gap between the existing and the needed human capital. The human capital needs of an enterprise can be met through various strategies, including internal training and development, sourcing through open-market transactions, outsourcing, and alliances (Lepak & Snell, 1999).

Transition economies in general can give good examples of human capital development in a restructuring environment. In transition economies experiencing dramatic structural changes, traditional lifetime utility maximizing models may not be appropriate methodological tools to study schooling and occupational choices. In recent years, significant investments in human capital both at the country level and at the individual enterprise level were made in countries of the former Soviet block, with the goal of increasing the competitiveness of emerging market economies in these countries. In Russia, the competitive strategies of enterprises faced a "tsunami" of changes in the first decade of the 21st century due to rapid changes in market conditions, ownership structure, and industry sector composition of the economy. During the Soviet period, people lived under the central-planned system. They made their initial choices of schooling, fields of study, and jobs within a system of priorities, preferences, and dominant practices. Their human capital decisions were largely determined by the socialist wage-setting system. As a result of this system, the earnings of workers and employees were inadequately associated with their education (Linz, 2000). The Russian program of privatization of state-owned enterprises was one of the most radical programs in the former Soviet block. The resulting new economic environment is characterized by stiff competition for markets and capital, including one of the main sources of competitive advantage, human capital (Russell, 2002). The economic reforms have resulted in an unprecedented shift from a labor market that was completely controlled and regulated by the government to a much more open arrangement that involves previously unavailable choices for acquiring or developing human capital. These choices include, among other things, open-market sourcing, training in overseas management development centers, and continuous education through partnerships with foreign universities (Clarke & Metalina, 2000; Fey & Bjorkman, 2001). Market liberalization and economic reform have had strong effects on human capital. On one hand, an appreciation of more educated employees was in favor; on the other hand, skills and experience acquired in the previous system became obsolete. Overall, the increase in global competition, as well as pressures generated by European integration and enlargement of the European Union, have forced Russian enterprises to improve dramatically their ability to acquire, retain, and manage human capital.

This new need for emphasis on human capital development is in sharp contrast to Soviet-era practices. In the past, Russian companies relied on the government allocation of labor resources. Under this model, an enterprise had only two options for changing its human capital composition. First, new employees were allocated to the enterprise by government regulators (and were trained at government-owned vocational schools or higher-learning institutions). Alternatively, enterprises could internally train those employees who were being promoted to new job functions or encourage them to get additional degrees through government-owned educational institutions (Ardichvili & Gasparishvili, 2001).

The early 1990s brought a complete change in the vocational education and professional development landscape. First, the Russian government had eliminated or significantly downsized many state-sponsored vocational training and professional development programs. Second, this downsizing created a market opportunity for numerous private providers of education and training. Finally, foreign competition also became a significant factor: subsidiaries of foreign companies created their own training and development facilities and new labor force entrants now have the option of completing their degrees abroad or in joint educational programs offered by

Russian and Western universities and professional development centers (Fey & Bjorkman, 2001).

Given the rapid changes in environmental conditions and available choices, a better understanding of emerging trends in human capital practices of Russian enterprises becomes a necessary prerequisite to the success of any human resource development and performance improvement initiatives. Despite the critical importance of such empirical research, related publications are all but nonexistent. Our recent comprehensive online database search has identified thousands of human-capital-related articles published in the West and in excess of 300 articles on human capital issues in Eastern Europe; however, fewer than a dozen of these dealt specifically with Russia (e.g., Clarke, 2002) and none have reported results of studies systematically documenting enterprise practices in this area. Therefore, the goal of the present study was to make a step toward closing this research gap by documenting human capital practices of Russian enterprises. Specifically, the study was guided by the following research questions:

(1) What are Russian firms' current approaches to human capital acquisition and development?
(2) Is there any evidence of strategic coordination of activities in various domains of human capital acquisition and development (e.g., are training and development activities aligned with hiring and promotion, performance appraisals, or compensation decisions)?
(3) How are these practices affected by companies' size and geographic location?
(4) Is there a difference in how companies acquire and develop the two main sources of their human capital: managers and nonmanagerial employees?

## THEORETICAL FRAMEWORK

The theoretical underpinnings of this study are provided by the human resource management architecture model developed by Lepak and Snell (1999). This model is grounded in three major theoretical streams of research: transaction cost economics, human capital theory, and the resource-based view of the firm. Transaction cost economics enables researchers to measure and compare the efficiency of two distinct human capital management strategies: market transactions or internal development (Williamson, 1985). Human capital theory, as advanced by Becker (1976), helps to identify the conditions under which investment in the development of human resources makes economic sense for an enterprise. Finally, the resource-based view of the firm suggests that human resources are a main competitive advantage of the enterprise, and human resources in core areas need to be developed internally to maintain the firm's competitiveness, whereas resources in noncore areas could be outsourced or procured through alliances (Barney, 1991).

Based on the above considerations, Lepak and Snell (1999) identify four core human capital strategies: internal development ("make"), external recruitment ("buy"), alliances, and contracting out. A review of recent research publications and business press articles suggests that Russian enterprises have a variety of choices under each of these categories. Thus, internal training and development involve both short-term strategies (e.g., specific job-related training) and longer-term strategies (e.g., training not related to the immediate job or long-term career development plans) (Clarke & Metalina, 2000; Fey & Bjorkman, 2001).

A group of researchers at the University of Illinois, headed by John Lawler and his colleagues in several different countries, has developed and implemented a comprehensive instrument for measuring human capital acquisition and development strategies, which covers training and development, staffing and recruitment, performance appraisals, evaluation, compensation, and promotion decisions (Bartlett, Lawler, Bae, Chen, & Wan, 2002). The authors suggest, among other things, that strategic human resource development (HRD) orientation is reflected not only in the choice of methods and approaches, but also in the number of hours spent on specific development activities and the number of employees involved in these activities.

In addition to trying to understand the general state of current human capital practices of a sample of Russian companies, we are also interested in detecting any differences in strategies based on such factors as size and geographic location. Thus, the size of the firm and location are organizational and structural factors that could increase the likelihood of a firm engaging in training activities. Large firms are more likely to have the resources necessary to establish training departments (Bartlett et al., 2002; Osterman, 1995). Similarly, the location of the operation might be related to the extent of HRD activities. For example, because recent studies in Russia have demonstrated the existence of a "significant capital-city effect with regard to the pace of transition in Russia" (Linz, 2000, p. 4), we cannot exclude the possibility that firms in Moscow will have an advantage in access to various facets of the labor market compared to firms located in provincial cities. In addition, because Moscow has the largest concentration of subsidiaries of multinational companies in Russia, indigenous firms in Moscow are more likely to be affected by Western management and HRD influences and thus more likely to be conducting sophisticated HRD activities and have more advanced knowledge of training requirements and techniques.

# METHOD

The data were collected at 270 enterprises in Moscow and four representative regional centers (one each in Siberia, in the Urals region, in Central Russia, and in Southern Russia). The sampling frame was drawn from a database of the Center for Opinion Research (COR) of the Moscow State University (MSU), and the final sample included small (up to 200 employees), medium-sized (from 201 to 500 employees), and large companies (more than 501 employees). The sample was fairly evenly distributed between these three groups. All companies in the sample were in the manufacturing sector of industry, which helped to control for potential industry classification differences.

The data collection was based on utilizing a short version of the survey instrument developed and tested earlier by John Lawler and his colleagues in a series of studies conducted to date in more than a dozen countries around the world (see, for example, Bartlett et al., 2002). The short version included a total of 68 Likert-scale questions. The instrument was translated into Russian by the representatives of COR at MSU. Back-translation and checks against the original were performed by independent experts. This process has enabled the researchers to identify and correct a number of errors that had arisen from interpretation differences.

The survey instrument was pilot tested at several enterprises located in Moscow. Because previous data collection experiences in Russia and other countries of the former USSR indicate that mail survey response rates tend to be extremely low, respondents were asked to fill out the questionnaires during personal meetings with the representatives of COR.

The descriptive/demographics section included three single-item questions, inquiring about the respondent's position in the company, the number of people the company employed, and the percentages of various employee categories. The remaining questions covered training and development, selection/recruitment and compensation practices, employee empowerment, and diversity and work/family balance issues. The scales for these questions consisted of 5-point Likert-type items (1 = strongly disagree, 5 = strongly agree).

Three groups of questions (training and development; selection, recruitment, and hiring; and compensation) included separate scales for managers and production workers. Thus the same group of questions would inquire about production workers and then about managers. The remaining two groups of questions, concerning employee empowerment and diversity and work/family issues, were general to both employee categories.

Six items on the Training and Development scale reflected short-term or long-term orientation in current approaches to developing human capital in the organization. The following are two sample items: "Training is primarily intended to prepare employees for their current jobs rather than provide broader knowledge" and "Training is viewed more as a short-term cost than a long-term investment."

Items on the Selection, Recruitment, and Hiring scale reflected staffing criteria, broad vs. narrow job ladders, and internal vs. external hiring sources. The scale consisted of 13 items, including these sample statements: "A candidate's personal references play a central role in staffing decisions" and "Except for entry-level positions, job vacancies are normally filled using the company's current employees." Eight items on the Compensation Practices scale reflected performance-based pay, internal vs. external equity, and incentives. The following are two sample items: "We strive to keep a large salary difference between high and low performers in the same position" and "Employee financial participation (e.g., gain sharing, profit sharing, or employee ownership, etc.) is extensive in this company."

Five Employee Empowerment items assessed the degree of employee autonomy and contribution to decision making. Nine Diversity items reflected gender and ethnic diversity and work/family balance issues. These items, as mentioned earlier, were not specific to production workers or managers. Sample items were: "Jobs are designed to allow employees many chances to use personal initiative or judgment in carrying out their work" and "The company makes special efforts to promote qualified members of underrepresented ethnic, regional, social, or religious groups."

The reliability tests were run separately for production/service workers and managers within the different scales. All $\alpha$ values for individual scales were in the 0.72–0.81 range, which is within generally accepted limits. As for the size of the organizations, we categorized them into three groups, companies up to 200 employees, companies between 201 and 500 employees, and companies with more than 500 employees (Table 1). For the geographical location comparison the 270 enterprises were categorized into two groups. Forty-four enterprises located in Moscow were grouped together and compared to enterprises located in the four representative regional

***Table 1.***  Company Size with Respect to the Number of Employees.

| Company Size | Frequency | Percentage |
|---|---|---|
| Less than 201 | 92 | 34.0 |
| 201–500 | 89 | 33.0 |
| More than 500 | 89 | 33.0 |
| Total | 270 | 100.0 |

***Table 2.***  Position of Respondents in Their Respective Enterprises.

| Position in the Company | Frequency | Percentage |
|---|---|---|
| Head of personnel department | 189 | 70.0 |
| Deputy head of PD/personnel manager | 63 | 23.3 |
| CEO or president | 10 | 3.7 |
| Vice-president | 8 | 3.0 |
| Total | 270 | 100.0 |

centers. A single dummy variable was used to distinguish firms in Moscow from firms elsewhere.

# RESULTS

Of 400 distributed survey instruments, 270 completed instruments were returned (68%). The majority of the respondents (93%) held positions as heads or deputy heads of the personnel department in their organization and the rest were either presidents or vice presidents (Table 2). Regarding the percentage of the company's workforce employed in various positions, statistics showed that geographical location did not make a difference. In contrast, the results showed that as the size of the organization increased, the percentage of office and clerical staff decreased and the nonmanagerial production/service workers percentage increased (Table 3).

The results also indicated that 57% of the enterprises employed temporary and/or contract workers. With regard to workforce change trends in different organizations, 40% of respondents indicated that over the past 3–5 years relative stability of workforce was more dominant, whereas 36% indicated a substantial decline and 34% a substantial growth.

The following sections present the results for five areas: training and development, hiring and selection, compensation, empowerment, and

***Table 3.*** Distribution of Enterprise Employees According to Their
Position and the Size of the Organization (Percentage).

| Title | Total (%) | Firm Size (1–200) | (201–500) | (>500) |
|---|---|---|---|---|
| Middle and upper-level managers | 8 | 8 | 9 | 7 |
| Professionals | 12 | 12 | 11 | 12 |
| Office and clerical staff | 6 | 8 | 6 | 4 |
| First-line supervisors | 6 | 6 | 6 | 5 |
| Nonmanagerial production and/or service workers | 67 | 64 | 67 | 70 |
| Other | 7 | 6 | 9 | 7 |

diversity. Because these constructs were measured on a 5-point Likert-type scale, we assumed that a mean score of 2.6 and above could be interpreted as an indication of a presence of a certain practice. Scores of 3.5 and higher are interpreted as a strong indication. Finally, scores below 2.5 suggest only weak evidence of certain practices.

### Training and Development

Respondents reported that their organizations spent an average of 90 h per year on training. Overall, enterprises spent more hours training their production and service workers ($\sim 100$ h) than training their managers ($\sim 79$ h). The highest divergence in training hours was observed in medium-sized enterprises (201–500 employees). These organizations were providing significantly more hours of training to their production and service workers (123 h per year) than to their managers ($\sim 70$ h per year). Large-size enterprises invested on average of 84 h in training both groups.

The number of training hours per year varied also depending on the geographic location of enterprise. Results showed that enterprises in Moscow invested, on average, 115 h of training per employee, with more training hours provided to production workers (147 h per year) than to managers (83 h per year). Enterprises in other regions of the country invested an average of 94 h of formal training per year in their production and service workers in comparison with around 78 h for managers (Table 4).

The study identified several significant trends in training and development practices. Overall, Russian companies in this study employed training more as a means of preparing people for their current jobs than of developing

*Table 4.*   Average Total Training Hours per Year.

| Employee Title | Firm Size | | | | Geographical Region | |
|---|---|---|---|---|---|---|
| | All | Small | Medium | Large | Moscow | Regions |
| Production and service workers | 100 | 98 | 122 | 82 | 147 | 94 |
| Managers | 79 | 81 | 70 | 85 | 83 | 78 |
| All employees | 90 | 90 | 96 | 84 | 115 | 86 |

their long-term potential ($M = 3.6$ for the overall sample) and emphasized multitasking and employees' ability to substitute for each other as needed ($M = 3.7$) (Table 5). At the same time, $t$-tests show that there was a statistically significant difference in long- vs. short-term orientation when two groups of employees (production workers vs. managers) were compared: the emphasis on current skill development was even more pronounced in production employee training than in management training ($M = 3.7$ vs. 3.4, respectively) (Table 6). In addition, management training programs emphasized more than the employee training programs the understanding of the organization's culture and values ($M = 3.5$ vs. 3.3). With respect to potential variations based on geographic location, no significant differences were found between Moscow and the regions.

Comparing firms according to size, we found that, in several cases, there were statistically significant differences between the large company group and the small and medium-size companies (taken together as one category). Large firms put more emphasis on interpersonal communication training, as well as on training aimed at developing employees' understanding of the company's culture and values. In addition, more respondents from large firms believed that their companies consider training to be a long-term investment (Table 7).

## Selection and Hiring

Russian enterprises in this study gave a clear preference to hiring full-time employees (1.8 on average in response to the question about preference for hiring part-timers). Furthermore, the predominant belief was that an employee, once hired, should expect to remain with the same company for as long as he or she wishes ($M = 3.6$). Most companies were using formal job descriptions in hiring and selection ($M = 3.8$). There was little evidence that the occupational advancement of employees was based on seniority

***Table 5.*** Means and Standard Deviations for Individual Questionnaire Items.

| Practice | Mean | SD |
|---|---|---|
| **Training** | | |
| Prepare for current job | 3.5988 | 1.0620 |
| Improve interpersonal skills | 3.4000 | 1.0494 |
| Employee acculturation | 3.4167 | 1.0483 |
| Short-term cost | 2.5091 | 1.1380 |
| Training for multitasking | 3.7012 | .9821 |
| Significant investments in training | 3.3795 | 1.1471 |
| **Selection** | | |
| Part-time employee hiring | 1.8206 | .7656 |
| Long-term commitment | 3.5988 | 1.0662 |
| Internal hiring | 3.3385 | 1.0175 |
| Extensive external recruiting | 3.2505 | 1.1494 |
| Emphasis on outside-company hiring | 3.3467 | .9954 |
| Planned transfer and promotion | 3.1209 | 1.1135 |
| Use of formal job descriptions | 3.7645 | 1.0063 |
| Multitasking expectations | 3.8324 | .8818 |
| Promotion based on seniority and tenure | 2.8173 | 1.0757 |
| Emphasis on testing and interviews | 3.3830 | 1.0910 |
| Selection based on performance | 3.7105 | .8737 |
| Personal references | 3.1673 | 1.0116 |
| Formal job analysis | 3.4273 | 1.0308 |
| **Compensation** | | |
| Higher benefits and pay | 2.5738 | .9768 |
| Performance-based pay | 3.3992 | 1.0319 |
| Competitive salaries | 3.4917 | 1.0422 |
| Compensation based on contribution | 3.7860 | .9798 |
| Pay based on individual and group performance | 3.8327 | .9023 |
| Pay based on seniority | 2.6959 | 1.0237 |
| Gain sharing | 2.6464 | 1.1129 |
| Pay based on formal job evaluations | 3.3474 | 1.0751 |
| **Empowerment** | | |
| Engagement in problem solving | 3.0038 | 1.1167 |
| Promoting personal initiative | 3.5202 | .8951 |
| Work in self-directed teams | 2.5098 | 1.0433 |
| Authority to make decisions | 2.7760 | 1.0325 |
| Sharing financial information | 3.2720 | 1.0857 |
| **Diversity** | | |
| Policies against sexual harassment | 2.9592 | 1.2974 |
| Recruit women | 3.5620 | 1.0458 |
| Recruit underrepresented groups | 2.9057 | 1.0260 |

***Table 5.*** (*Continued*)

| Practice | Mean | SD |
|---|---|---|
| Promote qualified women | 3.5306 | .9517 |
| Promote underrepresented groups | 3.0483 | 1.0181 |
| Provide counseling services | 3.2552 | 1.2117 |
| Flexible work schedules | 4.0344 | .8412 |
| Family-related time off from work | 4.2397 | .5708 |
| Help pay for childcare | 2.0512 | 1.1116 |

***Table 6.*** Means and Statistical Significance of *t*-Values for Comparisons between Two Occupational Groups.

| Item | Production Workers | Managers | |
|---|---|---|---|
| Practice | | Mean | Significance |
| Training | | | |
| Prepare for current job | 3.7743 | 3.4177 | 0.00* |
| Improve interpersonal skills | 3.2043 | 3.5917 | .003* |
| Employee acculturation | 3.3117 | 3.5224 | .233* |
| Training for multitasking | 3.7969 | 3.6016 | .139* |
| Selection | | | |
| Part-time employee hiring | 1.9478 | 1.6916 | .535* |
| Internal hiring | 3.2140 | 3.4630 | .997* |
| Emphasis on outside-company hiring | 3.4715 | 3.2201 | .186* |
| Multitasking expected | 3.9401 | 3.7235 | .000* |
| Emphasis on testing | 3.1647 | 3.5954 | .835* |
| Personal references | 3.0229 | 3.3106 | .447* |
| Compensation | | | |
| Gain sharing | 2.4537 | 2.8436 | .505* |

*Note:* In the interest of saving space, only items with statistically significant differences were included in Tables 6–8.
*Significant at .05 (2-tailed).

($M = 2.8$). Finally, the ability to perform current job responsibilities was more important than future potential as a base for being hired ($M = 3.7$). More respondents agreed that their firms were willing to promote from within than to hire from the outside; at the same time, there was more

*Table 7.* Means and Statistically Significant ANOVA-Values for Comparisons between Company Size Groups.

| | Size[a] Mean | | | SD | | | ANOVA | |
|---|---|---|---|---|---|---|---|---|
| | 1 | 2 | 3 | 1 | 2 | 3 | Size comparison | Significance |
| **Training** | | | | | | | | |
| Improve interpersonal skills | 3.040 | 3.132 | 3.416 | 1.144 | 1.099 | 1.008 | 1  3 | .030* |
| Employee acculturation | 3.258 | 3.116 | 3.541 | 1.103 | 1.123 | .945 | 2  3 | .011* |
| Short-term cost | 2.634 | 2.843 | 2.178 | 1.181 | 1.204 | 1.088 | 1  3 | .012* |
| | | | | | | | 2  3 | .000* |
| Multitasking training | 3.704 | 3.631 | 4.059 | .948 | 1.061 | .869 | 1  3 | .016* |
| | | | | | | | 2  3 | .004* |
| Significant investment in training | 3.085 | 3.172 | 3.809 | 1.113 | 1.202 | .975 | 1  3 | .000* |
| | | | | | | | 2  3 | .000* |
| **Selection** | | | | | | | | |
| Part-time employee hiring | 2.155 | 1.960 | 1.727 | 1.026 | .8861 | .599 | 1  3 | .002* |
| Extensive external recruiting | 3.177 | 3.211 | 3.523 | 1.166 | 1.196 | 1.113 | 1  3 | .048* |
| Planned transfer and promotion | 2.802 | 2.947 | 3.476 | 1.187 | 1.057 | 1.103 | 1  3 | .000* |
| | | | | | | | 2  3 | .003* |
| Emphasis on testing | 3.079 | 2.988 | 3.428 | 1.176 | 1.006 | .997 | 1  3 | .033* |
| | | | | | | | 2  3 | .008* |
| Formal job analysis | 3.100 | 3.315 | 3.625 | 1.038 | .998 | .998 | 1  3 | .001* |

**Table 7.** (*Continued*)

| | Size[a] Mean | | | SD | | | ANOVA | |
|---|---|---|---|---|---|---|---|---|
| | 1 | 2 | 3 | 1 | 2 | 3 | Size comparison | Significance |
| Compensation | | | | | | | | |
| Competitive salaries | 3.297 | 3.440 | 3.639 | 1.073 | 1.081 | .919 | 1 3 | .030* |
| Pay based on formal job evaluations | 3.092 | 3.287 | 3.580 | 1.133 | 1.086 | .933 | 1 3 | .004* |
| Diversity | | | | | | | | |
| Policies against sexual harassment | 2.979 | 2.625 | 3.260 | 1.330 | 1.265 | 1.242 | 2 3 | .015* |
| Recruit underrepresented groups | 2.700 | 2.971 | 3.041 | .983 | 1.062 | 1.013 | 1 3 | .047* |
| Promote underrepresented groups | 3.294 | 3.618 | 3.690 | .973 | .951 | .891 | 1 2 | .039* |
| | | | | | | | 3 | .004* |
| Provide counseling services | 2.927 | 3.356 | 3.494 | 1.266 | 1.159 | 1.141 | 1 2 | .026* |
| | | | | | | | 3 | .002* |
| Flexible work schedules | 3.868 | 4.011 | 4.229 | .884 | .898 | .693 | 1 3 | .028* |
| Help pay for childcare | 1.616 | 2.015 | 2.487 | .679 | 1.031 | 1.325 | 1 2 | .000* |

[a]Company size <201 employees coded 1. Company size 201–500 employees coded 2. Company size > 500 employees coded 3.
*Significant at .05.

willingness to hire from the outside for production worker positions than for managerial positions ($M = 3.2$ vs. 3.5).

Clear preference was given to potential employees and managers who could perform multiple functions ($M = 3.8$ for the overall sample). And such ability was even more important for production workers than for managers ($M = 3.9$ vs. 3.7). In addition, companies had in place much stricter selection and testing procedures for managers than for workers ($M = 3.6$ vs. 3.1) (see Table 6).

A comparison of hiring and selection practices in Moscow and regions yielded several statistically significant differences. First, companies in regions tended to promote from within more often than in Moscow ($M = 3.4$ vs. 3.1), paid more attention to external references ($M = 3.2$ vs. 2.8), and utilized more often formal job analysis ($M = 3.5$ vs. 3.2) (Table 8).

Several statistically significant differences were found between large firms, on the one hand, and small and/or medium-sized firms, on the other. Specifically, small firms were more willing to hire part-time employees; placed less emphasis on outside hiring, succession planning, and career development; less often used methods of scientific organization of labor; and utilized much less stringent selection-related testing than large firms.

### Compensations Practices

There was a fairly strong indication that companies were reluctant to establish a direct link between employees' seniority and tenure with a

***Table 8.*** Means and Statistical Significance of *t*-Values for Comparisons between Regions.

| Item | Moscow | Regions | |
| --- | --- | --- | --- |
| Practice | | Mean | Significance |
| Selection | | | |
| Internal hiring | 3.1084 | 3.3828 | .001* |
| Promotion based on seniority | 2.6207 | 2.8559 | .000* |
| Personal references | 2.8000 | 3.2381 | .072* |
| Formal job analysis | 3.2000 | 3.4680 | .515* |
| Empowerment | | | |
| Work in self-directed teams | 2.2286 | 2.5680 | .002* |

*Significant at .05 (2-tailed).

company and compensation ($M = 2.7$). There was also lack of emphasis on gain sharing, stock options, and employee stock ownership, although there was more emphasis on these practices as applied to managers ($M = 2.6$ for the overall sample and 2.8 and 2.4, respectively, for managers and workers). On the other hand, there was a clear preference for compensation based on individual or small team contribution ($M = 3.8$) and rewarding individual contribution based on performance, not on title or position in the organization ($M = 3.8$).

There were no statistically significant differences in compensation practices between Moscow and the regions. There were only two areas in which statistically significant differences were observed between size groups of firms. First, large firms placed a stronger emphasis on paying market rates for comparable jobs than did either small or medium-sized companies. Second, large firms used more formal measures of work performance in determining compensation levels than did small firms.

## Employee Empowerment

Even though respondents mostly agreed that jobs were designed to allow employees many chances to use personal initiative or judgment in carrying out their work ($M = 3.5$), employees at the majority of firms neither were working in self-directed work teams ($M = 2.5$) nor had the authority to make autonomous decisions at work ($M = 2.7$). There was some indication that companies tended to share financial and/or performance information with employees ($M = 3.2$).

## Diversity and Family Issues in the Workplace

What was the status of diversity and work/family balance in Russian enterprises? We found a mixed scorecard. Enterprises put some emphasis on promoting policies against sexual harassment in the workplace, as well as recruiting or promoting members of underrepresented ethnic, regional, or religious groups. However, because the mean scores for both these variables were around 2.9, we conclude that these policies have not yet assumed an overwhelming importance. On the other hand, there is evidence to suggest that more companies make a special effort to recruit and promote female employees ($M = 3.5$).

***Table 9.*** Correlations among Different Scales.

|  | Training | Selection | Compensation | Empowerment |
|---|---|---|---|---|
| Training | 1.00 | .469** | .293** | .181* |
| Selection | .469** | 1.000 | .365** | .249** |
| Compensation | .293** | .365** | 1.000 | .519** |
| Empowerment | .181* | .249** | .519** | 1.000 |

*Note:* $N = 270$.
*Correlation is significant at the .05 level (2-tailed).
**Correlation is significant at the .01 level (2-tailed).

As for work/family balance issues, organizations were willing to support employees through flexible scheduling. Respondents strongly agreed that enterprises allowed their employees to vary their work schedules and to take time off from work to meet family needs or deal with family emergencies ($M = 4.2$). On the other hand, most enterprises were not interested in helping their employees pay for childcare or providing daycare services for employees' children during work hours ($M = 2.0$). Small firms trailed both medium and large firms in recruiting and promoting underrepresented minorities and were less willing to provide their employees with flexible work hours or to pay for childcare.

### *Correlation between Scales: Evidence of Coordination?*

Correlations among the various items in the questionnaire were tested using the Pearson test. The results indicated that there was strong intercorrelation between all major components of the model (see Table 9). Especially strong correlation was found between training and selection practices and between compensation and empowerment.

## DISCUSSION

Pooling together the results for different areas of human capital (HC) acquisition and development allowed us to arrive at the following composite picture of the current state of HC practices at the surveyed Russian enterprises. First, the predominant tendency among Russian firms in this study was to emphasize current job-related needs, not a long-term human capital development strategy. Thus, training was predominantly oriented toward developing the ability to perform current job tasks, less so than developing the long-term potential of employees. And both selection and compensation procedures followed the same logic, emphasizing employees' ability to perform immediately needed job responsibilities rather than the ability to learn and grow.

Second, the majority of companies were pursuing different HC development strategies when dealing with two groups of employees (production workers and managers). Compared to strategies applied to production workers, the selection, compensation, and training and development of managers were more future oriented, with more attention paid to managers' ability to learn and grow. In addition, more time and money were being spent on developing the long-term potential of managers and their understanding of company values and culture and on selecting managers with long-term potential.

Third, firm size had a definite effect on differences in training and development, selection, and compensation practices. Thus, more respondents from large firms considered training to be a long-term investment, were paying more attention to developing employees' understanding of the company's culture and values, emphasized succession planning, and were more interested in promoting diversity.

Fourth, our assumption that there would be a significant difference between Moscow and the regional centers proved to be largely correct. For example, in Moscow individual and small-group performance played a much more important role in promotion and compensation decisions than seniority and tenure with the firm. At the same time, more firms in Moscow were basing their training, selection, and compensation decisions on considerations of meeting the needs of immediate, near-term projects than were firms in provinces. A possible explanation of this trend could be that human capital development approaches of firms in Moscow were less long-term oriented in response to a more competitive, dynamic, and market-oriented environment than were strategies of firms in other cities. The regional firms, in contrast, relied more on established rules and procedures, including the designing and structuring of jobs based on formal job task analysis, which had been highly developed in the Soviet era.

Fifth, correlation among all main elements of the human capital model suggests that Russian firms may be trying to coordinate selection, compensation, and training procedures. Furthermore, the study has provided some evidence that firms that empower their employees are also putting more emphasis on long-term training and on selection and compensation based on employees' long-term potential. However, the limitations of the survey-based data collection method employed in this study did not allow us to gather any conclusive evidence to suggest that these correlations were due to an existence of well-articulated strategies aimed at such coordination.

Finally, there were signs that diversity was gradually becoming an important issue for Russian enterprises of all sizes. At the same time, because the scores on the related scales were only moderately above average, we conclude that this issue has not yet become a major area of concern. Compared to diversity, companies' emphasis on helping their employees in balancing work and family life seemed to be much stronger.

### *Study Limitations and Recommendations for Further Research*

As indicated earlier, the major limitation of this study was the reliance on just one data collection method (quantitative survey). Because the human capital-related research in Russia is still in its exploratory stage, a combination of qualitative and quantitative methodologies aimed at an in-depth exploration of identified trends is warranted. Thus, one of the most important questions to ask in follow-up studies would be whether the evidence of correlation among various human capital-related activities also means that there is a well-articulated strategy of HC acquisition and development. The best way to conduct such follow-up studies would be based on qualitative interviews with key players from a sample of participants in this study, or a broader sample of organizations.

A longitudinal study of the evolution of the approaches to solving diversity and work/family balance issues would be another important future research direction. The present study shows that these issues are attracting some attention, with large firms leading the way. At the same time, even a quick perusal of the current Russian business press and employment Web sites shows that there are persistent signs of practices that would be in serious violation of employment laws should they have occurred in the United States or in Western Europe. Thus, one recent job ad, found by us on a major Russian job search Web site, specified preferred gender and age of successful candidates for a position. Again, to get rich data on this subject, quantitative methods are not enough. Qualitative interviews, coupled with a systematic secondary data analysis (e.g., review of a set of relevant business publications and online sources) would be advisable.

A promising future direction of research would be to compare human capital development strategies of endogenous firms and subsidiaries of multinational companies operating in Russia. One of the most interesting questions that such an investigation could help to answer is whether observed patterns of HC development are a result of subsidiaries' reaction to specific Russian economic, demographic, and sociopolitical realities or rather depend on the parent company's global strategy.

# REFERENCES

Ardichvili, A., & Gasparishvili, A. (2001). Human resource development in an industry in transition: The case of the Russian banking sector. *Human Resource Development International, 4*(1), 47–63.

Barney, J. B. (1991). Firm resources and sustainable competitive advantage. *Journal of Management, 17*, 99–120.

Bartlett, K., Lawler, J., Bae, J., Chen, S., & Wan, D. (2002). Differences in international human resource development among indigenous firms and multinational affiliates in East and Southeast Asia. *Human Resource Development Quarterly, 13*(4), 383–405.

Becker, G. (1976). *The economic approach to human behavior.* Chicago: The University of Chicago Press.

Clarke, S. (2002). Market and institutional determinants of wage differentiation in Russia. *Industrial and Labor Relations Review, 55*(4), 628–648.

Clarke, S., & Metalina, T. (2000). Training in the new private sector in Russia. *International Journal of Human Resource Management, 11*(1), 19–36.

Fey, C., & Bjorkman, I. (2001). The effect of human resource management practices on MNC subsidiary performance in Russia. *Journal of International Business Studies, 32*(1), 59–75.

Flamholtz, E., & Lacey, J. (1981). *Personnel management: Human capital theory and human resource accounting.* Los Angeles, CA: UCLA.

Lepak, D., & Snell, S. (1999). The human resource architecture: Toward a theory of human capital allocation and development. *Academy of Management Review, 24*(1), 31–48.

Linz, S. (2000). *Are Russians really ready for capitalism?* Working paper no. 268. William Davidson Institute, Ann Arbor, MI.

Osterman, P. (1995). Skills, training, and work organization in American establishments. *Industrial Relations, 34*(2), 125–147.

Penrose, E. (1959). *The theory of the growth of the firm.* London: Basil Blackwell.

Russell, R. (2002). The influence of ownership and organizational conditions on employee participation in Russian enterprises. *Economic and Industrial Democracy, 23*(4), 555–584.

Von Krogh, G., Ichijo, K., & Nonaka, I. (2000). *Enabling knowledge creation.* NY: Oxford University Press.

Wernerfelt, B. (1984). A resource-based view of the firm. *Strategic Management Journal, 5*, 171–180.

Williamson, O. E. (1985). *The economic institutions of capitalism: Firms, markets, relational contracting.* New York: Free Press.

# THE ADOPTION OF HR STRATEGIES IN A CONFUCIAN CONTEXT

Shyh-jer Chen

## ABSTRACT

*The traditional Confucian management system is considered distinctly different from Western-based management. This study draws data from indigenous Taiwanese firms listed on its public stock market and examines the associations among various human resource (HR) systems and organizational performance. First, factor analysis is used to explore a wide range of HR practices. Then, cluster analysis is used to classify indigenous Taiwanese firms with regard to their HR practices. Indigenous Taiwanese firms were found to use various HR systems, ranging from traditional Confucian HR to high-involvement HR practices. Companies that used high-involvement HR systems were found to perform better than those using a traditional Confucian HR system.*

There is an extensive body of research on the impact of human resource (HR) systems on organizational effectiveness in the American context (Appelbaum & Batt, 1994; Arthur, 1994; Batt, 2002; Delery & Doty, 1996; Huselid, 1995; Wright & Boswell, 2002) and an increasing number of studies on the effectiveness of high-involvement work systems[1] in cross-national

**The Global Diffusion of Human Resource Practices: Institutional and Cultural Limits**
**Advances in International Management, Volume 21, 145–169**
Copyright © 2008 by Emerald Group Publishing Limited
All rights of reproduction in any form reserved
ISSN: 1571-5027/doi:10.1016/S1571-5027(08)00006-5

settings. Cross-national transference of high-involvement work systems is reported to vary according to country and context (Bae, Chen, Wan, Lawler, & Walumbwa, 2003; Ferner, 1997; Guthrie, 2001; Harzing & Sorge, 2003; Von Glinow, Drost, & Teagarden, 2002). High-involvement work system technologies in East Asian countries (e.g., Korea, Taiwan, Thailand, and Singapore) have, for example, seemed to work better than those in European countries (e.g., Germany and Ireland) in both the international affiliates of multinational enterprises (MNEs) and locally owned enterprises (LOCs) (e.g., Bae et al., 2003; Chen, Lawler, & Bae, 2005; Doeringer, Lorenz, & Terkla, 2003; Ferner, 1997; Geary & Roche, 2001; Rowley & Benson, 2003; Takeuchi, Wakabayashi, & Chen, 2003). Most cross-national research examines convergence and divergence issues either by studying whether MNEs in host countries assume HR practices associated with those used in the local environment or retained those of the home country or by comparing the HR practices in MNE affiliates and LOCs. Few analyze why LOCs, particularly those located in developing economies, adopt global HR practices and how these practices affect organizational performance.

The traditional Confucian management system is distinctly different from Western-based management style. Chen (2001) has found several major differences between traditional Chinese management and Western management practices. One is that Chinese companies often serve family interests and Western companies serve those of the stockholders. He contends that this difference in interest leads to significant differences in the HR practices they implement. Lockett (1988) further pointed out that respect for age and hierarchy, group orientation, face, and the importance of relationships, which are embedded in Chinese culture, might undermine the development of HR management practices. Whereas that author attributes improved firm performance to the adoption of Western management methods, other researchers have shown traditional Confucianism to contribute to economic achievement and organizational effectiveness in such areas as Taiwan, Singapore, Hong Kong, and China (e.g., Khatri & Budhwar, 2002; Warner, 1995; Wilkinson, 1994; Xin & Pearce, 1996; Yang, 1994; Yeung & Tung, 1996).

Although cross-national cultural and institutional differences have often been found to mitigate the effective transfer of high-involvement work systems from the American context (e.g., Hofstede, 1980; Newman & Nollen, 1996), LOCs have recently been found to be deviating from conventional indigenous employment systems and adopting high-involvement work systems despite apparent cultural and institutional incompatibilities. Bae et al. (2003) used data from four countries – Korea, Singapore,

Taiwan, and Thailand – and found that the forces of globalization and competition have, to some extent, led to the adoption of American-based work systems. Rowley and Bae (2001) found that the 1997 Asian financial crisis pushed for change in some HR practices, such as seniority-based compensation, in favor of more performance-based HR practices in Korea.

Taiwan is a major economic player in East Asia and has attracted foreign investment from Europe, North America, and Japan since the 1950s. Many foreign companies (e.g., IBM, Texas Instruments, and Toshiba) established their affiliates in Taiwan several decades ago. Most HR studies of Taiwan have investigated the allocation of HR strategies of MNE affiliates (e.g., local responsiveness versus global integration) and the relationship between the utilization of HR strategies (e.g., high-involvement work systems versus control-based work systems) and organizational effectiveness (Bae et al., 2003; Chen et al., 2005).

This study, drawing data from indigenous Taiwanese firms listed on the Taiwan stock exchange, examines the relationship between various HR systems and organizational performance. Unlike previous research, I first use factor analysis to identify a wide range of HR practices and then classify the indigenous Taiwanese firms by cluster analysis according to the HR practices they use. The results show that Taiwanese firms using high-involvement HR systems perform better than those using traditional Confucian HR systems.

## CONFUCIANISM AND HR PRACTICES IN TAIWAN

Management practices in Taiwanese firms have traditionally been quite different from those prevalent in Western firms. These differences are rooted to a large extent in Confucian values. Confucianism emphasizes inter-personal obligations and hierarchical relationships as a means of maintaining social order and harmony, with several cardinal social relationships (e.g., parent and child, husband and wife, and ruler and subject). The notion of *guanxi,* indicating the importance of social networks or interpersonal connections, differs in many ways from networking used in Western countries (Hwang, 2001). In the idealized Western view, exchanges in business and the workplace are to be based largely on universal standards and cost–benefit calculations. People are supposed to be treated according to what they can contribute, not how they are related to a decision maker. In contrast, society and business under Confucian standards are quite particularistic. According to Confucian standards, decision makers are obligated to favor those with the closest social or hierarchical relationships. Traditional Confucian culture embedded in the value of family has been generalized into an indigenous management style in many Taiwanese firms, with important implications for HR practices within the companies. Harmony, trust, obligation, obedience, and authority are basic tenets of employment relationships. *Guanxi* is the core value.

It has often been mentioned that most indigenous Taiwanese firms are family-run businesses that use a traditional management style. Owners usually serve as chief managers and their relatives or close friends sit in such key positions as purchasing and finance. Small- and medium-sized enterprises are not the only firms to have these characteristics; they are also quite common in large-sized enterprises. A conglomerate known as the "Tainan Business Gang" is a good example of how Chinese family businesses are organized. The founders of the gang were two brothers surnamed Wu who established garment and textile companies around a century ago. Their companies rapidly expanded into a variety of industries, such as cement, construction, and consumer products. From the time it was established, family members have sat in most key positions in these companies (Chen, 2001). Using family members to do business can significantly reduce the need for a rigid bureaucratic decision-making process. Formosa Plastics Enterprise, founded by the world-renowned Wang Yong-qing, exemplifies this family business characteristic. Members of the Wang family are assigned to various crucial positions, including computer, petroleum, and hospital industries, to ensure the full control of the conglomerate.

Major positions in many indigenous Taiwanese companies are usually held by close family members or friends, because these people are thought to be the most loyal and trustworthy. Otherwise, recruitment in traditional Confucian management relies heavily on informal selection, often referrals from personal connections. Those hired without connections often do not enjoy the trust of the company. In traditional family businesses, personal reputation is even more important than a person's formal record of achievement (Chen, 2001). Although large-sized enterprises have more formal recruitment and selection procedures, trust and loyalty remain important. Large private-sector companies tend to use more formal mechanisms to select their employees, including physical and written examinations, interviews, and so forth. The use of formal selection mechanisms purports to impress the potential employees that the company holds an equal and impartial selection despite the consideration of trust and loyalty factors.

Most new graduates prefer to be hired by larger companies because they believe that these companies have more opportunity for advancement. Due to this promise of a future, they tend to stay longer at these firms. Although foreign affiliates are not quite as large as larger-sized indigenous firms, they are also preferred by new graduates. The work experience gained in these foreign affiliates could also be seen by indigenous firms as an index of employee ability, so after several years of service, many employees in foreign affiliates switch to other foreign firms or larger LOCs.

Training and development of employees is usually viewed as a cost rather than an investment; therefore, companies are reluctant to invest in developing employee skill level. This makes companies more likely to recruit people based on their current skills rather than their potential. In this sense, investment in training and development has traditionally been the responsibility of employees instead of employers. In recent decades, however, some large-sized enterprises have become more willing to provide formal in-house training and orientation to acclimate new employees to corporate culture and business strategy. Furthermore, some LOCs, especially high-tech companies, have started to promote company–university partnership activities, one being that the cooperating university provides higher education opportunities to qualified company employees who meet established university requirements. Getting in the way of these developments are instances of disloyalty. Rapid development in such high-tech industries as computers, design, and semiconductors has resulted in a shortage of high-tech professionals, leading to the raiding of one company's professional research and development team by another company. Instances such as these have, in addition to the increasing turnover rate in high-tech industries, discouraged some employers from investing in the training of professionals.

Compensation packages in Taiwan are complex and include base pay and various types of bonuses, including year-end bonuses, bonuses for best performance or innovation or length of service, spring and mid-autumn festival bonuses, and so forth. Base pay is traditionally related to seniority (Lee, 1995). If work performance can be evaluated as "above average," most workers are promoted along the pay grades established for their job titles. The pay grades in each job title are narrow to minimize possible negative and detrimental effects of pay raises on staff harmony and employment relationships. Theoretically, pay raises should be largely based on individual and team performance appraisals. Due to traditional cultural values that call for the avoidance of conflict between management and employees in Taiwan, managers are reluctant to assign their subordinates low performance scores. Therefore seniority is sometimes used as a proxy for performance. Employees with less tenure are more likely to receive low evaluations and fewer pay raises than those with more tenure. In addition, performance appraisals are not quite formalized and are rarely used for developmental purposes. The focus of such appraisals is usually on "proper" worker attitude and loyalty. Promotion may be rewarded for past performance or recognition of employee potential, but it is first rewarded for loyalty and is a sign of the trust managers and employers place in their employees.

Confucianism puts emphasis on authority and obedience, and the dyadic relationship between superior and subordinate is rigid. Decision making is not widespread and significant decisions are always made by top managers, resulting in less participation from the rank and file. Even though participation, to some extent, is allowed, the employees understand that their opinions about the operations of the business are considered suggestions and will possibly have limited influence. Furthermore, financial participation by outside or inside investors is unlikely because most family-run enterprises are afraid that outside capital will dissolve their ownership. Such practices are in stark contrast to high-involvement work systems, which emphasize such approaches as employee stock ownership, egalitarianism, and employee involvement in decision making. Table 1 summarizes and contrasts three crucial features of Confucian HR practices with those of high-involvement work practices based on Western management style.

It is worth noting that employment security is one of the important characteristics for both traditional Confucian management systems and high-involvement work systems; however, the two systems have their distinctive implications in employment security practices. In the Chinese context, employment security maintains a harmonious employment relationship. In contrast, employment security practice in Western context purports to increase employee work motivation and promote job performance.

Although fundamental to Chinese culture, critics propose that Confucianism is conservative, reactive (Lockett, 1988), and resistant to change. For example, the authoritative dyad of supervisor and subordinate has inhibited the feasibility of empowerment practices and hindered bottom-up initiation of action. Taiwan has experienced rapid growth in the past decades, with firms having the competitive advantage of relatively low cost producers. In such cases, Confucian management practices are more likely to promote disciplined and efficient workplace behavior. However, with the growing affluence of societies, companies must be more flexible and innovative in highly competitive, high value-added industries involving

***Table 1.***   Two Types of Human Resource Systems.

| | Confucian HR Practices | High-Involvement HR Practices |
|---|---|---|
| Selection and training | Informal selection | Extensive and formal selection |
| | Emphasis on *guanxi*, trust, and loyalty | Emphasis on company-wide values and culture |
| | Less training and orientation | Extensive and general training |
| Compensation and appraisal | Seniority-based pay | Performance-based pay |
| | Loyalty-based pay | Ability-based pay |
| | Little effort on performance appraisal | Extensive effort on performance appraisal |
| | Compressed wage structure | Dispersed wage structure |
| | Little use of formal performance appraisal | Developmental purpose of performance appraisal |
| Empowerment | Little involvement in decision making | High-involvement in decision making |
| | Less use of financial participation practices (e.g., gain-sharing, stock ownership, etc.) | More use of financial participation |
| | Authoritarian hierarchy | More autonomous jobs |
| | Less use of self-directed teams | More use of self-directed teams |

cutting-edge technologies. Therefore, a real issue confronting Taiwan is whether Confucian management can be transformed in a way that can enhance competitive advantage.

Various authors have contrasted Confucian management with the Western-based management system. In an earlier study, Negandhi (1973) established a stylized notion of the more traditional Taiwanese employment and compared the employment practices of indigenous Taiwanese firms with those of Japanese and American affiliates. He found substantial differences between indigenous firms and foreign affiliates. Most indigenous firms utilized selection procedures that were ad hoc and "based on the immediate whims of the supervisor," in contrast to the intensive, rigorous, and formal selection mechanism that existed in the American and Japanese affiliates.

# HR SYSTEMS IN TRANSFORMATION

I have examined stylized notions of traditional Confucian HR systems and used Taiwanese LOCs to help draw comparisons to the largely Western-based high-involvement HR systems. Although LOCs in Taiwan generally tend to utilize Confucian management systems more than high-involvement ones, preferences may be shifting. As Chen et al. (2005) observed, Taiwanese firms that have been exposed extensively to Western managerial techniques have tended to adopt some of them. One of most important reasons they do is to expand their family businesses beyond indigenous markets. Formosa Plastics Enterprise (Taiwan's largest petrochemical enterprise) and President Enterprises (Taiwan's largest food company) have established affiliates in the United States, as well as in Asian countries other than Taiwan. To "globalize," they are attempting to accept global standards and follow global HR practices. President Enterprises, for example, has tried to implement a 360-degree performance evaluation system.

The extent to which traditional family-owned enterprises diffuse in the market affects this transformation. Chen (2001) proposed that Chinese business in transition could be examined using two dimensions – corporate ownership (familial versus widely held) and management control (familial versus professional). As depicted in Fig. 1, if the companies are family owned and mostly managed by family, their Confucian HR system remains

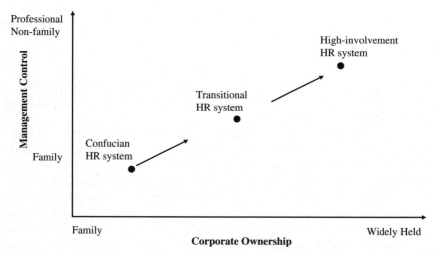

*Fig. 1.*  A Model for Transition of HR Systems.

dominant. If the management control of the company is under nonfamilial professionals and the ownership is diluted from outside capital, then high-involvement work systems can become prevalent.

Chen (2001) further observed that after these companies become listed on the stock exchange and are no longer closely held family enterprises, the founding family may continue to run the company. However, there are accountability demands from shareholders and increased competition from foreign companies (Chen, Ko, & Lawler, 2003). Because there are limits to the number of family members available and competent to manage an expanding company, professional managers are brought in, recruited as much for ability as for *guanxi*. Similar observations have been presented by Pyat, Ashkanasy, Tamaschke, and Grigg (2001).

Other factors than familial management control and corporate ownership may also affect the adoption of new HR practices. As is happening in other Confucian Asian countries, such as Korea (Bae & Lawler, 2000), Taiwan has been in a state of cultural and institutional flux, a factor possibly leading to the adoption of Western-influenced global "best practices" (i.e., high-involvement work system approaches). The factor favoring the transformation has been improving economic conditions and thus a tendency for employees to be more individualistic and less hierarchical (Hofstede, 1980). Employees, particularly younger ones, are less deferential to superiors, so cultural inhibitors to the effective implementation of high-involvement HR systems are less prevalent. Although Confucianism may long remain dominant in Taiwan's many small-sized enterprises, newer and larger companies are competing more extensively in the global market. Examples found in the high-technology industries are more prone to view high-involvement HR systems positively.

The other factor is the possible influence of HR systems of multinational corporation (MNC) affiliates in Taiwan. Yao (1999) has pointed out that the HR practices in Taiwanese LOCs have evolved, from very much a technical and administrative function in the 1960s and 1970s to a much more strategically involved management function today, particularly in larger companies. This has also involved considerable interaction with HR professionals in the growing number of MNC affiliates in Taiwan. Yeh's (1991) field study reports that LOCs have learned HR practices quickly from American affiliates. They have borrowed their recruiting criteria, compensation and promotion schemes, and methods of training. Farh (1995) indicates that many MNC and LOC HR professionals belong to the same HR associations, where they meet regularly to exchange information and share HR management practices and skills. The information sharing expedites the transition and diffusion of HR practices. Wu (2004) indicates that human resource management (HRM) in LOCs has generally moved toward learning and high-involvement HR practices.

The above discussions regarding the influences of globalization, competition, and MNC affiliates in Taiwan have led to the following hypothesis:

**Hypothesis 1.** Indigenous Taiwanese firms may use various HR systems, ranging from traditional Confucian HR practices to high-involvement HR practices.

## HR SYSTEMS AND FIRM PERFORMANCE

One line of strategic HR research has analyzed the impact of HR systems on the performance of a firm (e.g., Arthur, 1994; Delaney & Huselid, 1996; Huselid, 1995; Huselid, Jackson, & Schuler, 1997; Wright & Boswell, 2002). This research endeavored to find out whether high-involvement HR systems increase organizational performance. According to Barney (1991), crucial knowledge and abilities reside within the employees of the firm and HR systems that promote the acquisition and utilization of such knowledge will enhance organizational effectiveness, especially in the highly competitive, dynamic, and turbulent environments that most organizations face during globalization and rapid technological change. The high-involvement work system, with its emphasis on worker empowerment, training, and development, is seemingly best suited to achieve what are seen as critical objectives in the resource-based perspective. The resource-based view provides a useful and relevant framework for linking HR strategy with firm performance.

Most of the research on HR systems and organizational performance has been conducted in the United States using a high-involvement work system model that has in many ways been designed to fit the American context. However, there is considerable interest in the transferability of the American-based high-involvement work system model to other countries and cultures. American firms are trying to use these approaches in their international affiliates in which they attempt to manage host-country nationals working for them. LOCs in countries other than the United States are also applying these methods, specifically in East and Southeast Asia. For example, the pressures of globalization have played an important role in promoting interest in the use of high-involvement work system features by Korean companies (Rowley & Bae, 2001). The transference of HR techniques originally developed to suit Western culture to more collectivist and hierarchical Asian cultures would seem, in principle, a daunting task. This study attempts to cluster LOCs into various groups and then test the differences in organizational performance across various groups. I propose:

**Hypothesis 2.** Firms utilizing high-involvement HR practices are more likely to perform better financially than those utilizing traditional Confucian HR practices.

# METHODOLOGY

## Survey Data

The data used to test these hypotheses were gathered from 688 indigenous Taiwanese firms listed on the Taiwan stock exchange. I used listed companies for two reasons. First, compared to small-sized enterprises, the listed companies in the stock market tend to be larger and have more clearly established HRM functions and practices and would be more easily studied.[2] The second reason concerns the availability and reliability of financial data. Public companies are required to release and report returns on assets, annual sales, and operational expenditures. Because most other Taiwanese companies are reluctant to release or reveal their finances, the financial data made public by listed companies might serve as a relatively reliable source that could be used to evaluate organizational performance.

Questionnaires were mailed to each company's CEO (or senior general manager) and HR manager (or senior HR person). The HR manager or senior HR person was asked to fill out the part of the questionnaire that covered HR practices, and the CEO (or senior general manager) was asked to fill out the part of questionnaire that covered perceived organizational performance. This information was collected separately because the HR manager may not be fully familiar with the operation of company and its level of performance, and a single informant in each responding company could lead to common source variance problems (Podskoff & Organ, 1986; Podsakoff, MacKenzie, Lee, & Podsakoff, 2003). If the company was not able to provide two separate questionnaires, I mailed to the HR manager again to ask the HR manager to help in both parts of the questionnaire. A total of 93 completed questionnaires were returned. The return rate was 14%. Forty-one of 93 questionnaires were completed by the same person. The relatively low return rate is mainly attributable to the difficulty of collecting two completed questionnaires from one company. Low return rates are usual when doing surveys in Asian countries. For example, Takeuchi et al. (2003) had only a 15% response rate when investigating the HR practices of Japanese firms in China and Taiwan, and they also reported the difficulty of collecting data from both areas. Furthermore, Becker and Huselid (1998) also reviewed studies and reported an average of 17.4% response rate.

Logistic regression was used to test for sample selectivity bias. The dependent variable is dichotomous as responsive versus nonresponsive companies. The independent variables are size and age of firm. The two independent variables are not statistically significant (firm age, $p = .55$; firm size, $p = .53$) in differentiating the respondent and nonrespondent firms in the sample. The questionnaire was a Mandarin (Chinese) version of a questionnaire originally developed in English. The back-translated version was checked by two senior HR practitioners for work appropriateness, clarity, and conciseness.

## *Measures*

### *HR Practices*
It is not easy to identify commonly accepted measurements of HR work systems in previous research (Huselid, 1995; Zacharatos, Barling, & Iverson, 2005). Researchers usually develop their own measurements to fit the needs of their studies. Therefore, there is a large variety of measurement of HRM practices in use. For example, Huselid (1995) used 13 items to measure high-performance work systems. These items were factor-analyzed as employee skills and organization structure and employee motivation. Delery and Doty (1996) employed 7 practices (i.e., internal career opportunities, training, appraisal, employment security, participation, job description, and profit sharing) to conceptualize HR systems. Batt (2002) conceptualized high-involvement HR practices along 3 dimensions – skill level, work design, and involvement-enhancing HR incentives – investigating HR systems in communication industries. Other researchers have used various measures to examine different industry settings. In this study, I use 13 items to measure the HR practices of LOCs. They are based on the conceptual model of Confucian management and Western-based management styles presented in Table 1. They collect data on three key aspects – training and development, compensation and performance appraisal, and empowerment – and they are used to help identify and differentiate the characteristics of the two HR systems. All items in my questionnaire basically ask HR managers to

evaluate how descriptive a given statement is about the conditions in their organizations. All items use a 5-point Likert scale that ranges from "strongly disagree" to "strongly agree." Furthermore, the study focuses on examining the HR practices of only nonmanagerial and service workers to reduce the complexity of dealing with multiple HR architectures, because different HR configurations may be deployed in layers within an organization (Lepak & Snell, 1999).

### Corporate Financial Performance and Perceived Performance

I use two objective measures from financial data to capture organizational performance: return on invested capital (ROI) and return on total assets (ROA). Both measures of organizational performance have been widely used by companies to evaluate their profitability. ROI is measured in terms of yearly net income divided by a given year's invested capital and ROA is calculated as yearly net income divided by the average total assets for the year[3] (Bae & Gargiulo, 2004). The numbers were obtained from the *Taiwan Economic Journal* data bank. To minimize the effects of economic fluctuations, this study averaged ROI and ROA in 4 consecutive years (2001–2004).

In addition to collecting corporate financial performance from public data banks, this study also asked the general managers about their perceptions of organizational performance because public corporate financial data might not cover all dimensions of organizational performance. The survey of perceived organizational performance provides an alternative method to measure four items (i.e., employee productivity, profitability, customer's satisfaction with product quality, and market share) on a 5-point Likert scale. The Cronbach's $\alpha$ of the four items is .82. The perceived organizational performance variable was correlated with ROI and ROA. Both correlation coefficients for ROI and ROA were considered statistically significant at the .001 level.

### Control Variables

The variables used for control purposes include the size of the company, a collective bargaining agreement with the employees, the voluntary turnover rate at the firm level, sales growth, and the selling, general, and administrative expenses. Company size was measured as the natural logarithm of the number of full-time employees. HR managers were asked about whether there were formal collective agreements (or contracts) if there were unions or labor organizations. In this study, a dummy variable was used to measure whether companies had collective agreements (or contracts) with employees, rather than how many workers had been unionized.

Organizational turnover measures the quit rate of nonmanagerial employees. One question was used to measure this variable, asking, in the past year, approximately what percentage of the nonmanagerial workers had voluntarily left the company. These data were all provided by the respondents. Two variables were taken from published financial data sets. Sales growth measured the 3-year (2001–2003) trend in sales growth. The variable was from the *Market Observation Post System,* issued by the Taiwan Stock Exchange Corporation. The variable of selling, general, and administrative expenses was obtained from the *Taiwan Economic Journal* data bank.

# RESULTS

## *Exploratory Factor Analysis*

Before testing the hypotheses, I conducted an exploratory factor analysis to validate the measures of HR practices. The 13 HR practice items were submitted to a principal components analysis extraction with varimax rotation. Four factors emerged from these analyses with eigenvalues greater than 1, accounting for 61% of the variance (Table 2). Each of the 13 items was loaded on the factor with primary loadings of at least .54 and cross-loading not exceeding .38. The first factor was termed "empowerment" because it included empowering HR practices such as financial participation, self-directed teams, and job autonomy. The second factor was termed "training and development" because it related to whether firms viewed training as long-term investment and devoted resources to employees' training, orientation, and development. The third factor was "compensation" because it covered how firms compensated their employees. The fourth was termed "seniority" because it was related to how firms use tenure to promote or compensate employees. The Cronbach's α of the four factors was .67, .63, .75, and .66, respectively, which is reasonably acceptable.

## *Cluster Analysis*

This study attempts to explore how Taiwanese LOCs implement their HR practices – traditional Confucian system versus Western-based

***Table 2.*** Exploratory Factor Analysis for HR Practices.

| Factors and Items | 1 | 2 | 3 | 4 |
|---|---|---|---|---|
| *Empowerment (α = .67)* | | | | |
| Individual employees have considerable autonomy in their jobs | **.87** | .07 | −.18 | .03 |
| Employees often work in self-directed teams | **.75** | −.08 | −.02 | .21 |
| Employees rarely engage in problem solving or decision making in matters that are related to their jobs and working conditions (R) | **.56** | .08 | .24 | .07 |
| Employee financial participation (e.g., gain sharing, employee ownership, etc.) is extensive | **.55** | .34 | −.06 | .18 |
| *Training and Development (α = .63)* | | | | |
| The company devotes considerable resources to employee training and development | .09 | **.77** | −.12 | .2 |
| Training is viewed by management more as a short-term cost than as a long-term cost (R) | .07 | **.68** | .27 | −.11 |
| New employees undergo extensive orientation to learn the values and culture | −.02 | **.66** | .32 | .11 |
| The company extensively shares its performance data with its employees | .38 | **.54** | −.32 | .21 |
| *Seniority (α = .75)* | | | | |
| An employee's seniority is an important factor in determining pay (R) | .07 | .05 | **.89** | .18 |
| Promotion usually goes to the applicant who has worked the longest for the company (R) | .06 | .13 | **.78** | −.04 |
| *Compensation (α = .66)* | | | | |
| We strive to keep a large salary difference between high and low performers in the same position | .12 | .09 | −.07 | **.81** |
| Compensation is based more on performance than on an employee's job title or position | .10 | .04 | .12 | **.80** |
| An employee's pay is closely tied to individual or group performance | .35 | .25 | .12 | **.54** |
| Eigenvalue | 2.26 | 2.00 | 1.82 | 1.82 |
| Percentage of variance | 17.35 | 15.38 | 13.99 | 13.98 |

high-involvement system. The HR practice variables obtained from the exploratory factor analysis provided a basis for cluster analysis, which is a statistical method of categorizing objects (companies). Based on the selected measures, companies with similar characteristics can be grouped together. I used Ward's method because the results from this method tend to be more interpretable (Arthur, 1992). I applied cluster analysis to the four HR system variables extracted from factor analysis listed in Table 2.

The clustering (agglomeration) coefficient indicated large increases from four to three clusters (25.57), three to two clusters (27.95), and two to one cluster (60.10). To identify large relative increases in the cluster homogeneity and decide the cluster solution, I calculated the percentage change in the agglomeration coefficient. As indicated in Table 3, the percentage jumped precipitously from 10% in the five-cluster to 24% in the four-cluster solution, which was selected in this study.

Table 4 presents the results of the analysis for the four-cluster solution and shows the means and standard deviations of the four HR system variables. The variables in this table are all standardized with mean of 0 and standard deviation of 1. Because the variables had been standardized,

*Table 3.* Agglomeration Coefficient for Hierarchical Cluster Analysis.

| Number of Clusters | Agglomeration Coefficient | Change in Agglomeration Coefficient | Percentage Change in Coefficient to Next Level |
|---|---|---|---|
| 8 | 70.84 | 6.90 | 9.7 |
| 7 | 77.74 | 7.68 | 9.9 |
| 6 | 85.42 | 9.83 | 12.5 |
| 5 | 95.25 | 10.72 | 11.3 |
| 4 | 105.97 | 25.57 | 24.1 |
| 3 | 131.54 | 27.95 | 21.2 |
| 2 | 159.49 | 60.10 | 37.7 |
| 1 | 219.59 | – | – |

*Table 4.* Descriptive of HR Practice Clusters (Means and Standard Deviations of Standardized Values by Cluster).

| | Cluster 1 Confucian HR System (N = 22) | Cluster 2 Transformational HR System (N = 42) | Cluster 3 Collaborative HR System (N = 15) | Cluster 4 High-involvement HR System (N = 16) | |
|---|---|---|---|---|---|
| Variable | Mean (SD) | Mean (SD) | Mean (SD) | Mean (SD) | $F$-value |
| Empowerment | −.58 (.89)** | −.28 (.89)* | .43 (.65) | 1.10 (.62)** | 16.43** |
| Training | −1.01 (1.11)** | .03 (.61) | .28 (.41) | 1.05 (.72)** | 29.94** |
| Compensation | −.91 (.69)** | −.17 (.76) | .49 (.75)* | 1.22 (.59)** | 30.56** |
| Seniority (R) | −.59 (.71)** | .56 (.52)** | −1.41 (.47)** | .73 (.77)** | 53.03** |

*Note:* Test for the mean difference between the cluster and the rest of the sample.
*$p < .05$; **$p < .01$.

a positive score on a certain variable indicated that the average mean score on the variable was higher than the mean score for all the companies. For example, the score of the empowerment variable in cluster 4 was 1.10, indicating that the empowerment variable in this cluster was higher than the average score across the sample. To determine the objectiveness and show the uniqueness of each cluster, *t*-tests were performed to show the mean difference between the cluster and the rest of the sample (Table 4) (Arthur, 1992; Hambrick, 1983).

The four HR system clusters shown in Table 4 characterize the various systems used in LOCs in Taiwan. Two extreme clusters, 1 and 4, named "Confucian HR system" and "high-involvement HR system" match the two pure types of HR systems as presented in Table 1. Cluster 1 is composed of 22 companies for whom the standardized mean scores of the four factors were all negative and significantly lower than the mean for the rest of companies. The companies in this cluster follow traditional Confucian HR practice in that seniority determines compensation and promotion, they provide less training for employees, and they show less empowerment. In contrast, Cluster 4 consists of 16 companies for which the standardized mean scores of the four factors were all positive and significantly higher than the mean for the rest of companies. These companies provide training to their employees and empower them in the workplace. Seniority plays a reduced role with regard to compensation and promotion.

Cluster 2, named "transformational HR system," the largest in this study, is composed of 42 companies. Companies in this cluster have begun to adopt practices different from those found in a traditional Confucian HR system. They have changed the seniority system and have begun to invest more in employee training, though without statistically significance differences. In contrast, the empowerment score in this cluster is significantly below the average, indicating that the companies are reluctant to allow participation and autonomy, either in jobs or in sharing in financial matters.

Cluster 3, named the "collaborative HR system," consists of 15 companies. This cluster resembles the high-involvement HR cluster. Companies in this cluster tended not to see training their employees as a cost and were more willing to invest in them. These companies were more likely to use financial participation and team-based decision and compensation. The main difference between cluster 3 and cluster 4 was that the companies in cluster 3 continued to value and reward seniority highly. The significant difference in this variable indicated that age and tenure remain significant.

### HR System and Organizational Performance

Table 5 presents means, standard deviations, and correlations. The average age of firms was 30 years and average total number of employees was 1,283 (the logarithm of this variable is used in all subsequent analyses). Twenty-four percent of companies we investigated had signed agreements between employers and trade unions. Newer and larger firms tended to use high-involvement HR systems. Previous research has shown that newer firms tend to be likely to avoid traditional management styles and larger firms have more resources to devote HR practices (Arthur, 1992; Kochan, Katz, & McKersie, 1994). The voluntary turnover rate was 9.26% and did not appear to be significantly related to the four types of HR systems but has significant and negative correlation with ROI and perceived organizational performance. The three dependent variables (i.e., ROI, ROA, and perceived organizational performance) have high correlations with each other.

The second hypothesis of this study was that LOCs in Taiwan that use high-involvement HR systems are more likely to perform better financially after controlling for firm characteristics and operation variables. Operationally, I created three dummy variables for HR systems, coding "1" for cluster 4 (high-involvement HR), cluster 3 (collaborative HR), and cluster 2 (transformational HR). The reference group was cluster 1, the cluster of

***Table 5.*** Descriptive Statistics and Correlations.

| | Mean | SD | 1 | 2 | 3 | 4 | 5 | 6 | 7 | 8 | 9 | 10 | 11 | 12 |
|---|---|---|---|---|---|---|---|---|---|---|---|---|---|---|
| High-involvement HR | .17 | .38 | – | | | | | | | | | | | |
| Collaborative HR | .16 | .37 | –.20 | – | | | | | | | | | | |
| Transformational HR | .43 | .50 | –.40 | –.38 | – | | | | | | | | | |
| Confucian HR | .24 | .43 | –.25 | –.24 | –.48 | – | | | | | | | | |
| ROI (average 01–04) | .13 | .17 | .15 | –.05 | .05 | –.15 | – | | | | | | | |
| ROA (average 01–04) | 7.86 | 7.43 | .12 | –.03 | .11 | –.22 | .83 | – | | | | | | |
| Perceived performance | 3.13 | .73 | .19 | –.01 | –.08 | –.06 | .45 | .41 | – | | | | | |
| Firm age | 30.15 | 15.81 | –.02 | .15 | –.14 | .05 | –.10 | –.20 | .07 | – | | | | |
| Log firm size | 6.56 | 1.08 | .18 | .06 | –.15 | –.03 | –.08 | –.09 | .05 | .17 | – | | | |
| Collective agreement | .24 | .45 | .01 | .16 | –.12 | –.01 | –.17 | –.11 | –.02 | .16 | .02 | – | | |
| Voluntary turnover | 9.27 | 8.64 | .06 | .12 | .01 | –.18 | –.22 | –.12 | –.30 | –.10 | .23 | .03 | – | |
| Sales growth | .18 | .44 | .06 | –.07 | .01 | –.00 | .27 | .36 | .24 | .01 | .22 | .00 | .04 | – |
| Administrative expenditure | 20.16 | 1.26 | .03 | .07 | –.10 | .02 | .00 | –.10 | .08 | .00 | .61 | –.07 | .15 | .25 |

*Note:* Correlation coefficient greater than .21, $p < .05$; greater than .26, $p < .01$.

those using traditional Confucian HR systems. I expected high-involvement and collaborative HR systems to have a significantly positive effect on organizational performance in the regression model. Dependent variables were ROI, ROA, and perceived organizational performance[4].

Table 6 presents the results of the analysis of independent and control variables. Three regressions were statistically significant ($F = 2.604$; $p < .01$ for ROI; $F = 3.768$; $p < .001$ for ROA; and $F = 2.378$; $p < .05$ for perceived performance). The results show that the variable high-involvement HR system had significantly positive coefficients in all three regression models, indicating that LOCs in Taiwan experimenting with high-involvement HR practices enjoyed better financial performance than firms with traditional Confucian HR practices ($b = .126$; $p < .05$ for ROI; $b = 4.942$; $p < .05$ for ROA; and $b = .473$; $p < .05$ for perceived performance). The collaborative HR and transformational HR system variables in ROA regression were

***Table 6.*** Regression Results of Organizational Performance.

|  | ROI (2001–2004) | ROA (2001–2004) | Perceived Performance |
|---|---|---|---|
| Constant | .031** | 29.73*** | 2.367* |
|  | (.314) | (12.14) | (1.269) |
| High-involvement HR | .137** | 4.942** | .473** |
|  | (.057) | (2.219) | (.232) |
| Collaborative HR | .105* | 4.478** | .233 |
|  | (.059) | (2.272) | (.237) |
| Transformational HR | .088* | 3.527** | .104 |
|  | (.046) | (1.779) | (.186) |
| Firm age | −.0007 | −.089* | .002 |
|  | (.001) | (.046) | (.005) |
| Log firm size | −.028 | −.227 | −.007 |
|  | (.022) | (.854) | (.089) |
| Collective agreement | −.048 | −1.665 | −.044 |
|  | (.041) | (1.567) | (.164) |
| Voluntary turnover | −.004** | −.139 | −.029† |
|  | (.002) | (.084) | (.009) |
| Sales growth | .140† | 7.000† | .379** |
|  | (.042) | (1.617) | (.169) |
| Administrative expenditure | .012 | −1.009 | .040 |
|  | (.018) | (.708) | (.169) |
| $R^2$ | .236 | .291 | .205 |
| $F$ | 2.849*** | 3.768† | 2.378** |
| $N$ | 93 | 93 | 93 |

$*p < .10$; $**p < .05$; $***p < .01$; $†p < .001$.

positive and statistically significant at the .05 level, but ROI and perceived performance regressions showed no significant differences.

# DISCUSSION AND CONCLUSION

This study showed that Taiwanese LOCs should be clustered according to HR practices (i.e., those using traditional, transformational, collaborative, and high-involvement HR systems). Although researchers have highlighted the notions of pure traditional Confucian and high-involvement HR systems, I have found two other HR systems standing between them. Many researchers have discussed transferability and convergence in different aspects of HR practices and found that some HR practices tend to be more easily transferred (Brewster & Hegewisch, 1994; Wu, 2004; Yeh, 1991). Empirical research has indicated that the "hard" quantifiable technologies (e.g., training) are more likely to converge and transfer between companies from different countries than are the "soft" behavioral technologies (e.g., pay system and empowerment). This study shows that training and development practices are the most likely among the four HR practices to be changed. Of the four clusters, companies in three, all but the traditional HR system cluster, have adopted, to some extent, more general and extensive training. In contrast, empowerment practices are the least likely to transfer because the practice involves changing power and decision-making structures. If employees are endowed with more autonomy, the traditional authoritative employment relationship would be challenged. In my analysis, the transformational HR system (cluster 2) was the largest group in this study. Companies in this cluster have adopted training practices similar to those is the West while maintaining empowerment and compensation practices found in the traditional Confucian HR system.

In addition to examining the extent to which practices are more likely to be adopted, cultural sensitivity is often raised in examining the degree of transference and convergence. Triandis (1995) holds that national culture affects dominant values and norms and that management in general and HR in particular should be aligned with key aspects of national culture. He proposed the concepts of tight and loose cultures, referring to the degree to which those in a given culture conform to its standards with little variation. Bae and Lawler (2000) found that Korean culture is undergoing change toward more willingness to accept the strategic HRM concept. Taiwan has been found to have a trend similar to that in Korea and has made these changes in response to globalization and rapid economic growth (Kim,

Park, & Suzuki, 1990; Wu, 2004). Growing up in an environment of rapid modernization and globalization, the new generation in Taiwan is more individualistic and reluctant to be restrained by authoritarian, hierarchical, and collective cultures. These developments in the environment encourage companies to adopt a high-involvement HR system.

Much research has attributed Taiwan's rapid economic achievement and organizational performance in the past decades to traditional Confucian culture and values (Rowley & Bae, 2001; Warner, 1995; Wilkinson, 1994; Xin & Pearce, 1996; Yang, 1994; Yeung & Tung, 1996). The association observed has occurred not only in Taiwan but also in other Asian countries, such as Korea, Hong Kong, and Singapore, in which governments try to promote Confucian values (Bae et al., 2003). Some studies have questioned the positive association and expressed doubt that traditional Confucian values could promote growth, especially after the 1997 financial crisis. They question whether these values are the assets they were once thought to be. For example, some have expressed concern that *guanxi*-based recruitment and promotion could force out competent and high-potential employees, although the recruitment could guarantee trust and loyalty from employees. Furthermore, deference to authority and rigid hierarchical structures can distort information and negatively influence top-down decision making (Bae et al., 2003; Kirkman & Shapiro, 1997; Lockett, 1988). Regardless of whether Confucian values have a positive or negative effect, ad hoc inferences are usually not persuasive.

The study proposed a model for how Taiwanese firms could transform from a traditional Confucian HR system toward a more global standard. Several forces may play crucial roles in explaining the process of diffusion. First, in recent decades, Taiwan has become an important player in the global market. Many foreign multinationals have invested in Taiwan, bringing with them new HR practices. To gain competitiveness in global markets, the diffusion of the high-involvement HR system is occurring. Second, past decades have witnessed a growing number of Taiwanese with foreign MBA degrees, mostly from the United States, who came back and worked in foreign subsidiaries in Taiwan. Management principles have been incorporated into their management education and resulted in a change in traditional HR systems and practices. This is a very important institutional mechanism supporting the diffusion of global standard HR practices (Chen et al., 2005). In addition, the diffusion is more obvious in the information sector than in other sectors (e.g., traditional manufacturing) (Huang, Huang, & Uen, 1998). High-tech companies have received more serious competition in the global market and the emphasis on research and development has to dilute the influences of hierarchy and authoritarianism.

This study has found that corporations using Confucian HR systems performed significantly lower financially than those using high-involvement HR systems and other types of HR systems. As mentioned earlier, systems with traditional Confucian values do not easily adopt high-involvement HR system practices because extensive empowerment practices, worker participation, and autonomous job design seem to contradict rigid hierarchical organizational structure, collectivism, and seniority-based payment. However, Taiwanese cultural values are changing and there is a move toward individualism. Globalization has increased the interaction between LOCs and MNEs, and Taiwanese enterprises are implementing high-involvement practices. Furthermore, this study found that organizations' financial performance was improved by the adoption of high-involvement HR practices, meaning such HR practices are rewarded financially and will probably continue. The results somewhat support the convergence hypothesis stating that high-involvement HR systems can work well outside of the United States, even in various cultural contexts (Kerr, Dunlop, Harbison, & Myers, 1960; Pfeffer, 1994).

Finally, Fig. 1 presents a dynamic model stating that the adoption of HR practices in Taiwanese firms is significantly affected by the extent of familial control and familial ownership. Despite the limits of the cross-sectional data collected in current study, the model provides a preliminary starting point to include familial control and ownership and their effects on shaping HR practices in future research.

# NOTES

1. There are many terms to describe the HR system, such as high-performance work system, commitment-based work system, and high-innovative work system. These terms could be treated as having similar meanings despite different contents of HR practices in various studies.

2. Small-sized enterprises make up the majority of businesses in Taiwan. More than 60% of Taiwanese workers in the private sector are employed by companies with fewer than 30 employees. Less than 10% of Taiwanese workers are employed by companies with more than 500 employees.

3. Various researchers have different methods to calculate ROI and ROA. In this study, ROI is specifically calculated as net income divided by the sum of common equity, long-term debt, and preferred stock. ROA is computed from net income divided by average total asset. Refer to Sorensen (2002) and Bae and Gargiulo (2004).

4. To avoid the simultaneity between HR practices and firm performance, this study also used only 2004 ROI and ROA to regress HR practices in addition to using

averaged 2001 and 2004 ROI and ROA. The two results are very similar for both different measures of dependent variables.

# REFERENCES

Appelbaum, E., & Batt, R. (1994). *The new American workplace: Transforming work systems in the United States*. Ithaca and London: ILR.

Arthur, J. (1992). The link between business strategy and industrial relations systems in American steel minimills. *Industrial and Labor Relations Review, 45*, 488–506.

Arthur, J. (1994). Effects of human resource systems on manufacturing performance and turnover. *Academy of Management Journal, 37*, 670–687.

Bae, J., Chen, S., Wan, T. D., Lawler, J., & Walumbwa, F. (2003). Human resource strategy and firm performance in Pacific Rim countries. *International Journal of Human Resource Management, 14*, 1308–1332.

Bae, J., & Gargiulo, M. (2004). Partner substitutability, alliance network structure, and firm profitability in the telecommunications industry. *Academy of Management Journal, 47*(6), 843–859.

Bae, J., & Lawler, J. (2000). Organizational and HRM strategies in Korea: Impact on firm performance in an emerging economy. *Academy of Management Journal, 43*, 502–517.

Barney, J. (1991). Firm resources and sustained competitive advantage. *Journal of Management, 17*, 99–120.

Batt, R. (2002). Managing customer services: Human resource practices, quit rates, and sales growth. *Academy of Management Journal, 45*, 587–597.

Becker, B., & Huselid, M. (1998). High performance work systems and firm performance: A synthesis of research and managerial implication. In: K. M. Rowland & G. R. Ferris (Eds), *Research in personnel and human resource management* (pp. 53–101). Greenwich, CT: JAI Press.

Brewster, C., & Hegewisch, A. (Eds). (1994). *Policy and practice in European HRM: The Price Waterhouse Cranfield Survey*. London: Routledge.

Chen, M. (2001). *Inside Chinese business*. Boston, MA: Harvard Business School Press.

Chen, S., Ko, J., & Lawler, J. (2003). Changing patterns of industrial relations in Taiwan. *Industrial Relations, 42*(3), 315–340.

Chen, S., Lawler, J., & Bae, J. (2005). Convergence in human resource systems: A comparison of locally owned and MNC subsidiaries in Taiwan. *Human Resource Management, 44*(3), 237–256.

Delaney, J., & Huselid, M. (1996). The impact of human resource management practices on perceptions of organizational performance. *Academy of Management Journal, 39*, 949–969.

Delery, J. E., & Doty, D. H. (1996). Modes of theorizing in strategic human resource management: Tests of universalistic, contingency, and configurational performance predictions. *Academy of Management Journal, 39*, 802–835.

Doeringer, P. B., Lorenz, E., & Terkla, D. (2003). The adoption and diffusion of high-performance management: Lessons from Japanese multinationals in the West. *Cambridge Journal of Economics, 27*, 265–286.

Farh, J. L. (1995). Human resource management in Taiwan, the Republic of China. In: L. F. Moore & P. D. Jennings (Eds), *Human resource management on the Pacific Rim* (pp. 265–294). Berlin: Walter de Gruyter.

Ferner, A. (1997). Country of origin effects and HRM in multinational companies. *Human Resource Management Journal, 7*(1), 19–37.

Geary, J., & Roche, B. (2001). Multinationals and human resource practices in Ireland: A rejection of the "New Conformance Thesis". *International Journal of Human Resource Management, 12*(1), 109–127.

Guthrie, J. P. (2001). High-involvement work practices, turnover, and productivity: Evidence from New Zealand. *Academy of Management Journal, 44*, 180–190.

Hambrick, D. C. (1983). High profit strategies in mature capital goods industries: A contingency approach. *Academy of Management Journal, 26*(4), 687–707.

Harzing, A. W., & Sorge, A. (2003). The relative impact of country of origin and universal contingencies in internationalization strategies and corporate control in multination enterprises: Worldwide and European perspectives. *Organization Studies, 24*(2), 187–214.

Hofstede, G. (1980). Motivation, leadership and organization: Do American theories apply abroad? *Organizational Dynamics, 9*(1), 42–63.

Huang, I., Huang, J., & Uen, J. (1998). The relationships between human resource systems and organizational performance in high-tech companies in Taiwan. *Sun Yat-Sen Management Review, August* (International Issue), 643–656.

Huselid, M. A. (1995). The impact of human resource management practices on turnover, productivity, and corporate financial performance. *Academy of Management Journal, 38*, 635–672.

Huselid, M. A., Jackson, S., & Schuler, R. S. (1997). Technical and strategic human resource management effectiveness as determinants of firm performance. *Academy of Management Journal, 40*, 171–188.

Hwang, K. K. (2001). The deep structure of Confucianism: A social psychological approach. *Asian Philosophy, 11*, 179–204.

Kerr, C., Dunlop, J. T., Harbison, F., & Myers, C. A. (1960). *Industrialism and industrial man: The problems of labor and management in economic growth.* Cambridge, MA: Harvard University Press.

Khatri, N., & Budhwar, P. (2002). A study of strategic HR issues in an Asian context. *Personnel Review, 31*(2), 166–188.

Kim, K., Park, H., & Suzuki, N. (1990). Reward allocation in the United States, Japan, and Korea: A comparison of individualistic and collective cultures. *Academy of Management Journal, 33*(1), 188–198.

Kirkman, B., & Shapiro, D. (1997). Resistance to teams: Toward a model of globalized self-managing work team effectiveness. *Academy of Management Review, 22*, 730–757.

Kochan, T., Katz, H., & McKersie, R. (1994). *The transformation of American industrial relations.* New York: Basic Books.

Lee, J. (1995). Economic development and the evolution of industrial relations in Taiwan, 1950–1993. In: A. Verma, T. Kochan & R. Lansbury (Eds), *Employment relations in the growing Asian economies* (pp. 88–118). New York: Routledge.

Lepak, D. P., & Snell, S. A. (1999). The human resource architecture: Toward a theory of human capital allocation and development. *Academy of Management Review, 24*, 31–48.

Lockett, M. (1988). Culture and the problems of Chinese management. *Organization Studies, 9*(4), 475–496.

Negandhi, A. N. (1973). *Management and economic development: The case of Taiwan.* The Hague: Martinus Nijhoff.

Newman, K., & Nollen, S. D. (1996). Culture and congruence: The fit between management practices and national culture. *Journal of International Business Studies, 27*(4), 753–779.

Pfeffer, J. (1994). *Competitive advantage through people.* Boston, MA: Harvard Business School.

Podsakoff, P., MacKenzie, S. B., Lee, J., & Podsakoff, N. (2003). Common method biases in behavioural research: A critical review of literature and recommended remedies. *Journal of Applied Psychology, 88,* 879–903.

Podskoff, P. M., & Organ, D. W. (1986). Self-report in organizational research: Problem and prospects. *Journal of Management, 12,* 531–544.

Pyat, R., Ashkanasy, N., Tamaschke, R., & Grigg, T. (2001). Transitions and traditions in Chinese family businesses: Evidence from Hong Kong and Thailand. In: J. B. Kidd, X. Li & F. J. Richter (Eds), *Advances in human resource management in Asia.* New York: Palgrave.

Rowley, C., & Bae, J. (2001). The impact of globalization on HRM: The case of Korea. *Journal of World Business, 36*(4), 402–428.

Rowley, C., & Benson, J. (2003). Introduction: Changes and continuities in Asian HRM. *Asia Pacific Business Review, 9*(4), 1–14.

Sorensen, J. B. (2002). The strength of corporate culture and the reliability of firm performance. *Administrative Science Quarterly, 47,* 70–79.

Takeuchi, N., Wakabayashi, M., & Chen, Z. (2003). The strategic HRM configuration for competitive advantage: Evidence from Japanese firms in China and Taiwan. *Asia Pacific Journal of Management, 20,* 447–480.

Triandis, H. C. (1995). *Individualism and collectivism.* Boulder, CO: Westview.

Von Glinow, M. A., Drost, E. A., & Teagarden, M. B. (2002). Converging on IHRM best practices: Lessons learned from a globally distributed consortium on theory and practice. *Human Resource Management, 41*(1), 123–141.

Warner, M. (1995). *The management of human resources in Chinese industry.* London/New York: MacMillan/St. Martins Press.

Wilkinson, B. (1994). *Labor and industry in the Asia-Pacific: Lessons from the newly-industrialized countries.* Berlin: Walter de Gruyter.

Wright, P., & Boswell, W. (2002). Desegregating HRM: A review and synthesis of micro and macro human resource management research. *Journal of Management, 28,* 247–276.

Wu, P. (2004). HRM in Taiwan. In: P. S. Budhwar (Ed.), *Managing human resources in Asia-Pacific* (pp. 93–112). London, New York: Routledge.

Xin, K. R., & Pearce, J. (1996). Guanxi: Connections as substitutes for formal institutional support. *Academy of Management Journal, 39*(5), 1641–1658.

Yang, M. (1994). *Gifts, favors and banquets: The art of social relationship in China.* Ithaca, NY: Cornell University Press.

Yao, D. (1999). Human resource management challenges in Chinese Taipei. Paper presented at APEC Human Resource Management in Small and Medium-sized Enterprises Symposium, October 29–31, Kaohsiung, Taiwan.

Yeh, R. S. (1991). Management practices of Taiwanese firms: As compared to those of American and Japanese affiliates in Taiwan. *Asia Pacific Journal of Management, 8*(1), 1–14.

Yeung, I. M., & Tung, R. L. (1996). Achieving business success in Confucian societies: The importance of quanxi (connections). *Organizational Dynamics, 25*(2), 54–65.

Zacharatos, A., Barling, J., & Iverson, R. (2005). High-performance work systems and occupational safety. *Journal of Applied Psychology, 90,* 77–93.

# TOWARD A MODEL OF GENDER DIVERSITY IN THE WORKPLACE IN EAST ASIA: PRELIMINARY EVIDENCE FROM MANUFACTURING INDUSTRIES IN TAIWAN

I-Chieh Hsu and John J. Lawler

## ABSTRACT

*This chapter examines gender diversity with a focus on the proportion of females in companies in Taiwan. The investigation also examines the effect of the proportion of females on company performance. The research used two Taiwan government databases offering statistics of individual indigenous companies in the manufacturing industries in 1996 and 2001, with a sample size of 8,622 in 1996 and 8,731 in 2001. Results show that the proportion of females in managerial, professional, and administrative jobs is increasing and is positively associated with company performance. By contrast, the proportion of females in operational-level jobs is decreasing, and its association with company performance is inconsistent. This study extends previous gender diversity research in management*

The Global Diffusion of Human Resource Practices: Institutional and Cultural Limits
Advances in International Management, Volume 21, 171–190
ISSN: 1571-5027/doi:10.1016/S1571-5027(08)00007-7

*groups and suggests that women can be invaluable resources for business organizations in Taiwan.*

In the first decade of the 21st century, researchers studied a variety of phenomena associated with the domain of "diversity" (Jackson, Joshi, & Erhardt, 2003). Strategic management researchers studied diversity based on tenure, education, and functional background (Dwyer, Richard, & Chadwick, 2003). Diversity encompassing a wider range of attributes was also studied, such as diversity based on cognition (Kilduff, Angelmar, & Mehra, 2000; Miller, Burke, & Glick, 1998) and racio-ethnicity (Richard, 2000; Richard, Barnett, Dwyer, & Chadwick, 2004). However, issues surrounding gender diversity have not received sufficient attention from investigators (Dwyer et al., 2003). An examination of the literature suggests that different types of diversity have different effects on firm performance. Thus, Dwyer et al. (2003) conclude that knowledge of one type of diversity does not lead researchers to gain insight into other types of diversity. Furthermore, different types of diversity may have complex and interactive effects on firm performance, and future research into this problem is called for (Jackson & Joshi, 2001; Jackson et al., 2003). The fact that gender diversity is underexplored may impede this research quest.

In addition, past studies have generally focused on the top management team in their examination of diversity effect on firm performance (Dwyer et al., 2003; Finkelstein & Hambrick, 1996). Yet, researchers argue that strategic decision-making processes are an organization-wide phenomena, requiring participation from every level of organizational members (Hart, 1992; Hart & Banbury, 1994). In a strategic decision-making process, top management team members formulate a strategy and use structural or formal control systems to influence employees to behave in a way consistent with the achievement of organizational goals (Burgelman, 1983). Middle managers play important roles in influencing strategic decision making and implementation (Bower, 1970; Burgelman, 1994), whereas operating-level managers and employees may take initiative in productivity improvement and innovation (Hart, 1992; Imai, 1986). Thus, this chapter seeks to examine gender diversity, couched in terms of the proportion of females, and its effect on firm performance at the organizational level. This investigation will include various levels of organizational members, from managers and professionals to operational-level employees. Such an investigation has been recommended and considered important in the previous literature

(Dwyer et al., 2003). In so doing, this study also reflects the fact that the proportion of females in the workplace is on the increase, at both the managerial and other levels (Stringer, 1995).

The investigation will take place in an East Asian context, namely, Taiwan, whose economy has grown rapidly in the past few decades. The rapid economic development and industrialization led to rising female participation in the workforce in a variety of industrial contexts. However, although women increasingly participate in the workforce, government reports suggest that significant employer discrimination based on gender continues. The discrimination exists in pay and promotion opportunities for women relative to those for men (e.g., Council of Labor Affairs, 2000). Sadly, studies of gender diversity and its effect on firm performance in this economy are wanting. Is employer discrimination against women justified because of their low productivity and capability relative to men? Or is the discrimination against women not defensible? In this chapter, the authors will address these questions by examining gender diversity and its impacts on firm performance.

## LITERATURE REVIEW

Previous studies undertaken to investigate diversity in organizational settings have located their theoretical perspectives in either social identity theory or the resource-based view of the firm. According to social identity theory, belonging to a group based on a diversity attribute, such as gender or race, can lead to a psychological state in which a social identity or collective self-identity emerges (Tajfel, 1982). The social categorization process results in high frequencies of within-group communications in a variety of ways, because within-group members share similar views or culture, leading to the development of in-group attachment. Culturally homogeneous groups will tend to increase satisfaction and cooperation and reduce emotional conflicts (Williams & O'Reilly, 1998). Positive social relations and interactions are easily developed. Furthermore, social categorization often results in within-group solidarity and group member conformity to group norms and, at the same time, discrimination against those not in the group (Tajfel & Turner, 1985). Thus, Blau's (1977) theory of heterogeneity predicts that firms with various levels of diversity will result in different process dynamics and operating outcomes. Further work also suggests that diversity is associated with negative performance (Pelled, Eisenhardt, & Xin, 1999; Tsui, Egan, & O'Reilly, 1992). It appears that to the extent that diversity exists in an organization, discrimination and hostility will increase, whereas in a homogeneous organization, group cohesion and positive outcomes can be observed (Richard et al., 2004).

The resource-based view of the firm predicts otherwise. This view contends that organizations differ in their unique bundles of resources and capabilities. The most important task of a firm is to maximize performance outcomes through the optimal deployment of existing resources and capabilities, while at the same time developing its resource base to remain competitive in the future (Grant, 1996; Teece, Pisano, & Shuen, 1997). Among various types of resources, this view credits human resources as the most important resources a firm has (Pfeffer, 1994; Wright, McMahan, & McWilliams, 1994). The aggregation of the knowledge, skills, and capabilities of organizational members results in organizational competence (Mckelvey, 1983). More precisely, "human capital embraces the abilities and know-how of men and women that have been acquired at some cost and that can command a price in the labor market because they are useful in the productive process" (Parnes, 1984, p. 32). Thus, the resource-based view acknowledges the importance of human resources to positive outcomes of organizations.

Consistent with the above argument, researchers maintain that a competitive advantage based on a single resource or capability is easier to imitate than a competitive advantage derived from multiple resources or capabilities (Barney, 1991; Ulrich & Lake, 1990; Wernerfelt, 1984). In this respect, organizational human resources, especially with a variety of capabilities and competencies, are unique and capable of creating performance differentials for an organization (Bontis & Fitz-enz, 2002; Noe, Hollenbeck, Gerhart, & Wright, 2003). The process by which human resources create performance differentials requires complex patterns of coordination and input of other types of resources. The causal ambiguity and social complexity inherent in the process have made the human resource nonsubstitutable and inimitable (Teece et al., 1997; Wright et al., 1994). Thus, the resource-based view not only refers to men and women as human resources, but also encourages diversity in the workplace. The causal ambiguity and social complexity lying within the process whereby different groups of human resources interact to create organizational performance will bring competitive advantages to the organization.

Given the two contrasting theoretical views, empirical studies on diversity in the workplace have not resulted in conclusive findings. However, the evidence tends to be context-dependent. Richard (2000) studied the relationships among racial diversity, business strategy, and performance of

U.S. banks. Racial diversity, when implemented within banks pursuing a growth strategy, determines performance of banks. Similar findings also emerge from Richard and his colleagues' subsequent studies. Richard, McMillan, Chadwick, and Dwyer (2003) discovered that U.S. banks employing a racially diverse workforce would have better financial performance when the banks also adopted an innovation strategy. Richard et al. (2004) discovered that the innovative orientation of U.S. banks positively moderates the effect of racial and gender diversity on their financial performance, while the risk-taking propensity negatively moderates the effect. Finally, Dwyer et al.'s (2003) study concludes that gender diversity in management must be implemented in certain configurations of business strategy and organizational culture for it to produce good financial performance.

In addition to the above-mentioned studies, Kochan et al. (2003) examined diversity policies and practices in four companies with a case-study approach. They also examined business strategy, organizational culture, and human resource management practices in each of the four companies. Their findings suggest that racial or gender diversity has no direct effect on business performance.

The observation that the effect of gender diversity is context-dependent cannot be said to be conclusive. Our literature review reveals a study that demonstrates a positive association between organizational diversity practices and performance. Wright, Ferris, Hiller, and Kroll (1995) examined the effects of announcements of U.S. Department of Labor awards for exemplary affirmative action programs on stock price valuation of a firm. Announcements of the award are found to be associated with significant and positive excess returns. They conclude that quality affirmative action programs help improve a firm's competitive advantage and are valued by the market. The evidence suggests that to the extent that diversity practices are implemented in an organization, they may be beneficial to the organization.

## WOMEN IN ORGANIZATIONS IN TAIWAN

With only limited work conducted in the West (mainly North America) on the issue of diversity, this issue has received little attention in Taiwan. In view of this, this gender diversity study in Taiwan is conducted with a focus on the proportion of females. What is the proportion of females across various job categories in firms in Taiwan? What is the general trend for female participation in the workforce in recent years? Will a higher proportion of females contribute to organizational performance? These are the focal questions of this chapter. An examination into these questions will further our understanding of the dynamics of female participation in the workforce in Taiwan.

Throughout Chinese history, women have been the subjects of social injustice and male domination, enduring foot-binding, loveless marriages, widow suicide, widow obedience to the eldest son, concubinage, and female infanticide, even widow and concubines being buried alive with a deceased emperor. Taiwan, with its Chinese cultural heritage, has also inherited the Chinese legacy of female inferiority to men in social status and economic welfare.

Confucianism was often blamed for the tradition of the oppression of women in societies influenced by Chinese culture (Clark & Wang, 2004). Seemingly derogatory remarks are recorded in the Analects, traditionally attributed to Confucius: "Only women and small men seem difficult to look after. If you keep them close, they become insubordinate; but if you keep them at a distance, they become resentful." Mencius (2001, p. 3B2) also said, "When a daughter marries, her mother instructs her. Sending her off at the gate, she cautions her, saying, 'When you go to your family, you must be respectful, and you must be cautious. Do not disobey your husband.' To regard obedience as proper is the Way of a wife or concubine." Thus, it became a commonplace that the contempt for and denigration of women in Chinese societies are the direct result of Confucian values.

However, prior to the advent of Confucianism, a patriarchal system in China had already been steadily developing in the Shang Dynasty, between 1600 and 1050 BCE (Gu, 1989). The system was hierarchical, with the male patriarch atop the hierarchy. Women were seen as possessions of men, and the division of labor between men and women was decided by men. Confucianism and the interpretation of the yin–yang idea that emerged centuries later were used by emperors and literati to reinforce male predominance in the Chinese society.

Despite Taiwan's participation in the globalized economy and modernization of archaic patriarchal laws, education, and industrialization, oppression of women remains a fact of life in the workplace in Taiwan. According to a government report (Council of Labor Affairs, 2000), 7.55% of females encounter sexual harassment in the workplace, but in 65% of these offences, the employer did not take any action against the offender. Just 8.09% of females in the workforce think their organization has rules and regulations on sexual harassment. In addition, the percentage of female labor that believes it encounters discrimination against it in pay raises, work arrangement, promotion, and performance evaluation is 6.7, 19.2, 3, and 2.7, respectively. Studies have also shown that women with higher education are dissatisfied with the discriminatory work arrangement and opportunities for career development they face (e.g., Lien, 2005). All these suggest that women employees in Taiwan have not received treatment equal to that of their male counterparts.

However, several factors have increased the proportion of females in the workplace in Taiwan. The first of these is improved educational opportunities for females. According to a report (Directorate-General of Budget, Accounting, and Statistics, 2000), in 1999 females accounted for 48.8% of the population in Taiwan, but accounted for 51.4% of the students studying toward a higher degree. A trend has become clear: more women were awarded with and studying toward higher degrees in 1999 than in 1989 (Table 1). This has an effect on workforce participation rates of women, because women with higher degrees tend to seek a career in the workplace. Thus, it can be hypothesized that,

**Hypothesis 1.** The proportion of females in the workplace in Taiwan is increasing over time.

In addition to education, changing the legal environment is another way the Taiwan government attempts to secure female participation in the workplace. In 2002, the legislature mandated that no discrimination based on gender be

***Table 1.*** Degrees Awarded and Work Participation of Women in Taiwan in 1989 and 1999.

|  | 1989 | 1999 |
|---|---|---|
| Number of women as a percentage of the population with age above 15 and awarded with the following degrees | | |
| Junior high or below | 60.6 | 46.4 |
| Senior high | 28.4 | 33.3 |
| College or above | 11.0 | 20.3 |
| Number of female students studying toward a higher degree (in thousands) | 219 | 504 |
| Number of females as a percentage of total students studying toward a higher degree | 47.4 | 51.4 |
| Number of female students in postgraduate programs (in thousands) | 5 | 40 |
| Number of women in the workforce (in millions) | 3.16 | 3.86 |
| Participation of women in the workforce | 45.4 | 46.0 |

allowed in the workplace, including the offering of job opportunities. Of course, exactly how the law should be enforced has been the subject of much discussion both in the legislature and in the society at large (Wu & Lin, 2002). However, the law will certainly affect business operations in Taiwan.

Other factors may also contribute to an increase in the proportion of females in the workplace. National cultural change under the trend of globalization is one. Since 1990s, Taiwan has witnessed notable changes in its cultural traits, from being hierarchical and collectivist (Hofstede, 1997) to becoming more individualistic and egalitarian (Huang, 2001; Bae, Chen, Wan, Lawler, & Walumbwa, 2003). These new cultural traits are more often observed among those of the younger generation, who may be educated in the United States and who become the major entrepreneurial and professional elites of technology-based companies (e.g., information technology (IT) companies) in Taiwan. Following such changes, modern management systems are introduced and female participation in these companies is encouraged.

Furthermore, over the years companies in Taiwan, especially technology-based manufacturers, have developed themselves as manufacturers for Western multinationals. These technology-based manufacturers are exemplified by electrical and electronic companies, which include IT product manufacturers. The electrical and electronics industry has developed and grown so rapidly that in 1983 its annual production surpassed that of the textile industry and became the largest industry in Taiwan. In 2004 the annual production of the electrical and electronics industry was 169.8 billion U.S. dollars, an amount accounting for almost half (49.19%) of the total production of all manufacturing industries in Taiwan. Exports of this industry in that same year reached 86.62 billion U.S. dollars, half (49.8%) of Taiwan's total exports. Close cooperation between local and Western firms has led to companies in the electrical and electronics industry developing modern management systems. Using data collected in the industry in Taiwan, analysis shows that companies are becoming receptive to and starting to implement high-performance work systems (Huang, 2001; Uen, 1997), including emphasizing gender diversity (Bae et al., 2003). Thus, the electrical and electronics industry representing the rapid-growing technology sector in Taiwan should have a higher rate of female participation in the workforce and experience a higher rate of increase in the proportion of females than other industries in Taiwan.

**Hypothesis 2.** Increases in the proportion of females in the workplace should be more rapid in the electrical and electronics industry in Taiwan than in other industries.

Given the increases in the proportion of females in the workplace, how is organizational performance impacted? At a time when companies in Taiwan are undergoing changes to emphasize innovation and customer responsiveness, female participation in the workforce should increase the talent pool and cognitive diversity of these companies and thus increase chances that these goals are achieved. However, evidence suggests that issues of gender equity are not emphasized in the courses at the elementary, junior high, and senior high levels. Although students express their interest in the issues, teachers still prefer discussing biological health issues (Hong, Lawrenz, & Veach, 2005). If the concept of gender equity is not instilled in the formal education system at an early age, problems will still remain regarding how men and women should work together and appreciate each other's talents and abilities. Although the proportion of females may increase, women may be isolated and not treated fairly by their male colleagues and superiors. The mere presence of women in the workplace may not contribute to organizational performance. On the contrary, because of the time needed to coordinate and communicate between the two groups of organizational members, organizational performance may suffer. Social identity theory can then be applied to explain the negative impact of the proportion of females on performance. Due to a lack of investigation into the relationship between the proportion of females and organizational performance, two competing hypotheses are proposed based on social identity theory and the resource-based view:

**Hypothesis 3a.** The proportion of females in organizations is negatively related with organizational performance.

**Hypothesis 3b.** The proportion of females in organizations is positively related with organizational performance.

## RESEARCH METHODS

### Sources of Data

Two sets of government databases were used for the empirical investigation. The two databases, provided by the Directorate-General of Budget, Accounting, and Statistics, Executive Yuan, Taiwan, contain statistics for individual manufacturing companies in 1996 and 2001. Every 5 years, the Directorate-General of Budget, Accounting, and Statistics employs investigators to pay visits to a large sample of manufacturing companies randomly selected from all indigenous manufacturers for data collection. The latest two rounds of data collection took place in 1996 and 2001. The 1996 and 2001 databases contain data of 8,622 and 8,731 manufacturing companies, respectively. Thus, the large sample size is suitable for our empirical investigation.

For the 1996 database the size of the companies ranged from 1 employee to 20,150 employees, with a mean size of 120 employees (standard deviation = 503.62). The age of the companies ranged from 0 years (newly established) to 84 years, with a mean age of 13.62 years (standard deviation = 9.53). For the 2001 database the size of the companies ranged from 1 employee to 16,691 employees, with a mean size of 142 employees (standard deviation = 501.95). The age of the companies ranged from 0 years (newly established) to 89 years, with a mean age of 17.14 years (standard deviation = 10.31).

The 1996 database contains companies from 22 major manufacturing industries identified by the government. They are food and drinks, tobacco, textile, clothing, leather, timber and bamboo products, furniture, paper, printing, chemical material, chemical products, petroleum and coal products, rubber products, plastic products, nonmetal mineral products, basic metal, metal products, mechanical equipment, electrical and electronics, transportation vehicles, precision machinery, and other. The 2001 industry database was expanded into 24 categories. The rapid growth of the electrical and electronics industry led the government to divide this industry into 3. The 3 new industries are computers, telecommunications, and audiovisual products; electronic parts and components; and electrical mechanical products.

### Operationalization of Variables

#### The Proportion of Females

This variable is defined as the percentage of female members in an organization. The two databases provide statistics for two member groups within each of the organizations: managers, professionals, and administrative personnel as the first category and operatives and first-line workers as the second category. Thus, we are able to arrive at the percentage of women as managers, professional, and administrative personnel (administrative personnel for short) and the percentage of women as operatives and first-line workers (workers for short).

## Organizational Performance

Organizational performance is represented by company financial performance. Specifically, return on asset is used for the statistical examination.

## Control Variables

The control variables used are organizational strategy, human resource investment, percentage of liability, age and size of the company, and industry. Organizational strategy is represented by company R&D expenditures as a percentage of revenues, which indicates the extent to which a company pursues product differentiation for its competitive advantage (Miller, 1988). Human resource investment is represented by company salaries as a percentage of revenues, which indicates the extent to which a company is willing to pay its human resources for their talents and efforts (Pfeffer, 1998; Youndt, Subramaniam, & Snell, 2004). Company liability as a percentage of asset (percentage of liability), a measure of operational risk of a company, is also included as another control variable.

Size of a company is defined as the natural logarithm of the number of employees (Blau & Schoenherr, 1971; Snell, 1992). This logarithmic scale is also used to normalize the size variable, which might otherwise be badly skewed (Miller & Droge, 1986). Dummy variables (1 and 0) are assigned for each of the 22 industries in the 1996 database and each of the 24 industries in the 2001 database. When a company belongs to a certain industry, e.g., food and drinks, this industry is coded as 1, and the remaining industries are coded as 0.

# FINDINGS

Table 2 provides the means, standard deviations, and correlations of the study variables, including two measures of the proportion of females, return on asset, and control variables, including firm size, age, organizational strategy, human resource investment, and percentage of liability. Hypothesis 1 postulates a trend of increase in the proportion of females in organizations. *t*-tests were performed on the mean percentage of women as administrative personnel and the mean percentage of women as workers in manufacturing industries in 1996 and 2001. Table 3 presents the results. It can be seen that the percentage of women as administrative personnel increased between 1996 and 2001, but the percentage of women as workers decreased over the same time period. Hypothesis 1 is partially supported.

*Table 2.* Descriptive Statistics and Correlations.

| Variable | Mean | SD | 1 | 2 | 3 | 4 | 5 | 6 | 7 |
|---|---|---|---|---|---|---|---|---|---|
| *1996 Data*[a] | | | | | | | | | |
| 1. Percentage of women as administrative personnel | 0.44 | 0.26 | | | | | | | |
| 2. Percentage of women as workers | 0.39 | 0.28 | 0.08 | | | | | | |
| 3. Return on asset | 0.04 | 0.20 | 0.01 | -0.00 | | | | | |
| 4. Log of number of employees | 1.49 | 0.67 | 0.01 | 0.10 | -0.03 | | | | |
| 5. Company age | 13.62 | 9.53 | -0.07 | -0.02 | -0.04 | 0.41 | | | |
| 6. Salaries as a percentage of revenues | 0.21 | 0.19 | -0.05 | 0.04 | -0.08 | -0.23 | -0.12 | | |
| 7. R&D expenditures as a percentage of revenues | 0.00 | 0.05 | -0.03 | 0.01 | -0.04 | 0.05 | -0.04 | 0.14 | |
| 8. Percentage of liability | 0.50 | 0.57 | 0.03 | 0.01 | -0.71 | 0.10 | 0.05 | -0.06 | -0.02 |
| *2001 Data*[b] | | | | | | | | | |
| 1. Percentage of women as administrative personnel | 0.47 | 0.21 | | | | | | | |
| 2. Percentage of women as workers | 0.38 | 0.27 | 0.06 | | | | | | |
| 3. Return on asset | 0.03 | 0.12 | 0.02 | 0.03 | | | | | |
| 4. Log of number of employees | 1.72 | 0.54 | -0.13 | 0.13 | -0.04 | | | | |
| 5. Company age | 17.14 | 10.31 | -0.07 | -0.02 | -0.07 | 0.28 | | | |
| 6. Salaries as a percentage of revenues | 0.17 | 0.29 | -0.00 | 0.03 | -0.13 | -0.04 | -0.04 | | |
| 7. R&D expenditures as a percentage of revenues | 0.01 | 0.16 | 0.00 | -0.00 | -0.14 | 0.01 | -0.07 | 0.69 | |
| 8. Percentage of liability | 0.55 | 0.27 | 0.04 | 0.00 | -0.28 | 0.01 | 0.01 | -0.06 | -0.07 |

[a]$N = 8622$. Correlations with absolute values greater than .04 are significant at the .001 level; those greater than .03 are significant at the .01 level; those greater than .02 are significant at the .05 level (all two-tailed tests).
[b]$N = 8731$. Correlations with absolute values greater than .04 are significant at the .001 level; those greater than .03 are significant at the .01 level; those greater than .02 are significant at the .05 level (all two-tailed tests).

Hypothesis 2 postulates the rate of increase in the proportion of females in the electrical and electronics industry to be more rapid than in other industries. As reported earlier the electrical and electronics industry in 1996 was expanded into computer, telecommunications, and audiovisual products; electronic parts and components; and electrical mechanical products industries in 2001. Increases in the proportion of females are compared to those in other industries, which include food and drinks, tobacco, textile, clothing, leather, timber and bamboo products, furniture, paper, printing, chemical material, chemical products, petroleum and coal products, rubber products, plastic products, nonmetal mineral products, basic metal, metal products, and mechanical equipment industries. Table 4 presents the results.

***Table 3.*** A Comparison of the Proportion of Women in Organizations between 1996 and 2001.

| Measure | 1996 | 2001 | $t$-Value |
|---|---|---|---|
| Mean percentage of women as administrative personnel | 44 (SD = 26; N = 8,203) | 47 (SD = 21; N = 8,705) | 33.96*** |
| Mean percentage of women as workers | 39 (SD = 28; N = 8,546) | 38 (SD = 27; N = 8,704) | 8.67*** |

***$p < .001$.

***Table 4.*** A Comparison of the Proportion of Women in Organizations between 1996 and 2001 by Industry Sectors.

| Measures | 1996 | 2001 | $t$-Values |
|---|---|---|---|
| Mean percentage of women as administrative personnel in the electrical and electronics industry | 45 (SD = 21; N = 1,270) | 47 (SD = 19; N = 1,570) | 13.01*** |
| Mean percentage of women as administrative personnel in other industries | 44 (SD = 26; N = 6,065) | 47 (SD = 22; N = 6,206) | 28.21*** |
| Mean percentage of women as workers in the electrical and electronics industry[a] | 54 (SD = 27; N = 1,295) | 51 (SD = 27; N = 1,565) | 10.95*** |
| Mean percentage of women as workers in other industries | 35 (SD = 28; N = 6,349) | 34 (SD = 27; N = 6,211) | 7.40*** |

[a]The computer, telecommunications, and audiovisual products industry, electronic parts and components industry, and electrical mechanical products industry are combined into the electrical and electronics industry.
***$p < .001$.

It was found that increases in the percentage of women as administrative personnel in both the electrical and electronics and other industries are statistically significant. However, the increase from 1996 to 2001 in the electrical and electronics industry was 2%, as opposed to 3% in other industries. The rate of increase in the rapid-growing electrical and electronics industry was not higher than that in other industries. Furthermore, the percentage of women as workers in both industry sectors was on the decrease. Hypothesis 2 is not supported.

Hypotheses 3a and 3b are competing hypotheses, with one postulating a negative relationship between the proportion of females and organizational performance and the other a positive relationship. Table 5 presents regression results for these hypotheses. Analyses were completed for a return on asset measure of organizational performance using both 1996 and 2001 data. According to Table 5, the percentage of women as administrative personnel is consistently positively associated with organizational performance, whereas the effect of the percentage of women as workers is not consistent. Hypothesis 3b is partially supported. The percentage of women as workers is not associated with organizational performance in 1996, and the relationship is positive in 2001. Hypothesis 3a is not supported.

## DISCUSSION AND IMPLICATIONS

This chapter starts with an examination of the proportion of females in the manufacturing industries in Taiwan and proceeds with an examination of the applicability of two competing theoretical perspectives, social identity theory and the resource-based view, in the same industrial contexts. The examination of the proportion of females in organizations extends previous research in gender diversity in management. Findings of this chapter have the following implications.

First, the job categories in the manufacturing industries in Taiwan that show increases in the proportion of females are managers, professionals, and administrative personnel. In general, as time has passed, fewer and fewer women have chosen to be operatives and workers in organizations. As more women receive higher education, this may influence their choice of jobs after their graduation.

Second, the increase in the proportion of females as managers, professionals, and administrative personnel is not just observed in the more rapidly growing industries, long seen as attracting highly educated job candidates due to their booming success, but across all industries.

***Table 5.*** Regression Analysis: Return on Asset.

| Variable | Return on Asset | |
|---|---|---|
| | Model 1 | Model 2 |
| *1996 Data* | | |
| Percentage of women as administrative personnel | | 0.03(3.32)** |
| Percentage of women as workers | | −0.00(−0.12) |
| Log of number of employees | 0.04(4.65)*** | 0.04(4.34)*** |
| Age | −0.04(−4.18)*** | −0.03(−3.58)*** |
| Salaries as a percentage of revenues | −0.12(−14.74)*** | −0.12(−14.85)*** |
| R&D expenditures as a percentage of revenues | −0.04(−5.34)*** | −0.04(−5.56)*** |
| Percentage of liability | −0.72(−95.60)*** | −0.74(−98.96)*** |
| Industries: | | |
| Food/drinks | −0.02(−1.63) | −0.01(−1.35) |
| Tobacco | −0.01(−0.75) | −0.01(−0.84) |
| Textile | 0.02(2.14)* | 0.01(1.61) |
| Clothing | 0.01(1.27) | 0.00(0.16) |
| Leather | 0.00(0.35) | 0.00(0.52) |
| Timber | 0.02(1.82) | 0.01(1.70) |
| Furniture | 0.01(1.15) | 0.01(0.75) |
| Paper | −0.01(−0.60) | −0.00(−0.50) |
| Printing | −0.02(−2.27)* | −0.02(−2.14)* |
| Chemical materials | −0.00(−0.50) | −0.01(−0.72) |
| Chemical products | 0.01(1.57) | 0.01(1.53) |
| Petroleum/coal products | 0.00(0.55) | 0.00(0.39) |
| Rubber | −0.01(−0.83) | −0.01(−0.82) |
| Plastic | −0.02(−1.76) | −0.02(−2.10)* |
| Nonmetal mineral products | −0.01(−0.60) | −0.01(−0.91) |
| Basic metal | −0.02(−2.20)* | −0.02(−2.69)** |
| Metal products | 0.03(2.93)** | 0.02(2.53)* |
| Mechanical equipment | 0.01(1.06) | 0.01(1.10) |
| Transportation vehicles | 0.01(1.10) | 0.01(1.24) |
| Precision machinery | 0.00(0.39) | 0.01(0.67) |
| Other | 0.01(0.84) | 0.01(0.60) |
| Adjusted $R^2$ | 0.52 | 0.55 |
| F | 363.43*** | 360.95*** |
| df | 26          8,595 | 28          8,098 |

| Variable | Return on Asset | |
|---|---|---|
| | Model 3 | Model 4 |
| *2001 Data* | | |
| Percentage of women as administrative personnel | | 0.02(2.41)* |
| Percentage of women as workers | | 0.06(4.97)*** |
| Log of number of employees | 0.00(0.13) | −0.00(−0.13) |

**Table 5.** (*Continued*)

| Variable | Return on Asset | |
|---|---|---|
| | Model 3 | Model 4 |
| Age | $-0.09(-8.65)^{***}$ | $-0.09(-8.34)^{***}$ |
| Salaries as a percentage of revenues | $-0.17(-15.17)^{***}$ | $-0.17(-15.55)^{***}$ |
| R&D expenditures as a percentage of revenues | $-0.09(-8.12)^{***}$ | $-0.09(-7.76)^{***}$ |
| Percentage of liability | $-0.32(-31.16)^{***}$ | $-0.32(-31.41)^{***}$ |
| Industries: | | |
| Food/drinks | $-0.04(-3.53)^{***}$ | $-0.06(-4.55)^{***}$ |
| Tobacco | $-0.01(-0.48)$ | $-0.01(-0.49)$ |
| Textile | $-0.03(-2.15)^{*}$ | $-0.04(-3.33)^{**}$ |
| Clothing | $0.01(0.62)$ | $-0.02(-1.34)$ |
| Leather | $-0.01(-0.69)$ | $-0.02(-1.60)$ |
| Timber | $-0.01(-0.86)$ | $-0.02(-1.46)$ |
| Furniture | $-0.01(-0.79)$ | $-0.01(-1.25)$ |
| Paper | $-0.04(-3.85)^{***}$ | $-0.05(-4.23)^{***}$ |
| Printing | $0.02(1.91)$ | $0.02(1.55)$ |
| Chemical materials | $-0.03(-2.51)^{*}$ | $-0.03(-2.39)^{*}$ |
| Chemical products | $0.02(1.80)$ | $0.01(1.04)$ |
| Petroleum/coal products | $-0.01(-0.54)$ | $-0.01(-0.51)$ |
| Rubber | $-0.01(-0.74)$ | $-0.01(-1.19)$ |
| Plastic | $-0.02(-1.47)$ | $-0.03(-2.36)^{*}$ |
| Nonmetal mineral products | $-0.04(-3.04)^{**}$ | $-0.04(-3.25)^{**}$ |
| Basic metal | $-0.05(-4.25)^{***}$ | $-0.05(-4.41)^{***}$ |
| Metal products | $0.02(1.66)$ | $0.01(0.88)$ |
| Computers | $-0.06(-5.35)^{***}$ | $-0.08(-6.22)^{***}$ |
| Electronics | $-0.07(-5.51)^{***}$ | $-0.09(-6.91)^{***}$ |
| Electrical | $-0.02(-1.63)$ | $-0.03(-2.57)^{*}$ |
| Transportation vehicles | $-0.01(-1.10)$ | $-0.02(-1.45)$ |
| Precision machinery | $-0.00(-0.35)$ | $-0.02(-1.40)$ |
| Other | $-0.01(-1.21)$ | $-0.02(-2.15)^{*}$ |
| Adjusted $R^2$ | 0.15 | 0.15 |
| F | $54.14^{***}$ | $52.15^{***}$ |
| df | 28        8,691 | 30        8,636 |

$^{*}p<.05,$
$^{**}p<.01,$
$^{***}p<.001.$

This suggests that highly educated women do not have specific industry preferences. It is clear that not just advanced and relatively Westernized high-technology firms, but society in general in Taiwan is becoming more receptive to women in the workplace, especially in managerial, professional, and administrative jobs.

Third, the proportion of females as managers, professionals, and administrative personnel is positively related to organizational performance. This may suggest that in Taiwan the resource-based view is a better fit for this job category. As human resources for this island, women should be encouraged to work as administrative personnel and professionals and to move up the career ladder to serve in managerial positions.

Fourth, the fact that the percentage of women as workers is not associated with organizational performance in 1996, but positively associated with organizational performance in 2001, is intriguing. Again, this could point to the fact that society is changing. Previously, companies hired women for low-value-added jobs such as operatives and workers to reduce personnel costs through pay differentials between men and women. Social identity theory may be applicable under such circumstances. Women, seen as physically inferior creatures, played insignificant roles in organizations so that how they performed had only trivial effects on financial performance. However, manufacturing companies in Taiwan have learned to appreciate and use the talents and abilities of women in a way that improves organizational performance. Women, once thought of as liabilities for companies, have gradually become important human resources.

## Limitations

This study has limitations. First, regrettably, the databases used for the empirical investigation do not provide detailed breakdowns of the data on female participation in the workplace by job categories. Presumably, female participation in managerial positions can differ from that in professional and administrative jobs. However, the data provide only the total number of women in the two broad job categories in an organization. Thus, this study has not been able to explore the contribution of the female manager in Taiwan to the financial performance of her organization.

Second, although this study uses two databases with a 5-year time lag to examine trends in the proportion of females in organizations, the databases do not allow longitudinal examinations of individual companies through time, as information regarding company identity has been removed by the government. The positive associations revealed from the analyses are cross-sectional by nature. Further investigation into these associations is still needed to unveil the underlying causal mechanisms.

## CONCLUSION

This is an early attempt to examine with scientific rigor the proportion of females in the workplace and its effect on organizational performance in Taiwan. Such an examination has been lacking for the Taiwan economy. The contribution of this study does not lie just in its examination of changes in the proportion of females across differing major job categories, but also in its examination of the effect of the proportion of females on organizational performance as an organization-wide phenomenon. The latter has been called for (e.g., Dwyer et al., 2003), but no previous research has followed the line of enquiry undertaken by this study.

Further, this study suggests, in contrast to previous research that concludes that diversity is context-dependent in its effect on organizational performance, that in Taiwan women seem to have a beneficial effect on organizational performance regardless of industrial contexts. Although this study is cross-sectional and no causal relationship should be inferred, the findings are encouraging. The findings show support for the resource-based view and suggest the importance of ongoing research following the line of enquiry reported in this chapter.

## REFERENCES

Bae, J., Chen, S.-j., Wan, T. W. D., Lawler, J. J., & Walumbwa, F. O. (2003). Human resource strategy and firm performance in Pacific Rim countries. *International Journal of Human Resource Management, 14*(8), 1308–1332.

Barney, J. (1991). Firm resources and sustained competitive advantage. *Journal of Management, 17*, 99–120.

Blau, P. M. (1977). *Inequality and heterogeneity*. New York: Free Press.

Blau, P. M., & Schoenherr, R. (1971). *The structure of organizations*. New York: Basic Books.

Bontis, N., & Fitz-enz, J. (2002). Intellectual capital ROI: A causal map of human capital antecedents and consequents. *Journal of Intellectual Capital, 3*(3), 223–247.

Bower, J. (1970). *Managing the resource allocation process*. Boston: Harvard Business School Press.

Burgelman, R. A. (1983). A model of interaction of strategic behavior, corporate context, and the concept of strategy. *Academy of Management Review, 8*, 61–70.

Burgelman, R. A. (1994). Fading memories: A process theory of strategic business exit in dynamic environments. *Administrative Science Quarterly, 39*, 24–56.

Clark, K. J., & Wang, R. R. (2004). A Confucian defense of gender equity. *Journal of American Academy of Religion, 72*(2), 395–422.

Council of Labor Affairs. (2000). *Investigation report on women equity at employment* (in Chinese). Taiwan: Council of Labor Affairs.

Directorate-General of Budget, Accounting and Statistics, Monthly Bulletin of Statistics. (2000). *The general situation of women in education and employment*. Taiwan: Directorate-General of Budget, Accounting and Statistics.

Dwyer, S., Richard, O. C., & Chadwick, K. (2003). Gender diversity in management and firm performance: The influence of growth orientation and organizational culture. *Journal of Business Research, 56*, 1009–1019.

Finkelstein, S., & Hambrick, D. C. (1996). *Strategic leadership: Top executives and their effects on organizations*. St. Paul, MN: West.

Grant, R. M. (1996). Toward a knowledge-based theory of the firm. *Strategic Management Journal, 17*(Winter Special Issue), 109–122.

Gu, Y.-L. (1989). Examining women status in present-day Taiwan (in Chinese). *Social Construction, 69*, 20–22.

Hart, S. (1992). An integrative framework for strategy-making processes. *Academy of Management Review, 17*(2), 327–351.

Hart, S., & Banbury, C. (1994). How strategy-making processes can make a difference. *Strategic Management Journal, 15*, 251–269.

Hofstede, G. (1997). *Cultures and organizations: Software of the mind*. NY: McGraw-Hill.

Hong, Z.-R., Lawrenz, F., & Veach, P. M. (2005). Investigating perceptions of gender education by students and teachers in Taiwan. *Journal of Educational Research, 98*(3), 156–163.

Huang, T. (2001). Human resource management in Taiwan. In: P. S. Budhwar & A. D. Yaw (Eds), *Human resource management in developing countries* (pp. 56–74). London: Routledge.

Imai, M. (1986). *Kaizen*. New York: Random House.

Jackson, S. E., & Joshi, A. (2001). Research on domestic and international diversity in organizations: A merger that works? In: N. Anderson, D. Ones, H. Sinangil & C. Visweswaran (Eds), *Handbook of work and organizational psychology* (pp. 206–231). London: Sage.

Jackson, S. E., Joshi, A., & Erhardt, N. L. (2003). Recent research on team and organizational diversity: SWOT analysis and implications. *Journal of Management, 29*(6), 801–830.

Kilduff, M., Angelmar, R., & Mehra, A. (2000). Top management-team diversity and firm performance: Examining the role of cognitions. *Organization Science, 11*, 21–34.

Kochan, T., Bezrukova, K., Ely, R., Jackson, S., Joshi, A., Jehn, K., Leonard, J., Levine, D., & Thomas, D. (2003). The effects of diversity on business performance: Report of the diversity research network. *Human Resource Management, 42*(1), 3–21.

Lien, B. Y.-H. (2005). Career development and the needs of young college-educated women in Taiwan. *Journal of Career Development, 31*(3), 209–223.

McKelvey, B. (1983). *Organizational systematics: Taxonomy, evolution and classifications*. Berkeley, CA: University of California Press.

Mencius. (2001). Mengzi (Mencius). In: P. Ivanhoe, & B. Van Noorden (Trans.), *Readings in classical Chinese philosophy* (pp. 111–155). New York: Seven Bridges Press.

Miller, C. C., Burke, L. M., & Glick, W. H. (1998). Cognitive diversity among upper-echelon executives: Implications for strategic decision processes. *Strategic Management Journal, 19*, 39–58.

Miller, D. (1988). Relating Porter's business strategies to environments and structure: Analysis and performance implications. *Academy of Management Journal, 31*(2), 280–308.

Miller, D., & Droge, C. (1986). Psychological and traditional determinants of structure. *Administrative Science Quarterly, 31*, 539–560.

Noe, R. A., Hollenbeck, J. R., Gerhart, B., & Wright, P. M. (2003). *Human resource management: Gaining a competitive advantage* (4th ed.). Boston: McGraw-Hill.

Parnes, H. S. (1984). *People power*. Beverly Hills, CA: Sage.

Pelled, L. H., Eisenhardt, K. M., & Xin, K. R. (1999). Exploring the black box: An analysis of work group diversity, conflict, and performance. *Administrative Science Quarterly, 44*, 1–28.

Pfeffer, J. (1994). *Competitive advantage through people: Unleashing the power of the workforce*. Boston, MA: Harvard Business School Press.

Pfeffer, J. (1998). *The human equation: Building profits by putting people first*. Boston, MA: Harvard Business School Press.

Richard, O. C. (2000). Racial diversity, business strategy, and firm performance: A resource-based view. *Academy of Management Journal, 43*(2), 164–177.

Richard, O. C., Barnett, T., Dwyer, S., & Chadwick, K. (2004). Cultural diversity in management, firm performance, and the moderating role of entrepreneurial orientation dimensions. *Academy of Management Journal, 47*(2), 255–266.

Richard, O. C., McMillan, A., Chadwick, K., & Dwyer, S. (2003). Employing an innovation strategy in racially diverse workforces. *Group and Organization Management, 28*(1), 107–126.

Snell, S. A. (1992). Control theory in strategic human resource management: The mediating effect of administrative information. *Academy of Management Journal, 35*(2), 292–327.

Stringer, D. M. (1995). The role of women in workplace diversity consulting. *Journal of Organizational Change Management, 8*(1), 44–51.

Tajfel, H. (1982). *Social identity and intergroup relations*. Cambridge, UK: Cambridge University Press.

Tajfel, H., & Turner, J. (1985). The social identity of intergroup behavior. In: S. Worchel & W. Austin (Eds), *Psychology and intergroup relations* (pp. 7–24). Chicago: Nelson-Hall.

Teece, D. J., Pisano, G., & Shuen, A. (1997). Dynamic capabilities and strategic management. *Strategic Management Journal, 18*, 509–533.

Tsui, A., Egan, T., & O'Reilly, C. (1992). Being different: Relational demography and organizational attachment. *Administrative Science Quarterly, 37*, 549–579.

Uen, J. (1997). *The configurations of human resource systems and their implications for organizational performance in high-tech companies in Taiwan*. Working paper, National Sun Yat-sen University, Kaohsiung, Taiwan.

Ulrich, D., & Lake, D. (1990). *Organizational capability*. New York: Wiley.

Wernerfelt, B. (1984). A resource based view of the firm. *Strategic Management Journal, 5*, 171–180.

Williams, K., & O'Reilly, C. (1998). Forty years of diversity research: A review. In: B. M. Staw & L. L. Cummings (Eds), *Research in organizational behavior* (pp. 77–140). Greenwich, CT: JAI Press.

Wright, P., Ferris, S. P., Hiller, J. S., & Kroll, M. (1995). Competitiveness through management of diversity: Effects on stock price valuation. *Academy of Management Journal, 38*(1), 272–287.

Wright, P. M., McMahan, G. C., & McWilliams, A. (1994). Human resources and sustained competitive advantage: A resource-based perspective. *International Journal of Human Resource Management, 5*(2), 301–326.

Wu, C.-J., & Lin, C.-C. (2002). Gender equity at work vs. impacts on women at employment (in Chinese). *Central Daily News*, March 9.

Youndt, M. A., Subramaniam, M., & Snell, S. A. (2004). Intellectual capital profiles: An examination of investments and returns. *Journal of Management Studies, 41*(2), 335–361.

# CROSS-NATIONAL DIFFERENCES IN THE DETERMINATION OF PAY FAIRNESS JUDGMENTS: DO CULTURAL DIFFERENCES PLAY A ROLE?

Greg Hundley and Carlos Sánchez Runde

## ABSTRACT

*Data from samples of managers from eight countries, Thailand, Nigeria, Philippines, Peru, Uruguay, Argentina, Spain, and the United States, are used to explore cross-national differences in how individuals make judgments about an individual's pay. A policy-capturing instrument is used to elicit judgments about the ways that variations in individual employee job performance, business unit performance, seniority, schooling, and need affect judgments about pay fairness. Significant between-country differences are found in the sensitivities of pay fairness judgments. However, these differences are not well explained by differences in individualism/collectivism reflected either by a priori categorizations of national culture or direct measures of horizontal/vertical collectivism. Implications for the explanation of cross-national differences are explored.*

The Global Diffusion of Human Resource Practices: Institutional and Cultural Limits
Advances in International Management, Volume 21, 191–210
Copyright © 2008 by Emerald Group Publishing Limited
All rights of reproduction in any form reserved
ISSN: 1571-5027/doi:10.1016/S1571-5027(08)00008-9

# INTRODUCTION

This study is concerned with the estimation and explanation of cross-national differences in the ways that individuals make judgments about the fairness of an employee's pay. For global businesses confronting the tension between the need to integrate global business processes efficiently and the need to adapt to the demands of local conditions (Bartlett & Ghoshal, 2002), the degree to which similar human resource management practices can be used in different national contexts is of great interest. Because the perceived fairness of pay differentials is an important element of pay satisfaction (Folger & Konovsky, 1989) and a key ingredient in a successful compensation system (Milkovich & Newman, 2005), a better understanding of cross-national differences in pay fairness judgments offers insight into whether different pay systems should be applied in different national contexts. Whereas cross-country similarities in pay fairness judgments support the use of common methods for determining relative pay, cross-country differences verify accounts of pay systems applicable in one nation failing in others (Ouchi, 1981) and support recommendations that pay policies should be targeted to local conditions.

We explore whether differences in the determinants of pay fairness judgments can be explained by differences in national culture. Culture is frequently implicated as a cause of cross-national differences in ways that organizational members respond to organizational characteristics. The most common approach compares samples from a very small number of countries, typically two or three, and ascertains the degree to which the findings are consistent with country differences in a cultural characteristic – such as individualism/collectivism – that has been hypothesized to affect reaction to the practice (Oyserman, Coon, & Kemmelmeier, 2002). Typically, recourse is made to a priori characterization of country cultures, and there is no information as to whether between-sample differences arise from between-sample differences in the relevant cultural attributes. This is particularly problematic in organizational research in which country samples are not representative of the country's population and/or differ from those samples used in the earlier studies, such as those of Hofstede (1981, 1983), that have been used to classify country cultures. Consequently, we collect information on cultural values directly from the samples that provide reactions to the pay practices, thus enabling an assessment as to whether the cross-country differences that are observed in the sample can actually be attributed to cultural differences.

# DETERMINANTS OF PERCEPTIONS OF PAY FAIRNESS: THE RESEARCH RECORD

This study extends and advances the lines of inquiry pursued by Bond, Leung, and Wan (1982), Kim, Park, and Suzuki (1990), Hundley and Kim (1997), and Zhou and Martocchio (2001), who have investigated the way in which individual performance affected judgments about reward allocation in the United States and some Asian nations. Bond et al. (1982) found that college students in the United States and Hong Kong used the equity principle for reward allocation; that is, they felt that a reward should increase as an individual's performance contribution increased. Kim et al. (1990), in a comparison of the United States, Japan, and Korea, found that adherence to the equity principle was more pronounced in the most individualistic of these countries (the United States) than it was in the most collectivistic (Korea). Hundley and Kim's (1997) comparison of Korean and U.S. business students found that a number of factors in addition to individual performance were used to make judgments about the fairness of an employee's pay, and examined the roles of seniority, educational attainment, family needs, and work effort. They concluded that differences in pay judgments between different national cultures would be better viewed as a matter of degree, rather than of absolute differences. Thus, for example, whereas individual performance had a larger impact in the United States, it also was a major factor in Korean judgments. Zhou and Martocchio (2001) found that both American and Chinese managers viewed individual performance as the main criterion for awarding bonuses, but unlike their American counterparts, the Chinese awarded bonuses to even the lower level performers.

The investigations conducted so far have several shortcomings. First, except for Zhou and Martocchio (2001), they involve comparisons of undergraduate business students. Proceeding directly from these samples to inferences about the effects of national culture on reactions to workplace practices is a hazardous exercise. Because business students in the United States and comparison countries have similar educational experiences, differences in their responses may be relatively small compared to differences observed between samples that are more representative of the national populations and/or do not share similar educational backgrounds that affect their responses to managerial issues. Because the samples are also likely to have relatively small differences in cultural values, the cross-country differences may underestimate the effects of the large cultural differences between typical members of the respective national populations.

Second, except for Hundley and Kim (1997), the previous studies have been confined to judgments about bonus allocations. In studying compensation decision making and analyzing employee responses, it is more appropriate to evaluate a wider range of pay determinants. Specifically, it is well known that individuals take stock of their overall relative level of pay compared to others (not just their bonus allocations). Any employee's pay level is best seen as the result of decisions on a number of key variables (or determinants) that determine a pay structure. Compensation experts (Milkovich & Newman, 2005) argue that a variety of factors go into determining relative pay and the ways that these variables translate into a pay structure affect perceptions of pay fairness. Third, studies so far do not provide any direct information about the aspects of national culture, if any, that affect judgments about pay fairness. In common with nearly all other findings of national differences in management practices, the results are explained by ex post resort to classifications of national cultures, such as the one provided by Hofstede (1981). Although cross-national differences in the standards for pay determination are observed, there has been no test as to whether or how these differences are actually attributable to different value systems, and there is no information as to the sorts of values that actually affect decision making about fair pay.

## THEORETICAL FRAMEWORK

The foundation of the study is provided by models of the factors that individuals use in making judgments about the fairness of an employee's pay:

$$j_i = \sum_{k=1}^{5} \beta_{ki} x_{ki} + \varepsilon_i$$

where $j_i$ is the $i$th respondent's judgment on pay fairness, which increases (decreases) with degree of perceived over (under) payment, and the $x_k$ are measures of fair pay determinants. The $\beta_{ki}$ are individual-specific regression coefficients capturing the sensitivity of judgments to changes in pay fairness determinants. Estimates of the sensitivities of pay fairness judgments within each country (or other relevant aggregation of individuals) are provided by the means, $\bar{\beta}_{ki}$, of the relevant individual-specific regression coefficients.

Five employee characteristics are assumed to affect judgments about the fairness of the pay received by an employee. These are: (1) individual job performance, (2) organizational performance, (3) seniority, (4) educational attainment, and (5) employee need. All of these variables are recognizable as factors that may explicitly or implicitly affect decisions that are relative in at least some of the countries in the study. Each has been the subject of considerable interest to human resource specialists and social scientists concerned with pay structures. Individual job performance has been the focus of psychological equity theorists (Adams, 1965) for whom judgments about the fairness of an individual's reward depend on how his or her ratio of inputs (job performance) to outcomes (financial rewards) compares with a similar ratio for an actual or hypothetical referent other. Seniority and educational level are primary examples of the status-attainment measures associated with the "status-value" school (Berger, Zelditch, Anderson, & Cohen, 1972; Cook, 1975; Jasso & Rossi, 1977; Jasso, 1978; Stolte, 1987), which argues that judgments about the fairness of an individual's income are determined by the degree to which the individual occupies positions and holds qualifications that are generally valued in his or her society. Employee need has been proposed as a factor by an eclectic group, including Deutsch (1975, 1985) and Jasso and Rossi (1977). Whereas organizational performance has apparently not been previously considered in the pay fairness literature, it is likely to be an important variable, given the interest in profit sharing and organization-wide variable pay programs in the United States and many other nations.

Like the earlier studies, our investigation of possible explanations of cross-national differences in the ways that pay fairness judgments are made starts with the possible effects of individualism and collectivism. Although precise definitions of individualism/collectivism vary somewhat (Hofstede, 1983; Earley, 1993; Oyserman et al., 2002), it is generally agreed that individualists emphasize independence of the self, value mostly their own success, and make decisions on an avowedly rational basis. Collectivists emphasize interdependence with others, give priority to the goals of the larger group with which they identify, and maintain communal relationships, even where relationships may not be seen, in a rational sense, as advantageous to themselves.

We explore a more refined, and arguably more powerful, approach to individualism/collectivism put forward by Triandis and his associates (Singelis, Triandis, Bhawuk, & Gelfland, 1995; Triandis, 1996; Triandis & Gelfland, 1998), who have proposed that individualism and collectivism be considered in two categories: vertical and horizontal. In vertical collectivism (VC) the individual's needs are subordinate to the interests of a larger abstract collectivity (such as work organization, family, or nation) with which the individual identifies. Horizontal collectivism (HC) is the degree to which the individual takes his or her peers (co-workers, friends, and neighbors) into account. Whereas many writers have assumed that collectivist values also support hierarchy (as in the case of East Asian countries with a strong Confucian heritage and that are assumed to be VC), there are examples in which collectivist values and horizontal values coexist (a commune, for example).

In a similar vein, two categories of individualists are proposed. In vertical individualism (VI) differences based on forms of legitimate competition are accepted, so that differences based on individual worth or contribution are valued. In horizontal individualism (HI) the individual is valued as a unique person, apart from others, without any regard to differences based on achievement or status.

Predictions about how culture affects the sensitivity of pay fairness judgments to each of the four types of fair pay determinants (individual performance, organizational performance, status attainment (measured by seniority and education), and employee need) are summarized in Fig. 1. Variations in individual job performance are expected to have a greater effect on perceived pay fairness in individualistic societies, with the impact greatest where there is a vertical orientation. Organizational performance, however, has a greater effect in collectivistic societies.

The importance of individual performance as a determinant of pay fairness increases with VI. Because individualists emphasize the independence of self, individual performance is more likely to be considered an appropriate unit for measuring performance. Because vertical individualists also believe that individuals can be different, they are more likely to accept differences in measured performance as legitimate or efficacious. Pay fairness judgments will be less sensitive to individual performance variations in more collectivistic societies in which individuals are seen as inherently interdependent and in which, for several reasons, individual performance may be seen as an inappropriate basis for rewards, for example, because it displaces individuals' attentions toward measured individual outputs and away from cooperative behaviors. There is evidence from single country samples in the United States (Moorman & Blakely, 1995) and China (Kirkman, Lowe, & Peng, 2000) that the propensity to value organizational citizenship behaviors (such as providing encouragement to fellow employees) increases with collectivism. Individual performance criteria are likely to be relatively less important for the horizontal collectivists who, as collectivists, will see individualistic criteria as reducing

|  | Individualistic (Independent self) | | Collectivistic (Interdependent self) | |
|---|---|---|---|---|
| Vertical (Different self) | Individual performance | [1] | Individual performance | [2,3] |
|  | Group performance | [3,4] | Group performance | [1] |
|  | Status attainment | [2] | Status attainment | [1] |
|  | Need | [3,4] | Need | [2] |
| Horizontal (Similar self) | Individual performance | [2,3] | Individual performance | [4] |
|  | Group performance | [3,4] | Group performance | [2] |
|  | Status attainment | [4] | Status attainment | [3] |
|  | Need | [3,4] | Need | [1] |

*Fig. 1.* The Effects of Horizontal/Vertical Individualism/Collectivism on the Relative Sensitivities of Pay Fairness Judgments to Variations in Pay Determination Criteria. *Note:* Numbers assigned to each characteristic show the ranking of national culture types according to the degree to which pay fairness judgments will be sensitive to variations in the employee characteristic. For example, the ranking of [1] given to job performance in the vertical individualism quadrant indicates that job performance has a greater effect on perceived fair pay in this culture than it does in any other.

group cooperation and harmony and, as horizontalists, will devalue individual differences in rewards.

Organizational performance is expected to have a greater impact on pay fairness judgments in more collectivistic groups. Because collectivists see individuals as interdependent, group performance is more likely to be seen as an appropriate basis for measuring performance. Because collectivists with a vertical orientation are more willing to countenance differences between individuals, they are also willing to accept differences in performance between aggregations or groups of people.

Status-related attributes are expected to be more important in vertical societies, with the effect of a specific attribute depending on the value attached to that attribute in society. Thus, as proposed by Hundley and Kim (1997), the individual's education level and seniority will have a much greater effect on judgments about the individual's pay level.

Employee need is expected to play a greater role in societies that are collectivistic rather than individualistic and to have the greatest effect in a horizontal collectivistic society. Because collectivists see individuals as being interdependent, the welfare of other individuals is more likely to have ramifications for others. To the extent that taking care of others fosters group harmony, collectivists will favor needs criteria.

## DATA AND RESEARCH METHOD

The data used to estimate the pay fairness model described above are generated by a policy-capturing method that was used to elicit judgments from sample members about the fairness of the pay received by hypothetical individuals presented in vignette form in an instrument entitled the Pay Fairness Survey. Each vignette describes a production manager who is paid a salary held constant in all cases within a country and is characterized by systematically varying levels of five factors hypothesized to affect judgment of the degree to which the individual is under (or over) paid: individual job performance relative to peers, profitability of the individual's business unit, seniority, educational level, and the number of family dependents. Each respondent provided his or her opinion about the fairness of a given pay level on a 9-point scale ranging from "greatly underpaid" ($-4$) to "greatly overpaid" ($+4$). The vignettes specify two alternative levels of each of the fair pay determinants, so that each respondent was provided with every possible combination of levels of the five determinants in $2^5 = 32$ vignettes. To fix a standard for evaluation, the questionnaire provided information regarding the "fair" annual salary level for a hypothetical manager characterized by average amounts of the five determinants. The fair salary was set to the average for the position according to local salary surveys and compensation experts. Instructions for the Pay Fairness Survey are provided in Appendix A, and the coding scheme for the values of the pay fairness determinants to be entered in the pay fairness regression model are provided in Appendix B.

To generate measures of horizontal and vertical individualism and collectivism, the respondents provided answers on the extent to which they agreed or disagreed with 25 items from the INDCOL questionnaire, an instrument developed by Triandis and colleagues (Singelis et al., 1995; Triandis, 1996; Triandis & Gelfland, 1998). Measures of HI, VI, HC, and VC were constructed from the means of the items specified in Appendix C.

## SAMPLES

Data were collected from samples of individuals with managerial experience enrolled in management development programs in eight countries: Thailand, Nigeria, Philippines, Peru, Uruguay, Argentina, Spain, and the United States.

## RESULTS

The means of the coefficients of the individual pay fairness models for each country estimated by Swamy's (1971) stochastic regression method are reported in Table 1.[1] For all pay fairness determinants, the coefficients were in the expected direction, with increases in individual performance rating, business unit profitability, seniority, education, and employee need

***Table 1.***   Effects of Pay Determinants on Judgments of Pay Fairness: Eight Countries.

| | Individual Performance | Profitability | Seniority | Education | Need | Hofstede Individual. Score |
|---|---|---|---|---|---|---|
| | $\|\beta_{1k}\|$ | $\|\beta_{2k}\|$ | $\|\beta_{3k}\|$ | $\|\beta_{4k}\|$ | $\|\beta_{5k}\|$ | |
| Thailand | 1.20** | .75** | 2.10** | 1.09** | .53** | 21 |
| Nigeria | 1.36** | .69** | 1.37** | 1.20** | .14 | n.a. |
| Philippines | 1.01** | .71** | 1.22** | .72** | .26* | 32 |
| Peru | 1.72** | 1.72** | 1.11** | 1.31** | .33** | 17 |
| Uruguay | 2.32** | 1.98** | .71** | .90** | .28** | 36 |
| Argentina | 1.91** | 1.48** | .91** | .88** | .29** | 46 |
| Spain | 1.72** | 2.20** | 1.04** | .49** | .33** | 54 |
| USA | 1.74** | .29* | 1.37** | .93** | .25* | 93 |

*Note:* Coefficients are given in absolute values. All original coefficients were negative.
$^*p<.001$
$^{**}p<.0001$

associated with a decrease in the extent to which the individual on a specific (fixed) salary is deemed to be overpaid or an increase in the extent to which the individual is underpaid. For convenience, absolute values of the mean coefficients are reported in Table 1. With the exception of the employee needs in the Nigerian model, all variables were adjudged to be statistically different from 0 at conventional levels of significance.

To begin assessment of cultural effects, Hofstede's oft-used scale of individualism/collectivism was assigned to the seven countries for which it was available. Four of these (Thailand, Philippines, Peru, and Uruguay) are low in individualism. Nigeria, which was excluded from Hofstede's studies, is categorized as collectivistic based on other evidence (Oyserman et al., 2002). Argentina and Spain are around the midpoint based on Hofstede's scale and the United States is the most individualistic of all countries.

At this level, there are some indications of support for the hypothesis that pay fairness judgments are less sensitive to individual performance in the more collectivistic countries. The individual performance coefficients for the three non-Latin collectivist nations (Thailand, Nigeria, Philippines) are smaller than the coefficients for the other nations. The pattern is not complete, however, as the two Latin nations classified as highly collectivistic (Peru and Uruguay) have sizable coefficients – at least as big as those of the highly individualistic United States.

The hypothesis that the effects of organizational financial performance are greater in more collectivistic societies is supported only insofar as the organizational performance coefficient is much smaller in the United States than it is in any other society. The pattern is much less clear when all countries are compared. Pay fairness judgments in the three non-Latin collectivistic countries are less sensitive to organizational performance than are the judgments in the other nations, including those (notably Peru and Uruguay) that are ranked as equally collectivistic. The strongest pattern is revealed by the results for the Latin countries, which have relatively very large profitability coefficients – several times larger than the coefficients in other countries.

The most notable pattern is the generally greater performance orientation of the Latin countries (Peru, Uruguay, Argentina, and Spain) relative to the other nations, including the United States. In each of these four countries, the coefficients for both the individual performance variable and the business performance variable are generally much greater than the coefficients of the other countries. There is no trade-off between the effects of individual and group performance metrics, as those countries that are sensitive to individual performance are also sensitive to group performance.

There is no strong across-country pattern for the effects of educational attainment and seniority. Consistent with the arguments that pay determination is more sensitive to these types of status variables in the more collectivistic countries, the effects of seniority and education are relatively large in Thailand and Nigeria. The effects of seniority and education are also lowest of all in Uruguay and Argentina. However, the effects of seniority on pay fairness judgments is second highest in the individualistic United States.

The effect of employee need is greatest in the relatively collectivistic Thailand. Interestingly, the magnitude of the family need effect is of approximately equal size in all other countries, except Nigeria, including the individualistic United States.

Summary statistics for the measures of horizontal individualism/ collectivism from the INDCOL instrument are shown in Table 2. These measures are used as data to test if, and to what extent, the cross-country differences in the sensitivity of pay fairness judgments could possibly be attributable to cultural differences.

Cronbach $\alpha$'s show that, in a number of cases, the cultural scores are not reliable or valid measures of the cultural attribute. Based on an arbitrary cutoff of $\alpha = .65$, HC is poorly measured in all countries, except the United States, and is not used in the analysis except for Thailand. VI is reasonably well measured. Measures of HI are deemed to be reliable in all countries.

The most remarkable result to emerge from the study is the uniformity of the cultural measures across national samples. In general pairwise comparisons of VI scores reveal that none of the pairs have significantly different scores at anything approaching conventional standards of statistical significance. The United States has higher HI than the Latin nations specifically. There is little to distinguish between the nations on the VC scores, as none of the pairs are significantly different.

Overall, these measures exhibit considerable similarity in the cultural traits of the samples of experienced managers in executive training or graduate programs. As such, they contrast markedly with the results from the work of Triandis and his co-workers, who with samples of under-graduate students from generally non-business programs found significant differences between nations (Triandis, 1996).

These results directly imply that the between-nation differences observed in the sensitivity of pay fairness judgments by experienced managers are not due to cultural differences along the dimensions of vertical/horizontal individualism/collectivism that have been posited above.

***Table 2.*** Vertical Individualism, Horizontal Individualism, Vertical Collectivism, and Horizontal Collectivism: Mean Scores by Nation.

|  | VI | HI | VC | HC |
|---|---|---|---|---|
| Thailand | 4.93 | 6.30 | 7.12 | 6.88 |
| SD | (1.04) | (1.47) | (1.08) | (.88) |
| α | .25 | .82 | .76 | .34 |
| Nigeria | 5.08 | 7.17 | 7.67 | 7.20 |
| SD | (1.50) | (1.34) | (.74) | (.95) |
| α | .72 | .85 | .43 | .52 |
| Philippines | 5.28 | 7.60 | 7.23 | 6.99 |
| SD | (1.38) | (1.05) | (.99) | (1.12) |
| α | .65 | .87 | .66 | .43 |
| Peru | 5.26 | 6.39 | 7.44 | 7.39 |
| SD | (1.22) | (1.34) | (.97) | (.81) |
| α | .66 | .73 | .72 | .44 |
| Uruguay | 5.17 | 6.59 | 7.45 | 7.51 |
| SD | (1.51) | (1.50) | (.78) | (.91) |
| α | .55 | .82 | .49 | .62 |
| Argentina | 5.19 | 6.57 | 6.79 | 7.08 |
| SD | (1.23) | (1.53) | (1.61) | (.77) |
| α | .67 | .81 | .68 | .54 |
| Spain | 4.83 | 5.89 | 7.38 | 7.32 |
| SD | (1.42) | (1.29) | (.84) | (.89) |
| α | .73 | .69 | .56 | .63 |
| USA | 5.21 | 7.89 | 6.93 | 6.88 |
| SD | (1.29) | (.74) | (1.01) | (1.27) |
| α | .84 | .67 | .77 | .73 |

# DISCUSSION AND CONCLUSIONS

The empirical work provides evidence of substantial differences between nations in the ways in which judgments about the fairness of an employee's pay are formed. To this extent, it is tempting to argue that there is support for the idea that the design of pay systems varies across nations and invoke differences in national culture as an explanation of the cross-country differences.

The between-country differences in the determinants of pay fairness do not fit well with the "cultural" explanations offered above or elsewhere. For example, pay fairness judgments are not consistently less sensitive to individual performance variations in countries typically regarded as more collectivistic according to Hofstede's country rankings. Contrary to predictions, the judgments about pay fairness are often less sensitive to variations in organizational performance in the more collectivistic nations. Seniority is adjudged to be more important in the United States than in most of the other, less individualistic societies. We need to explore explanations for the failure to find the expected connection between national culture and reaction to a management practice. There are three lines of explanation. None of these are mutually exclusive, and each has distinctive implications for future research.

The first possibility is that the national samples explored in this study are not equally representative of the cultural attributes of the countries from which they are drawn. In an era of globalization, selection into managerial ranks could be biased toward individuals who subscribe to an occupational culture that values similar bases for rewards across nations. Thus even if cultural differences do exist on average, they will not be fully revealed in the samples of managers, obscuring any effects of cultural differences on cross-national differences in the determination of pay fairness judgments. Our data show that samples drawn from executive programs do not exhibit cross-national differences that are necessary for cross-cultural differences in pay fairness judgments.

A second possibility is that reactions to pay systems are simply not affected by culture in the ways proposed. To make this point, we consider the responses to performance-based financial reward systems by more collectivistic individuals. The usual theory sees collectivists who subordinate their interests to the group, recognize intragroup interdependencies, and seek to promote group harmony as placing less value on pay methods that differentiate between individuals and greater value on those that recognize the overall importance of the group as an entity. We note, however, that the collectivist subordinates his or her interests to in-groups with which he or she identifies and not to any group or organization in his or her environment. And there may be cases in which even within collectivistic societies, the work group or organization is not necessarily an in-group – the focus of behaviors and attitudes that might be considered collectivistic. Further, even strong individualists may subordinate their interests to in-groups, most notably the family (Hofstede, 1983). The importance of in-group/out-group identification is demonstrated by Earley (1993), who showed that individuals with collectivist values engage in less free-riding when working in groups with which they share a common identity, but are just as inclined to free-ride as individualists when working in groups that they do not identify as an in-group.

Consequently, the way in which individualism/collectivism mediates the reaction to a management practice will depend on the extent to which the work group or organization is viewed as a valid in-group. An examination of employment systems in countries with reputedly collectivistic cultures shows that the position of the work group as an important in-group can vary considerably. Work organizations in the established corporate sector of collectivist Japan are very influential in-groups for core employees, who are extensively socialized in the organization as a family member and who enjoy lifetime employment but have limited opportunities in the external labor market if they leave. Thus, the Japanese employee will exhibit work behaviors and attitudes consistent with a view of the work organization as a strong in-group. In some parts of China, however, the work organization is less likely to exert strong in-group influences. The work organization in the rapidly growing market-oriented part of the economy does not provide for the general welfare of the employee and his or her family. In a highly active and fluid labor market, qualified experienced employees face a strong demand for their services, as evidenced by high labor mobility. Qualified workers and managers who are now conditioned by decades of rapid economic growth and expanding opportunity may see individual achievement as instrumental in furthering the interests of an important in-group, such as their family, and strongly endorse performance-based pay.

Some work situations in the individualistic United States encourage collectivistic orientations among workers. These especially occur in lines of work or locations in which workers from similar backgrounds are gathered together in places where alternative opportunities are limited, encouraging militant union activity (Kerr & Siegel, 1954) and active resistance to individual piece rates (Whyte, 1955).

A third possibility is that nation-specific factors dominate any effects of culture. Specific elements of national experience condition expectations and perceptions of management practices in ways that influence judgments about pay fairness. Viewed in a historical vacuum, the intended results of pay-for-performance systems are elegant and simple. With a presumed valuable reward (money) contingent on performance, higher levels of measured performance accrue to those who are more productive. A second-order effect is that overall levels of organizational efficiency and competitiveness increase, so that pay for performance may be appealing to collectivists as well as achievement-oriented, competitive individualists. It is possible that pay for performance may be seen as good for an entire economy. The problem is, however, that some workers, perhaps even a large majority, because of their experiences may not see it this way.

Participants in long-industrialized market economies might be exposed to considerable skepticism about pay-for-performance outcomes. These include goal displacement, in which focus on imperfectly measured performance causes key aspects of performance to be neglected, for example, neglecting maintenance or product quality or safety. Ironically, the problem of goal displacement may be seen as more pronounced in more individualistic cultures, in which employees will advance their own self-interest by focusing narrowly on only those aspects of performance for which they will be rewarded. However, according to Deci (1975) and Kohn (1993), pay for performance of all types may confound or even offset the advantages of other intrinsic motivators, such as opportunities for personal growth and performance of intrinsically interesting work. Further, the acceptance of, and efficacy of, pay for performance will depend very much on the employee's judgment that the performance measure actually measures performance. The problems associated with merit pay and the deleterious consequences for performance motivation (Heneman & Werner, 2003) are well known. Organization-wide performance measures, such as profitability, are likely to present similar issues in that individuals have reason to believe that the measures are not transparent.

Cross-national differences in reactions to management practices may have more to do with beliefs about how the systems will work that are conditioned by the experiences or expectations of participants in the system and have relatively little to do with presumed deep-seated cultural values that endure across the generations. For example, the warm response to both individual and group performance as criteria for pay increases in the Latin American samples may be understandable in the case of managers who have a stake in global competitiveness and see aggressive pay for performance as a means toward this end. Given the slow growth of their economies and organizations in the heavily interventionist, state-protected years covering much of the post-WWII era, they will be attracted to reward systems that hold the promise of promoting and rewarding work effort – and are seen to be consistent with the ethos of the modern market economy.

Granick's (1979) survey shows that managerial compensation varies widely across national settings, sometimes in surprising ways. Notably, socialist systems (such as the Soviet Union) were characterized by short-term bonus systems for the ability to meet organizational goals and termination and demotion for failure to meet performance objectives – characteristics that were shared with the most market-oriented of all economies. This not only illustrates how superficially similar systems can exist in widely varying national cultures and economic systems, but also provides testimony as to how the systems can be associated with different outcomes. Granick has noted that the Soviet variant, in which bonuses were tied to quantifiable measures of firm performance, such as profitably, could produce unintended consequences associated with goal displacement. The systems characteristic of a particular nation can be understood only in the context of a wide variety of collateral mechanisms, such as several variables related to promotional systems.

## NOTES

1. Swamy's (1971) stochastic regression method is used to estimate country means of the pay fairness regression coefficients.

## REFERENCES

Adams, J. S. (1965). Inequity in social exchange. In: L. Berkowitz (Ed.), *Advances in experimental social psychology* (Vol. 2, pp. 267–299). New York: Academic Press.

Bartlett, C. A., & Ghoshal, S. (2002). *Managing across borders: The transnational solution.* Boston, MA: Harvard Business School Press.

Berger, J., Zelditch, M., Anderson, B., & Cohen, B. P. (1972). Structural aspects of distributive justice: A status-value formulation. In: J. Berger, M. Zelditch & B. Anderson (Eds), *Sociological theories in progress* (Vol. 2, pp. 119–146). Boston: Houghton Mifflin Company.

Bond, M. H., Leung, K., & Wan, K. C. (1982). How does cultural collectivism operate? The impact of task and maintenance contribution on reward distribution. *Journal of Cross-Cultural Psychology, 13,* 186–200.

Cook, K. S. (1975). Expectations, evaluations and equity. *American Sociological Review, 40,* 372–388.

Deci, E. (1975). *Intrinsic motivation.* New York: Plenum Press.

Deutsch, M. (1975). Equity, equality and need: What determines which value will be used as the basis of distributive justice? *Journal of Social Issues, 31,* 137–149.

Deutsch, M. (1985). *Distributive justice: A social-psychological perspective.* New Haven: Yale University Press.

Earley, P. C. (1993). East meets west meets mideast: Further explorations of collectivistic and individualistic work groups. *Academy of Management Journal, 38*(2), 319–348.

Folger, R., & Konovsky, M. A. (1989). Effects of procedural and distributive justice on reactions to pay raise decisions. *Academy of Management Journal, 32,* 115–130.

Granick, D. (1979). Managerial incentive systems and organizational theory. In: C. J. Lammers & D. J. Hickson (Eds), *Organizations alike and unlike: International and inter-institutional studies in the sociology of organizations* (pp. 76–96). London: Routledge & Kegan Paul.

Heneman, R. L., & Werner, J. (2003). *Merit pay: Linking pay to performance in a changing world.* Greenwich, CT: Information Age Publishing.

Hofstede, G. (1983). *Culture's consequences: International differences in work-related values.* Beverly Hill: Sage Publications.

Hundley, G., & Kim, J. (1997). National culture and the factors affecting perceptions of pay fairness in Korea and the United States. *International Journal of Organizational Analysis, 5,* 325–341.

Jasso, G. (1978). On the justice of earnings: A new specification of the justice evaluation function. *American Journal of Sociology, 83,* 1398–1419.

Jasso, G., & Rossi, P. H. (1977). Distributive justice and earned income. *American Sociological Review, 42,* 639–651.

Kerr, C., & Siegel, A. (1954). The inter-industry propensity to strike. In: A. Kornhauser (Ed.), *Industrial conflict.* New York: McGraw-Hill.

Kim, K. I., Park, H., & Suzuki, N. (1990). Reward allocation in the United States, Japan, and Korea: Comparison of individualistic and collectivistic cultures. *Academy of Management Journal, 33,* 188–198.

Kirkman, B. L., Lowe, K. B., & Peng, D. (2000). The role of procedural justice, perceived organizational support, and individualism-collectivism in motivating organizational citizenship behavior of employees in the people's republic of China Presented at the annual meeting of the Academy of Management, Toronto, Canada.

Kohn, A. (1993). *Punished by rewards: The trouble with gold stars, incentive plans, A's, Praise and other Bribes.* Boston, MA: Houghton Mifflin.

Milkovich, G. T., & Newman, J. M. (2005). *Compensation* (8th ed.). Homewood, IL: Richard D. Irwin.

Moorman, R. H., & Blakely, G. L. (1995). Individualism-collectivism as an individual difference predictor of organizational citizenship behavior. *Journal of Organizational Behavior, 16,* 127–142.

Ouchi, W. G. (1981). *Theory Z: How American business can meet the Japanese challenge.* Reading, MA: Addison-Wesley.

Oyserman, D., Coon, H. M., & Kemmelmeier, M. (2002). Rethinking individualism and collectivism: Evaluation of theoretical assumptions and meta-analyses. *Psychological Bulletin, 128,* 3–72.

Singelis, T. M., Triandis, H. C., Bhawuk, D., & Gelfand, M. J. (1995). Horizontal and vertical dimensions of individualism and collectivism: A theoretical and measurement refinement. *Cross-Cultural Research, 29,* 240–275.

Stolte, J. (1987). The formation of justice norms. *American Sociological Review, 52,* 774–784.

Swamy, P. (1971). *Statistical inference in random coefficient regression models.* New York: Springer-Verlag.

Triandis, H. C. (1996). The psychological measurement of cultural syndromes. *American Psychologist, 51,* 407–415.

Triandis, H. C., & Gelfland, M. J. (1998). Converging measurement of horizontal and vertical individualism and collectivism. *Journal of Personality and Social Psychology, 74,* 118–128.

Whyte, W. F. (1955). *Money and motivation.* Harper: New York.

Zhou, J., & Martocchio, J. J. (2001). Chinese and American managers' compensation award decisions: A comparative policy-capturing study. *Personnel Psychology, 54*, 115–145.

## APPENDIX A. INSTRUCTIONS FOR PAY FAIRNESS SURVEY INSTRUMENT

We are interested in your views about the fairness of the pay received by people who work for organizations. People who work in organizations differ in a lot of ways. We have made up descriptions of 32 different individuals working at a specific type of job. For each individual described below please mark the degree to which you consider the hypothetical individual to be underpaid, or overpaid, or if you consider them to be fairly paid.

(a) On the scale provided, please mark the individual as being Fairly Paid (0) if you think that the salary is about right for the person doing the job; that is, the salary is fair payment.
(b) Please mark Extremely Overpaid (+4) only if you think that the salary is way too much for the person described. That is, if, taking everything into account, you think that they are very much overpaid.
(c) Please mark Extremely Underpaid (−4) if you think that the salary is way too little payment for the person described. That is, if, taking everything into account, you think that they are very much underpaid.
(d) If you think that the salary is a bit too much or a bit too little, that is, if you think it belongs somewhere between the Extremely Underpaid and the Extremely Overpaid, then mark the position that matches the degree of underpayment or overpayment of the salary.

To help make your judgments, we describe below an individual who can be regarded as fairly paid given his circumstances. This description will be repeated at the top of each page of the questionnaire.

*A Fairly Paid Manager.* Mr. Lee is a manager for ABC Corporation, a manufacturing company of 12,000 employees organized into 7 major product divisions. He has worked for the company for 6 years. During this period, his division has been the fourth most profitable, with a profit rate of 10.8% of sales (average profitability for the company). He has an associate degree (2 years) from a community college. He has two dependents: a wife and a child. Across all similar workers he is ranked as an average employee. That is, on the ABC Corporation rating scale, which goes from 1 (bottom 20% of performers) to 5 (top 20% of performers), he gets a score of 3. Mr. Lee's annual salary is $100,000.

Given his qualifications and background, Mr. Lee is considered to be fairly paid at this salary.

## APPENDIX B. CODING SCHEME FOR PAY FAIRNESS DETERMINANTS

| | |
|---|---|
| Individual performance | 1 if ranked in second highest quintile |
| | 0 if ranked in second lowest quintile |
| Profitability | 1 if business unit profits second highest (out of 7) |
| | 0 if profits second lowest (out of 7) |
| Seniority | 1 if 10 years with company |
| | 0 if 2 years with company |
| Education | 1 if university degree |
| | 0 if high school graduate |
| Need | 1 if four dependent |
| | 0 if no dependents |

## APPENDIX C. ITEMS FOR HORIZONTAL AND VERTICAL INDIVIDUALISM AND COLLECTIVISM

*Vertical individualism*
Winning is everything
It annoys me when other people perform better than I do
It is important to me that I do my job better than others
Competition is the law of nature
When another person does better than I do, I get tense and aroused
Some people emphasize winning, I am not one of them (reverse score)
I am accountable for my results

*Horizontal individualism*
Being a unique individual is important to me
I would rather depend on myself than on others
My personal identity independent of others is very important to me
My personal identity is very important to me
I am a unique person, separate from others

I enjoy being unique and different from others

*Vertical collectivism*
I usually sacrifice my self-interest for the benefit of my group
Family members should stick together, no matter what sacrifices are
  required
Parents and children must stay together as much as possible
It is my duty to take care of my family, even when I have to sacrifice what
  I want
It is important to me that I respect decisions made by my groups

*Horizontal collectivism*
My happiness depends very much on the happiness of those around me
I like sharing little things with my neighbors
The well-being of my co-workers is important to me
If a co-worker gets a prize I would feel proud
I respect the majority's wishes in groups of which I am a member
The work group or team should be accountable for the results versus the
  individual
It is important to consult close friends and get their ideas before making
  a decision

# INDIVIDUALISM AND COLLECTIVISM IN LEBANON: CORRELATIONS WITH SOCIOECONOMIC FACTORS AND EFFECTS ON MANAGEMENT AND HUMAN RESOURCES PRACTICES

Khalil M. Dirani

## ABSTRACT

*The aim of this chapter is to study individualism and collectivism as two construct indicators of social patterns in Lebanon using Triandis's (1995) framework of individualism and collectivism. This study explores the Lebanese autostereotypes and views of their extreme individualism and collectivism compared to the common opinion held by cross-cultural research. The study sheds light on how social patterns of different Lebanese individuals are distributed across four "cultural syndromes," namely vertical and horizontal collectivism and vertical and horizontal individualism. These four social patterns will be tested against various contextual factors such as age, gender, and education. The results may provide a better idea for managers and human resources practitioners of how to prepare training and evaluation programs for their employees.*

The Global Diffusion of Human Resource Practices: Institutional and Cultural Limits
Advances in International Management, Volume 21, 211–233
ISSN: 1571-5027/doi:10.1016/S1571-5027(08)00009-0

*Findings from 161 respondents showed that the subjects tested tended to be individualistic in their choices, and this suggests that the classification in the literature of the Lebanese as collectivists was based on the fact that there was no evidence to the contrary. Also, results showed a positive correlation between sociodemographic measures (gender, age, education, income, occupation, and location) and individualism. The author argues that these findings might have been the result of the evolution of the Lebanese family in the past 25 years. Suggestions for the use of these results in management and human resources practices and theory are given.*

# INTRODUCTION

International and comparative human resources development research, regardless of specific topics studied, continuously refers to culture or social patterns. This means that culture is a matter of central importance for such research (Ardichvili & Kuchinke, 2002). Both conceptual and empirical research is abundant when it comes to culture and in almost all disciplines of social science. Still, it is rare to find such research in the Arab world in general and in Lebanon in particular (Dirani, 2006). "Culture," in the anthropological sense of the word, has been defined in many ways. Hofstede's shorthand definition is "the collective programming of the mind which distinguishes one category of people from another" (Hofstede, 1980, p. 25). This definition can be associated with any category of people and is applicable to whole nations (Hofstede, 1984). One way to look at culture is through the constructs of individualism and collectivism. These constructs became popular at the national level after the publication of Hofstede's *Cultural Consequences* (1980). The terms individualism and collectivism are used by many people in different parts of the world and are given various meanings by different disciplines (Triandis, 1995). Triandis suggested that individualism and collectivism are also applicable at the individual level. He came up with four categories of individualism and collectivism based on four kinds of self: independent or interdependent (Markus & Kitayama, 1991) and same or different. The combinations of these four types can be categorized as horizontal individualism (HI; independent/same), horizontal collectivism (HC; interdependent/same), vertical individualism (VI; independent/different), and vertical collectivism (VC; interdependent/different).

This chapter, unlike other comparative studies, explores social patterns within the Lebanese context and tests whether there is preference among the Lebanese people with respect to the four determinants of social patterns (HI, VI, HC, and VC). In addition, the chapter provides empirical evidence as to whether Lebanese people converge or diverge on the four determinants with different contextual factors, including gender, age, education, income, and demographic location.

The common approach typically compares samples from different countries or regions and establishes whether there are differences in the cultural characteristics (such as individualism and collectivism) among these countries at the national level (Hofstede, 1991). Two problems arise from such research. First, the findings would ignore testing for differences within the relevant countries, where the samples are not representative of the country's population. Second, with the new age of globalization and technology, the notion of a priori characterization of macrolevel country cultures (as findings from earlier studies in the 1980s such as Hofstede's research in 1981) renders such research as limited and inaccurate with respect to the new characterizations of cultures. As a result, this study explores microlevel or within-country social patterns of Lebanese people, taking into account their different backgrounds. This is not to proclaim that this research is all inclusive; there are some limitations that will be discussed in a later section of this chapter.

Cross-cultural research and organizational and management research at the international level are abundant. However, this is not the case when talking about the Arab countries, in general, and about Lebanon, in particular. Organizational and cross-cultural research in that region is limited and country-specific research is rare (Miller & Sharda, 2000; Robertson, Al-Habib, AlKhatib, & Lanoue, 2001; Sidani & Gardner, 2000). This study takes a small step in attempting to fill the gap by exploring two constructs of social patterns, namely individualism and collectivism, in a sample of 161 Lebanese individuals at the microlevel. Empirical research has provided strong evidence of divergence among countries with respect to norms, values, and customs. Most of this research was done at the country level (e.g., Hofstede, 1984), assuming homogeneity of these cultures and labeling nations according to their mainstream trends. But deviations from the mainstream do occur even in homogeneous cultures as illustrated by the existence of subcultures, such as the subcultures of teenagers and working women, and thus the term "national culture" (Hofstede, 1984) will be decomposed into components of "social patterns" (Triandis, 1995) and the latter will be tested by two of its constructs, individualism and collectivism, and four of their subconstructs, VI, HI, VC, and HC.

It is beyond the scope of this research to discuss all possible variations in the social patterns of the Lebanese people. Rather, drawing mostly on ground-breaking research on different cultures, such as that of Hofstede (1991), Kluckhohn and Strodtbeck (1961), and Triandis (1995), I aim to explore the social patterns of the Lebanese people with respect to the two selected cultural dimensions. The study suggests that, contrary to what one might believe, or what the literature has portrayed, the Lebanese people are more individualistic in general and the degree of their individualism might vary with different sociocultural factors such as gender, age, education, occupation, salary, and demographic location.

## Research Questions

The study was guided by the following research questions:

(a) How do Lebanese individuals autostereotype themselves within the four subconstructs of individualism and collectivism?
(b) How do horizontal and vertical individualistic and horizontal and vertical collectivistic groups of Lebanese society measure on different sociocultural factors, including gender, age, education, demographic location, and occupation?

## Literature Review

The constructs of individualism and collectivism have a long history in the social sciences (Wagner, 1995), but became especially popular after the publication of Hofstede's *Cultural Consequences* (1980). The terms individualism and collectivism are used by many people in different parts of the world and are given various meanings by different disciplines (Triandis, 1995). The following section will be an overview of individualism and collectivism constructs and explain their importance in cross-cultural and social sciences. The section will start with a historical overview of individualism and collectivism, followed by a definition of the terms, a presentation of the main research utilizing this construct and conducted at the cross-cultural and individual levels, and the limitations of the construct, and concluding with how individualism and collectivism contribute to the theoretical framework of this research.

## Definition

According to Hofstede (1991), "individualism stands for a society in which the ties between individuals are loose; everything is expected to look after himself or herself and his or her immediate family only" and "collectivism stands for a society in which people from birth onwards are integrated into strong, cohesive in-groups, which throughout people's lifetime continue to protect them in exchange for unquestioning loyalty" (pp. 260–261). Triandis (1995) defined individualism and collectivism as follows:

> Individualism consists of loosely linked individuals who view themselves as independent of collectives; as primarily motivated by their own preferences, needs, rights, and the contracts they have established with others; give priority to their personal goals over the goals of others; and emphasize rational analyses of the advantages and disadvantages to associating with others. (p. 2)

> Collectivism is a social pattern consisting of closely linked individuals who see themselves as parts of one or more collectives (family, co-worker, tribe, nation); are primarily motivated by the norms of, and duties imposed by, those collectives; are willing to give priority to the goals of these collectives over their own personal goals; and emphasize their connectedness to members of these collectives. (p. 2)

## History

The constructs of individualism and collectivism have long been significant in social views about human nature and the relationships among human beings. Kagitcibasi and Berry (1989) considered the constructs as "universal dimensions." Since 1980, much research and discussion have been conducted on individualism and collectivism, to the extent that Kagitcibasi (1994) regarded the 1980s as the decade of individualism and collectivism. The terms individualism and collectivism have a history of more than 300 years (Triandis, 1995) and many terms in the literature have meanings that overlap with individualism and collectivism. Tonnies (1964) introduced the terms Gesellschaft (society) and Gemeinschaft (community), which correspond to the constructs of individualism and collectivism in a societal context. According to Tonnies (1964), the term Gemeinschaft referred to the traditional agricultural community, which is noted for solidarity and trust. On the other hand, the term Gesellschaft referred to industrial urban society, which is noted for an unrelated and competitive population.

It appears that all societies must deal with tensions between collectivism and individualism and that there are some of both everywhere. Nevertheless, differences in emphasis appear to be real. Thus individualism is to a large extent a characteristic of Western society, and this may engender a bias in psychological theory that is predominantly Western. Today, the majority of cultures share at least some aspects of collectivism. The West, where individualism is more widespread, constitutes less than 30% of humanity, and even there ethnic minorities and lower socioeconomic status groups tend to be more collectivistic (Singelis, Triandis, Bhawuk, & Gelfand, 1995).

Individualism and collectivism have been interdisciplinary. Various scholars (e.g., Kim, Triandis, Kagitcibasi, Choi, & Yoon, 1994; Oyserman, Coon, & Kemmelmeier, 2002; Smith & Bond, 1993; Triandis, 1995) have provided comprehensive coverage of individualism and collectivism. Others have used individualism and collectivism (e.g., Hui & Yee, 1994) as a framework in their research and conceptual studies. As a construct, individualism and collectivism have been used for a long time in, and touch on central concerns of, philosophy, economics, anthropology, and all other social sciences (Triandis, 1995).

*Levels of Analysis*
Individualism and collectivism research takes place at two distinct levels of analysis, individual and societal. As formulated by Hofstede (1980), collectivism and individualism are societal-level concepts and not attributes of individuals. Similarly, Trompenaars (1994) drew upon sociological literature to derive dimensions of cultural differences that might affect behavior in business organizations. Many researchers have, however, transposed the constructs into an individual difference or personality variable – the degree to which individuals endorse values, norms, and attitudes associated with cultural individualism or collectivism. The central feature of this dimension is a tendency to give priority to personal interests or to in-group interests and a tendency to value independence, emotional detachment, personal achievement, and competition versus interdependence, emotional closeness, group achievement, and cooperation (Triandis, 1995). Another major theme (Markus & Kitayama, 1991) concerns thinking about or construing the self as an independent entity motivated by personal standards or as an interdependent part of social groups motivated by social expectations.

*Societal Level.*   The promise of individualism and collectivism as "perhaps the most important dimension of cultural difference in social behavior across the diverse cultures of the world" (Triandis, 1988, p. 60) renders them as attractive constructs for explaining cross-cultural variation. At the cultural level, Hofstede (1980) showed a correlation of .82 between individualism and the level of national economic development. But this correlation failed to provide information about causation. At the same time, Marsella and Choi (1994) argued the link between incompatibility and collectivism. Some researchers challenged both arguments (Triandis, 1995). It is important to keep the cultural and individual levels of analysis separate and not assume the correlation between the two levels to be 1.0. In some studies the correlation was high (e.g., Schwartz, 1994), but in other cases it was low (e.g., Hofstede, Bond, & Luk, 1993).

*Individual Level.* Hofstede (1980, 1991) proposed that psychological relationships like person–organization fit, organizational assessments of individual merit, and individual compliance with organizational demands, among others, are all affected by the prevalence of individualistic or collectivist norms in society. Of course, a number of other cultural dimensions (power distance, masculinity–femininity, uncertainty avoidance) are also considered significant components of social processes, but the moderating function of individualism and collectivism is often clearly implied in explaining relationships among psychological and/or behavioral variables.

Triandis, Leung, Villareal, and Clark (1985) developed a model in which psychological, rather than cultural, constructs were described as immediate determinants of individual behavior. They tried to measure individualism and collectivism at the individual level and used the terms "idiocentrism" and "allocentrism," respectively, in an attempt to differentiate the individual level from the cultural level of analysis. They conceptualized idiocentrism and allocentrism as stable personality dispositions that affect individual action and judgment. Accordingly, culture would be considered as a theoretical concept determined by the prevalence of individual behavior within a group (Triandis, 1988). Within this framework, individualism and collectivism would be "syndromes" through which culture is defined (Triandis, 1995). Therefore, culture would take a causal construct for individualism and collectivism, and internal individual determinants of behavior would be viewed as proximal causal mechanisms. This model of individualism and collectivism implicitly treats culture as a moderator variable. Specifically, it defines culture in terms of the preponderance of individual tendencies and at the same time assigns some causal properties to culture (Triandis et al., 1985). However, this distinction between levels of analysis, though important in methodological terms, is often not attended to, and commonly the terms individualism and collectivism are used at both levels. This usage is also open to a problem of circularity (Bierbrauer, 1994), which means the lack of independent measurement at the two levels combined with the use of correlations between them. Schwartz (1990, 1994) pointed out that the individualism and collectivism dichotomy is not sufficient because it leaves out some universal goals and values that do not serve the in-group, such as equality for all, social justice, a world at peace, and preserving the natural environment. Similarly, some values, such as maturity, may serve both individual and group goals.

*Lebanese Culture*
This section presents different indigenous sociocultural variances that influence, in one way or another, human resources and management practices in Lebanon.

Hofstede's research (1991) on cultural differences and their impact on management suggested that the Arab countries, including Lebanon, share a high collectivist orientation; the Arab countries were ranked 26/37 with a 38 index with respect to the value dimension of individualism and collectivism. This means that there is a preference for group as opposed to individual decision making, whereas group harmony, consensus, and cooperation are valued higher than individual initiative. In Lebanon, there is emphasis on compliance, obedience, and shared responsibility, along with a preference for consultative and participative decision-making styles that maintain and reinforce consensus. Rewards are based on tenure and loyalty to the group and motivation derives primarily from the sense of belonging, whereas the role of leadership is to foster a supportive atmosphere and group culture, thereby facilitating team effort and integration.

The few empirical studies on the Arab countries tend to confirm Hofstede's findings. Ali (1993) and Ali, Taqi, and Krishnan (1997) found that Arab people, including the Lebanese, are collectivists in their orientation, loyal and committed to the group, whether the immediate family, the extended family, or the work group. Ali and colleagues (1997) also found that managers prefer participative and consultative decision making. Al-Rasheed (2001) argued that Arab managers are more authoritarian decision makers and do not prefer delegating authority to their subordinates. Thus, although consultation may take place, decisions are never made jointly with or delegated to subordinates. Elsayed-Elkhouly and Buda (1996) found that Arab managers seek harmony within groups and care for friendly relationships. This explains their preference for solving conflicts on the bases of collaboration between the parties involved. Still, Bjerke and Al-Meer (1993) considered that Arab managers demand loyalty, obedience, and compliance from subordinates, suggesting a social distance between managers and employees, which may be attributed to beliefs about authority in traditional societies (Dedoussis, 2004).

Barakat (1993) found that individual relationships among the Lebanese are characterized as hierarchal and collectivist. Individuals' respect for authority, seniority, and hierarchy was evident by age, family, sex, and education. Weir (1999) found strong emphasis in Arab culture in general on the masculine role through establishing a good working relationship with supervisors, cooperating with peers, and having employment security. Tayeb (1997) found that individuals have an affiliation-oriented nature, which renders important the personal, family, and group values, and less important the individuals' private life and independence from family. Interpersonal ties produce intense loyalties (Ali, 1993), binding people within systems of traditional and personalized authority structures in which advancement often depends more on non-work-related factors such as family connections and affiliations rather than the individual's own skills and merit (Al-Aiban & Pearce, 1993). In Lebanon, individuals identify with their families and local social groups more than with national groups. Bierbrauer (1994) found that the collectivistic groups in Lebanon had a greater preference for abiding by the norms of tradition and religion and were less willing to let state law regulate in-group disputes.

Khalaf (1987) studied the structural–functional aspects of the "Lebanese family system" and its influence on individuals' career development. He concluded that kinship has been, and is likely to remain, Lebanon's most solid and enduring tie and that the family, not the individual, has been the basic social unit. He also found that the family, through its economic interests, affiliations, and values, has a major effect on the development of vocational preference and on achievement motivation and individual accomplishments. Therefore, to a large extent, the family largely defines individuals' status in society, their occupation, and their social and political prestige.

Various studies have shown that the Lebanese people rank the family first in terms of importance among all social institutions (Kazarian, 2005). Some of these studies indicated that the Lebanese family had shifted from an extended family structure to a nuclear family frame (Faour, 1998). Traditionally, the extended family included parents, children, sons' families, and other kin, whereas the nuclear family included the parents and their dependent children. The traditional family is considered to be more vertical than the nuclear family in its relation structure. In a traditional family, members would be dependent on and unequal to the self of others in the family, and the male elder of the family would be an undisputed superior head, who commands and expects unswerving loyalty from the collective. At the same time, male members of the family may have more of a say in family matters than female members and may have more important roles within the family. On the other hand, the modern nuclear family is more horizontal in its in group relationships. Members are considered inter-dependent and equal to the self of the other family members. They share family authority based on egalitarian bases rather than sex, and decision making usually follows democratic procedures. Both forms of family are heterogeneous with respect to their levels of verticality and horizontality. Some other forms that describe the transformation of the Lebanese family are hierarchy versus horizontal, conservative versus liberal, patriarchal versus conjugal, and traditional versus modern (Kazarian, 2005).

Lebanese respondents believe in a collectivist orientation. Their identity is based on the Lebanese social system. They are emotionally dependent on their institutions and organizations. Their private lives are not as much so (Trompenaars, 1994). When handling interpersonal conflicts, the Lebanese tend to use an avoiding and integrating style (Elsayed-Elkhouly & Buda, 1997). Individuals in managerial positions tend to use more assertive and less accommodating styles with their subordinates, to be rigid with instructions, to have a highly authoritarian tone, and to rely on personal contacts, and their social positions and family influences are ever-present factors (Badawy, 1980).

Overall, the Lebanese take a modern approach to an individual's ability for leadership and internal control of supervisors over subordinates. Badawy (1980) classified the Lebanese as collectivists. Triandis (1995) supported the idea that there are degrees of collectivism within collectivistic cultures.

The utilization of women's capabilities in the Arab world through political and economic participation remains the lowest in the world (Pheraon, 1993). However, in Lebanon, the culture supports an active role in society for women. The Lebanese society has made significant advances in providing women with greater job opportunities. As a result, women now hold professional positions in traditional and nontraditional careers. Some also hold public offices and are engaged in the social and political activities in the government. In general, Lebanese women pursue careers that contribute to the support and development of their families. Thus, although job opportunities are still limited compared to those in the United States, the author would assume that the status of Lebanese females in the world of work is similar to that of American women in the 1970s.

## Theoretical Framework

The framework of this study is provided by Triandis's model for individualism and collectivism. Triandis proposed four categories of individualism and collectivism based on four kinds of self-identification: independent or interdependent (Markus & Kitayama, 1991) and same or different. The combinations of these four types can be categorized as HI (independent/same) and HC (interdependent/same), VI (independent/different), and VC (interdependent/different). In collectivist cultures, horizontal includes a sense of social cohesion and of oneness with members of the in-group. Vertical includes a sense of serving the in-group and sacrificing for the benefit of the in-group and doing one's duty. In both individualist and collectivist cultures, the vertical dimension accepts inequality, and rank has it is privileges. This is reflective of the "different self." In contrast, the horizontal dimension emphasizes that people should be similar on most attributes, especially status. This reflects the "same self," which does not want to stand out. This typology accounts for data collected by Chen, Meindl, and Hunt (1994) and Daun (1991, 1992). Four universal dimensions of individualism and collectivism emerged as a result of Triandis's work (1995). The first dimension defined the self as independent in collectivism and independent in individualism (Reykowski, 1994). This would be reflected in various aspects of daily life, including the extent to which individuals share resources with group members and conform to the norms of the group. Scales for the measurement of this aspect have been developed by Singelis (1994) and by Gudykunst, Matsumoto, Ting-Toomey, Nishida, and Karimi (1994). The second dimension considered personal and communal goals as closely aligned in collectivism and not at all aligned in individualism. One could identify collectivism when group goals have priority and individualism when personal goals have priority (Schwartz, 1994). A scale for measuring this aspect has been developed by Yamaguchi (1994). The third dimension considered that cognitions that focus on norms, obligations, and duties guide much of social behavior in collectivist cultures. Those that focus on attitudes, personal needs, rights, and contracts (Miller & Sharda, 2000) guide social behavior in individualistic cultures. The fourth dimension emphasized the stress on relationships that is common in collectivist cultures even when these relationships are disadvantageous. In individualist cultures, the emphasis is on rational analyses of the advantages and disadvantages of maintaining a relationship (Mills & Clark, 1982; Kim et al., 1994). The four aspects can be measured independently, and they have been found to correlate substantially (Triandis, 1995). The importance of this point is that individualism and collectivism are "real" in the sense that the measurements of the four aspects do converge. Thus, individualism and collectivism are not just intuitive, theoretical entities. A summary of the four subconstructs of collectivism and individualism is presented in Table 1.

The problem with the constructs of individualism and collectivism is that there is a lack of systematic analyses of hypotheses derived from the terms. At the same time, the overwhelming dominance of the Western perspective in psychology has underestimated the importance of studying alternative views of human nature (Triandis, 1995). Narrow scales do not capture the richness of the constructs. But findings of many studies indicate that these constructs had probably been defined in an overly inclusive global manner that is not justified conceptually (Triandis, 1995). Another problem with individualism and collectivism is the level of analysis for the constructs. From a conceptual point of view, the problem is that many researchers assume it is appropriate to use the same dimensions to describe individuals and cultures. Thus, they adopt either a reductionist, person-logical view of culture or a reductionist, cultural view of persons. At the same time, scores on the dimensions are treated as equally appropriate for comparing individual persons and comparing cultures, with no empirical test of this assumption, thereby adding to the conceptual confusion in the literature (Fijneman, Willemsen, & Poortinga, 1996; Schwartz, 1994). Much work has yet to be done to establish the optimal conceptualization and measurement of individual difference variables.

*Table 1.* Culture, Self, and Orientation.

|  | Vertical | | Horizontal | |
|---|---|---|---|---|
|  | Collectivism | Individualism | Collectivism | Individualism |
| Triandis (1995) | Interdependent | Independent | Interdependent | Independent |
| Kind of self | Different from others | Different from others | Same as others | Same as others |
| Fiske (1992) | Communal sharing | Market pricing | Communal sharing | Market pricing |
| Orientation | Authority ranking | Authority ranking | Equality matching | Equality matching |
| Rokeach (1973) | Low equality | Low equality | High equality | High equality |
| Values | Low freedom | High freedom | Low freedom | High freedom |

*Source:* Adapted from *Individualism and Collectivism* (Triandis 1995, p. 51).

## Method

The data used to answer the research questions were elicited from two groups. The first group of responses was based on the judgments of undergraduates from a major university located in Beirut. The other group consisted of individuals with work experience and was composed of employees and managers in the banking sector in Beirut and other cities.

### Measurement Instruments

Most instruments used in the various cross-cultural research studies (e.g., Hofstede, 1980) were developed in the West, but a few were developed in other cultures, such as the Chinese Value Survey developed by non-Western social scientists (Chinese Culture Connection, 1987). At the individual level, several instruments have been devised to measure individualism and collectivism variables. This research study adapts Triandis's collectivism–individualism instrument to measure the individual tendencies in Lebanon.

### Measures

To generate measures of horizontal and vertical collectivism and individualism, the respondents were asked to rank their answers to 20 items from the INDCOL questionnaire developed by Triandis and colleagues. The questionnaire included a set of scenarios. Each scenario is followed by four options. Respondents were asked to place themselves mentally in that situation and rank these options by placing a "1" next to the option they consider the best or the most "right" or "appropriate," placing a "2" next to their second option, a "3" next to their third option, and a "4" next to the "least good" option. The following is an example:

Which of the following activities is likely to be most satisfying to you? (Please rank your answer.)

(a) Thinking about yourself _____ (HI)
(b) Doing things for others _____ (VC)
(c) Linking with others _____ (HC)
(d) Beating your competitors _____ (VI)

Measures of HI, VI, HC, and VC were constructed from the means of the items specified in the Appendix. The horizontal types refer to emphasis on equality and the perception of people having more or less the same self, as is typically found in homogeneous cultures. The vertical types refer to acceptance of inequality. Vertical collectivists are willing to sacrifice themselves for the benefit of the collective.

*Participants*
Of 300 questionnaires randomly distributed by the researcher, 182 respondents filled out the questionnaires, with a response around 61%. Although the instructions were clear, upon data entry 21 questionnaires were discarded because respondents did not rank their answers but rather chose one best answer. Thus, only 161 questionnaires were analyzed. Data were collected in the summer of 2006.

*Results*

Altogether, 161 usable questionnaires were analyzed, including 73 students (45%) and 88 employees (55%), with diverse social and demographic backgrounds. Ninety-seven respondents (60%) were females and 64 (40%) were males. With respect to age, 85 (53%) respondents were 25 years old or younger and 76 (47%) participants were older than 25 years. Regarding education, there were 93 (58%) respondents with undergraduate college studies, 13 (8%) respondents pursuing a master's degree, 35 (22%) respondents who had already completed their master's degrees, and 20 (12%) respondents with other diplomas. For income, 85 (52%) indicated that their salaries were less than $500 per month, and this is expected because around half of the respondents were students pursuing under-graduate degrees. Seventeen (10%) respondents reported a salary between $501 and $1,000, 22 (14%) had a salary between $1,001 and $1,500, 18 (10%) had a salary between $1,501 and $2,000, and 24 (14%) had a salary of more than $2,000 per month. The majority of the respondents ($n = 123$; 76%) were from Beirut, and few ($n = 38$; 24%) lived in other cities and towns at the time of survey. These results are summarized in Table 2.

The mean scores obtained from this study show that the Lebanese, in general, tend to be more individualistic ($M = 101.6$) rather than collectivis-tic ($M = 96.2$) within the society. Regarding the four subconstructs of individualism and collectivism, the respondents autostereotyped themselves as fitting more within HI ($M = 54.1$). On the other hand, they showed almost equal bias with respect to VI ($M = 48.2$), HC ($M = 48.7$), and VC ($M = 48.5$). This result might be due to the evolution of the family form from a traditional to a more modern democratic one.

Analysis of gender differences on the four subconstructs showed no differences between females and males (see Table 2). Both females and males equally prefer HI over the other three subconstructs. Similar results were found with respect to age. Respondents who were less than or

***Table 2.*** Vertical Individualism, Horizontal Individualism, Vertical Collectivism, Horizontal Collectivism: Mean Scores.

| Demographic | | N | | VI | HI | VC | HC | IND | COL |
|---|---|---|---|---|---|---|---|---|---|
| Gender | Male | 64 | M | 48.0 | 53.7 | 48.6 | 47.8 | 101.7 | 96.4 |
| | | | SD | 6.89 | 5.96 | 6.69 | 7.12 | 9.43 | 11.2 |
| | Female | 97 | M | 48.5 | 54.0 | 48.4 | 48.2 | 102.5 | 96.6 |
| | | | SD | 5.40 | 5.81 | 5.57 | 5.46 | 7.50 | 7.80 |
| Age | ≤25 | 85 | M | 48.7 | 53.7 | 48.1 | 47.7 | 102.4 | 95.8 |
| | | | SD | 5.70 | 6.04 | 6.57 | 6.79 | 8.68 | 10.1 |
| | >25 | 76 | M | 47.9 | 54.1 | 48.8 | 48.5 | 102.0 | 97.3 |
| | | | SD | 6.39 | 5.67 | 5.34 | 5.34 | 7.88 | 8.09 |
| Income/month | <$500 | 80 | M | 47.9 | 53.7 | 48.3 | 48.0 | 101.6 | 96.3 |
| | | | SD | 5.61 | 6.09 | 6.83 | 6.82 | 8.67 | 10.7 |
| | $501–1,000 | 17 | M | 47.2 | 53.4 | 49.9 | 48.9 | 100.6 | 98.8 |
| | | | SD | 4.93 | 6.23 | 5.19 | 4.56 | 7.11 | 6.57 |
| | 1,001–1,500 | 22 | M | 47.3 | 52.5 | 49.0 | 49.9 | 99.8 | 98.9 |
| | | | SD | 6.74 | 6.12 | 4.95 | 6.03 | 8.24 | 8.02 |
| | 1,501–2,000 | 18 | M | 53.8 | 54.6 | 48.1 | 43.5 | 108.4 | 91.6 |
| | | | SD | 6.34 | 5.50 | 7.95 | 4.74 | 9.11 | 9.11 |
| | >$2,000 | 24 | M | 48.3 | 55.6 | 48.0 | 48.1 | 103.9 | 96.1 |
| | | | SD | 6.53 | 4.92 | 4.13 | 4.98 | 6.95 | 6.95 |
| Occupation | Student | 73 | M | 48.1 | 54.3 | 47.7 | 47.8 | 102.4 | 95.5 |
| | | | SD | 6.03 | 6.11 | 6.92 | 7.17 | 9.40 | 10.9 |
| | Employee | 88 | M | 48.5 | 53.6 | 49.0 | 48.3 | 102.1 | 97.3 |
| | | | SD | 6.09 | 5.67 | 5.10 | 5.26 | 7.35 | 7.65 |
| Education | Undergraduate | 93 | M | 47.9 | 54.1 | 47.9 | 48.1 | 102.0 | 96.0 |
| | | | SD | 5.91 | 5.95 | 6.39 | 6.89 | 8.78 | 10.3 |
| | Graduate courses | 13 | M | 49.2 | 53.2 | 50.9 | 46.7 | 102.4 | 97.6 |
| | | | SD | 5.82 | 5.16 | 4.01 | 4.31 | 6.56 | 6.56 |
| | MS degree | 35 | M | 48.6 | 54.2 | 48.5 | 48.2 | 102.8 | 96.7 |
| | | | SD | 6.81 | 6.59 | 5.10 | 5.75 | 8.93 | 8.44 |
| | Other | 20 | M | 49.2 | 52.3 | 49.4 | 48.6 | 101.5 | 98.0 |
| | | | SD | 5.64 | 4.35 | 6.88 | 3.96 | 5.82 | 7.14 |
| Location | Beirut | 123 | M | 48.1 | 54.4 | 48.2 | 47.9 | 102.5 | 96.2 |
| | | | SD | 5.77 | 5.80 | 5.82 | 5.91 | 7.98 | 9.04 |
| | Major city | 22 | M | 51.6 | 52.1 | 48.5 | 46.6 | 103.7 | 95.0 |
| | | | SD | 5.83 | 5.59 | 4.75 | 5.69 | 7.05 | 7.47 |
| | Town | 16 | M | 44.9 | 52.3 | 50.4 | 51.1 | 97.2 | 101.5 |
| | | | SD | 6.52 | 6.25 | 8.78 | 7.90 | 10.9 | 11.9 |

equal to 25 years of age and those who were older than 25 years tended to be more horizontal individualists in their preferences. Similar results were recorded for occupation and education, for which the tendency was toward HI. This supports the democratic progress of the Lebanese society and does not support the notion of male dominance within the Lebanese culture. With respect to income, there were no surprises except that respondents with salaries between \$1,501 and \$2,000 showed high VI tendencies ($M = 53.8$), almost equal to their HI tendencies ($M = 54.6$). This finding is attributed to the fact that people who get such salaries are in managerial positions and generally tend to be authoritarian and demand obedience from their followers. This finding is supported by the reviewed literature. For demographic location, the results were similar to the general trend of individuals tending to be horizontal individualists in Beirut and small towns. But for other cities, individual tendencies were split between vertical individualists ($M = 51.6$) and HI ($M = 52.1$).

Cronbach's $\alpha$ measures demonstrated acceptable reliability estimates. They ranged between .46 and .58. A Cronbach's $\alpha$ of 1.0 identifies a perfectly reliable instrument, $\alpha$ between .70 and .90 indicates high reliability, and $\alpha$ between .50 and .60 indicates moderate to low levels of reliability (Hair, Anderson, Tathman, & Black, 1998).

The reliability measures resulting from the current study were as follows: (a) VI Cronbach's $\alpha = .52$; (b) HI $\alpha = .44$; (c) VC $\alpha = .52$; (d) HC $\alpha = .54$; (e) individualism $\alpha = .46$; and (f) collectivism $\alpha = .585$. Table 3 includes a summary of Cronbach's $\alpha$ reliability results for all scales.

*Relationship Measures*

Pearson's correlation coefficient was used to determine the relationships between the different variables. Pearson's correlation coefficient enables a determination of the strength of the linear relationship between the variables under examination. Correlations above .70 are referred to as highly positive relationships, correlations between .40 and .60 as moderate positive relationships, and between .10 and .30 as small or weak positive relationships (Hair et al., 1998).

Correlation coefficients were computed to answer the following question: Are the four social patterns (VI, HI, VC, HC) correlated to demographics (measured by gender, age, education, location, occupation, and income) in the Lebanese society? The correlation matrix is presented in Table 3.

Pearson correlation results indicated that there are significant moderate relationships among the social patterns themselves, among the different demographic variables, and between age and VI ($r = -.32$, $p < .01$).

***Table 3.*** Correlations among Social Patterns and Demographics
($n = 161$).

| Variable | 1 | 2 | 3 | 4 | 5 | 6 | 7 | 8 | 9 | 10 | 11 | 12 |
|---|---|---|---|---|---|---|---|---|---|---|---|---|
| VI | (.52) | | | | | | | | | | | |
| HI | −.01 | (.44) | | | | | | | | | | |
| VC | −.19* | −.41** | (.52) | | | | | | | | | |
| HC | −.29** | −.28** | .13 | (.54) | | | | | | | | |
| IND | .73** | .67** | −.42** | −.40** | (.46) | | | | | | | |
| COL | −.32** | −.45** | .76** | .75** | −.54** | (.58) | | | | | | |
| Gender | −.01 | −.04 | .07 | .05 | −.03 | .07 | 1.0 | | | | | |
| Age | .17* | .00 | −.02 | −.06 | .12 | −.06 | −.50 | 1.0 | | | | |
| Education | −.03 | .10 | −.02 | .06 | .05 | .03 | −.01 | .25** | 1.0 | | | |
| Location | .04 | .12 | −.09 | −.07 | .11 | −.11 | −.10 | −.06 | .20* | 1.0 | | |
| Occupation | .02 | .06 | −.03 | .02 | .05 | −.02 | .03 | .71** | .29** | .11 | 1.0 | |
| Income | .00 | −.05 | .06 | .10 | −.03 | .10 | −.12 | .61** | .19* | −.09 | .52** | 1.0 |

*Note:* VI, vertical individualism; HI, horizontal individualism; VC, vertical collectivism; HC, horizontal collectivism; IND, individualism; COL, collectivism. Gender: 1, male; 2, female. Age: 1, less than 25; 2, 25–34; 3, 35–44; 4, 45–54; 5, more than 54. Education: 1, bachelor's degree; 2, master's coursework; 3, master's degree; 4, other. Location: 1, Beirut; 2, major city other than Beirut; 3, town. Occupation: 1, student; 2, employee; 3, other. Income: 1, less than $500; 2, $500–$1,000; 3, $1,001–$1,500; 4, $1,501–$2,000; 5, more than $2,000.() Cronbach's α reliability coefficient.
*$p = .05$.
**$p = .01$.

This means that students, in general, were more individualistic in their behavior than employees.

## Discussion

The results of this study suggest that the Lebanese see themselves different from how others see them. Respondents characterized themselves as more individualistic at the personal level. The sample scored higher on the VI scale than the HI, VC, and individual collectivism scales. This finding substantiates Triandis's (1995) and Wagner's (1995) findings that variations in individualism and collectivism can occur at the individual level.

On the other hand, the findings question conventional wisdom and older comparative studies (e.g., Hofstede, 1981) that characterize the Lebanese society as highly collectivistic. A simple explanation for such contradiction is that the Lebanese became more individualistic in their orientation in the 25 years since those studies.

This research supports the proposal that individualism and collectivism depend on who the "others" are with respect to the subjects' groups. In other words, respondents in this study exhibited individualistic behaviors toward out-groups similar to those found in individualistic cultures.

This chapter examined the social values in Lebanon and their effect on human resource development and management. Several implications are drawn. One of these is that individualism and collectivism in the Lebanese social context inside and outside management are subject to a variety of environmental influences. Examining the effects of these environmental factors provides a more complete understanding of the dynamics underlying choices and activities in Lebanese firms and society in general.

The literature had shown the Lebanese family as the most fundamental institution and most important social structure in Lebanon (Khalaf, 1987; Super, 1988). The Lebanese family is a closely knit patriarchal one. Lebanese, unlike Americans, find it extremely difficult to leave their family. In fact, they tend to give up their independence and individuality and submit to the rule of the father. The consequences of such a situation in relation to work are very significant. The dependent life that an individual leads in the family is reflected in work. Employees display little initiative or independent judgment at work and shy away from the exercise of creative thinking. They try to evade innovative decision making and, as a result, take comfort in submission to their superiors. On the other hand, leaders' power and authority, and the rules, laws, and regulations developed by those in power reinforce their own leadership and control (Hofstede, 1984). Moreover, Lebanese workers are less likely to be driven by an internalized need for achievement than their Western counterparts (Jabbra, 1989). Although individuals tend to accept new ideas and exhibit readiness to challenge traditional and social values, they are highly influenced by the family system and their loyalty is mainly toward their families and not toward their work, their organization, or their nation (Sharabi, 1988).

## Conclusion and Limitations

Scholars have looked at culture in more depth in the Western context. In Lebanon, little research had been known to target the concept of national culture, let alone research that focuses on individual social patterns. This research provides a roadmap for how to measure individualism and collectivism at the individual level in the Lebanese social context.

It is important to note that, although individualism and collectivism do not offer a full explanation, they nevertheless provide an underlying substantiation for explanations that may turn out to be very varied. Still, a number of limitations with respect to methodology are worth mentioning. First, the researcher relied on groups of individuals that might not best represent the whole society. The author would not know how other samples might have answered, and this limits the ability to generalize the findings to the entire population. Another limitation is that this study used only one measure of collectivism and individualism. Future research should use multiple, complementary methods and instruments. It is worth mentioning that the survey was conducted in English and not in Arabic. The author assumed, based on his personal knowledge of Lebanon, that all participants were qualified enough in the English language to answer the items in English. Future research should use translated instruments to eliminate this limitation.

There is a problem regarding levels of analysis. From a methodological point of view, labels are sometimes used interchangeably to refer both to persons within a society who differ on the personality variable (individual level) and to all members of a society or other cultural group who are treated as reflecting the presumed level of individualism and collectivism in their group (culture level).

This study has both practical and theoretical indications. For practitioners this research study provides empirical evidence that can help human resources and management practitioners with information that might be very significant when preparing training programs and other professional development activities. For researchers, this research would add to the literature base and provide scholars with empirical data and insight to understand the subconstructs of individualism and collectivism in the Lebanese context. Finally, this research can create an avenue for future research that will lead to improvements in Lebanese corporate practices.

# REFERENCES

Al-Aiban, K., & Pearce, J. (1993). The influence of values on management practices: A test in Saudi Arabia and the United States. *International Studies of Management and Organization, 23*(3), 35–53.

Ali, A. (1993). Decision making style, individualism, and attitudes toward risk of Arab executives. *International Studies of Management and Organization, 23*(3), 53–74.

Ali, A., Taqi, A., & Krishnan, K. (1997). Individualism, collectivism and decision making styles of managers in Kuwait. *The Journal of Social Psychology, 137*(5), 629–637.

Al-Rasheed, A. (2001). Features of traditional Arab management and organization in the Jordan business environment. *Journal of Traditional Management Development, 6*(1–2), 27–53.

Ardichvili, A., & Kuchinke, K. P. (2002). The concept of culture in international and comparative HRD research: Methodological problems and possible solutions. *Human Resource Development Review, 1*(2), 145–166.

Badawy, M. K. (1980). Styles of mideastern managers. *California Management Review, 22*(1), 51–58.

Barakat, H. (1993). *The Arab world: Society, culture, and state.* University of California Press: Berkeley.

Bierbrauer, G. (1994). Toward an understanding of legal culture: Variations in individualism and collectivism between Kurds, Lebanese, and Germans. *Law and Society Review, 28*(2), 243–264.

Bjerke, B., & Al-Meer, A. (1993). Culture's consequences: Management in Saudi Arabia. *Leadership and Organization Development Journal, 14*(2), 30–36.

Chen, C. C., Meindl, J. R., & Hunt, R. G. (1994). *Collectivism and differential rewards allocation: A study of the Chinese allocation preferences.* Working paper. Rutgers University, Newark, NJ.

Chinese Culture Connection. (1987). Chinese values and the search for culture-free dimensions of culture. *Journal of Cross-Cultural Psychology, 18*, 143–164.

Daun, A. (1991). Individualism and collectivity among Swedes. *Ethnos, 56*, 165–172.

Daun, A. (1992). Modern and modest: Mentality and stereotypes among Swedes. In: H. C. Triandis (Ed.), *Individualism and collectivism.* Boulder, CO: Westview Press.

Dedoussis, E. (2004). A cross-cultural comparison of organizational culture: Evidence from universities in the Arab world and Japan. *Cross Cultural Management, 11*(1), 15–34.

Dirani, K. M. (2006). Socio-cultural factors that influence HRD practices in Lebanon. *Human Resource Development International, 9*(1), 35–50.

Elsayed-Elkhouly, S., & Buda, R. (1996). Organizational conflict: A comparative analysis of conflict styles across cultures. *International Journal of Conflict Management, 7*(1), 71–76.

Elsayed-Elkhouly, S., & Buda, R. (1997). A cross-cultural comparison of value systems of Egyptians, Americans, Africans and Arab executives. *International Journal of Commerce and Management, 7*, 102–119.

Faour, M. (1998). *The silent revolution in Lebanon: Changing values of the youth.* Beirut, Lebanon: American University of Beirut.

Fijneman, Y. A., Willemsen, M. E., & Poortinga, Y. H. (1996). Individualism-collectivism: An empirical study of a conceptual issue. *Journal of Cross-Cultural Psychology, 27*, 381–402.

Fiske, A. P. (1992). The four elementary forms of sociality: Framework for a unified theory of social relations. *Psychological Review, 99*, 689–723.

Gudykunst, W. B., Matsumoto, Y., Ting-Toomey, S., Nishida, T., & Karimi, H. (1994). Measuring self construals across cultures: A derived etic analysis. Paper presented at the International Communication Association convention, Sydney, Australia, July.

Hair, J. J. F., Anderson, R. E., Tathman, R. L., & Black, W. C. (1998). *Multivariate data analysis.* Upper Saddle River, NJ: Prentice-Hall International, Inc.

Hofstede, G. (1980). *Culture's consequences.* Beverly Hills: Sage.

Hofstede, G. (1984). *Culture's consequences: International differences in work-related values.* Beverly Hills: Sage.

Hofstede, G. (1991). *Cultures and organizations: Software of the mind.* Maidenhead: McGraw-Hill.

Hofstede, G., Bond, M. H., & Luk, C.-L. (1993). Individual perceptions of organizational cultures: A methodological treatise on levels of analysis. *Organizational Studies, 14*, 483–503.

Hui, C. H., & Yee, C. (1994). The shortened individualism–collectivism scale: Its relations with demographic and work-related variables. *Journal of Cross-Cultural Psychology, 25,* 417–433.

Jabbra, J. (1989). *Bureaucracy and development in the Arab World.* Leiden, The Netherlands: E. J. Brill.

Kagitcibasi, C. (1994). A critical appraisal of individualism–collectivism: Toward a new formulation. In: U. Kim, H. C. Triandis, C. Kagitcibasi, S.-C. Choi & G. Yoon (Eds), *Individualism and collectivism: Theory, method and applications* (pp. 52–65). Newbury Park, CA: Sage Press.

Kagitcibasi, C., & Berry, J. W. (1989). Cross-cultural psychology: Current research and trends. *Annual Review of Psychology, 40,* 493–531.

Kazarian, S. (2005). Family functioning, cultural orientation, and psychological well-being among university students in Lebanon. *The Journal of Social Psychology, 145*(2), 141–152.

Khalaf, S. (1987). *Lebanon's predicament.* New York: Columbia University Press.

Kim, U., Triandis, H. C., Kagitcibasi, C., Choi, S.-C., & Yoon, G. (1994). *Individualism and collectivism: Theory, method and applications.* Newbury Park, CA: Sage Press.

Kluckhohn, F. R., & Strodtbeck, F. L. (1961). *Variations in value orientations.* New York: Peterson.

Markus, H. R., & Kitayama, S. (1991). Culture and self: Implications for cognition, emotion, and motivation. *Psychological Review, 98,* 224–253.

Marsella, A., & Choi, S. (1994). Psychological aspects of economic development and modernization in East Asian countries: Some issues and thoughts. *Psychologia: An International Journal of Psychology in the Orient, 32,* 201–213.

Miller, G., & Sharda, B. D. (2000). Organizational structure in the Middle East: A comparative analysis. *International Journal of Comparative Sociology, 41*(4), 315–329.

Mills, J., & Clark, M. S. (1982). Exchange and communal relationships. In: H. C. Triandis (Ed.), *Individualism and collectivism.* Boulder, CO: Viewpoint Press.

Oyserman, D., Coon, H. M., & Kemmelmeier, M. (2002). Rethinking individualism and collectivism: Evaluation of theoretical assumptions and meta-analyses. *Psychological Bulletin, 128*(1), 3–73.

Pheraon, N. A. (1993). *A comparative study of the career maturity, achievement motivations and self-esteem of college women in two cultures: Saudi Arabia and Lebanon.* Unpublished doctoral dissertation. Columbia University, NY.

Reykowski, J. (1994). Collectivism and individualism as dimensions of social change. In: U. Kim, H. C. Triandis, C. Kagitcibasi, S.-C. Choi & G. Yoon (Eds), *Individualism and collectivism: Theory, method and applications* (pp. 276–292). Newbury Park, CA: Sage Press.

Robertson, C., Al-Habib, M., AlKhatib, J., & Lanoue, D. (2001). Beliefs about work in the Middle East and the convergence versus divergence of values. *Journal of World Business, 36*(3), 223.

Rokeach, M. (1973). *The nature of human values.* New York: Basic Books.

Schwartz, S. H. (1990). Individualism–collectivism. Critique and proposed refinements. *Journal of Cross-Cultural Psychology, 21,* 139–157.

Schwartz, S. H. (1994). Beyond individualism and collectivism: New cultural dimensions of values. In: U. Kim, H. C. Triandis, C. Kagitcibasi, S.-C. Choi & G. Yoon (Eds), *Individualism and collectivism: Theory, method and applications* (pp. 85–122). Newbury Park, CA: Sage Press.

Sharabi, H. (1988). *Neopatriarchy: A theory of distorted change in Arab society.* Oxford: Oxford University Press.

Sidani, Y. M., & Gardner, W. L. (2000). Work values among Lebanese workers. *The Journal of Social Psychology*, *140*(5), 597–609.

Singelis, T. M. (1994). The measurement of independent and interdependent self construals. *Personality and Social Psychology Bulletin*, *20*, 580–591.

Singelis, T. M., Triandis, H. C., Bhawuk, D. S., & Gelfand, M. (1995). Horizontal and vertical dimensions of individualism and collectivism: A theoretical and measurement refinement. *Cross-Cultural Research*, *29*, 240–275.

Smith, P. B., & Bond, M. H. (1993). *Social psychology across cultures*. Boston: Allyn and Bacon.

Super, D. (1988). Vocational adjustment: Implementing a self-concept. *Career Development Quarterly*, *36*, 351–357.

Tayeb, M. (1997). Islamic revival in Asia and human resource management. *Employee Relations*, *19*(4), 352–364.

Tonnies, F. (1964). *Community and society*. Mineola, NY: Dover Publications.

Triandis, H. (1988). Collectivism and individualism: A reconceptualization of a basic concept in cross-cultural social psychology. In: G. K. Verma & C. Bagley (Eds), *Cross-cultural studies of personality, attitudes and cognition* (pp. 60–95). London: Macmillan.

Triandis, H. (1995). *Individualism and collectivism: New directions in social psychology*. Oxford: Westview.

Triandis, H. C., Leung, K., Villareal, M., & Clark, F. L. (1985). Allocentric vs. idiocentric tendencies: Convergent and discriminant validation. *Journal of Research in Personality*, *19*, 395–415.

Trompenaars, F. (1994). *Riding the waves of culture: Understanding cultural diversity in business*. New York: Irwin.

Wagner, J. A. (1995). Studies of individualism-collectivism: Effects on cooperation in groups. *Academy of Management Journal*, *38*(2), 152–172.

Weir, D. (1999). Management in the Arab World. In: M. Warner (Ed.), *Regional encyclopedia of business and management: Management in emerging countries*. USA: Business Press Thomson Learning.

Yamaguchi, S. (1994). Empirical evidence on collectivism among the Japanese. In: U. Kim, H. C. Triandis, C. Kagitcibasi, S.-C. Choi & G. Yoon (Eds), *Individualism and collectivism: Theory, method and applications* (pp. 175–188). Newbury Park, CA: Sage Press.

# APPENDIX. SELECTED ITEMS FOR VERTICAL AND HORIZONTAL INDIVIDUALISM AND COLLECTIVISM

| | |
|---|---|
| Vertical individualism | To each according to contribution |
| | Has worked for a competitor before |
| | Someone who has been successful in previous business ventures |
| | You consider which position will most likely benefit you in the future |
| | It gives you prestige |
| | Compute each person's charge, according to what that person ordered |

## APPENDIX. (*Continued*)

| | |
|---|---|
| Horizontal individualism | To each equally |
| | Is easy to get along with |
| | Someone with the same business interests |
| | You assemble all the facts and make up your mind |
| | It allows you to set your own goals |
| | Each person decides how much to contribute to the total, and if it does not cover the bill, each person is assessed inversely proportional to what she or he has contributed |
| Vertical collectivism | To each according to status within the organization |
| | Is a respected member of the community |
| | A senior, successful, experienced member of the community |
| | You discuss it with your boss and support his position |
| | It helps your community |
| | The group leader pays the bill or decides how to split it |
| Horizontal collectivism | To each according to need |
| | Is a relative |
| | A close friend |
| | You discuss it with your friends and take their views into consideration |
| | It links you with friends |
| | Split it equally, without regard to who ordered what |

# FAMILY-FRIENDLY EMPLOYMENT PRACTICES: IMPORTANCE AND EFFECTS IN INDIA, KENYA, AND CHINA

Peng Wang, John J. Lawler, Kan Shi, Fred Walumbwa and Ming Piao

As technological changes and concomitant shifts in job demands have enabled women to become increasingly active in the labor force, there have been profound changes in family structure. The dual-earner family has increasingly substituted for the more traditional single-earner family. Men are becoming more active in the family domain (Pleck, 1985), just as women are increasing their participation in the labor force. With these shifts, a demand for a better balance between work and home life has greatly increased. Imbalance in the relationship between work and family can be a source of stress that has adverse effects on an individual's work attitude and well-being (e.g., Bacharach, Bamberger, & Conley, 1991; Frone, Russell, & Cooper, 1992). Employers who fail to respond to these needs of their employees may incur costs due to higher turnover rates, reduced productivity, and poor morale. Accordingly, American companies have started to develop family-friendly programs for their employees based on the assumption that such efforts will enhance productivity, attract higher

The Global Diffusion of Human Resource Practices: Institutional and Cultural Limits
Advances in International Management, Volume 21, 235–265
Copyright © 2008 by Emerald Group Publishing Limited
All rights of reproduction in any form reserved
ISSN: 1571-5027/doi:10.1016/S1571-5027(08)00010-7

quality employees, improve job satisfaction and organizational commitment, and maintain a stable workforce (Daley, 1998; Mergenhagan, 1994).

Although the relationships between family-friendly policies and organizational outcomes have not yet been firmly established, the assumption of
positive effects by such policies is prevalent among employers. There is a
continuing debate as to whether family-friendly policies have a positive
effect on employees in general or only on employees who can directly benefit
from such policies. Knowledge of such relationships can help employers to
design the most cost-efficient family-friendly policies.

The majority of family-friendly policy research has been conducted in
North America. Our knowledge of family-friendly policies in developing
economies and more collectivist societies is lacking. We are unaware of
any extensive study investigating the effects of family-friendly policies in
collectivist cultures, despite evidence that suggests such cultures hold values
quite distinct from those in individualist cultures (Kiggundu, 1989; Aryee,
Fields, & Luk, 1999). Multinational corporations (MNCs) frequently
transfer domestic employment practices to other cultural contexts. Therefore, research on family-friendly policies in cultures different from the
United States can equip employers to design employment policies in an
international context.

This study addresses this deficiency by examining family-friendly policies
and their effects on employees in three collectivist and developing countries:
China, Kenya, and India. The purpose of this study is twofold. First, we try
to understand family-friendly policies in these societies, such as the types of
family benefits offered, the perceived importance of these policies by
employees, and the relationships between the perceived importance of these
policies and employees' demographic characteristics. Second, we explore the
relationship between family-friendly policies and work-related attitudes,
specifically job satisfaction and organizational commitment. We also try
to provide some insights toward resolving the debate as to whether the
effects of family-friendly policies are general or specific. These findings may
improve our knowledge of family-friendly policies in collectivistic and
developing societies and provide some information for MNC managers who
will be implementing family-friendly policies in such countries.

# FAMILY-FRIENDLY HUMAN RESOURCE POLICIES

With higher female labor force participation and the greater prevalence of
dual-career families, family responsibilities ever more overlap work

responsibilities. Companies have begun to respond to the changing nature of the workforce by offering family-friendly policies that are intended to help employees manage family responsibilities while remaining productive workers. Examples of family-friendly policies include child and dependent care, flexible leave polices, and time off for family emergencies (Daley, 1998; Folsom & Botsch, 1993; Greenfield, 1997; Ezra & Deckman, 1996). Some benefits frequently offered by employers are not considered family-friendly policies because they are not primarily directed toward the management of family responsibilities. Examples of those benefits are educational assistance for the employee, mortgage assistance, holidays, and employee wellness programs.

It would appear that few organizations select family-friendly programs systematically or evaluate program effects. Survey results, for example, have shown that most public agencies in the United States offer some family-friendly benefits (U.S. Department of Labor, 1996), but the numbers and types of programs offered vary widely. Employers generally seem to believe that their organization will benefit from the provision of family-friendly programs, such as by enhanced productivity, improved job satisfaction and organizational commitment, and decreased turnover. Though some research has started to explore the linkage between organizational gains and family-friendly programs, these relationships have not yet been determined. For example, there has been a debate as to whether family-friendly policies have positive effects on employees in general or only on some specific employee groups. Some scholars have argued that these policies might affect workers in general, regardless of whether they benefit directly from these policies (Grover & Crooker, 1995; Baron & Kreps, 1999; Johnson, 1995). In contrast, other researchers insist that the effects of family-friendly policies on organizational outcomes may be moderated by individual characteristics that enable workers to benefit from family-friendly programs (Daley, 1998; Greenfield, 1997; Durst, 1999). Family-friendly programs may even result in resentment among people who do not need such benefits (Herzberg, Mausner, & Synderman, 1959; Pasternak, 1994). Research is thus needed to improve our knowledge of the relationship between family-friendly policies and organizational outcomes. Failure to understand these relationships may lead to the provision of costly benefits that yield little direct return to the organization.

Most studies of family-friendly programs have been conducted with North American samples (Greenhaus & Parasuraman, 1999). We know little about family-friendly policies and their effects on organizations in other societies, for example, the developing and collectivistic countries. Two detailed case studies conducted by the Gender in Agribusiness Project at the University of Illinois, under a grant from the U.S. Agency of International Development, provide insights into the potential role well-designed family-friendly practices could play in firms operating in developing countries. Lawler and Atmiyanandana (2001) provide evidence by way of a case study suggestive of the utility of family-friendly policies in these societies. Most of the production workers employed by Sun Valley (Thailand), a poultry processor that is a wholly owned subsidiary of Cargill, are women, which is typical of light manufacturing companies in much of Asia. Although the company had been successful after initiating operations in the early 1990s, it still suffered from high absenteeism, high turnover, and lower than desired productivity. The women employed by Sun Valley were often the principal source of income for their families, because they either were divorced or widowed with children or had husbands that were unemployed because of limited opportunities in the rural area in which the plant was located. It was apparent that absenteeism and turnover problems were often linked to family responsibilities of these women (i.e., sick children, infirm parents, work demands on family farms). Productivity was diminished in part because of turnover and absenteeism. The company achieved significant reductions in turnover and absenteeism, as well as increased productivity, after revamping it human resource (HR) system, adding numerous family-friendly policies. Employees were given more latitude in terms of taking short-term and long-term leaves to deal with family problems, certain educational and medical expenses were covered for children, and the company provided on-site educational program to help these employees, most of whom had limited education, complete additional years of schooling and thus qualify for better jobs. Some of the policies were culturally based. For example, supervisors were taught to be empathetic to employee concerns and often helped resolve family difficulties. This tied into the cultural norm that bosses in Thailand are supposed act as wise and benevolent elder "brothers" or "sisters." To be sure, the company implemented other changes in its HR system unrelated to family issues, but interviews with many of the workers in the company conducted by Lawler and Atmiyanandana (2001) indicated that the family-friendly policies innovations were perhaps most appreciated by the workers.

Another case study of a Cargill subsidiary involved in cotton production in Zimbabwe also demonstrated the efficacy of utilizing certain family-friendly policies in developing economies with strong collectivist cultural orientations (Cloud, 1999). Here again the opportunity for female employees to take leaves of absence to handle various family matters was viewed very positively by these workers. It should be noted that the family-friendly policies seen as highly important in both of these instances were significantly different from the norm in the United States, in large part because both countries are developing. For example, day care, a major issue for families in the United States, was a significant issue in neither Thailand nor Zimbabwe. This is because of the prevalence of extended families, so that children are normally cared for by grandparents or others in the home. When a child became seriously ill, the mother would feel compelled to take time off to care for the child and seek medical attention. Longer-term (i.e., multimonth) leaves were often also necessary in rural settings to allow these women time to assist with seasonal work on family farms. In Zimbabwe, with its serious AIDS epidemic, the company also provided advice on avoiding HIV infection.

The importance of the particular policies we have discussed is partly linked to the fact that both cases involve rural workers in very traditional settings. The need for family-friendly policies might be just as pervasive in the urban centers of these countries, though the specific policies may be different. In the Thai case, for example, young, professional dual-career couples are quite common and the extended family is being supplanted by the nuclear family in these situations. The issues of quality child care is thus of increasing importance. Many of these couples can afford servants at this point, but with further economic development, the supply of servants will decline (as they move to higher-paying jobs) and day care is apt to become a more important issue.

Our discussion to this point leads to several observations:

(1) Many American companies generally believe that family-friendly policies have a positive impact on work-related outcomes.
(2) Empirical evidence demonstrating such a linkage, along with the careful assessment of policies that would follow from such information, is lacking.
(3) The issue of the role of family-friendly policies in other parts of the world, particularly developing countries, has been virtually ignored.
(4) The evidence that is available on this issue of family-friendly policies in developing countries suggests that such efforts are potentially important in light of the growing role of women in the labor forces of these countries and the challenges to traditional family life generated by economic development and modernity.

(5) Not surprisingly, almost nothing is known about what policies will work best in these circumstances, in which cultural and economic forces are quite different from those in the United States.

# THE IMPACT OF FAMILY-FRIENDLY POLICIES ON WORK ATTITUDES

Job satisfaction is defined as a pleasurable or positive emotional state resulting from the appraisal of one's job in general (Locke, 1976) and has been viewed as a multidimensional construct. Examples of job satisfaction dimensions include satisfaction with co-workers, satisfaction with supervisors, and satisfaction with work in general. In this study, we are interested in only one facet of job satisfaction, satisfaction with work in general. Affective commitment is a value-sharing, attitudinal attachment to the organization (Mathieu & Zaiac, 1990). Job satisfaction and organizational commitment have been regarded as two important attitudinal issues in the workplace because of their linkages with various workplace outcomes such as work and job withdrawal (Hanish & Hulin, 1991; Jaros, Jermier, Koehlor, & Sincich, 1993; Mowday, Porter, & Steers, 1982; Boles & Barry, 1996). Moreover, these outcomes have such effects in both predominantly collectivist and predominantly individualist cultures (Robert, Probst, Drasgow, Martocchio, & Lawler, 2000). Thus assessing the impact of family-friendly policies on these basic work-related outcomes is a useful means of assessing the potential impact of family-friendly policies in developing economies.

Theoretical arguments suggest that family-friendly polices can influence work satisfaction and affective commitment in two different ways. First, these policies may affect workers in general, regardless of whether they can benefit directly from these policies. By providing family-friendly policies, a company may promote an image of treating employees well, engendering a positive affective response by employees regardless of any actual or potential personal benefit from such policies (Grover & Crooker, 1995; Baron & Kreps, 1999; Johnson, 1995). There is some empirical evidence to support a general effect from family-friendly policies. For example, Kirchmeyer (1995) found that employee commitment was enhanced when organizations provided resources to help employees fulfill family and other nonwork responsibilities. Grover and Crooker (1995) showed that employees were more attached to organizations that offered family-friendly polices even though they might not personally benefit from the policies. Rogers and Rodgers (1989) found that employees in companies that did not offer family-friendly policies experienced higher levels of stress, greater absenteeism, and lower job satisfaction.

**Hypothesis 1a.** Family-friendly policies will be positively related to employee affective commitment.

**Hypothesis 1b.** Family-friendly policies will be positively related to employee job satisfaction.

Second, an individual's perception of the organization can be influenced by two types of information: the way others are treated by the organization and the way the individual himself or herself is treated by the organization. When an individual benefits directly from an organization's family-friendly policies, he or she may judge these policies as fair and consequently develop a more positive affect toward the company compared to those who do not benefit directly (Scholl, 1981). As an example of such a process at work (though not directly related to family-friendly policies), Greenberg (1981) compared workers' attitudes toward the government policy of gas rationing and observed that employees who took mass transit to work presented more positive attitudes than those who drove to work. More specifically, in the area of family-friendly policies, Grover (1991) found that people who benefited from a parental leave program rated that policy higher than people who could not utilize it. Thus the interrelationship between family-friendly policies and work attitudes, including work satisfaction and affective commitment, may not be linear (Herzberg et al., 1959), but may be moderated by some individual characteristics that enable workers to benefit from family-friendly programs. Compared to unmarried or childless counterparts, married workers or working parents face more actual or potential family responsibilities, including arranging for child care, caring for sick children or other family members, and dealing with other family-related matters. Although men have increasingly invested in the family domain, women are still chiefly responsible for these duties (Higgins, Duxbury, & Irving, 1992; Hochschild, 1989). So female workers with family responsibilities may have greater need to balance work and family responsibilities, making them benefit more from family-friendly programs and thus judge these policies more positively, leading to higher levels of work satisfaction and affective commitment.

Research evidence supports the specific effects of family-friendly polices on subpopulations. For example, Scandura and Lankau (1997) reported that flextime was related to higher organizational commitment and job satisfaction for those having family responsibilities. Marquart (1991) and Dawson, Mikel, Lorenz, and King (1984) found that users of on-site child-care facilities in the private sector were more satisfied with their jobs than those who did not use on-site care. Grover and Crooker (1995) found that the commitment of parents with young children was more influenced by child-care referral services than was that of parents without young children. The National Council of Jewish Women (NCJW, 1987) found that pregnant women in more family-friendly companies were more satisfied with their jobs and were more likely to return to work. Durst (1999) and Osterman (1995) observed that organizations with more women have gained more from providing family-friendly benefits. Kim (1998) reported that female employees desire greater family-related assistance from employers. He also found a significant difference in the family leave policy's impact on organizational commitment between male and female employees.

**Hypothesis 2a.** Family-friendly polices will be more positively related to employee affective commitment and job satisfaction for those with children than for those without children.

**Hypothesis 2b.** Family-friendly polices will be more positively related to employee affective commitment and job satisfaction for married workers than for unmarried workers.

**Hypothesis 2c.** Family-friendly polices will be more positively related to employee affective commitment and job satisfaction for female workers than for male workers.

Prior research has demonstrated the importance of controlling for the effects of potentially confounding demographic variables in the assessment of work–family relationships (Burley, 1994). Gender, parental status, marriage, family financial status, age, and tenure were expected to influence these relationships and are thus used as control variables in this study.

# RESEARCH METHODS

*Sample*

Survey data were collected from 11 banks located in India (New Delhi), Kenya (Nairobi), and China (Beijing). Questionnaires were distributed to groups of employees within each of the banks. The researchers oversaw the distribution of the questionnaires to the participants and explained the reason for the study. Participants were assured of anonymity. For the current study, only full-time nonmanagerial respondents were included in the sample. After deletion of cases with missing data, we had a useable sample of 448, with 136 respondents from India, 122 from Kenya, and 190 from China. Sample demographic characteristics are presented in Table 1.

## Measures

The survey utilized a variety of scales to measure major constructs in the study. Several steps were taken to ensure scale reliability and validity (as discussed below). The questionnaire was administered in English in India and Kenya, but translated into Chinese for the Chinese sample. Two bilingual speakers of Chinese and English performed the translation independently and then met to resolve discrepancies between the two translated versions. The resulting translation was then given to two

***Table 1.*** Sample Demographic Characteristics.

| Variable | India | Kenya | China | Combined |
|---|---|---|---|---|
| Total respondents | 136 | 122 | 190 | 448 |
| Age[a] | 35.7 (9.2) | 32.5 (6.3) | 32.5 (6.3) | 33.2 (7.4) |
| Gender | | | | |
| Male | 101 | 84 | 83 | 268 |
| Female | 35 | 36 | 107 | 178 |
| Unreported | 0 | 2 | 0 | 2 |
| Marital status | | | | |
| Never married | 40 | 45 | 30 | 115 |
| Married or living together | 96 | 77 | 160 | 333 |
| Parental status | | | | |
| With children | 89 | 93 | 131 | 313 |
| Without children | 46 | 29 | 59 | 134 |
| Unreported | 1 | | | 1 |
| Organization tenure[a] | 10.6 (8.3) | 6.9 (6.4) | 7.7 (5.0) | 8.3 (6.7) |
| Family financial status[a] | 3.2 (0.9) | 2.2 (0.2) | 2.7 (0.7) | 2.7 (0.9) |
| Education | | | | |
| Some high school | 9 | 21 | 0 | 30 |
| Some college or diploma | 19 | 51 | 71 | 141 |
| University degree | 56 | 41 | 113 | 210 |
| Post-graduate degree(s) | 52 | 9 | 7 | 67 |

[a]Reported as means with standard deviations in parentheses.

additional bilingual translators, who back-translated the questionnaire into English. In situations in which the back-translation was not equivalent to the original version, discussion among translators was held to resolve differences. Given the educational backgrounds of the white-collar workers in this study, it was possible to administer the questionnaires in English in both Kenya and India, where most educated individuals in major urban centers are fluent in English. Natives of both countries with professional expertise in the HR management field initially reviewed the English-language questionnaires in Kenya and India, indicating that most of the respondents would be able to understand the instrument. In fact, virtually all students in Kenya are taught at all grade levels in English and large numbers of more educated Indians attend English-language schools or study English from an early age. We also received no feedback from the participants to suggest that they could not understand the questionnaires.

*Family-Friendly Policies*
A list of 18 family-friendly programs was developed after discussion with HR experts and a review of the relevant literature, including prior surveys conducted in the United States. Examples of family-friendly programs in this list are on-site child care, resource and referral service for child care or elder care, flexible work schedules, working at home, leave for family reasons, and educational assistance for children or spouse. Short descriptions of each program were provided to ensure respondents understood the program in a similar way. Respondents were asked to answer "yes" if the particular program was provided by their organization, "no" if the program was not offered. The responses were dummy coded as $-1 =$ no and $1 =$ yes. Respondents also indicated how important each program was to them. Responses were made on a 4-point scale, ranging from 0, representing "not needed," to 3, representing "essential service." "No opinion" responses were treated as another expression of "not needed."

*Work Satisfaction and Affective Commitment*
We used the Job Descriptive Index (Smith, Kendall, & Hulin, 1969) to measure satisfaction with work in general (9-item form). Affective commitment was assessed using a 10-item scale developed by Mowday, Steers, and Porter (1979). Example items included "This organization has a great deal of personal meaning for me" and "I would be very happy to spend the rest of my career with this organization." Responses were made on a 5-point scale, with 1 representing "strongly disagree" and 5 representing "strongly agree."

*Control Variables*

Gender, marital status, and parental status were each coded as dummy variables (0 for female, unmarried, or nonparent; 1 for male, married, or parent). Individuals were defined as parents if they had at least one child under the age of 18. Age and organizational tenure were the actual value in years. Financial status was measured on a 5-point scale, ranging from 1 for "Our family's financial resources are not enough to get by on" to 5 for "Money is not an issue for our family." Country was also used, with a dummy variable indicating the company was located in China and a second indicating that it was located in Kenya, with India serving as the reference category.

*Data Analysis*

The entire sample was broken into two groups. The first sample was composed of 100 randomly selected participants (26 were from India, 29 from Kenya, and 45 from China). Thirty-nine were females and 59 were males. The average age was 32.4 (SD = 6.5), and job tenure was 7.7 years (SD = 6.6). As for education, 6.5% of the respondents finished only high school, 24% had some college work, and about 69% graduated from university or graduate school. The second sample consisted of the remaining 348 participants, including 110 respondents from India, 93 from Kenya, and 145 from China (see below for discussion of other demographic characteristics of this sample).

Various analyses were conducted in this study. We first did exploratory factor analysis of family-friendly policies using the first sample. Then, using the second sample, we did confirmatory factor analysis to validate the results of the exploratory factor analysis. We then examined scale equivalence across countries. Next, regression analyses were used with the second sample to test the hypotheses regarding the general or specific effects of family-friendly policies.

# RESULTS

## The Family-Friendly Policy Construct

### Exploratory Factor Analysis

We define the *motivating force of a family-friendly policy* as the product of its perceived availability multiplied by its importance to the respondent (i.e., availability × value). If the program is available and is perceived as important, then the value of this variable will be high (maximum value of 3); if the program is not available, yet perceived to be important, then the value will be low (with the lowest possible value being −3).

The smaller sample was first used for exploratory factor analysis to determine the underlying dimensions of motivating force. Factor analysis involved the use of principal axis factoring with varimax rotation. Three factors with eigenvalues greater than 1.0 emerged, explaining a 43% variance. Only items with loadings greater than .40 were kept in the scale. The first factor was named as "dependent care service" and included four items on child care and elder care. The second factor was "facilitating flexible time" and had three items. The third factor was named "assistance with family responsibilities" and included seven items. The extracted factors and item loadings are presented in Table 2.

## Confirmatory Factor Analysis

The second sample was used to examine the three-factor structures obtained from exploratory factor analysis. It was performed using analysis of moment structures (AMOS) with maximum likelihood estimation (Arbuckle & Wothke, 1999; Byrne, 2001). Each item was allowed to load on only its factor. The loading of the first item in each factor was fixed at 1.00 for identification purposes (see Byrne, 2001). The factors were allowed to correlate with one another. In assessing the model, we relied on several

***Table 2.***   Exploratory Factor Analysis Results.

|  | Factor 1 | Factor 2 | Factor 3 |
| --- | --- | --- | --- |
| Child-care referral service | .669 | | |
| On-site child-care facility | .733 | | |
| Elder-care referral service | .776 | | |
| On-site elder-care facility | .640 | | |
| Flexible work schedule | | .711 | |
| Work at home | | .443 | |
| Personal/family leave | | .685 | |
| Subsidize cost of child's education | | | .410 |
| Subsidize cost of spouse's education | | | .558 |
| Transportation of children | | | .587 |
| Job referral for child or spouse | | | .545 |
| Nursing area | | | .670 |
| Paid long-distance call to home on business travel | | | .692 |
| Parenting workshop | | | .657 |

standard fit indices to examine the overall model fit: the ratio of $\chi^2$ to degrees of freedom ($\chi^2/df$), goodness-of-fit index (GFI), comparative-fit index (CFI), and root mean square error of approximation (RMSEA). Fit indices for the three-factor model indicated a satisfactory fit of the data. The $\chi^2/df$ had a value 2.04, GFI was .95, CFI was .94, and RMSEA was .05. All the standardized item loadings were significant ($p < .0001$) and greater than .40.

*Scale Equivalence*
One of the pressing issues in cross-cultural research is establishing construct comparability in different samples (Little, 1997). To establish the equivalence of the scales developed here across the three countries, we used a combination of mean and covariance structures (Byrne, 2001; Little, 1997) and simultaneous factor analysis in several populations (Jöreskog, 1971; Sörbom, 1974). Following Byrne (2001), we first conducted item analysis on the scales used in the study to assess whether individual items were invariant across the three countries. On the basis of these analyses, one item from the commitment scale was excluded in the AMOS analyses conducted later because it did not function the same way in two countries.

Having established the invariance of individual scale items across the three countries, we then tested for invariant factor structures in our full theoretical model (i.e., estimation of a measurement model in which all constructs are included simultaneously). Progressively restricted models were fitted to multisample data to test the assumption that factor loadings were equivalent across samples. To do this, we followed the procedure recommended by Fitzgerald, Drasgow, Hulin, Gelfand, and Magley (1997) by forming multi-item indicators for each of the constructs and assuming covariation among the latent variables. This procedure minimizes the extent to which the indicators of each construct share variance and has the ability to generate more stable parameter estimates (Robert et al., 2000). Three multi-item indicators were created for the work satisfaction and commitment scales. However, in the case of the family-friendly program factors, we used the individual items rather than multi-item constructs. This was necessitated by the fact that two of the factors revealed by our exploratory factor analysis consisted of only three or four indicators.

The loading of the first indicator in each factor was fixed at 1.00 for identification purposes (see Byrne, 2001). In Model A (unrestricted), each indicator was allowed to load on only its factor, but the factor loadings and covariances were allowed to vary across countries. In Model B (restricted factor loading), factor loadings were restricted to be invariant across the three countries, but the covariances were free to vary across three countries. In Model C, an additional restriction of equal intercepts across countries for each item was added. Acceptance of Model C (fully restricted model) would imply that indicators provided approximately equivalent measurement of the same constructs across the three countries (Little, 1997).

The fit indices demonstrated a satisfactory fit of the data for Model A, the least restricted model. The $\chi^2/df$ was 1.43, GFI was .84, CFI was .91, and RMSEA was .04, indicating very good fit for a complex model. Fit statistics marginally decreased, but were still satisfactory, for the more constrained Model B: the $\chi^2/df$ was 1.47, GFI was .83, CFI was .90, and RMSEA was .04. The factor loadings and standard errors from Model B are presented in Table 3. All the estimated factor loadings were significant and reasonably close to 1.00, suggesting that the indicators measured their latent traits well, even under rigorous constraint. In addition, because Models A and B are nested, their differences in $\chi^2$ can be compared to their differences in $df$; the ratio was $70.87/30 = 2.36$. These fit statistics indicated that the factor loadings are approximately equal across the three countries. For Model C, the $\chi^2/df$ was 1.64, CFI was .97, and RMSEA was .04, indicating a satisfactory fit to the data under further rigorous constraints. Given that Model C provided an adequate fit to the data after we set very rigorous constraints on parameters across countries, we concluded that the assumption of measurement equivalence was acceptable.

***Table 3.*** Factor Loadings and Standard Errors in the Measurement Model.

| Construct | Factor Loadings | | | | | | |
|---|---|---|---|---|---|---|---|
| | 1 | 2 | 3 | 4 | 5 | 6 | 7 |
| Dependent-care service | 1.00 | 1.23 (0.27) | 1.70 (0.31) | 0.98 (0.22) | | | |
| Facilitating flexible time | 1.00 | 0.94 (0.15) | 0.47 (0.15) | | | | |
| Assistance with family responsibilities | 1.00 | 0.77 (0.16) | 0.89 (0.14) | 0.68 (0.14) | 1.15 (0.22) | 0.84 (0.18) | 0.52 (0.11) |
| Work satisfaction | 1.00 | 0.91 (0.11) | 0.88 (0.10) | | | | |
| Affective commitment | 1.00 | 1.09 (0.11) | 0.95 (0.09) | | | | |

*Note:* All factor loadings are significant at the .001 level.

## Hypothesis Testing

As described below, we used multiple regression, rather than structural equation modeling techniques, to test our principal hypotheses. This was done as many of the control variables are dichotomous and do not meet the normality assumption for covariance structure models. Hence, having established the validity of the family-friendly policies scales using fairly rigorous methods, we needed to construct scales for the regression analysis that were simply the sums of the corresponding items.

Table 4 presents means, standard deviations, and reliabilities for all summated rating scales based on the data from the second sample, with each item assigned a weight of 1. Overall, the scales had satisfactory reliability coefficients in each country, with the possible exceptions of .46 for flexible time in Kenya, .56 for flexible time in the pooled sample, and .51 for dependent care service in Kenya. The reliability estimates for the other measures were above .70 in the combined sample and could therefore be classified as acceptable for research purposes (Nunnally & Bernstein, 1994). Table 5 summarizes the correlations between the major variables. As seen from the Table 5, the three family-friendly policy factors were each significantly and positively correlated. Each policy factor was significantly and positively associated with work satisfaction and affective commitment. These results confirmed prior findings that family-friendly polices are associated with positive organizational outcomes.

Our principal hypotheses were tested by regressing work satisfaction and affective commitment on the three policy factors and control variables.

***Table 4.*** Scale Means, Standard Deviations, and Reliabilities.

| Scale | Pooled Sample | | | Indian Sample | | | Chinese Sample | | | Kenyan Sample | | |
|---|---|---|---|---|---|---|---|---|---|---|---|---|
| | M | SD | α | M | SD | α | M | SD | α | M | SD | α |
| Dependent-care service | −.96 | .93 | .68 | −.78 | 1.0 | .80 | −1.11 | .8 | .67 | −.94 | 1.0 | .51 |
| Assistance with family responsibilities | −.87 | .77 | .78 | −.62 | .81 | .79 | −.91 | .59 | .72 | −1.09 | .89 | .79 |
| Facilitating flexible time | −.05 | 1.0 | .56 | .36 | 1.12 | .62 | −.47 | .8 | .62 | .12 | 1.06 | .46 |
| Work satisfaction | 2.25 | .59 | .87 | 2.39 | .57 | .86 | 2.06 | .57 | .85 | 2.38 | .58 | .88 |
| Affective commitment | 3.42 | .72 | .85 | 3.63 | .7 | .82 | 3.27 | .65 | .87 | 3.43 | .79 | .86 |

This was conducted first with a pooled sample of all participants, then on various subpopulations. The subpopulations included parents versus nonparents, married versus not married, and males versus females. Tables 6a and 7a present the regression results (standardized coefficients) for work satisfaction and affective commitment, respectively. As we did analysis on subpopulations, it was necessary to test for the significance of differences in the values of the coefficients associated with the family-friendly policy factors (using the unstandardized coefficients) to test

***Table 5.*** Correlations among Summated Rating Scales.

| Variable | 1 | 2 | 3 | 4 | |
|---|---|---|---|---|---|
| Dependent-care service | 1.00 | | | | |
| Facilitating flexible time | .283** | 1.00 | | | |
| Assistance with family responsibilities | .602** | .445** | 1.00 | | |
| Work satisfaction | .210** | .233** | .210** | 1.00 | |
| Affective commitment | .147** | .286** | .199** | .547** | 1.00 |

**Correlation is significant at the 0.01 level (two-tailed).

***Table 6a.*** Regression Results for Work Satisfaction.

| Variable | Pooled Sample | Parents | Nonparents | Married | Unmarried | Female | Male |
|---|---|---|---|---|---|---|---|
| Age | .23** (.01) | .23** (.01) | −.02 (.02) | .24** (.01) | .19 (.02) | .22* (.01) | .23$^†$ (.01) |
| Gender | .11* (.06) | .12* (.07) | .02 (.13) | .13* (.07) | .00 (.14) | | |
| China (dummy variable) | −.11 (.08) | −.08 (.10) | −.10 (.16) | −.03 (.10) | −.15 (.17) | −.13 (.11) | −.03 (.14) |
| Kenya (dummy variable) | .13$^†$ (.10) | .15 (.12) | .22$^†$ (.20) | .22* (.12) | .35* (.21) | .11 (.12) | .21 (.17) |
| Marriage | −.01 (.09) | .02 (.13) | .03 (.15) | | | .06 (.13) | −.09 (.13) |
| Parent | .04 (.10) | | | .05 (.12) | −.11 (.22) | .03 (.14) | .05 (.16) |
| Family financial status | .10$^†$ (.04) | .12$^†$ (.05) | .00 (.08) | .10 (.05) | .09 (.08) | .10 (.05) | .11 (.06) |
| Tenure | −.01 (.01) | −.09 (.01) | −.13 (.03) | −.03 (.01) | −.33$^†$ (.02) | −.09 (.01) | −.14 (.01) |
| Dependent care | .09 (.04) | .16* (.05) | −.07 (.08) | .15* (.05) | −.02 (.09) | .15$^†$ (.05) | .02 (.07) |
| Flexible time | .09 (.03) | .06 (.04) | .18 (.07) | .07 (.04) | .12 (.07) | .11 (.04) | .07 (.06) |
| Assistance with family responsibilities | .11 (.05) | .10 (.06) | .11 (.12) | .11 (.06) | .10 (.11) | .06 (.07) | .16 (.08) |
| Overall $F$ | 6.77** | 6.38** | 1.75$^†$ | 7.40** | 2.23* | 4.04** | 2.06* |
| $R^2$ | .18 | .21 | .17 | .25 | .24 | .17 | .14 |
| Adjusted $R^2$ | .16 | .18 | .07 | .21 | .13 | .13 | .07 |

*Note:* Standard errors are in parentheses. *Significant at .05 level; **Significant at .01 level; $^†$Significant at .10 level.

Hypotheses 2a–2c. The results of *t*-tests for the values of the differences in these coefficients between subpopulations are reported in Table 6b for work satisfaction and Table 7b for affective commitment.

Counter to Hypothesis 1b, none of the family-friendly policy factors contribute to work satisfaction in the pooled sample (Table 6a). Hypotheses 2a–2c propose the specific effects of family-friendly policies on subpopulations rather than for employees generally. Our findings show that dependent care was significantly associated with work satisfaction among parents (of minor children), married employees, and females, but not among nonparents, unmarried employees, and males. These results lend some support for our argument that family-friendly policies will influence the former subpopulations more than the latter. However, this finding is weakened when we test for the significance of these differences (Table 6b). Only one of the three differences (supporting Hypothesis 2a) is supported. Therefore Hypotheses 2b and 2c are at best only weakly supported in the case of work satisfaction for dependent care. The other two family-friendly policy factors, flexible time and assistance with family responsibilities, did not show any significant effect on work satisfaction among any subpopulation.

***Table 6b.*** *t*-tests for Subpopulation Differences in Coefficients for Family-Friendly Policy Factors with Work Satisfaction as Dependent Variable.

| Variable | Parents | Nonparents | *t*-Value |
|---|---|---|---|
| Dependent care | 9.69E−02 (.047) | −4.37E−02 (.08) | 1.52[†] |
| Flexible time | 3.49E−02 (.038) | .105 (.071) | −0.87 |
| Assistance with family responsibilities | 7.08E−02 (.06) | .105 (.12) | −0.25 |
| Variable | Married | Unmarried | *t*-Value |
| Dependent care | 9.66E−02 (.046) | −1.28E−02 (.086) | 1.12 |
| Flexible time | 3.97E−02 (.038) | 7.16E−02 (.069) | −0.40 |
| Assistance with family responsibilities | 8.11E−02 (.06) | 8.01E−02 (.111) | 0.01 |
| Variable | Female | Male | *t*-Value |
| Dependent care | 9.39E−02 (.054) | 1.20E−02 (.065) | 0.97 |
| Flexible time | 6.26E−02 (.044) | 3.99E−02 (.056) | 0.32 |
| Assistance with family responsibilities | 4.58E−02 (.072) | .116 (.083) | −0.64 |

*Significant at .05 level; **Significant at .01 level; [†]Significant at .10 level.

***Table 7a.***   Regression Results for Affective Commitment.

| Variable | Pooled Sample | Parents | Nonparents | Married | Unmarried | Female | Male |
|---|---|---|---|---|---|---|---|
| Age | .24** (.01) | .19* (.01) | .13 (.02) | .27** (.01) | .01 (.02) | .26* (.01) | .21† (.01) |
| Gender | .05 (.08) | .07 (.09) | −.04 (.14) | .04 (.09) | .00 (.17) | | |
| China (dummy variable) | −.05 (.10) | .05 (.13) | −.25* (.17) | .01 (.12) | −.22† (.21) | −.02 (.14) | −.03 (.17) |
| Kenya (dummy variable) | .06 (.12) | .03 (.15) | .27* (.22) | .06 (.15) | .39* (.26) | .02 (.15) | .18 (.21) |
| Marriage | .06 (.11) | .07 (.17) | .05 (.16) | | | .06 (.16) | .08 (.16) |
| Parent | −.11 (.12) | | | −.03 (.14) | −.42* (.28) | −.12 (.17) | −.10 (.19) |
| Family financial status | .08 (.05) | .08 (.06) | .07 (.09) | .08 (.06) | .18 (.10) | .09 (.06) | .09 (.08) |
| Tenure | .01 (.01) | .06 (.01) | −.11 (.03) | .03 (.01) | .00 (.03) | .04 (.01) | −.08 (.01) |
| Dependent care | .03 (.05) | .14† (.06) | −.20† (.09) | .03 (.06) | .04 (.11) | .16† (.07) | −.13 (.08) |
| Flexible time | .22** (.04) | .22** (.05) | .22† (.08) | .22** (.05) | .20† (.09) | .30** (.05) | .12 (.07) |
| Assistance with family responsibilities | .06 (.07) | .01 (.08) | .13 (.13) | .09 (.07) | −.02 (.14) | −.05 (.09) | .18 (.10) |
| Overall $F$ | 5.77** | 5.32** | 3.75** | 5.89** | 2.23* | 5.37** | 1.33 |
| $R^2$ | .16 | .18 | .30 | .21 | .24 | .21 | .09 |
| Adjusted $R^2$ | .13 | .15 | .22 | .17 | .13 | .17 | .02 |

*Note:* Standard errors are in parentheses. *Significant at .05 level; **Significant at .01 level; †Significant at .10 level.

The results are somewhat different – and somewhat more supportive of our hypotheses – in the case of affective commitment. Flexible time schedules contribute to the affective commitment in the pooled sample, as well as in all subpopulations except males. This finding supports Hypothesis 1a. Neither of the two other family-friendly policy factors demonstrated an overall impact within the pooled sample. However, dependent care showed a significant and positive association with affective commitment among parents and a significant and negative association among nonparents. Dependent care had a significant and positive effect on commitment among female workers, but an insignificant effect among male workers. *t*-tests (Table 7b) revealed that dependent care had more significant effects on commitment among parents and females than among nonparents and males. These findings support Hypotheses 2a and 2c. Flexible time showed a significant and positive effect on commitment among females, but not among males, with this difference being significant and thus supporting Hypothesis 2c. However, none of the family-friendly policy factors show more positive effect on affective commitment among married workers than among unmarried workers, therefore countering Hypothesis 2b. And also

**Table 7b.** *t*-tests for Subpopulation Differences in Coefficients for Family-Friendly Policy Factors with Affective Commitment as Dependent Variable.

| Variable | Parents | Nonparents | *t*-Value |
|---|---|---|---|
| Dependent care | .108 (.06) | −.158 (.086) | 2.54** |
| Flexible time | .151 (.048) | .15 (.08) | 0.01 |
| Assistance with family responsibilities | 9.52E-03 (.076) | .137 (.128) | −0.86 |

| Variable | Married | Unmarried | *t*-Value |
|---|---|---|---|
| Dependent care | 2.15E−02 (.057) | 3.38E−02 (.105) | −0.10 |
| Flexible time | .151 (.047) | .147 (.085) | 0.04 |
| Assistance with family responsibilities | 8.27E−02 (.074) | −1.82E−02 (.136) | 0.65 |

| Variable | Female | Male | *t*-Value |
|---|---|---|---|
| Dependent care | .122 (.066) | −9.90E−02 (.08) | 2.13* |
| Flexible time | .206 (.053) | 7.81E−02 (.07) | 1.46† |
| Assistance with family responsibilities | −4.07E−02 (.087) | .16 (.102) | −1.50† |

*Significant at .05 level; **Significant at .01 level; †Significant at .10 level.

counter to Hypothesis 2c, assistance with family responsibilities showed a significantly more positive effect among males than females.

In sum, Hypothesis 1a was supported by the effects of flexible time but not supported by the effects of dependent care and assistance with family responsibilities. Hypothesis 1b was not supported by any family-friendly policy factors. Hypothesis 2a was supported by the effects of dependent care on work satisfaction and affective commitment, but not supported by the effects of other family-friendly policy factors. Hypothesis 2c was partially supported by the effects of dependent care and flexible time on affective commitment. Hypothesis 2b was not supported by any family-friendly policy factors.

### Analyses of Individual Family-Friendly Policies

In the previous analyses, we examined how family-friendly policies appear to influence work satisfaction and affective commitment. However, exploring family-friendly policies only in this manner may miss information about each individual policy. Thus, we provide a further descriptive analysis of the perceived availability and importance of individual family-friendly policies, as well as the relationships of importance with individual characteristics.

*Availability of Family-Friendly Policies in China, India, and Kenya*
Responses to the availability of each family-friendly policies were analyzed to obtain the percentage of people who answered "yes." Of 18 policies, only 6 in the combined sample, 6 in India, 5 in Kenya, and 3 in China were rated available by more than 20% of the respondents, indicating that most family-friendly programs were not widely used in these countries. The 6 most widely used policies in the combined sample were leave for family emergency (82.1%), personal and family leave (56.8%), flexible schedule (26.6%), subsidized child-care cost (24.6%), and health insurance for immediate family (21.2%). When we took a deeper look at the three country samples, we found that leave for family emergency (62.6% in India, 89.6% in Kenya, and 93.5% in China) and family and personal leave (67.9% in India, 74.5% in Kenya, and 35.1% in China) were consistently listed within the 5 most widely used policies. Subsidized child-care cost (23.7% in India and 47.2% in Kenya), flexible schedules (45% in India and 35.8% in Kenya), and health insurance for immediate family members (21.4% in India and 31.1% in Kenya) were within the 5 most widely used policies in both the Indian and the Kenyan samples.

*Desired Family-Friendly Policies*
Perceived importance of each family-related program was originally measured on a 4-point Likert-like item, ranging from 0 (not needed) to 3 (essential service). To make the following descriptive results more easily understood, we recoded the responses as 1 (not needed), 2 (somewhat important), 3 (important), and 4 (essential service). Table 8 presents the mean ratings of importance for each of these 18 family-friendly policies. Regardless of country, 16 of these 18 ratings were greater than 2.0 (somewhat important), indicating that the respondents found most of these programs to be important.

Table 9 shows the five most important and five least important policies in each country sample and the combined sample. Consistency in the rankings was observed. Six policies were ranked as most important more than twice. They were leave for family emergency (four times), health insurance for immediate family (three times), subsidized child-care cost (three times), subsidized child education cost (three times), leave for family and personal reasons (three times), and child referral service (twice). In addition, another six policies were ranked as least important more than twice, including work

***Table 8.*** Ratings of Importance for Family-Friendly Policies.

| Policy | India | | Kenya | | China | | Combined | |
|---|---|---|---|---|---|---|---|---|
| | Mean | SD | Mean | SD | Mean | SD | Mean | SD |
| Child-care referral | 2.12 | 0.90 | 2.84 | 1.13 | 2.30 | 0.89 | 2.39 | 1.00 |
| Bring child to work in emergency | 1.86 | 0.88 | 1.99 | 1.06 | 1.88 | 0.84 | 1.90 | 0.92 |
| Subsidize child-care cost | 2.34 | 0.94 | 2.84 | 1.01 | 2.33 | 0.86 | 2.47 | 0.95 |
| Child-care facility | 2.15 | 0.92 | 2.62 | 1.11 | 2.32 | 0.91 | 2.34 | 0.98 |
| Elder-care referral | 2.25 | 0.88 | 2.37 | 1.01 | 2.33 | 0.90 | 2.32 | 0.92 |
| Elder-care facility | 2.25 | 0.89 | 2.06 | 0.95 | 2.28 | 0.90 | 2.22 | 0.91 |
| Leave for family emergency | 2.80 | 1.00 | 3.26 | 0.79 | 3.12 | 0.78 | 3.06 | 0.88 |
| Flexible schedule | 2.39 | 0.98 | 2.54 | 0.94 | 2.00 | 0.67 | 2.25 | 0.96 |
| Work at home | 1.97 | 0.91 | 1.58 | 0.84 | 1.86 | 0.77 | 1.82 | 0.85 |
| Leave for family and personal reasons | 2.88 | 0.96 | 2.80 | 0.97 | 1.88 | 0.87 | 2.44 | 1.04 |
| Subsidize child's education cost | 2.34 | 0.84 | 2.75 | 0.84 | 2.34 | 0.73 | 2.45 | 0.81 |
| Subsidize spouse's education cost | 1.95 | 0.70 | 2.31 | 0.92 | 1.95 | 0.88 | 2.07 | 0.76 |
| Health insurance for immediate family | 2.74 | 0.86 | 2.94 | 0.91 | 2.08 | 0.77 | 2.52 | 0.92 |
| Transportation of children | 2.05 | 0.95 | 2.33 | 0.95 | 2.04 | 0.76 | 2.12 | 0.88 |
| Job referral for immediate family | 2.03 | 0.80 | 2.33 | 0.90 | 2.08 | 0.77 | 2.13 | 0.82 |
| Lactation facilities | 2.04 | 0.85 | 2.46 | 1.03 | 2.30 | 0.80 | 2.26 | 0.89 |
| Paid call to home when traveling | 2.29 | 0.88 | 2.51 | 0.96 | 2.07 | 0.80 | 2.26 | 0.89 |
| Parenting seminars | 1.95 | 0.81 | 2.39 | 0.92 | 1.91 | 0.77 | 2.05 | 0.85 |

at home (four times), bring child to work in emergency (four times), subsidized spouse education cost (four times), parenting seminars (three times), transportation for child to and from school (twice), and job referral service for immediate family (twice). Some exceptions were also observed in the Chinese sample. For example, though family and personal leave was ranked as one of the five most important policies in the Indian and Kenyan samples, it was regarded as one of five least important programs in the Chinese sample. As another example, on-site child-care facilities and elder-care referral services were rated within the six most important programs in China but not in India and Kenya.

*Individual Characteristics and Desired Family-Friendly Policies*
Table 10 presents the simple correlations between a variety of individual characteristics and the importance ratings of each family-friendly policy. Employees who had children rated seven family-related programs as more important, including child-care referral ($r = .16$, $p < .01$), subsidized child-care cost ($r = .15$, $p < .01$), on-site child-care facilities ($r = .13$, $p < .05$), subsidized spouse education cost ($r = .11$, $p < .05$), transportation for child

Table 9. List of Respondents' Ratings of Five Most and Five Least Important.

| Rank | India | | Kenya | | China | | Combined | |
|---|---|---|---|---|---|---|---|---|
| | Most important | Least important | Most important | Least important | Most important | Least important | Most important | Least important |
| 1 | Leave for family and personal reasons | Bring child to work in emergency | Leave for family emergency | Work at home | Leave for family emergency | Work at home | Leave for family emergency | Work at home |
| 2 | Leave for family emergency | Work at home | Health insurance for immediate family | Bring child to work in emergency | Subsidize child's education cost | Leave for family and personal reasons | Health insurance for immediate family | Bring child to work in emergency |
| 3 | Health insurance for immediate family | Subsidize spouse's education cost | Subsidize child-care cost | Elder-care facility | Subsidize child-care cost | Bring child to work in emergency | Subsidize child-care cost | Parenting seminars |
| 4 | Flexible schedule | Parenting seminars | Child-care referral | Subsidize spouse's education cost | Elder-care referral | Parenting seminars | Subsidize child's education cost | Subsidize spouse's education cost |
| 5 | Subsidize child's education cost | Job referral for immediate family | Leave for family and personal reasons | Job referral for immediate family | Elder-care referral | Subsidize spouse's education cost | Flexible schedule | Transportation of children |

***Table 10.*** Correlations between Individual Characteristics and Importance Ratings of Family-Friendly Policies.

| Individual Policy | Parent | Sex | Marriage | Tenure | Family Financial Status | Age |
|---|---|---|---|---|---|---|
| Child-care referral | 0.16** | −0.03 | 0.11* | 0.08 | −0.25** | −0.06 |
| Bring child to work in emergency | 0.04 | 0.10 | 0.01 | −0.06 | −0.06 | −0.07 |
| Subsidize child-care cost | 0.15** | −0.03 | 0.07 | −0.04 | −0.17** | −0.12 |
| Child-care facility | 0.13* | −0.03 | 0.08 | 0.02 | −0.24** | −0.02 |
| Elder-care referral | 0.08 | 0.03 | 0.08 | 0.12* | −0.10 | 0.04 |
| Elder-care facility | 0.08 | −0.05 | 0.14** | 0.07 | −0.10 | 0.05 |
| Leave for family emergency | −0.09 | −0.02 | −0.04 | −0.10 | −0.03 | −0.14 |
| Flexible schedule | −0.10 | 0.03 | −0.10 | −0.03 | 0.05 | −0.08 |
| Work at home | −0.02 | −0.02 | 0.06 | 0.00 | 0.01 | 0.04 |
| Leave for family and personal reasons | 0.06 | 0.11* | −0.06 | 0.10 | −0.02 | 0.06 |
| Subsidize child's education cost | 0.10 | 0.07 | 0.02 | 0.07 | −0.13** | −0.02 |
| Subsidize spouse's education cost | 0.11* | 0.04 | 0.04 | 0.00 | −0.14** | 0.00 |
| Health insurance for immediate family | −0.03 | 0.08 | 0.14* | 0.00 | 0.00 | −0.05 |
| Transportation of children | 0.17** | 0.00 | 0.04 | 0.00 | −0.19** | 0.00 |
| Job referral for immediate family | 0.15** | 0.03 | 0.12* | 0.16** | −0.15** | 0.11 |
| On-site nursing room | 0.16** | −0.02 | 0.19** | 0.07 | −0.14 | 0.05 |
| Paid call to home when traveling | 0.02 | −0.03 | −0.03 | −0.02 | −0.01 | 0.00 |
| Parenting seminars | 0.13 | 0.03 | 0.08 | 0.05 | −0.15** | −0.02 |

*Significant at .05 level; **Significant at .01 level.

to and from school ($r = .17$, $p < .01$), job referral service for immediate family ($r = .15$, $p < .01$), and on-site nursing rooms ($r = .16$, $p < .01$). This was followed by married workers, who rated five programs as more important, such as child-care referral service ($r = .11$, $p < .05$), elder-care facility ($r = .14$, $p < .01$), health insurance for immediate family ($r = .14$, $p < .05$), job referral for immediate family ($r = .12$, $p < .05$), and on-site nursing room ($r = .19$, $p < .01$). Males were more likely to rate family and personal leaves as more important ($r = .11$, $p < .05$). Workers with more years in the organization rated elder-care referral service ($r = .12$, $p < .05$) and job referral service ($r = .16$, $p < .01$) as more important. Workers with better family financial status rated eight family-related programs as less important: child-care referral service ($r = -.25$, $p < .01$), subsidized child-care cost ($r = -.17$, $p < .01$), child-care facility ($r = -.24$, $p < .01$), subsidized child education cost ($r = -.13$, $p < .01$), subsidized spouse education cost ($r = -.14$, $p < .01$), child transportation ($r = -.19$, $p < .01$), job referral for immediate family ($r = -.15$, $p < .01$), and parenting seminars ($r = -.15$, $p < .01$). Finally, employees' age was not correlated with any of the family-friendly policies.

## DISCUSSION AND IMPLICATIONS

This study has sought to address the dearth of empirical evidence as to the potential impact of family-friendly polices in developing countries with collectivist cultures. To fill this gap, this large-scale study empirically investigated the number and types of family-friendly policies and their personal importance in three collectivist countries. This study also explored the effects of family-friendly polices on various worker attitudes, such as affective commitment and work satisfaction.

This study showed that over 20% of the respondents rated only 6 of 18 policies as available in the pooled sample. Among these, only 2 policies (leave for family emergency and leave for personal and other family reasons) were perceived available by more than 50% of the respondents. Not surprisingly, these findings thus indicated that family-friendly programs in these countries are not in wide use compared to the United States. Apart from differences in the level of economic development, one possible explanation for these findings is that collectivist cultures enable workers to seek help with housework or child care from their relatives and friends. For example, it is very common in China for parents to help their children with household maintenance and child rearing. Help from workers' extended families and personal networks may minimize their needs for assistance from an employer to meet family responsibilities. Another reason may be that these countries are still surplus-labor economies, so employers might not need to utilize family-friendly polices to attract and retain workers, as their American counterparts often do. However, some factors that have not been explored in this study may also contribute to the provision of family-friendly polices. For example, employers may offer more family-friendly policies in larger organizations and in tighter labor markets. Moreover, with rapid economic development, traditional familial relationships may be breaking down, particularly among the more affluent of the urban population. Future studies can help to get a clearer picture by controlling for the effects of these factors.

Results showed that family emergency days off was ranked as one of the five most important family-friendly polices in all three countries, which is consistent with McKeen and Burke (1994), who found that family emergency days off was one of the five most important policies for managerial women employees. Other important policies were mostly related to family expenses, such as health insurance for immediate family, subsidized child-care cost, and subsidized child education cost. Work at home and being able to bring a child to work in emergencies were rated consistently as among the five *least* important policies. Previous research has found that work at home exerts significantly negative influence on satisfaction with work–family balance (Saltzstein, Ting, & Grace, 2001) and is more stressful for employees with children at home or facing great demands for household care (Christense, 1988; Hall, 1990; Metzger & Von Glinow, 1988; Saltzstein et al., 2001). Interruptions by children and household maintenance work may make it hard for workers to concentrate on their work. In addition, work pressures may inhibit workers' ability to fulfill family responsibilities. As a result, the increased conflict between work and family may make workers unable to take advantage of working at home. Bringing children to work may have similar negative effects on both work productivity and the relationship with children, therefore being disfavored by workers.

Leave for personal and other family reasons was ranked as one of the five *most* important policies in India and Kenya, but as one of five *least* important policies in China. This inconsistent finding may be due to the difference in worker composition. Examination of the sample composition showed that male workers were a much higher proportion of the Indian and Kenyan samples than the Chinese sample. The difference in worker composition may result from government policies utilized since the founding of the People's Republic of China in 1949 that enable Chinese women to participate more extensively in the labor force. Women traditionally assume more family responsibilities than men. Women's traditional supportive image is likely to hold back their upward mobility in organizations (Naff, 1997; Kim, 1998). Though personal and family leave can help women to reconcile work–family conflict, it may also increase the conflict between women and supervisors, who value productivity at work. It may put women at more of a disadvantage at work, thus making it a less desirable policy for women employees in China. Some support for this notion was offered by Kim (1998), who found that female employees perceived a marginally more negative, though not statistically significant, impact of family leave policies on their career advancement than male employees.

The study showed that parents with minor children and married workers rated family-friendly policies as more important than parents without minor children and unmarried employees, whereas the employees with better family financial situations rated family-friendly policies as less important. Taken together, these findings suggested that perceived family pressures might influence individual's perception of the importance of family-friendly policies. Being a parent means increased family work on child care. Being married incurs more responsibilities to take care of the household, the marriage partner, and other immediate family members. Increased family pressure may make these workers desire greater support from employers for family responsibilities.

Regression results showed support for both sides of the debate about whether family-friendly programs have generally positive effects on employees or have diverse effects on various subpopulations. Our findings suggest that different family-friendly policy factors cannot be similarly explained by either a general- or specific-effect hypothesis. In particular, we found that flexible time has positive effects on affective commitment among the whole workforce and the majority of subpopulations. This type of family-friendly policy may contribute to building a positive image of the organization and thus should be offered to employees regardless their need for such a benefit. In contrast, we found that dependent care has various effects on employees who have different needs for such benefits, supporting the argument of specific effects of family-friendly policies related to affected groups. Dependent care even showed a negative association with affective commitment among nonparents, which is consistent with the argument that family-friendly programs may produce a sense of inequality and result in negative outcomes among people who do not need such benefits (Herzberg et al., 1959; Pasternak, 1994). These results have suggested that dependent care should be cautiously tailored to meet employees' specific needs. We did not find any positive effects for assistance with family responsibilities, suggesting that this type of family-friendly policy may be less useful for employers. The finding that all family-friendly policy factors have insignificant effects on work satisfaction in the pooled sample may not be generalized to other facets of job satisfaction, because we measured only one facet of job satisfaction (i.e., satisfaction with the work itself). Further research is needed to examine the effects of family-friendly policies on other facets of job satisfaction. The unexpected finding that assistance with family responsibilities has more positive effects on commitment among males than among females is hard to explain. It may reflect the fact that men are becoming more active in the family (Pleck, 1985) and assuming more family responsibilities than before. Employer assistance with family responsibilities may help male workers to balance work and family duties and enable them to achieve their work goals, which are usually primary in men's lives. Further studies are needed to explain why this type of family-friendly polices showed more significant effects on men than on women.

The current study provides several theoretical and practical implications for future research in family-friendly policies. Theoretically, the current study has extended previous research by attempting to improve our understanding of a much broader array of family-friendly policies in countries with different cultures compared to the United States. Generally, very few family-friendly programs have been utilized in these countries. We suggest that cultural forces might play an important role on the unpopularity of these programs in collective countries. For example, easy access to relatives or friends for help can reduce employee need for help from employers with their family responsibilities, thus making the family-friendly policies unnecessary in the organizations. However, would be useful if future research compared family-friendly policies directly between individualist and collectivist cultures within a single study.

Despite a commonly held assumption among managers that utilization of family-friendly policies is beneficial for organizations, previous research has not yet established firm and unequivocal relationships between family-friendly programs and work-related outcomes. Scholars have not resolved the debate about whether family-friendly programs have generally positive effects on employees or have diverse effects on various subgroups. This study shows support for both sides of the debate and suggests that different family-friendly policies cannot be similarly explained by either general- or specific-effect hypotheses. The way organizations offer family-friendly policies should depend on the nature of their effects on employees. For example, organizations may offer family-friendly policies to all the employees if these policies have a positive effect on employees in general. Instead, if the policies have a positive effect on only some subpopulations, organizations should tailor these policies to specific employee needs to make them more cost-efficient.

As with all research, our study is bound by certain limitations that warrant further attention. First, the use of cross-sectional data precludes definitive assertions regarding causality and directionality. Longitudinal designs are needed in future research to avoid such problems. However, the optimal time lag for a given relationship is crucial in longitudinal studies. In the absence of appropriate time lags, longitudinal data might provide biased parameter estimates that may be worse than those obtained from cross-sectional data (Frone et al., 1992). Second, we measured only affective commitment and one facet of job satisfaction: satisfaction with the work itself. We did not investigate the effects of family-friendly policies on other work-related attitudes and behaviors, such as other facets of job satisfaction and withdrawal behaviors. Exclusion of various work-related outcomes inhibited our ability to make a complete benefit analysis of family-friendly policies. Third, we measured the effects of family-friendly policies on various subpopulations such as females versus males, parents versus nonparents, and married workers versus unmarried workers. However, the subpopulations may not be homogeneous. For example, mothers and fathers or parents with younger children and those with older children may show different patterns regarding the effects of family-friendly policies. Future studies might sample a wider range of individual characteristics and thus reveal the effects on more diverse employee groups.

Despite these limitations, the present study makes an important contribution to our understanding of the effects of family-friendly policies on worker attitudes. This area of research still merits further empirical investigation before conclusive generalizations can be made. Therefore, we hope that the results of the current study will stimulate further investigation into the field of family-friendly policies.

## ACKNOWLEDGMENTS

The authors acknowledge support for this project received under research grants from the Illinois Center for International Business Education and Research and the University of Illinois Campus Research Board.

## REFERENCES

Arbuckle, J. L., & Wothke, W. (1999). *AMOS 4.0 user's guide*. Chicago: Smallwaters.

Aryee, S., Fields, D., & Luk, V. (1999). A cross-cultural test of a model of the work-family interface. *Journal of Management*, 25(4), 491–511.

Bacharach, S. B., Bamberger, P., & Conley, S. (1991). Work-home conflict among nurses and engineers: Mediating the impact of role stress on burnout and satisfaction at work. *Journal of Organizational Behavior*, 12(1), 39–53.

Baron, J. N., & Kreps, D. M. (1999). *Strategic human resources: Frameworks for general managers*. New York: Wiley.

Boles, J. S., & Barry, B. J. (1996). On the front lines: Stress, conflict, and the customer service provider. *Journal of Business Research*, 37(1), 41–50.

Burley, K. A. (1994). Gender differences and similarities in coping responses to anticipated work-family conflict. *Psychological Reports*, 74, 115–123.

Byrne, B. M. (2001). *Structural equation modeling with AMOS: Basic concepts, applications, and programming.* Mahwah, NJ: Lawrence Erlbaum Associates.

Christense, K. (1988). *Women and home-based work: The unspoken contract.* New York: Holt, Rinehart, and Winston.

Cloud, K. (1999). *Case study: Cargill Zimbabwe.* Champaign, IL: Gender in Agribusiness Project University of Illinois.

Daley, D. (1998). An overview of benefits for the public sector: Not on the fringe anymore. *Review of Public Personnel Administration, 19*(3), 5–22.

Dawson, A. G., Mikel, C. S., Lorenz, C. S., & King, J. (1984). *An experimental study of the effects of employer-sponsored childcare services on selected employee behaviors.* Washington, DC: Department of Health and Human Services, Office of Human Development Services.

Durst, S. (1999). Assessing the effect of family friendly programs on public organizations. *Review of Public Personnel Administration, 19*(3), 19–33.

Ezra, M., & Deckman, M. (1996). Balancing work and family responsibilities: Flextime and childcare in the Federal Government. *Public Administration Review, 56*(2).

Fitzgerald, L. F., Drasgow, F., Hulin, C. L., Gelfand, M. J., & Magley, V. J. (1997). Antecedents and consequences of sexual harassment in organizations: A test of an integrated model. *Journal of Applied Psychology, 82,* 578–589.

Folsom, D., & Botsch, R. (1993). Is your company family friendly? *Business and Economic Review, 39*(3), 13–15.

Frone, M. R., Russell, M., & Cooper, M. L. (1992). Antecedents, and outcomes of work-family conflict: Testing a model of the work-family interface. *Journal of Applied Psychology, 77*(1), 65–78.

Greenberg, J. (1981). The justice of distributing scarce and abundant resources. In: M. J. Lerner & S. C. Lerner (Eds), *The justice motive in social behavior* (pp. 289–316). New York: Plenum.

Greenfield, C. A. (1997). Mobilizing resources for work force effectiveness: The role of work/life benefits and programs. *Employee Benefit Plan Review, 52*(3), 29–30.

Greenhaus, J. H., & Parasuraman, S. (1999). Research on work, family, and gender: Current status and future directions. In: G. N. Powell (Ed.), *Handbook of gender and work* (pp. 391–412). Newbury Park, CA: Sage Publications.

Grover, S. L. (1991). Predicting the perceived fairness of parental leave policies. *Journal of Applied Psychology, 76,* 247–255.

Grover, S. L., & Crooker, K. J. (1995). Who appreciates family-responsive human resource policies: The impact of family-friendly policies on the organizational attachment of parents and non-parents. *Personnel Psychology, 48,* 271–288.

Hall, D. (1990). Promoting work/family balance: An organization-change approach. *Organizational Dynamics, 18*(1), 4–18.

Hanish, K. A., & Hulin, C. L. (1991). General attitudes and organizational withdrawal: An evaluation of a causal model. *Journal of Vocational Behavior, 39,* 110–128.

Herzberg, E., Mausner, B., & Synderman, B. B. (1959). *The motivation to work* (2nd ed.). New York: Wiley.

Higgins, Duxbury, & Irving (1992). Work-family conflict: A comparison of dual-career and traditional-career men. *Journal of Organizational Behavior, 13,* 389–411.

Hochschild, A. (1989). *The second shift: Working parents and the revolution at home.* New York: Viking.

Jaros, S. J., Jermier, J. M., Koehlor, J. M., & Sincich, T. (1993). Effects of continuance, affective, and moral commitment on the withdrawal process: An evaluation of eight structured equation models. *Academy of Management Journal, 6*, 951–995.

Johnson, A. A. (1995). The business case for work-family programs. *Journal of Accountancy, 180*(2), 53–58.

Jöreskog, K. G. (1971). Simultaneous factor analysis in several populations. *Psychometrika, 36*, 409–426.

Kiggundu, M. N. (1989). *Managing organizations in developing countries: An operational and strategic approach.* West Hartford, CT: Kumarian Press.

Kim (1998). Organizational culture and New York state employees' work-family conflict: Gender differences in balancing work and family responsibilities. *Review of Public Personnel Administration, 18*(2), 57–72.

Kirchmeyer, C. (1995). Managing the work-non-work boundary: An assessment of organizational responses. *Human Relations, 48*, 515–536.

Lawler, J. J., & Atmiyanandana, V. (2001). *Case study: Cargill Sun Valley (Thailand).* Champaign, IL: Gender in Agribusiness Project, University of Illinois.

Little, T. (1997). Mean and covariance structures (MACS) analyses of cross-cultural data: Practical and theoretical issues. *Multivariate Behavioral Research, 32*, 53–76.

Locke, E. A. (1976). The nature and causes of job satisfaction. In: M. Dunnette (Ed.), *Handbook of industrial and organizational psychology* (pp. 1297–1350). Chicago, IL: Rand McNally.

Marquart, J. (1991). How does the employer benefit from childcare. In: J. S. Hyde & M. J. Essex (Eds), *Parental leave and childcare.* Temple University.

Mathieu, J., & Zaiac, D. M. (1990). A review and meta-analysis of the antecedents, correlates, and consequences of organizational commitment. *Psychological Bulletin, 108*, 171–194.

McKeen, C. A., & Burke, R. J. (1994). The women-friendly organization: Initiatives valued by managerial women. *Employee Counseling Today, 6*(6).

Mergenhagan, P. (1994). Job benefits get personal. *American Demographics, 16*(9), 30–36.

Metzger, R. O., & Von Glinow, M. A. (1988). Off-site workers: At home and abroad. *California Management Review, 30*(3), 101–111.

Mowday, P., Porter, l., & Steers, R. (1982). *Employee-organization linkages: The psychology of commitment, absenteeism, and turnover.* New York: Academic Press.

Mowday, R. T., Steers, R. M., & Porter, L. W. (1979). The measurement of organizational commitment. *Journal of Vocational Behavior, 14*, 224–247.

Naff, C. C. (1997). Colliding with a glass ceiling: Barriers to the advancement of women and minorities. In: C. Ban & N. M. Riccucci (Eds), *Public personnel management: Current concerns and future challenges* (2nd ed.). New York: Longman.

National Council of Jewish Women (NCJW). (1987). *Accommodating pregnancy in the workplace.* New York: National Council of Jewish Women.

Nunnally, J. C., & Bernstein, I. H. (1994). *Psychometric theory.* New York: McGraw-Hill.

Osterman, P. (1995). Work/family programs and the employment relationship. *Administrative Science Quarterly, 40*, 681–700.

Pasternak, C. (1994). Questioning friendly policies. *HR Magazine, 39*(6), 30.

Pleck, J. H. (1985). *Working wives/working husbands.* Thousand Oaks, CA: Sage publications.

Robert, C., Probst, T. M., Martocchio, J. J., Drasgow, F., & Lawler, J. J. (2000). Empowerment and continuous improvement in the United States, Mexico, Poland, and India:

Predicting fit on the basis of dimensions of power distance and individualism. *Journal of Applied Psychology, 85,* 643–658.

Rogers, E. S., & Rodgers, C. (1989). Business and the facts of family life. *Harvard Business Review, 67,* 121–129.

Saltzstein, A. L., Ting, Y. S., & Grace, H. (2001). Work-family balance and job satisfaction: The impact of family-friendly policies on attitudes of federal government employees. *Public Administration Review, 61*(4), 452–467.

Scandura, T. A., & Lankau, M. (1997). Relationships of gender, family responsibility and flexible work hours to organizational commitment and job satisfaction. *Journal of Organizational Behavior, 18*(4), 377–391.

Scholl, R. W. (1981). Differentiating organizational commitment from expectancy as a motivating force. *Academy of Management Review, 6,* 589–599.

Smith, P. C., Kendall, L. M., & Hulin, C. L. (1969). *The measurement of satisfaction in work and retirement.* Chicago: Rand-McNally.

Sörbom, D. (1974). A general method for studying differences in factor means and factor structures between groups. *British Journal of Mathematical and Statistical Psychology, 27,* 229–239.

# INTERNATIONAL HUMAN RESOURCE MANAGEMENT IN THE INDIAN INFORMATION TECHNOLOGY SECTOR: A COMPARISON OF INDIAN MNCS AND AFFILIATES OF FOREIGN MNCS IN INDIA

Mary Mathew and Harish C. Jain

## ABSTRACT

*The information technology (IT) sector has gained prominence since 1990. However, studies on the human resource management (HRM) policies and practices of multinational corporations (MNCs) have been few and far between. In this paper we study the Indian IT sector using both qualitative and quantitative approaches. For the quantitative research design, we used structured measurement tools developed by the Global HRM Project. Data were collected from 36 IT MNCs of Indian and foreign origin (U.S. and European) located in Bangalore and Hyderabad in India. We tested four hypotheses that were verified using the Mann–Whitney test of mean rank. We assessed the flow of HRM*

The Global Diffusion of Human Resource Practices: Institutional and Cultural Limits
Advances in International Management, Volume 21, 267–297
ISSN: 1571-5027/doi:10.1016/S1571-5027(08)00011-9

*practices and the differences in HR practices between Indian and foreign MNCs. For the qualitative design we used an unstructured approach to gather secondary data sources and used anecdotal data gathered over a decade through our interactions with the Indian IT industry. We used the narrative style to show past and current Indian business culture, level of technology, and implications for foreign direct investment in the Indian IT sector. We state two qualitative hypotheses for this part of the research study. We find the current business culture and level of technology of Indian IT MNCs moderately similar to those of foreign MNCs, and more so U.S. MNCs. We find no differences between Indian and foreign MNCs in HRM practices. We assume that the unexpected similarity in international human resource management (IHRM) practices is probably due to: (1) the nature of information technology, (2) closing levels of R&D between Indian and foreign MNCs, and (3) similar business cultures of Indian and foreign MNCs. IT-intensive global organizations are likely get a step closer to global IHRM standardization.*

# INTRODUCTION

The role of import and export of human resource management (HRM) practices in parent multinational companies (MNCs) is critical in understanding international human resource management (IHRM) (Jain, Lawler, & Morishima, 1998). The direction of HRM flow (export and import) has undergone a metamorphosis with time. In previous times, parent MNCs controlled the operations of their international affiliates or subsidiaries in other countries by exporting their standardized HRM practices into the affiliate to ensure business effectiveness. This is what Perlmutter (1969) referred to as an ethnocentric approach. According to this approach, parent-to-affiliate HRM practice flows were achieved by sending expatriates to manage the HR practices of the affiliate or through ways of maintaining a dependence on the parent and ensuring communication with the parent (Rosenzweig & Nohria, 1994). The ethnocentric flow met with local culture clashes and local laws (Schneider, 1988; Martin & Beaumont, 1998; Bae, Chen, & Lawler, 1998; Ferner & Quintanilla, 1998). Certain contextual factors like business, organizational, and social environments of parents and affiliates largely determined these variations. With time, localization or local embeddedness was noted (Rosenzweig & Nohria, 1994). This localization was based on local resource dependency, union representation, and affiliate size. The HRM practices that prevailed in the affiliate's country were to be a reflection of the social fabric of that country.

As time progressed some HRM practices got exported back to the parent or host organizations whenever necessary. This is called reverse diffusion (Edwards, 1998). Taking cues from terms like "national business systems" and "industrial orders," which are alternative ways of organizing economic activities, varying organizational isomorphisms are now documented (Ferner & Quintanilla, 1998). This reversal of flow gave rise to a number of studies assessing the differences in parent–affiliate HRM practices. What was missing was a sectoral emphasis on HRM research designs. A multisectoral emphasis was noted in some studies (Ferner & Quintanilla, 1998; Kelly, 2001). However, even in these, sector is not a predominant focus of the study. This is because the role of technology was not considered a moderator variable of IHRM differences. At present, technology has gained priority in IHRM research designs. This is because some technologies create new isomorphisms of economic activity. The boundary-less world of virtual organizations (Bartlett & Ghoshal, 1989) creates borderless multinational organizations. An exciting sector that has emerged in new markets, namely India and China, but missing until recently in IHRM research, is the information technology (IT) sector. Keeping the IT sector in perspective, this chapter attempts to throw light on IHRM in IT multinationals of Indian origin. A comparison of U.S. and non-U.S. IT organizations located in India is made to assess their flow of HRM practices. Implications for research in this context are also discussed.

# LITERATURE REVIEW

Since the 1980s, there have been a variety of studies and publications dealing with IHRM. A common theme is the role of HR practice flow from the MNC parent to recipient affiliate organizations. Looking at the early literature, scholars considered best practices of HRM to understand why HRM failed in its objectives. Organizations were classified in terms of HR usage into "nonstarters," "fads," and "dead letters" (Jain & Murray, 1984). Jain and Murray (1984) outline the best HRM practices at that time. They examine such HRM practices as job analysis, human resource planning, selection and placement, employee training and development, performance appraisal, wage and salary administration, employee participation, employee relations records, and HR research.

The literature can be classified into writings of American and European origin. Both the European- and the American-origin studies have contributed significantly to the understanding of HRM practices. The research designs used differed, however. The research designs can be classified into empirical and nonempirical, of which empirical takes both the case-study and the survey research approaches. These studies aimed at identifying best practices for IHRM. Table 1 shows the survey research studies in IHRM. Ten studies reported in this table covered varying HR practices in multiple countries and looked at samples of parents and subsidiaries. Eight studies examined hypotheses related to IHRM. The table lists the methods used, as described by these authors. Intercountry differences were documented in these studies. The Euronet Cranfield Survey covered a large sample of over 6,300 organizations and 1,055 returned responses (Cleveland, Gunnigle, Heraty, Morley, & Murphy, 2000). The researchers studied host-country practices of U.S.-owned subsidiaries in Europe. Using discriminant analysis on a series of HR practices to predict the country of the U.S. affiliate, they found labor relations to be the most important predictor. Further, they examined levels of similarity of U.S. firm HRM practices in European subsidiaries. The similarity was less in countries such as Denmark, Germany, and Sweden and more in Ireland and the United Kingdom. This indicates that HRM practices of affiliates in Ireland and the United Kingdom are similar to those of the host country and minimal accommodation is required by the host country while operating in these foreign countries. Another study examined 700 organizations and measured the impact of high-performance work systems (HPWS) originating from host countries in the East Asian markets (Bae, Chen, Wan, Lawler, & Walumbwa, 2003). Using two-stage least-squares regression, the researchers found that locally owned firms had greater success in implementation of HPWS than Japanese, European, and U.S. affiliates in the area. U.S. affiliates did a bit better than other multinationals. The authors that used the case-study approach and provided qualitative case data in the context of IHRM were Ferner and Quintanilla (1998), Martin and Beaumont (1998), Edwards (1998), Shekshnia (1998), Muller (1998), Teagarden et al. (1995), Turner, D'Art, and Gunnigle (2002), Kelly (2001), Shih, Chiang, and Kim (2005), Papalexandris and Panayotopoulou (2004), Zhang (2003), Ferner and Varul (2000), Jain (1991), Edwards, Ferner, and Sisson (1996), Schneider (1988), and Belanger, Edwards, and Wright (1999). Among these authors Jain (1991), Martin and Beaumont (1998), Belanger et al. (1999), and Turner et al. (2002) also contribute to the body of knowledge with qualitative hypotheses testing. Jain (1991) considered eight case studies of Indian origin

***Table 1.*** Showing Quantitative Survey Research Literature in IHRM.

| Author | Year/Journal | Sector | Sample |
|---|---|---|---|
| Rosenzweig and Nohria | 1994/JIBS | 10 two-digit SIC industry categories ranging from food processing to electronics and wholesale trade | U.S. companies (MacMillan & Co Corporate Affiliations database), parents in Canada, France, Germany, Japan, The Netherlands, Sweden, Switzerland, UK, 249 completed samples using a questionnaire |
| Roth and O'Donnell | 1996/AMJ | Scientific measuring instruments and controls, surgical and medical instruments | Questionnaire used in mail survey, from directories of IDCA (international), ACFIA (USA), DFCAE (Japan), obtained 100 completed responses from foreign subsidiaries in USA, UK, Canada, Japan, Germany |
| Bae, Chen, and Lawler | 1998/TIJHRM | 20 two-digit SIC industry categories | Questionnaire on nonmanagerial employees, 138 Korean companies (40 indigenous Korean and 98 affiliates (USA, Europe, Japan)), 52 Taiwanese companies (26 indigenous Taiwanese and 26 affiliates), affiliates subsidiaries and JVs. |
| Horwitz and Smith | 1998/TIJHRM | Several industries, 50% manufacturing | Labor market flexibility questionnaire, 626 responses from organizations in South Africa (local and foreign owned) (South African Central Statistical Services Register of Companies) |
| Ngo, Turban, Lau, and Lui | 1998/TIJHRM | Manufacturing, trading, finance/banking, and others | Organizations with over 50 employees in Hong Kong, 253 responses from 99 local Chinese firms, 82 USA, 39 Japanese, 34 British |
| Ryan, McFarland, Baron, and Page | 1999/Personnel Psychology | Not mentioned | Managerial and nonmanagerial responses from 959 organizations of 22 countries, organizations having 1,000 or more employees (Dun and Bradstreet's database) |

**Table 1.** (*Continued*)

| Author | Year/Journal | Sector | Sample |
|---|---|---|---|
| Bae and Lawler | 2000/AMJ | 20 two-digit SIC industry categories | Single business units with 50 or more employees in 138 Korean companies (40 Korean owned, 41 U.S. subsidiaries and joint ventures, 42 European subsidiaries and joint ventures, 15 Japanese joint ventures and subsidiaries) |
| Cleveland, Gunnigle, Heraty, Morley, and Murphy | 2000/IBAR | Not mentioned | 1,022 samples of U.S.- and European-owned MNCs, namely Denmark, France, Germany, Ireland, UK, Sweden, USA, EURONET Cranfield Survey |
| Carpenter, Sanders, and Gregersen | 2001/AMJ | Not mentioned | 245 MNC companies (Standard & Poors 500, Fortune 500, PC-COMPUSTAT, Directory of Corporate affiliations) |
| Bae, Chen, Wan, Lawler, and Walumbwa | 2003/IJHRM | Not mentioned | 683 organizations from Korea, Thailand, Taiwan, Singapore, subsidiaries of MNCs and locally owned organizations |

using HR variables of manpower planning, layoff policies, compensation and promotion, training, performance appraisal, decision-making and management styles, participative mechanism and work group, union–management relations, and grievances.

Belanger et al. (1999) described the case of Alcan in the aluminum sector. Kelly (2001) analyzed the increasing role of HR personnel in MNCs. Martin and Beaumont (1998) described diffusion of best practices in Asea Brown Boveri (ABB). Using the Cranfield survey of HR practices, Turner et al. (2002) commented on industrial relations systems of MNCs. Some of these studies examined how MNCs' HRM practices were incorporated into new cultures of affiliates and factors that facilitated that fit. In doing so, scholars considered different variables in the context of IHRM. Some of them were clashes of local national culture, business characteristics of the organization, and HR practices; the role of IT in facilitating IHRM; and classification of parent-affiliate practice philosophy. Schneider (1988) looked at specific HRM practices and their fit with the local national cultures. Implied in her study was the need to verify potential clashes generated by the philosophy of a specific HRM practice. She discussed the practices of staffing, planning, appraisal, compensation, selection, and socialization in her study. Doz and Prahalad (1986) stated that as the variety of strategic control configurations increased in the international affiliate's home territory, HRM needed to balance the polarized strategies of localizing the international affiliate's culture and maintaining loyalty to the MNC's corporate interests for the success of MNCs in such foreign territories. The authors found a relationship between business characteristics and HRM. They stated that, "export platforms that are an integral part of a global manufacturing network for a business and ... large integrated subsidiaries which contain significant research, product development and manufacturing capabilities ..." needed extensive and substantial strategic controls over small importing subsidiaries that acted as internal agents for the parent MNC. One solution was to manage MNC businesses abroad through technology. HRM systems are used to manage relationships between the affiliate and the host MNC, together with information-processing systems and corporate control systems (Pucik & Katz, 1986). Some scholars identified business characteristics and practice philosophy. They referred to these as "counteracting pressures for internal consistency" that ensured that "the affiliate HRM practices resemble local practices" (Rosenzweig & Nohria, 1994). This is called *coercive isomorphism*. Selective imitation of local HR practices, on the other hand, is called *mimetic isomorphism* and varies from intentions to adapt to local HR practices just to fit in for the sake of competition, namely *normative isomorphism* (DiMaggio & Powel, 1983 in Rosenzweig & Nohria, 1994).

Our literature review of IHRM notes scholars using various samples (within country and between countries), data collection methods, and independent, dependent, and control variables of HRM practices. The huge investments and coordinated activities required to do stratified sampling designs in which sample sizes of a minimum of 30 in each cell can be obtained are a challenge. Also, data collected from a parent headquartered in one country requires comparison with its counterpart in the affiliate's country in a paired manner to provide meaningful insights. This requires coordinated research groups much like the approach of the Globe and Euronet Cranfield studies.

In the studies reported here, hardly any attention has been paid to IHRM in the context of the IT sector. IT is a fast-growing sector and requires closer examination in terms of IHRM. The dynamics of IHRM in the IT sector is prominent in research studies by Budhwar, Luthar, and Bhatnagar (2006a) and Budhwar, Varma, Singh, and Dhar (2006b). These authors examine HRM systems of the business process outsourcing (BPO) sector and call centers in the Indian IT sector, respectively. Call centers, unlike BPOs, are preferably classified as IT-enabled services, in which software and hardware development per se is not a focus. However, IT-enabled voice-based customer support is a focus. Data collected from 11 call centers in India in their study show the centers to be formal and bureaucratic. HR heads hold positions on the boards of directors. The centers have a written HR strategy and the HR managers appear to have recruitment as their most critical task. They seem to be operating with a business culture similar to those in developed countries. The BPO study (Budhwar et al., 2006a) conducted around the region of Delhi in India used a mixed methodology of 51 interviews with BPO managers, self-administered questionnaires, and secondary data. The work of the BPOs covers areas of accounting, finance, consulting, telecommunications, banking, insurance, health, pharmaceutical, energy, and travel in the sample. The BPOs have linkages with foreign MNCs from the United States, the United Kingdom, Germany, Finland, Switzerland, and France. The authors give an inventory of tasks done at Indian BPOs, including R&D. Their data highlight the tasks in Indian BPOs in training and development, performance appraisal and compensation, and employee turnover and retention. The authors conclude by saying:

> Indian BPOs are highly structured, tightly controlling, bureaucratic, formalized, monitored and scripted, though aiming for a "total customer satisfaction" philosophy. Most HR practices of recruitment, training, compensation and performance appraisal are formal and structured. These activities are similar to outsourcing centres operating in developed countries.

Although it appears that the call centers and BPOs have similar IHRM practices, it is important to realize that they differ from a technological point of view. The former is a user and the latter a developer of technology. Within the BPO sector, too, organizations vary in their level of technology from mere code developers to IT R&D developers. This certainly has implications for IHRM and accommodation. From our literature review we see a trend in IHRM, swaying away from the ethnocentric approach over the past decades toward a market-driven one much like what Perlmutter (1969) called the worldwide standard or global HRM. This leads us to the research questions addressed in this paper:

- Was there a change in business culture before and after the IT sector boom in India?
- Is the current IT business culture in India similar to that of foreign MNC affiliates of developed countries?

- What is the level of R&D in India and is there evidence of foreign direct investment (FDI) in the IT sector?
- What is the direction of flow of IHRM practices in this sector?
- What are the differences in HRM practices between foreign and Indian IT companies?
- What research designs are essential to control effects and study IHRM practices in these contexts?

Insights into these questions will provide a greater understanding of the current status of IHRM in Indian and foreign MNCs in India.

## METHODOLOGY

The aim of this study is to understand the IHRM practices of Indian MNCs located in India as well as foreign MNCs having subsidiaries in India. With the insights drawn from literature, we decided to use both (i) qualitative and (ii) quantitative approaches to gain an understanding.

The first part of this paper describes the qualitative approach. An unstructured qualitative approach is used with the objective of understanding the past and current status of business culture, FDI, and technology levels in the Indian location. We assume that these findings will have a bearing on the similarity of IHRM practices between Indian and foreign MNCs. *In describing similarity we use the term accommodation, which is seen in prior literature to mean affiliate adjustments to parent IHRM practices.* When foreign MNCs operate in a given location with a business culture equivalent to that of its parent, chances are high that accommodation of IHRM practices between these Indian and foreign MNCs is low. Hence low accommodation is indicative of similarity in business culture between these Indian and foreign MNCs.

Taking cues from past literature and personal experiences we propose the following qualitative hypotheses:

**Hypothesis 1.** Cultural preparedness for performance orientation in the Indian location needs lower accommodation in IHRM practices of foreign MNCs and Indian MNCs located in India.

**Hypothesis 2.** Evidence of FDI in R&D for IT in India implies low accommodation requirements in IHRM practices of foreign MNCs and Indian MNCs located in India. Because the technologies are similar in technology level in the Indian and foreign locations, their HRM policies and practices should be similar (low accommodation).

To verify these hypotheses we used reliable secondary data sources and previous literature on Indian HRM. Additionally, we used historical and anecdotal documentation of our experiences and interactions with various actors in Indian and foreign IT companies through meetings, consultations, and training and development sessions from 1998 to 2008. Analyzing these unstructured qualitative data and summing the parts into a whole, we develop a narrative on Indian business culture from the past to the present to assess if the present Indian business culture matches that of foreign MNCs in their home country. If it does, then we infer that there will be a low accommodation of IHRM practices between the Indian and the foreign MNCs.

We assumed that as IT development and R&D activities increase in India, the IHRM practices will also approximate those of the foreign MNCs. This is because there are strict regulations and management practice controls maintained when R&D output in the form of licensed software, trade secrets, copyrights and patents is globally traded. This puts Indian and foreign IT organizations possibly at par on these practices. Hence we conceptualized this part of the study as presented in Fig. 1.

Figure 1 shows that if the domestic business culture has similarities to the in-house business culture of foreign MNCs, both low- and high-end

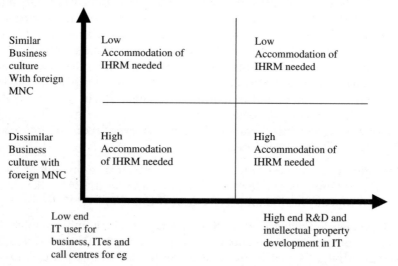

*Fig. 1.* Relationship between Business Culture, Accommodation Need, and Technology Level.

technology sectors of IT in India will approximate IHRM practices in the foreign MNCs. If this is the case, we expect to see a low need for accommodation of IHRM practices in IT companies in India, i.e., they will have IHRM practices similar to those of foreign MNCs.

The objective of the second part of the Indian study was to understand the HRM practices followed in the Indian MNC IT industry. We did a survey of Indian and foreign IT MNCs located in India. First, we analyzed the flow of HRM and followed with an analysis of the differences in HRM practices. We compared Indian IT MNC HRM practices with those of foreign MNC practices. We surveyed production/service workers and managers. The following hypotheses were proposed.

**Hypothesis 3.** Production/service workers and managers of Indian and foreign MNCs differ in their perceptions (mean ranks) regarding the influence of the parent organization on the HRM practices.

**Hypothesis 4.** Production/service workers and managers of Indian and foreign MNCs differ in their perceptions (mean ranks) regarding the adoption of HRM practices from other international affiliates.

**Hypothesis 5.** Production/service workers and managers of Indian and foreign MNCs differ in their perceptions (mean ranks) regarding HRM practices in training and development, staffing, compensation practices, and employee empowerment.

**Hypothesis 6.** Production/service workers and managers of Indian and foreign MNCs differ in their perceptions (mean ranks) regarding goal achievement, knowledge transfer from the parent to the affiliate and from the affiliate to the parent, and business strategy.

The methodology reported for this survey broadly follows that of the University of Illinois Global HRM Project. The survey used two questionnaires:

(a) Employment Practices Survey (EPS)
(b) Organizational Background and Environment Survey (OBES)

The EPS questionnaire dealt with background information: HRM flows and HR practices in the organization. The OBES questionnaire dealt with questions about the relationship of the company with its parent company and local business, the social environment of the company, and the demographics of the organization. Practices measured in the questionnaires are largely from the literature that has emerged since the early 1980s. In this paper we report the following:

(a) Background questions about the organization (these items were on a nominal scale and the organizations are described under the heading of organizational sample description).

Other background questions were items using a 5-point rating scale, with appropriate anchor definitions. They are listed from (b) to (d):

(b) The degree to which local laws restrict the HRM practices of the affiliate.
(c) The degree to which a strict code of conduct is provided by the parent.
(d) The degree to which a quality HR information system (HRIS) is present.
(e) The directions of flow of HRM practices from parent to affiliate (4 items).
   • Affiliate's HRM practices are determined by parent.
   • Affiliate adopted HRM practices from other international affiliates of the parent.
   • Affiliate's HRM practices adopted by parent.
   • Local companies in affiliate's geographic area have HRM practices similar to those of the affiliate.

Items (f) to (i) below were rated on a 5-point Likert-type scale with appropriate anchor definitions. The questions in the section of HR practices (f) were given to two different employee groups: production and service (P&S) workers and managers. The questions in the business environment section, (g) to (i), were obtained from HR managers.

(f) The differences in various HRM practices of foreign and Indian MNCs. Practices assessed were *training and development practices* (7 items, $\alpha = 0.75$, $n = 36$ (for all practices)), *staffing practices* (17 items, $\alpha = 0.88$), *compensation practices* (7 items, $\alpha = 0.98$), *employee empowerment* (4 items, $\alpha = 0.86$).
(g) The degree to which business goals were achieved (7 items, $\alpha = 0.72$).
(h) Flow of knowledge transfer (to affiliate from parent and to parent from affiliate, 4 items, $\alpha = 0.87$).
(i) Their business strategy–product differentiation, quality, and prices in comparison with competitors (3 items, $\alpha = 0.83$).

## Organizational Sample Description from the Survey

Bangalore and Hyderabad are representative of Indian IT. Data were collected from these IT hubs. The contact information of potential IT companies for data collection was obtained from the company's Web site and also from various IT databases such as the NASSCOM database and the Karnataka IT directory. The companies were subsequently contacted via telephone to make appointments with the HR head or HR manager for data collection. Most of the foreign sample was from U.S. parent and a few non-U.S. (essentially European) parent companies. Unlike the American and European parent MNCs and international affiliates, Indian IT organizations refer to their international affiliates as branches and units. Ten HR heads and 5 senior HR managers responded from Indian MNCs. Thirteen HR heads and 8 senior HR managers responded from foreign MNCs. Table 2 gives the details of the number of organizations contacted and number that responded.

Of the 21 foreign MNCs that responded to the survey, 16 were U.S. based and the remaining 5 were European based and all were operating in Bangalore and Hyderabad. Among the Indian IT MNCs, 13 were from software solutions, 1 was from telecommunications, and 1 was from product development. Of the foreign MNCs, 11 were from software solutions, 4 from telecommunications, and 6 from semiconductor software and design. Among the Indian MNCs, 10 were from organizations with employee size fewer than 1,000 and having no expatriates (which meant that they did not have HR expatriates either). Among the foreign MNCs, 15 had organizational sizes fewer than 1,000 and had a total of 5 expatriates and 1 HR expatriate. Three Indian MNCs had 5,000–15,000 employees and reported up to 200 HR managers.

In this sample, the largest foreign MNCs had 5,000 employees and reported up to 23 HR managers. Among the Indian organizations, 10 in the sample were started by the parent itself, 3 were acquired by the parent, 1 was a joint venture with the parent, and 1 was a spin-off of the parent. Among the foreign MNC affiliates in India, 16 were started by the foreign parent

***Table 2.*** Number of MNCs Contacted and Responding.

| Type of Organization | Number of Companies Contacted | Number of Companies Responding |
| --- | --- | --- |
| Indian IT MNC in India | 20 | 15 |
| Foreign IT MNC affiliate in India | 35 | 21 |
| Total | 55 | 36 |

and 3 were acquired by a foreign parent. One-half of both foreign and Indian organizations in the sample had been in business for 1–10 years. Twelve of 15 Indian MNCs stated that their growth over the years was substantial and 16 of 21 foreign MNCs stated the same. None in the sample claimed that their growth was on the decline. None of the businesses in the sample had unions.

### Data Analysis

Hypotheses 1 and 2 were addressed in a qualitative manner. For Hypotheses 3–6, we used Mann–Whitney $U$-tests for nonparametric randomly drawn independent samples. The sample size was not large. It consisted of three groups of organizations: Indian IT organization affiliates, the U.S. IT MNC affiliates, and European MNC affiliates. The groups were compared using the Mann–Whitney $U$-test. The U.S. and European MNC values were combined to form the foreign MNC score.

Data for general questions were analyzed using descriptive statistical analysis and graphic representations. Data in the form of rating scales covering the HR practices from both questionnaires were also analyzed using descriptive statistics, namely frequency distribution analysis per item and combined means for each HR practice computed as an average of the items for each group and their standard deviations.

## QUALITATIVE FINDINGS

The following narrative describes the status of Indian HRM, as it has changed through the decades after Indian independence from Britain in 1947. This is followed by a description of IT R&D, technology status, FDI presence, and foreign R&D presence in the IT hubs of India.

### HRM before and after the IT Boom in India

Prior to the current IT sector in India, we divide the Indian HRM practices in a historical perspective, as follows:

- Postindependence and HRM in India
- Postliberalization and HRM in India
- IT sector introduction in India and HRM

Economically, India has come a long way in developing and maintaining a growing and vibrant human resource management system. Economic and population growth has been moderated by a secular, democratic political system.

Indians from 1940 to early 1970s were guided by the philosophies and values of the heroic Mahatma Gandhi. Although his values were deep seated in Hindu learning, the secularism of religion is seen in India. Scoville, Lawler, and Yi (2005) noted the existence of harmonious polarization of religious value systems in India. The authors traced the epistemology of ethics that evolved around non-Western frameworks. For instance, the Parsee Tata Group, one of the most powerful industrial organizations in India, promoted the values of secularism in its 1999 code of conduct that barred any discrimination at work (Chopra, 2003 in Scoville et al., 2005).

Although India is predominantly Hindu, many other religions are actively practiced; and secular tolerance is practiced. A majority of the workers in India follow Indian values (though predominantly Hindu in origin) acquired through the socialization process, such as humility, openness, masking of conflicts, respect for God, respect for elders and superiors, respect for men, and a sheltered role for women. These values became embedded in the business cultural workings of both public and private sector organizations in India post-Indian independence.

The personnel management of these public and private organizations, as the function was popularly called then, was known as a welfare function. It had a very low strategic importance. Management of industrial relations also gained prominence at the same time. As in the Western industrialized countries, the ratio of blue-collar workers to white-collar officers was high in Indian organizations. Most workers were employed in the manufacturing and retail sectors. In the 1970s, the Indian personnel manager's job description contained tasks related to union–management relations, recruitment and promotions, and change management, namely, impact on retrenchment, retention, and retraining (Akhilesh, Sekar, & Mathew, 1991; Akhilesh & Mathew, 1991).

High-technology organizations began to spring up in Bangalore. Science and technology organizations in aerospace, electronics, machine tools, telecommunications, space science, and computerized manufacturing employed many management trainees. Engineering schools were established to service the supply side of manpower for human resources needed for these organizations. Personnel managers were engaged in recruitment, training, job rotation, and welfare. Industrial relations officers engaged in active negotiations with unions of these large organizations. Promotions remained seniority based. Most high-technology organizations were in the public sector and a large number of them were located in Bangalore. Bangalore became an aerospace hub. This density of science and technology organizations in Bangalore made the garden city a historic R&D base of India.

The critical liberalization of India's economic policy in 1991, put in place by the then Finance Minister and later Prime Minister Dr. Manmohan Singh, brought radical changes to the Indian economy. Additionally, a sea change was also seen in the job description of the personnel manager. The change from personnel manager to human resource manager was evident. Organizational development activities such as change management, HRD, and appraisals were also incorporated into the HRM function.

In the 1980s, the first foreign multinational, the U.S. IT organization Texas Instruments, began to operate in Bangalore. With its entry, the MNC became one of the many actors that lobbied with the federal government for supportive telecommunication infrastructure, paving the way for a viable entry of the Internet later in the 1990s.

The postliberalization period of HRM in India is certainly fused with the entry of information technology businesses. However, a great deal has been written regarding the era of liberalization and Indian HRM (Singh, 1990; Akhilesh & Nagaraj, 1990; Saha, 1992; Kanungo & Mendonca, 1996; Rao, Silveria, Shrivastava, & Vidyasagar, 1994; Sodhi, 1994; Krishna & Monappa, 1994; Venkata Ratnam, 1995, 1998; Budhwar, 2003). Indian HRM gained a strategic role due to competition from the entry of MNCs into the various industrial sectors of India. Outsourcing of American business activities into India saw HRM grow as a global profession. The Indian value system referred to earlier was reduced in importance. Quality, customer satisfaction, cash flow, global orientation, project management, time management, deadlines, and task- and performance-related goals gained importance in the value system of Indian personnel. This paved the way for HR professionals to have a more strategic role in the Indian economy. Interestingly, both the public and the private sector organizations showed these changes. For instance, Budhwar and Boyne (2004) reported:

> This research compared HRM in public and private sectors in the context of a developing country. We anticipated significant differences in the HRM practices of Indian public and private-sector firms, but the research found little support for this supposition ... The entry of IT business in India was related to business culture. As greater quality, customer consciousness, R&D productivity, telecommunications infrastructure and literacy programs were being emphasized, the Indian IT sector began its ascent. Since IT is a technology that links spatial distances, the new organizational design of virtual organizations put IHRM in a new light. This created two types of MNCs, that is, Indian origin MNCs doing business in

*India and abroad and foreign origin MNCs doing business in India, outside of the country of their parent organization.*

With the Indian globalization and liberalization policy, as well as changes in economic planning, the IT sector grew at a fast pace in India. Certain characteristics of the Indian IT sector are worth noting. First, the impact of the entry of American MNCs into India is seen. Indian labor worked for the United States from out of India. These American affiliates in India were designed like American offices in America. Further, American MNCs began to bring quality work into India. Thus R&D activities in the IT sector began in India. Table 3 illustrates some of these actors in India. Hence, when an American IT MNC entered a developing country such as India, setting up an international affiliate, the organization was designed almost like an American one in appearance. Second, the technology infrastructure was shared; that is, the American affiliate in India and the American organization in the United States shared one proprietary IT network. Indian employees were often using the American organization's network system from India when engaged in outsourcing for those American clients. This ensured information security, an important business variable for IT organizations in competitive markets. Third, moving yet a step further, a new flow (beyond the reverse flow Edwards, 1998) was taking place. The Indian-owned IT MNC opened offices on American soil. These were generally marketing and software production offices. Confidentiality of business information and being close to the customer were reasons for this choice of proximity.

The MNC strategy, motivated by mere cost cutting, might lose popularity as strategic alliances between complementary organizations, using the collaborator model, gain dominance. Real estate locations opposite those of their American collaborators and strategic partners became important for the Indian IT MNCs. They thus moved to set up offices in the United States. It is, therefore, important to also analyze the Indian IT organizations and their HR practices in these foreign locations.

Thus, the growth of the IT sector in India is witnessing an exchange of MNCs flowing both toward India and out of India. Foreign MNCs are entering and setting up their international affiliates in India. Similarly, Indian-origin MNCs are moving to foreign countries and setting up base there. TCS India is one example of an organization that has set up bases globally. This reciprocal effect creates a change in perspective for studies in IHRM practices and needs a typology different from that of Perlmutter (1969). This reverse flow of outsourcing brings a clarity that differences in

*Table 3.*   MNC R&D Investors in India.

| Company Name | Location and Year of Establishment | Number of Employees (2003) | Area of R&D |
|---|---|---|---|
| Texas Instruments | Bangalore, 1984 | 900 | VLSI and embedded software enabling or within a chip |
| Oracle India Development Centre | Bangalore, 1994 Hyderabad, 1999 | 2,700 (4,000 by year end) | Oracle's database products, applications, business intelligent products, application development tools |
| Sun Microsystems' India Engineering Centre | Bangalore, 1999 | 500 | Sun's software, including Solaris and Sun One |
| i2 technologies R&D Centre | Bangalore, Mumbai, 1988 | 1,000 | Company's global development delivery |
| IBM's Software Lab India | Bangalore, 1998 | Not available | IBM software such as Websphere, DB2, Lotus, Tivoli, and Rational. Middleware and business intelligence |
| SAP Labs India | Bangalore, 1998 | 750 by September 2003 | Does 10% of SAP's total R&D work here |
| Philips Innovation Campus | Bangalore, 1996 | 895 (1,000 by end of 2003) | Develops software for Philips, almost all Philips products with software have development here |
| HP Labs | Bangalore, 2002 | 20 | High-level research on futuristic technologies, focus on emerging markets |

*Source:* Express Computer (2003).

business culture between Indian and American organizations are minimizing. Indian organizations are picking up the business culture of performance-oriented American organizations.

The Indian IT sector is considered unique. The IT and BPO sectors alone employ 700,000 employees directly and approximately 2.5 million workers indirectly. Projected figures indicate that India needs 2.3 million direct workers and 6.5 million indirect workers and can generate $60 billion U.S. in export revenues by 2010 (Nasscom–McKinsey Report, 2005). However, the competition and economic development of these IT organizations are different from those of other industrial sectors in India. Although this should have caused a divide between the sectors, the permeable character of IT appears to have had a positive spillover effect on non-IT sectors of India.

Despite the fact that the IT industry is 2 decades old in India, there are only a few scholarly studies in the area of Indian IT sector management (Mathew & Chattopadyay, 2002; Mathew & Subramanya, 2003; Chattopadyay, 2004; Goswami & Mathew, 2005; Goswami, 2005). Reasons can be attributed to difficulty in respondent cooperation for questionnaire-based data collection. Indian IT personnel in Indian companies are extremely busy with their time schedules and their competitive environments are stressed beyond fatigue and patience. Indian IT personnel work long hours and appear to enjoy it. Their main activity is manpower planning, recruitment, and selection. Line managers also share much of these activities. The density of HR personnel to every 100 employees (non-HR IT personnel) is low (Mathew & Subramanya, 2003).

## *Conclusions for Hypotheses 1 and 2*

We have briefly traced the growth of HRM in India to understand the current status of business culture and how this compares with the culture of the developed countries that are used in this study for comparison. For qualitative Hypothesis 1, we come to the judgment that the business cultures between Indian and foreign MNC organizations match moderately; for example, in Western countries, the business culture is customer and performance oriented. In comparison, our study indicates that Indian MNCs are customer and performance oriented as well. For qualitative Hypothesis 2, we find that the level of technology is high for foreign MNCs located in India. The level of technology between Indian and foreign MNC organizations in India is comparable, to some extent.

# RESULTS OF THE SURVEY

Additionally, this study also aimed at understanding differences between HRM practices of Indian and foreign IT MNCs. The results are discussed below. First, we address general questions and provide descriptive findings of the background of the sample.

### Do the Indian Laws and Regulations Constrain Employment Practices in Indian IT?

The respondents of the Indian IT MNC strongly agree (11 of 15) that the Indian laws and regulations on employment practices constrain some employment practices in their organizations. About 6 foreign MNCs agree with most of the Indian-owned organizations. However, a majority of foreign MNCs (12 of 21) strongly disagree that the Indian laws and regulations put a constraint on employment practices in their organizations.

### Do the Parent Companies have a Comprehensive Code of Conduct that Specifies the Ethical Standards of the Affiliate?

Thirteen of the 15 Indian IT organizations felt there was a comprehensive code of conduct given by their parent organization. Nineteen of the 21 foreign affiliates stated that there was a very limited code of conduct.

### Is There a Quality HR Information System?

When asked whether they had access to a fully computerized online information system, the majority of the Indian and foreign MNC IT organizations agreed that they did. However, a majority of both groups felt that the reliability and quality of their HRIS were poor.

### Conclusions for Hypotheses 3–6

Respondents were asked regarding IHRM flow for P&S workers and managers separately. The results were used to run a Mann–Whitney $U$-test of mean rank differences between the responses of foreign and Indian firms for P&S and managerial employees. Table 4 indicates that there was a perceived statistical difference for both P&S employees and managers on two flows. These were the parent MNC's role regarding the HR practices of Indian MNCs and affiliates of foreign MNCs and the adoption of HRM practices from international affiliates of the parent MNC organizations. Hence Hypotheses 3 and 4 are valid. Respondents from Indian MNCs (who are close to the parents in this context) felt this influence to be higher than those from foreign MNCs. Perceptions do differ.

***Table 4.*** Flow of HRM Practices in Foreign MNCs vs. Indian IT Companies.

| Variable | Production and Service Workers | | Managers | | Production and Service Workers | | Managers | |
|---|---|---|---|---|---|---|---|---|
| | Mean rank Indian (N=15) 1 | Mean rank foreign (N=21) 2 | Mean rank Indian (N=15) 3 | Mean rank foreign (N=21) 4 | Mann–Whitney U-test (N=36) 1,2 | p-value 1,2 | Mann–Whitney U-test (N=36) 3,4 | p-value 3,4 |
| HRM practices determined by parent company | 24.90 | 13.93 | 23.73 | 14.76 | 61.5 | 0.01** | 79.0 | 0.01** |
| HRM practices adopted from international affiliates | 22.90 | 15.36 | 22.57 | 15.60 | 91.50 | 0.05* | 96.5 | 0.05* |

$*p \leq 0.05$
$**p \leq 0.01$

Although not reported here in the table, Mann–Whitney tests done at the subcategory level of the sample indicate that Indian and U.S. organizations differed in their mean rankings of whether the HRM practices were adopted from the affiliate to the parent. This was higher for the Indian sample ($p = 0.05$), again showing evidence of a reverse flow (Edwards, 1998), possibly because of parental proximity.

Parental influence on Indian MNCs in India is high. The need to adopt from international affiliates abroad was also high for Indians. The mean ratings are shown in Table 5. Comparisons are made among MNCs of Indian origin and U.S. and non-U.S. (European) origin. The combination of U.S. and European origin was termed as foreign-origin MNCs. When we examined the univariate statistics, the four practices, namely training and development, staffing, compensation, and employee empowerment, showed midrange values hovering around the median of 3. There is not much perceived difference between the ratings for P&S vs. managers. The mean values indicated marginally higher values among the European MNCs for training and development as well as compensation practices.

A comparison of the mean rankings is provided, using the Mann–Whitney $U$-test, for pairs of countries, shown in Table 6. No significant differences were found at the practice levels for the pairs (that is, India vs. United States and Europe). We can with confidence reject Hypothesis 5, implying standardization of IHRM practices in the IT industry, irrespective of country. It is possible that the nature of IT and the nature of IT tasks demand fairly universal HRM practices. Such can be the case for IT organizations irrespective of the geographic location. Development of design, architecture, and code per se, as well as hardware design, involves similar tasks all over the globe. Hence the nature of a task as done in the United States or Europe or India is similar and has similar time lines, project management requirements, and quality requirements. The quality requirements have standardized training and skill development requirements. Managing these IT knowledge workers is becoming increasingly a universal HRM practices package, perhaps confined to this sector only. Similarity in the office designs and interiors of Indian and foreign MNCs makes it difficult to distinguish whether one is in India or the United States. Due to collaborative tasks, an IT worker at a computer monitor in Bangalore, for example, and an American colleague (across the sea) develop code together. This may create a feeling of being in any one geographic location, typical of the boundaryless virtual organization (Bartlett & Ghoshal, 1989). There are no statistical differences for compensation practices as well. The pay differentiation between the countries, in the

***Table 5.*** Combined Item Means for HRM Practices of Foreign and Domestic IT Firms in India.

| Variable | Foreign (N = 21) | | Indian (N = 15) | | U.S. (N = 16) | | European (N = 5) | |
|---|---|---|---|---|---|---|---|---|
| | Production and service workers mean (SD) | Managers mean (SD) | Production and service workers mean (SD) | Managers mean (SD) | Production and service workers mean (SD) | Managers mean (SD) | Production and service workers mean (SD) | Managers mean (SD) |
| Training and development | 3.66 (0.48) | 3.63 (0.54) | 3.74 (0.44) | 3.54 (0.61) | 3.62 (0.52) | 3.60 (0.60) | 3.82 (0.29) | 3.74 (0.31) |
| Staffing practices | 3.40 (0.29) | 3.42 (0.30) | 3.26 (0.25) | 3.31 (0.27) | 3.39 (0.30) | 3.40 (0.32) | 3.44 (0.28) | 3.48 (0.26) |
| Compensation practices | 3.47 (0.32) | 3.53 (0.35) | 3.12 (0.62) | 3.15 (0.68) | 3.42 (0.32) | 3.48 (0.36) | 3.64 (0.27) | 3.68 (0.25) |
| Employee empowerment | 3.46 (0.34) | | 3.32 (0.36) | | 3.48 (0.35) | | 3.38 (0.32) | |

*Table 6.* Comparison of HRM Practices – European and U.S. IT Sector Affiliates in India.

| Variable | Production and Service Workers | | Managers | | Mann–Whitney $U$-test | | $p$-value | |
|---|---|---|---|---|---|---|---|---|
| | Mean rank European ($N=5$) 1 | Mean rank US ($N=16$) 2 | Mean rank European ($N=5$) 3 | Mean rank US ($N=16$) 4 | ($N=21$) 1,2 | ($N=21$) 3,4 | ($N=21$) 1,2 | ($N=21$) 3,4 |
| Training and development | 15.8 | 9.5 | 14.70 | 9.84 | 16 | 21.5 | 0.04* | 0.12 |
| Staffing practices | 12.20 | 10.63 | 13.30 | 10.98 | 34 | 28.5 | 0.62 | 0.34 |
| Compensation practices | 13.00 | 10.38 | 14.60 | 9.88 | 30 | 22 | 0.40 | 0.13 |
| Employee empowerment | 12.10 | 10.66 | | | 34.5 | | 0.63 | |

*$p \leq 0.05$
**$p \leq 0.01$

sample, seems to be closing in. The only statistical difference between Europe and the United States is in the practice of training and development. The ratings are higher for Europeans than for U.S. respondents.

Tables 7–9 provide data regarding Hypothesis 6. The respondents of the IT organizations provided data on the organizational and business environments of the Indian and foreign MNC affiliates. Table 7 shows the combined item mean ratings and standard deviations of goal achievement, knowledge and technology transfer, and business strategy. Comparisons are made between India, the United States, and Europe.

In Table 7, the U.S. MNC subsidiaries have a higher rating for goal achievement compared to the other two countries. They score moderately above the expected levels for employee productivity, delivery of products and services to local and international markets, profitability, and customer satisfaction. For the next aspect of knowledge and technology transfer (to and from the affiliate), the U.S. MNC affiliates score higher on knowledge and technology transfer from the parent to the affiliate. In contrast, for knowledge transfer to the parent from the affiliate, the Indian organizations score higher than the other two countries. European MNCs score lower on knowledge and technology transfer to their parent. When asked about the importance of providing product differentiation, quality, and prices in comparison with competitors, Indian IT MNCs score the highest means, followed by U.S. and then the European MNCs.

***Table 7.*** Importance of Organizational and Business Environments.

| Variable | | Foreign ($N=19$) Mean (SD) | Indian ($N=14$) Mean (SD) | U.S. ($N=16$) Mean (SD) | European ($N=3$) Mean (SD) |
|---|---|---|---|---|---|
| Goal achievement | | 4.09 (0.67) | 3.86 (0.60) | 4.22 (0.64) | 3.42 (0.38) |
| Knowledge and technology transfer | To the affiliate from the parent company | 3.75 (0.99) | 3.55 (1.10) | 3.86 (1.02) | 3.25 (0.79) |
| | From the affiliate to the parent company | 3.48 (0.85) | 3.83 (1.01) | 3.74 (0.67) | 2.33 (0.58) |
| Business strategy | | 3.93 (0.67) | 4.33 (0.51) | 4.09 (0.56) | 3.11 (0.69) |

***Table 8.*** Importance of Organizational and Business Environments in European vs. Indian IT Companies.

| Variable | | Mean Rank European (N = 3) 1 | Mean Rank Indian (N = 14) 2 | Mann– Whitney U-test (N = 17) 1,2 | p-value 1,2 |
|---|---|---|---|---|---|
| Goal achievement | | 6.00 | 9.64 | 12 | 0.25 |
| Knowledge and | To the affiliate | 7.50 | 9.32 | 16.5 | 0.56 |
| technology | To the parent | 3.00 | 10.29 | 3 | 0.02* |
| transfer | | | | | |
| Business strategy | | 5.67 | 9.71 | 11 | 0.20 |

*$p \leq 0.05$
**$p \leq 0.01$

***Table 9.*** Importance of Organizational and Business Environments in European vs. U.S. IT Companies.

| Variable | | Mean Rank European (N = 3) 1 | Mean Rank US (N = 16) 2 | Mann– Whitney U-test (N = 19) 1,2 | p-value 1,2 |
|---|---|---|---|---|---|
| Goal achievement | | 4.50 | 11.03 | 7.5 | 0.06 |
| Knowledge and | To the affiliate | 5.83 | 10.78 | 11.5 | 0.15 |
| technology | To the parent | 2.83 | 11.34 | 2.5 | 0.01** |
| transfer | | | | | |
| Business strategy | | 3.17 | 11.28 | 3.5 | 0.01** |

*$p \leq 0.05$
**$p \leq 0.01$

To obtain a better understanding of these differences and address Hypothesis 6, a Mann–Whitney U-test was conducted on mean rankings between the three countries. Only pairs of countries for which significant differences were noticed are reported. Although not shown in the tables it was seen that there is no statistical difference between Indian and foreign MNCs in goal achievement, knowledge transfer from the parent to the affiliate, knowledge transfer from the affiliate to the parent, and perceived business strategy. Hence Hypothesis 6 can be confidently rejected.

Some differences were found, however, between Indian and non-U.S. samples (Europe), in Table 8. This table shows significant differences in knowledge and technology transfer from the affiliate to the parent organization. The rankings indicate that this practice is higher in Indian MNCs than in European MNCs. Additionally, Table 9 compares the United States with Europe on the organizational and business environments. There are significant differences in two areas, namely, knowledge and technology transfer from affiliate to parent and business strategy. In both cases the United States scores higher than Europe.

# CONCLUSIONS

This is a preliminary study, as noted earlier, aimed at investigating IHRM practices in the IT sector of India. The Indian IT sector is experiencing fast growth with the entry of MNCs. The outflow of Indian IT through outsourcing and also the setting of Indian offices on-site at foreign locations are on the increase.

We encountered two problems. These were (a) cooperation from IT organizations in obtaining responses from HR and business CEOs and (b) lack of sufficient data within stratified sample cells to test varying country difference hypotheses with parametric tests. Field studies in competitive sectors, in which the speed of managerial delivery is high, showed that managers lacked the time to provide detailed responses to lengthy questionnaires.

It appears that Indian IT MNCs are experiencing ethnographic flows between parents and affiliates. They are also influenced by IHRM flows of foreign affiliates. U.S. leadership in business practices such as goal achievement, employee productivity, and customer satisfaction indicates that U.S. organizations have a business culture that is different from that of the others in the sample. In addition, parent-to-affiliate knowledge transfer is higher for U.S. and lower for non-U.S. affiliates. Indian affiliates bring back knowledge to their parents, retrieving knowledge from their environments. Indians are concerned about product differentiation, quality, and prices; these were the very features that helped scale up the IT industry in India. A partial difference is evident between Indian and foreign MNCs regarding their business environments, although this is apparent in knowledge transfer flows only.

Indian business culture and technology levels are getting closer to those of foreign MNCs. With time, if this gap closes further, there is a likelihood of fewer differences in IHRM practices. The historical narrative of Indian HRM shows India moving from a traditional anti-industrialization culture to a global market-driven culture with liberalization and IT sector growth. We conclude from our qualitative narrative that the Indian and foreign business cultures are moderately approximate, as also seen by Budhwar et al. (2006b). The level of technology is moderately the same. Therefore, the degree of accommodation on HRM practices of foreign and Indian IT organizations is likely to be low.

We need to be cautious in drawing the above conclusions because (a) the sample size is too small to make inferences from the Mann–Whitney tests and (b) the IHRM practices between MNC IT sector organizations are likely to be minimally different because of the virtual organization and borderless MNC effects. We can say with some confidence, however, that IHRM in IT MNCs, irrespective of country of origin, are likely to be standardized.

The implications for research designs are plentiful. These include the implication that sample matching in terms of parent–affiliate age, technology level, and business culture requires strict control. Measurement variables are by now clearly known and do not appear to be a black box, as does the process of sample design. Both qualitative and quantitative approaches are popular to use when they complement each other. There is a need for collaborative research groups working across countries to collect data of this nature.

# REFERENCES

Akhilesh, K. B., & Mathew, M. (1991). Technological change and emerging HR issues: An analysis. *Personnel Today, XII*(2), 29–37.

Akhilesh, K. B., & Nagaraj, D. R. (1990). HRM 2000. India: Wiley Eastern.

Akhilesh, K. B., Sekar R., & Mathew, M. (1991). Personnel profession as perceived by young personnel executives: A national survey, in role, performance & challenges for young personnel executives, back ground conference papers, NIPM, pp. 6–25.

Bae, J., Chen, S.-J., & Lawler, J. J. (1998). Variations in human resource management in Asian countries: MNC home-country and host-country effects. *International Journal of Human Resource Management, 9*(4), 653–670.

Bae, J., Chen, S., Wan, T. W. D., Lawler, J. J., & Walumbwa, F. O. (2003). Human resource strategy and firm performance in Pacific Rim countries. *International Journal of Human Resource Management, 14*(8), 1308–1332.

Bae, J., & Lawler, J. J. (2000). Organizational and HRM strategies in Korea: Impact on firm performance in an emerging economy. *Academy of Management Journal, 43*(3), 502–517.

Bartlett, A. C., & Ghoshal, S. (1989). *Managing across borders*. USA: Harvard business School Press.

Belanger, J., Edwards, P., & Wright, M. (1999). Best HR practice and the multinational company. *Human Resource Management Journal, 9*(3), 53–70.

Budhwar, P. (2003). Employment relations in India. *Employee Relations, 25*(2), 132–148.

Budhwar, P., & Boyne, G. (2004). Human resource management in the Indian public and private sectors: An empirical comparison. *International Journal of Human Resource Management, 15*(2), 346–370.

Budhwar, P., Luther, H., & Boyne, J. (2006a). Dynamics of HRM systems in BPOs operating in India. *Journal of Labor Research, 37*, 339–360.

Budhwar, P., Varma, A., Singh, V., & Dhar, R. (2006b). HRM systems of Indian call centres: An exploratory study. *The International Journal of Human Resource Management, 17*(5), 881–889.

Carpenter, M. A., Sanders, W. G., & Gregersen, H. B. (2001). Bundling human capital with organizational context: The impact of international assignment experience on multinational firm performance and CEO pay. *Academy of Management Journal, 44*(3), 493–511.

Chattopadyay, U. (2004). *Organizational designs for patent productivity in the ICT sector*. Unpublished Doctoral thesis, Department of Management Studies, Indian Institute of Science, Bangalore, India.

Cleveland, J. N., Gunnigle, P., Heraty, N., Morley, M., & Murphy, K. R. (2000). US multinationals and human resource management: Evidence on HR practices in European subsidiaries. *IBAR – Journal of the Irish Academy of Management, 21*(1), 9–28.

Doz, Y., & Prahalad, C. K. (1986). Controlled variety: A challenge for human resource management in the MNC. *Human Resource Management, 25*(1), 55–71.

Edwards, P., Ferner, A., & Sisson, K. (1996). The conditions for international human resource management: Two case studies. *The International Journal of Human Resource Management, 7*(1), 20–40.

Edwards, T. (1998). Multinationals, labor management and the process of reverse diffusion: A case study. *International Journal of Human Resource Management, 9*(4), 696–709.

Ferner, A., & Quintanilla, J. (1998). Multinationals, national business systems and HRM: The enduring influence of national identity or a process of 'Anglo-Saxonization'. *International Journal of Human Resource Management, 9*(4), 710–731.

Ferner, A., & Varul, M. Z. (2000). Internationalization and the personnel function in German multinationals. *Human Resource Management Journal, 10*(3), 79–96.

Goswami, S. (2005). *Innovation measurement and organizational competencies in IT organizations*. Unpublished Doctoral thesis, Department of Management Studies, Indian Institute of Science, Bangalore, India.

Goswami, S., & Mathew, M. (2005). Definition of innovation revisited: An empirical study on Indian information technology industry. *International Journal of Innovation Management (IJIM), 9*(3), 371–383.

Horwitz, M. F., & Smith, D. A. (1998). Flexible work practices and human resource management: A comparison of South African and foreign owned companies. *International Journal of Human Resource Management, 9*(4), 590–607.

Jain, H. C. (1991). Is there a coherent human resource management system in India? *International Journal of Public Sector Management, 4*(3), 18–30.

Jain, H. C., Lawler, J. J., & Morishima, M. (1998). Multinational corporations, human resource management and host-country nationals. *International Journal of Human Resource Management*, 9(4), 553–566.

Jain, H., & Murray, V. (1984). Why the human resources management function fails. *California Management Review*, 26(4), 95–110.

Kanungo, R. N., & Mendonca, M. (1996). Corporate leadership in the context of liberalization in India. *The Social Engineer*, 5(2), 114–136.

Kelly, J. (2001). The role of the personnel/HR function in multinational companies. *Employee Relations*, 23(6), 536–557.

Krishna, A., & Monappa, A. (1994). Economic restructuring and human management. *Journal of Industrial Relations*, 29, 490–501.

Martin, G., & Beaumont, P. (1998). Diffusing 'best practice' in multinational firms: Prospects, practice and contestation. *International Journal of Human Resource Management*, 9(4), 671–695.

Mathew, M., & Chattopadyay, U. (2002). Another new agenda for the HR professional: Patent productivity. *Paper in proceedings of Human Resources Development in Asia, Trends and Challenges*, pp. 703–708.

Mathew, M., & Subramanya, T. (2003). *A preliminary survey of HR practices in Indian information technology (IT) organizations*. Working Paper. Department of Management Studies, Indian Institute of Science, Bangalore.

Muller, M. (1998). Human resource and industrial relations practices of UK and US multinationals in Germany. *International Journal of Human Resource Management*, 9(4), 732–749.

Nasscom–McKinsey Report (2005). Extending India's leadership of the global IT and BPO industries. New Delhi: NASSCOM.

Ngo, H-Y., Turban, D., Lau, C-M., & Lui, S-Y. (1998). Human resource practices and firm performance of multinational corporations: Influences of country origin. *International Journal of Human Resource Management*, 9(4), 632–652.

Papalexandris, N., & Panayotopoulou, L. (2004). Exploring the mutual interaction of societal culture and human resource management practices: Evidence from 19 countries. *Employee Relations*, 26(5), 495–509.

Perlmutter, H. (1969). The tortuous evolution of the multinational corporation. *Columbia Journal of World Business*, 4, 9–18.

Pucik, V., & Katz, J. H. (1986). Information, control, and human resource management in multinational firms. *Human Resource Management*, 25(1), 121–132.

Rao, T. V., Silveria, D. M., Shrivastava, C. M., & Vidyasagar, R. (1994). *HRD in the new economic environment*. New Delhi: Tata/McGraw-Hill.

Rosenzweig, P. M., & Nohria, N. (1994). Influences on human resource management practices in multinational corporations. *Journal of International Business Studies*, 25(2), 229–251.

Roth, K., & O'Donnell, S. (1996). Foreign subsidiary compensation strategy: An agency theory perspective. *Academy of Management Journal*, 39(3), 678–704.

Ryan, A. M., McFarland, L., Baron, H., & Page, R. (1999). An international look at selection practices: Nation and culture as explanations for variability in practice. *Personnel Psychology*, 52(2), 359–391.

Saha, A. (1992). Basic human nature in Indian tradition and its economic consequences. *International Journal of Sociology and Social Policy*, 12(1–2), 1–50.

Schneider, S. C. (1988). National vs. corporate culture: Implications for human resource management. *Human Resource Management*, 27(2), 231–246.

Scoville, J. G., Lawler, J. J., & Yi, X. (2005). Non-western ethical frameworks: Implications for human resources and industrial relations. Chapter 4. In: J. W. Budd & J. G. Scoville (Eds), *The ethics of human resources and industrial relations*. Illinois, USA: Labor and employment relations association series.

Shekshnia, S. (1998). Western multinationals' human resource practices in Russia. *European Management Journal*, 16(4), 460–465.

Shih, H.-A., Chiang, Y.-H., & Kim, I.-S. (2005). Expatriate performance management from MNCs of different national origins. *International Journal of Manpower*, 26(2), 157–178.

Singh, J. P. (1990). Managerial culture and work related values in India. *Organization Studies*, 11(1), 75–101.

Sodhi, J. S. (1994). Emerging trends in industrial relations and human resource management in Indian industry. *Indian Journal of Industrial Relations*, 30(1), 19–37.

Teagarden, M. B., Glinow, V. M. A., Bowen, D. E., Frayne, C. A., Nason, S., Huo, Y. P., Milliman, J., Arias, M. E., Butler, M. C., Geringer, J. M., Kim, N.-H., Scullion, H., Lowe, K. B., & Drost, E. A. (1995). Toward a theory of comparative management research: An idiographic case study of the best international human resources management project. *Academy of Management Journal*, 38(5), 1261–1278.

Turner, T., D'Art, D., & Gunnigle, G. (2002). Multi-national corporations: A challenge to European trade unions? *Irish Journal of Management*, 23(1), 125–141.

Venkata Ratnam C. S. (1995). Economic liberalization and the transformation of industrial relations policies in India. In: A. Verma, T. A. Kochan, & R .D. Lansbury (Eds), *Employment relations in the growing Asian economies*. Routledge: London.

Venkata Ratnam, C. S. V. (1998). Multinational companies in India. *International Journal of Human Resource Management*, 9(4), 567–589.

Zhang, M. (2003). Transferring human resource management across national boundaries: The case of Chinese multinational companies in the UK. *Employee Relations*, 25(6), 613–626.